THE EDUCATION OF TEACHERS IN ENGLAND, FRANCE AND THE U.S.A.

by C. A. RICHARDSON, HÉLÈNE BRÛLÉ, HAROLD E. SNYDER

GREENWOOD PRESS, PUBLISHERS
WESTPORT, CONNECTICUT

PREFACE

This volume containing three national studies on the education of teachers is published by Unesco as part of a general programme for furthering the cause of universal compulsory education. One of the prevailing difficulties that besets the extension of schooling is the shortage of qualified teachers. In singling out this problem Unesco has prepared two booklets: the first, to examine the position in three highly developed educational systems (England and Wales, France, U.S.A.) which have evolved characteristically different methods for training their teachers; and the second (published under the title *Rural Teacher Training*) to describe a number of institutions in different countries which are coming to grips with the problem of the supply of rural teachers.

The two volumes have a particular application in the 1953 International Conference on Public Education, convened in Geneva by the International Bureau of Education and Unesco. The conference is to discuss at some length the training and status of primary school teachers, and a world-wide study of the problem will be presented by the IBE. The conference itself and the recommendations it formulates will be further steps towards achieving Unesco's purposes.

Apart from being a contribution to this conference, the present volume may be of wide use to all educators and administrators who are concerned with the place of the teacher in the educational system. The three authors present detailed studies of conditions in their own countries; while writing as individual authorities (and being free, therefore, to express their opinions) they have attempted to keep in mind the reader who is unfamiliar with the country. The studies share this aim of being interpretative and objective; and in form they are as comparable as is possible. The fact that the French study deals exclusively with primary teachers (the *instituteurs*) whereas the two others cover both primary and secondary teachers does not detract from this comparability, but arises naturally from the national systems of education described.

Mr. C. A. Richardson, author of the English study, was formerly the Chief Inspector for the Training of Teachers, Ministry of Education, England.

Mrs. Hélène Brûlé, author of the French study, is Head, Ecole normale d'institutrices, Tours, Indre-et-Loire.

Dr. Harold Snyder, editor of the U.S. study, is director of the Washington Seminar of the American Friends Service Committee, has directed several international projects of the American Council on Education, and was Research Associate and Assistant to the Director of the staff of the Council's Commission on Teacher Education.

While thanking the three contributors—and the team of educators who assisted Dr. Snyder—Unesco should place on record the constant interest shown by Dr. Karl Bigelow, Professor of Education, Teachers' College, Columbia University, in the project as a whole. It is fitting that a brief introduction by this distinguished authority should take its place at the beginning of the volume.

CONTENTS

INTRODUCTION

by KARL W. BIGELOW

The significance of education for personal and social accomplishment and happiness has never been more widely or more fully appreciated than today. In the great democracies of the West, in the nations that have embraced communism, and in those countries and territories that have newly achieved independence or stand upon its brink—everywhere the quantity and quality of schooling are matters of lively concern. Belief in the power of education was never stronger; demands for its extension and improvement were never greater.

And everywhere one result is to focus attention upon the teachers, for these constitute the most vital factor in any educational system. Upon their number, their devotion, and their quality the effectiveness of all educational arrangements must chiefly depend. How can young people of adequate promise be attracted in suitable quantities to the teaching profession? How should selection be made among the applicants? What particular form of education should be provided in order to fit them for their teaching tasks? When should it commence and how long should it last? What provision should be made to facilitate their continued growth in professional competence after they have entered the schools? How should institutions for the preparation of teachers be organized, controlled, and financed? What compromises—if any—should be made between considerations of quantity and quality? What salaries and other provisions are essential?

These and many other related questions occupy the thought of educationists, legislators, and citizens everywhere. The problems raised are difficult. But they are also vital. In the complex modern world—in the most, as well as in the least, advanced areas—a sufficient corps of good teachers is essential.

Unesco, therefore, performs a valuable service in publishing this account of the education and status of teachers in three of the leading nations of the world. Similar in many ways, England, France and the United States have also their characteristic differences. Both similarities and differences are revealed in this study.

The history of all three demonstrates that in these highly developed democracies universal compulsory education has become a cornerstone of national policy. On the other hand, the role of the State—the central government—in establishing schools, determining and sharing in educational costs (including teachers' salaries), and providing for the education of teachers has varied in reflection of the differences in national political institutions and ideas. For example, the role of the French Ministry is greater than that of the British, while no corresponding institution exists in the United States, where control over education is delegated to the 48 States and, by them, largely to the particular localities. The thoughtful reader, comparing these different pictures will, however, be most struck by the common problems and trends. Some of them may be mentioned: the lengthening period of teacher preparation; the mounting problem of maintaining an adequate supply of qualified teachers; the growing emphasis on child study as a key element in professional training; the increased awareness of the necessity that teachers be prepared to adjust educational practice to changing social circumstances; the struggle with the problems of what are the best proportions of general and professional education in the preparation of teachers and of how these components may best be related to one another; the more vivid awareness of the importance of providing continuous opportunities for teachers in service to increase their understanding and competence.

To read of these similarities—as well as of the dissimilarities—can have many values to educationists and lay citizens everywhere. A sense of solidarity may well ensue. And a recognition of what each country may learn from others. Discussions of the ideas and practices here set forth can stimulate and suggest. It is to be hoped that this book may lead to many such discussions.

It is also to be hoped that similar accounts of conditions in other countries may be forthcoming. Then the discussions will prove even more rewarding. In addition one must hope that such discussions may often involve educationists from many countries. Unesco's Seminar on the Education and Training of Teachers, held in England in 1948, proved—not for the first nor for the last time—how rewarding such international examinations of common problems can be.

Finally it is to be hoped that reading and discussing may increasingly be supplemented by seeing. The post-war expansion of international exchanges of teachers and teacher educators, vigorously encouraged and assisted by Unesco, has proved of notable value. Through such experiences educationists have gained much: greater appreciation and tolerance; new insights capable of application in their own circumstances; a renewed sense of the worth of the teacher's work.

Teachers College, Columbia University

PART I

THE TRAINING OF TEACHERS IN ENGLAND AND WALES

by C. A. RICHARDSON

FOREWORD

The system of teacher training in England and Wales is now so vast and complex that it would be impossible to consider it in exhaustive detail within the scope of a study such as that which follows. Nevertheless it is hoped that all the essential points have been covered and covered adequately.

One point of terminology requires a brief note of explanation. The term 'Institute of Education' was originally applied to area training organizations of the C type (see the text) as distinct from the A type known as 'Schools of Education'. For reasons which will appear in the sequel it is now common practice to use 'Institute of Education' as practically synonymous with 'Area Training Organization', whatever the type.

A possible source of confusion in this connexion has particular reference to London. For many years one of the departments of London University, the main business of which is concerned with the training of teachers, has been known as the 'Institute of Education'. It retains this name although it is now, as a central college, an integral part of the wider London Institute of Education, namely the Area Training Organization. The two uses of the name in the case of London should be borne in mind.

Where a reference is obviously intended to apply to both men and women I have followed the English custom and used the masculine term to cover both sexes.

INTRODUCTION

The training of teachers in England and Wales has not been a static system but an evolutionary process. For the most part this process has gone on gradually but steadily. Twice during the last 30 years, however, it has culminated in comparatively sudden and revolutionary changes, after which it has settled down again to a steady rhythm of development. The first of these revolutions took place round about 1926, and the second round about 1946; the latter is, indeed, so recent that the training system is only now settling down again into a steady stride.

Although the changes when they came were revolutionary, they were end-results of a process of educational thought and discussion. This had in course of time taken coherent shape in ideas which had gathered so great a weight of public opinion behind them as to give rise to an irresistible demand for action.

To understand the position, some description should first be given of the development of public education in England, from its beginnings in the earlier part of the nineteenth century, followed by an exposition of the parallel development of the means whereby a supply of teachers has been provided appropriate to the stage reached by the educational system at any given time.

Broadly speaking there have been four fairly well-marked phases in the development of the educational system in England and Wales, associated respectively with the Education Acts of 1870, 1902, 1918 and 1921, and 1944.

Some provision for public education was instituted long before 1870, in the first half of the century, the first schools being the result of voluntary effort—mainly, though not entirely, on the part of religious bodies. These 'voluntary schools', as they were called, and their successors have remained, as we shall see in subsequent chapters, an integral and important part of the system of public education, and are likely to continue as such in the future.

The first government grants in aid of public education were made as early as 1832, but the system was not brought into something like coherent and orderly form on a national scale until the passing of the Act of 1870. This Act established what was known as 'Elementary

Education', given in 'Public Elementary Schools'. It did not make education compulsory or free, but it enabled school boards to draw up by-laws making attendance compulsory and remitting fees when the circumstances of parents warranted this. Provision appropriate to the times having been made for dealing with the difficult question of religious instruction, the secular element in the education given in elementary schools consisted of instruction in the rudiments of knowledge and skill, particularly in regard to reading, writing and arithmetic—'the three R's'. In 1891 elementary education was made free through the medium of a special grant voted by Parliament, and, as such, was available to all who cared to take advantage of the facilities available.

With the establishment of local authorities—in the first instance the county councils in 1888—it became possible to begin the development for older and abler pupils of a system of 'higher education' given in 'secondary' or in 'technical' schools according as the ability of the pupil was mainly of the 'academic' and verbal or of the practical kind.

This phase culminated in the Act of 1902, in accordance with which local education authorities (LEAs) were set up. Every county and county borough became a LEA for both elementary and higher education, while boroughs with a population of over 10,000 and urban districts with a population of over 20,000 became LEAs for elementary education alone, higher education in their areas being administered by the appropriate county council. Central administration had been vested in 1899 in a Board of Education uniting the old Education Department and the Department of Science and Art.

The war of 1914–18, acting at first as a brake on educational progress, ultimately became a stimulus to further progress. This was largely due to the enhanced appreciation of the value of education which large numbers of people gained from the new and varied kinds of experience resulting from war conditions. The result was the Education Act of 1918 supplemented and consolidated by the Act of 1921. These Acts brought about great changes. Local authorities were required to produce schemes which, in combination, aimed at the establishment of 'a national system of public education available for all persons capable of profiting thereby'. In regard to elementary education, power was given to set up nursery schools for children between the ages of two and five, while the upper limits of the age of compulsory school attendance, which, after many vicissitudes, had settled at 12, was raised to 14 with power to the local authority to extend that age to 15. Incidentally the difficulties in the way of extension to 15 were such that very few authorities had been able to put it into operation even by 1939 when the second great war broke out.

Part-time attendance at school was abolished and provision made for the transfer of some of the older and abler children for whom the Act required that suitable educational provision should be made, from elementary schools to what were known as 'central schools'. The level of the education given in these central schools was intermediate between that of the secondary schools and that of the elementary schools. They were administered under the regulations for elementary education.

Local authorities were required to co-operate in preparing suitable children for the higher education given in secondary and technical schools and in making arrangements for the transfer of the children to these schools at appropriate ages, while a new feature, though not one of special importance for the purpose of this study, was introduced in the form of a compulsory system of part-time education after leaving the elementary school.

The Act also made provision for wide extension of the school curriculum in certain directions, especially in regard to practical work and physical education.

The re-organization of education envisaged in these far-reaching Acts took many years to come to fruition; indeed it was by no means complete, especially in rural areas, at the outbreak of war in 1939, while comparatively little progress had been made in the establishment of part-time education beyond the elementary school.

Owing mainly to the recommendations of a committee (known as the 'Hadow committee' from the name of its chairman) which was set up to review the position after the Act had been in operation for some years, progress during the period 1920–39 was not in fact through the establishment of central schools, which never became widespread, but through the reorganization of elementary education, from the age of seven upwards, into junior and senior schools, with the dividing line at 11 years of age. The general pattern in an area was that of senior schools providing suitable courses of instruction according to age and capacity for all children of 11 and upwards who had not been transferred to secondary schools, each of these senior schools drawing its pupils from a number of neighbouring junior schools.

The position was entirely altered by the Act of 1944, with the abolition of the distinction between elementary and higher education and its replacement by a distinction between 'primary' and 'secondary' education. All children were to receive primary education up to the age of 11 plus, and secondary education thereafter. The age of compulsory school attendance was raised to 15 with possible future extension, when circumstances allowed, to 16.

The schools of the country have been reorganized and re-classified on this basis, either as primary or as secondary. An anomaly in the system at present is the existence of a number of old 'all-age' (5–14) elementary schools. Where it has not been found possible to dispense with these in their present form, they have been temporarily retained and classified as 'primary', but they are due for elimination in course of time.

One other important feature of the Act was provision for establishing 'special educational treatment' for children mentally or physically handicapped. The training of teachers for this work constitutes a special problem which will be referred to in a later chapter.

The conception of primary education is fairly straightforward. It is the direct descendant, though with a quite different outlook and great improvements and extensions both in content and in method, of the earlier 'elementary education' for younger children. The new conception of secondary education is, however, a different matter, and it is of the greatest importance that the present system should be thoroughly understood.

A chief aim of the 1944 Act was the provision of secondary education for *all* children of 11 plus and upwards in schools administered under one set of regulations and enjoying parity of status and esteem. During the preceding 50 years, however, great developments had taken place in educational thought, accompanied by a very considerable amount of experiment and research. One result of this was a growing understanding of the fundamental nature and importance of the differences between individual children in capacity and bent. Accordingly the Act required that the secondary education provided for any child should be suitable to his age, ability and aptitude, due consideration being given, in all the circumstances of the case, to the wishes of his parents.

This embodied a new conception of secondary education as something which was the right of every child, and not merely of those who were specially gifted, but the education had to be adapted to the child's capacity and interests.

Clearly it was impossible to cater exhaustively for the infinite varieties of child-mind. In the result secondary education has been divided, in effect, into three types, secondary grammar, secondary technical, and secondary modern. These three types are for the most part provided by different schools bearing the corresponding names, but in some cases two, in others all three, types are provided on the same school premises by means of 'departments', 'sides' or 'streams'.

Broadly speaking, one may say that the grammar schools and the secondary technical schools are intended for the abler children—at present there is accommodation for about 15 per cent to 20 per cent of each of the age-groups affected. The secondary modern schools cater for the rest, through the medium of a wide and general education biased on the practical side. But, as has been said, all types of secondary school are administered under the same set of regulations, and are officially regarded as equal in status.

The grammar schools are the direct descendants of what were formerly known as 'secondary schools', and are in general identical with the latter, not only in regard to school premises but also in regard to the nature of their staffing and equipment and the kind of education they provide. The secondary technical schools (of which there are at present only a few) are, with their practical bias, a new type of school though representing in some ways a development of what were known as 'junior technical schools', for children of 13 or 14 to 16. Most of the children in grammar and technical schools stay on till 16, though by statute they are only compelled to stay till 15. The majority leave by 16, though an increasing number stay on till 17 or 18, as 'sixth forms', with a view to entering the professions or comparable occupations, or proceeding to a university.

The modern schools are the descendants, via the central and senior schools, of the upper ranges of the old elementary schools, though with a much wider and much more enlightened curriculum which has been shaped by the developments in educational ideas. Most of the children in these schools leave at 15 but a small, and slowly increasing, number stay on for a year or so longer, a tendency which is encouraged within the limits of the accommodation and facilities available.

It will be clear that the growth of the educational system, as outlined in the foregoing, has made steadily increasing demands on teaching power in regard to both quantity and quality. The corresponding stages through which the method of supplying teachers to meet these demands has passed can be listed in chronological order, though with a certain amount of overlapping, as follows: (a) the monitorial system; (b) the pupil-teacher system; (c) the student-teacher system; (d) training colleges for non-graduates; (e) university training departments for graduates; (f) training college examination boards or delegacies; (g) area training organizations.

The early voluntary schools relied on the monitorial system to make good the deficiency in the number of adult teachers. The principle of this system was that selected older pupils, known as 'monitors', learnt their lessons from the teacher in charge of the school and then passed on the knowledge they had acquired to the younger children.

It was not long before the inadequacies of this system began to make themselves felt in an acute form, and in 1840 a movement started as a result of which monitors were replaced by what were known as 'pupil-teachers'. These were boys and girls who served an apprenticeship of five years, from the age of 13, during which they gained experience in teaching and at the same time continued their own education under the instruction of the head teacher of an elementary school. As training colleges began to come into existence arrangements were made for some of them to admit a number of the best pupil-teachers, after they had finished their apprenticeship, for a further period of instruction.

Under the Act of 1902, the Board of Education was enabled to insist that entrants to training colleges should normally have taken a four-year course in a secondary school. All the forces at work, including the professional interests of the teachers themselves, were combining to demand a higher standard of professional qualification for teachers. This led to the gradual disappearance of the pupil-teacher system. In its latter stages it became the practice in some areas to collect the pupil-teachers into centres, each of which was attached, when possible, to a secondary school.

The pupil-teacher system has long since ceased to exist, but it was succeeded, along a line largely separate from the main line of development in training, by the 'student-teacher' system. The student-teacher continued in a course of general education till the age of 17, when he entered upon a year of preliminary training in an elementary school interspersed by periods of continued attendance at his secondary school. The supply of teachers from this source was never more than a trickle, and a departmental committee set up in 1925 to review the training of teachers recommended against the continuance of the system. It continued to linger on even up to 1939, but lapsed during the war and has not been renewed.

Meantime the establishment of training colleges had continued apace. These colleges began to come into existence in increasing numbers during the latter part of the nineteenth century. As might have been expected, in view of the way in which the educational system developed, the first colleges were 'voluntary colleges' set up mainly by religious organizations, and like the voluntary schools, these colleges have continued, and will continue, to play a large and vital part in the general system of education.

As time went on, however, the voluntary colleges were unable to carry the full burden of training and, with the passing of the 1902 Act, it became possible for local education authorities to found and maintain training colleges. These LEA colleges have continued to increase in number, but until recent years they were far fewer than the voluntary colleges. With the increasing demand for teachers, and the re-organization of training which began to come into operation in 1946, many more LEA colleges have been set up, and the disparity in number between them and the voluntary colleges is rapidly decreasing.

In 1893, new regulations enabled universities to establish grant-aided departments for the training of teachers. Full advantage was taken of this, and it was not very long before all universities and university colleges had opened what were known as 'university training departments'. Graduates who wished to become teachers could, after completing their degree course, take a year of training in one of these departments.

The report of the 1925 committee was followed by great changes. Up till that time the Board of Education had exercised an extremely close system of control over the training colleges. The examination of students in training at the end of their course had been conducted entirely by the Board, with His Majesty's inspectors acting as examiners through the formation of panels in the various subjects. But after 1926 the conduct of the examinations was handed over almost entirely to bodies acting under the aegis of universities. These bodies were known as training college examination boards or delegacies, and they included members both of the staffs of training colleges and of the staffs of universities.

Although the main function of the delegacies was examining, it was necessary for them, in order to perform this function effectively, also to concern themselves with the content of the syllabuses and schemes of work in the training colleges. This they did mainly through sub-committees known as 'boards of studies' which reported through a general board of studies to the governing council of the delegacy itself.

In the course of a few years the delegacies established an intricate and effective system of supervision over the training of teachers in the colleges. The course of training settled down to a pattern which was very much the same for all delegacies. In addition to the professional subjects, each student was required to select a number of general subjects of study from a list divided into Group A and Group B. The subjects in Group A were those generally known as 'academic', such as English, history, geography, mathematics, the sciences. In Group B were the 'practical subjects', such as handicraft, domestic science, music, art, gardening and rural science, etc. In making his selection a student had to include subjects from both groups.

Most general subjects could be taken at either of two levels, the 'ordinary' and the 'advanced'. Qualification could be obtained by taking four or five subjects (there was some variation in this number among the delegacies) at ordinary level, or a smaller number if some of the subjects were taken at advanced level.

Nevertheless, in spite of this delegation of a large measure of responsibility for training to regional bodies, the Board of Education continued to exercise a strict and detailed control over the scheme of work and syllabuses in training colleges, although it had long given up such close control in the case of the schools. No doubt this was because the Board attached great importance to training, which was regarded as a key activity. Even after the delegacies had been established, and although a college had first to obtain for its courses the approval of the delegacy with which it was associated, the syllabuses for these courses had finally to be submitted to the Board and were carefully scrutinized by H.M. inspectors before being approved.

The régime of the delegacies continued until 1946. In one respect it failed to achieve adequately one of the aims in the minds of those who were responsible for setting it up. It had been hoped that one of the results of the work of the delegacies would be to bring about a measure of liaison between training colleges and universities which would be of mutual benefit. This did in fact happen to some extent, though with considerable variations from one area to another; but on the whole the results were disappointing, no doubt partly because the complex machinery of examination and consideration of syllabuses absorbed most of the time and energy available.

It was for this and many other reasons, including especially the development in educational ideas and the corresponding demand for more and better qualified teachers, that during the last war, in spite of many obvious pre-occupations, the Board of Education set up a committee to review the existing position in regard to the training of teachers and to make recommendations for its improvement. This committee was known as the 'McNair committee' from the name of its chairman, Sir Arnold McNair.

As a result of the report of this committee, changes have taken place which are probably more profound than any in the history of training. They began to come into operation in 1946. The general position, which has resulted from them, will be fully considered in subsequent chapters, but a brief description of the general pattern will be given here.

The delegacies have disappeared and their place has been taken by bodies called 'area training organizations', familiarly known as ATOs, with functions and responsibilities far wider than those of the delegacies. The Ministry of Education, as it has now become, has given up all detailed control over training courses and handed over full responsibility for approving these to the councils of the ATOs acting on the advice of their academic (or professional) boards. The Ministry continues to exercise only a very general control, acting in this through a central national advisory council which will be described later.

As we shall see in Chapter II, all the relevant educational interests are represented on the council and committees of an ATO—the university, the training colleges, the local education authorities, and the practising teachers. The constituent members of an ATO, as an institution, are the training colleges and university training departments, now known as university departments of education (UDEs), in the area concerned. It is important to note the position of the UDEs. They were outside the purview of the delegacies but, while retaining their status as mainly autonomous departments of universities, they now, as constituent members, also come under the aegis of ATOs in ways to be described later.

There are two types of area training organizations, though both exercise the same functions, known as A type and C type as a result of the labels attached to the schemes which adumbrated them in the report of the McNair committee. This division into two types was, in fact, due to differing views in that committee. In the result choice as to type was left to the universities and other interested parties in the various regions. Three of the latter—Reading, Liverpool and Cambridge—opted for Scheme C; the remainder for Scheme A.

The difference between A and C lies in the position occupied by the university in the scheme. In scheme A the ATO is a 'school of education' of the university and the latter is pre-eminent in its governance although, as already stated, other interests are represented on the council and committees. Such an ATO is financed through the University Grants Committee.

An ATO under scheme C is an autonomous institution though closely associated with the university which is represented, as an equal among others, on its council and committees. An ATO of this kind is financed directly by the Ministry of Education.

Further results and implications of this division will be considered in Chapter II, but it is important to be clear from the outset on one point of terminology to which a brief reference has been made in the preface.

It was originally intended that ATOs of A type should be called 'schools of education' and those of C type 'institutes of education'. In practice, however, it has come about that all ATOs are now generally referred to as 'institutes of education'. The two terms are practically synonymous—sometimes it is convenient to use one, sometimes the other—though 'Area Training Organization' remains the official title[1]. Some A-type ATOs have retained 'school of education' in their own nomenclature.

The channels of supply, as they now exist, of teachers from the training institutions to the schools can be simply indicated. The non-graduate training colleges, with a two-year course (apart from certain exceptions to be described in Chapter I), train teachers mainly for primary schools and secondary modern schools. A number, comparatively small at present, of these teachers take in addition to their two-year course a post-initial course of the kind to be described in Chapter VII. The university departments of education train teachers mainly for all types of secondary school. The secondary grammar and technical schools are staffed mainly by graduates; the secondary modern schools with a preponderance of non-graduates and a leaven of graduates.

As will be seen later, there are certain exceptions to these general rules. For example, some graduates go into primary schools, and certain UDEs now make provision for training these. Some training colleges run courses for graduates or for those intending to graduate, while some of the non-graduate products of the colleges, especially in the 'practical' subjects, find their way into grammar schools.

---

1 See note in the foreword on a special usage in the case of London.

In the pattern of the long historical process which has led to the results described, certain main threads are discernible. One is the increasing degree of delegation of power and responsibility by the Board, later the Ministry, of Education to external bodies both regional and central. Another is the growing association of the universities with the conduct of the training of teachers. This has come about with an inevitability which considerable resistance from some quarters has not been able to halt, though it has sometimes slowed down the process temporarily.

A third main thread of development is of a different kind. It is concerned with educational principles, whereas the first two are concerned to a considerable degree with organization and administration.

During the last 50 years there has come about in England—though not only in England—a marked change consisting in a shift of focus in the educational process to the individual. Although the training colleges have always been pioneers and leaders in educational thought, and developments in the schools owe much to them, the change referred to first became clearly apparent in the schools themselves, especially the infant schools. The effect of the success of the comparatively new individual method of education in its application to younger children gradually spread through the whole educational system, and its influence on general thought and opinion was such that the principle of fitting education to the needs, abilities, and interests of the individual pupil was formally embodied in the great Education Act of 1944.

The effect on the training colleges has been twofold; not only are the students trained in the most effective way of applying individual methods to the children they will teach, but they are themselves studied as individuals, so that the professional training and the general education of each may be adapted to his special characteristics. The student is not regarded as one who, by hook or by crook, must somehow be got through a final examination which sets fixed limits and fixed patterns to which everyone must conform; he is regarded as a human being to be studied and understood sympathetically so that whatever potentialities he may have, even if comparatively humble in some respects, may be developed to the fullest possible extent.

The concentration on the student in training as an individual throws into relief another development which has become more clearly apparent in recent years. This is based on a principle which has been held in some degree ever since systematic training began. It is that the training college is not only an institution for giving its students an adequate training in professional methods of teaching, but also an institution for making a vital contribution to the general education of its students. For the latter it is indeed what the university is for its undergraduates, though it works under limitations, especially in regard to time, to which the university is not subject.

Professional competence and adequate and suitable general education are not of course strictly separable. However slick a teacher may be in applying the tricks of his trade, he cannot exercise the kind of general influence on his pupils which it is proper and desirable that he should unless he is an educated person in the fullest sense of the term. On the other hand, however well educated a person may be he cannot apply his capacity for teaching with the fullest effectiveness unless he has been professionally trained.

The last point raises an interesting and important question. It has often been held that some people are so gifted by nature—they are sometimes called 'born teachers'—that they can teach well without any professional training. This argument has been used to suggest the retention of the present practice, a practice which will be mentioned later, of granting the status of 'qualified teacher' to a graduate, or other of comparable qualification, who has had no professional training. But the argument misses the point. Nobody could deny with reason that the 'born teacher' may teach well without training. The real point is that he could apply his great natural gift far more effectively if he had been trained in the most effective ways of doing so. If we allow him to teach without training we may gain much from his potentiality, but at the same time we are wasting much of that potentiality.

There is one other point which may well be referred to here. It was said earlier that in 1926 the delegacies took over from the Board of Education 'almost' the whole responsibility for the examination of students in training. An exception was the examination and assessment of practical teaching. The examination of teaching practice had always been carried out for the Board of Education by H.M. inspectors. At a suitable time towards the end of the college course, generally between January and April, each college submitted to H.M. inspectors a list of the students completing the course, giving a provisional list of marks for practical teaching. With this list for reference H.M. inspectors visited the schools to observe the practice of the students teaching in them. In doing this they were concerned not so much with the marks of individual students as with the general standard of the college marking. After their school visits H.M. inspectors met the college staff in conference and, as a result of the ensuing discussion, a final list of teaching marks was drawn up and approved by H.M. inspectors.

The Board of Education retained control of this part of the training college examinations not only because of the importance they attached to it but also because at that time H.M. inspectors were the only body of people with the width and type of experience necessary to the conduct of the examination of practical teaching. But it was an anomaly in the system. The proper function of H.M. inspectors is to inspect, not to examine; moreover, with the steady increase in the scope of H.M. inspectors' official duties, the additional burden of examining, always very heavy, became well-nigh insupportable. Accordingly, with the coming of the new institutes of education the opportunity has been taken of handing over to these institutes responsibility for examining practical teaching. This could not be done all at once, for the institutes had to discover, or gradually to create, an alternative body of examiners with the requisite type of experience. Meanwhile H.M. inspectors continued to lend a hand where necessary; but the process of transfer of responsibility is now almost complete.

As has been said, the general control exercised by the Ministry, as such, over teacher training has now been considerably relaxed. Nevertheless the Ministry is kept in close touch with what is happening through the work of H.M. inspectors.

Every training institution drawing grant from the Ministry is, by regulation, open to inspection, and certain H.M. inspectors are, in fact, assigned to the inspection of training institutions. These H.M. inspectors, often with specialist colleagues, visit the training institutions from time to time and discuss matters of common concern with the principals and staffs. These discussions have proved very fruitful, and cordial relations exist between H.M. inspectors and the training world to the benefit of both.

At long intervals, a more formal inspection of every college is held, known as a 'full inspection'. A panel of inspectors visits the college for the best part of a week to discuss and assess every aspect of the work, subsequently reporting to the Minister.

The Ministry also appoints assessors to the councils and academic boards of the ATOs. The function of these will be described later.

It might seem logical to follow this historical introduction by a description in detail of the system of organization and control of the training of teachers through the ATOs as it now exists; but such a description will probably be better understood if something is said first about the nature of the training institutions themselves. To that matter we will now turn.

CHAPTER I

THE TRAINING INSTITUTIONS

ORIGIN

As we have seen, training colleges began to come into existence about the middle of the last century, springing up here and there to meet the need of particular bodies for teachers, and were at first established voluntarily and mainly by religious organizations. Colleges set up and administered by local education authorities came considerably later and in much smaller numbers, but recently there has been a great expansion in LEA provision, especially since the end of the last war. This has been necessary to meet the pressing need for teachers and it has been greatly aided by the fact that, after the war, a large number of colleges administered by LEAs came into being under the emergency training scheme. With the winding up of the emergency scheme many of these colleges have become available for the permanent training system.

The individual, indeed almost haphazard, way in which the first training colleges came into being had one disadvantage which gives some substance to a criticism often made against the colleges—that they are traditionally isolationist. This is undoubtedly true. The first colleges were so scattered, and were intended to meet such special needs, that there was very little stimulus or opportunity towards their making contact with one another and pooling their ideas and experience. This set up an attitude of self-sufficiency which is only now breaking down. The establishment of the delegacies after 1926 helped to bring the colleges into contact with one another, but full advantage was not taken of the opportunities thus provided. With the coming of the area training organizations or institutes, however, the picture is already changing radically. The way in which the work of the institutes is carried on involves a considerable degree of contact between the staffs of different colleges, not only at the conference table but through visits paid by members of the staff of one college, for various purposes, to other colleges. Moreover one of the functions of an institute, a function to which the McNair committee gave considerable weight, is to survey the resources in college staffing and equipment of its area as a whole and to consider how best these resources can be pooled and co-ordinated to the advantage of all.

Another criticism levelled with some truth against certain colleges is that their code of discipline is unduly rigid and severe. This again arises from the nature of the origin of the colleges. It is not surprising that institutions set up by religious bodies during the last century should have been bound by strict codes of conduct and discipline. This tradition has died hard, and amelioration in accordance with modern ideas allowing greater flexibility and latitude, without a lowering of moral standards, has been rather slow in coming. In this respect the colleges have lagged behind the universities, although both are dealing with young people of about the same age. But there has been a steady improvement in this matter, much accelerated of late, in the colleges as a whole. No doubt closer association with the universities has had something to do with this.

FINANCE

Apart from the students' contributions, almost the whole of the income of a voluntary college comes from the Ministry. The college fees for students must be approved by the Ministry, which pays to the college in respect of each recognized student a grant equal to the tuition fee and a grant equal to the boarding fee less an appropriate contribution from the student. These grants must be applied towards the payment of fees. The day maintenance grant is paid, through the college, to a day student by the Ministry, but is not available to the college as income. At present the fees approved for a college are fixed for three years, at the end of which period they are reviewed, and are based on estimates of expenditure submitted by the college and carefully scrutinized by the Ministry.

Voluntary colleges may also receive capital grants from the Ministry. The object of these grants is not to enable new voluntary colleges to be established, but to help existing ones to make themselves efficient and, if necessary, to extend to an economical size. A voluntary college which existed on April 1945, the date when the capital grant regulations came into force, may receive grant at a rate not exceeding 50 per cent on capital expenditure over £500 involved by: (a) improvement, extension or replacement of its accommodation, and (b) provision of furniture and equipment necessitated by (a). The remaining proportion of the capital expenditure must come from purely voluntary sources.

The case of LEA colleges is different. Before 1946 an authority providing a training college received in grant 50 per cent of its net recognizable expenditure, the other 50 per cent being met from the local rates. The students were charged fees as in voluntary colleges. But, under the new grant system, a providing LEA receives 100 per cent grant on all its net recognizable expenditure, capital and maintenance. The total of such expenditure for all providing LEAs is then aggregated into a pool. All LEAs, including providing LEAs, are required to contribute between them the amount of the pool, the contribution of each being determined by the ratio of the number of children on its school registers to the total number for the whole country. These contributions rank for the Ministry's grant, and, in the result, the Ministry contributes 60 per cent of the total expenditure and the combined LEAs 40 per cent.

The reason for the change in the grant system is that the training of teachers is now regarded as a national service. It is true that many training colleges tend for various reasons to attract students from particular localities, especially from the localities in which they are situated; but when the students come out as qualified teachers they are regarded as available, in principle, for work in any part of the country, and they do in fact distribute themselves widely. This desirable scattering process is hampered at the moment by economic and domestic difficulties, especially in regard to housing, the influence of which is such as to keep individual teachers tied to certain regions, but it is a process to be encouraged so that it may operate fully again when times are easier.

The 100 per cent grant is paid to the providing LEA on condition that no tuition fee is charged to recognized students, and that the charge to such students in respect of boarding shall be assessed on an approved scale, the student paying this grant to the college as in the case of voluntary colleges. Since grant is not based on fees there is no need for a systematic approval of fees for recognized students, except when such students are rich enough to be called upon to pay the full boarding fee, in which case the Ministry consults with the LEA as to what fee it would be reasonable to charge. Other forms of aid to students and to practising teachers will be considered later, but it should be added here that the 'private' student, that is one who is admitted to a college without signing the declaration that, when trained, he will teach in schools grant-aided by the Ministry, is required to pay full boarding and tuition fees.

The large majority of students in the training colleges are, of course, non-graduates. The university departments providing one-year professional courses for graduates came into the field rather later, pioneered by such institutions as the London Day Training College. Formerly they were known as 'university training departments' but this name has now been changed to 'university departments of education'.

Hitherto there have been two types of university students in training, the four-year and the one-year. The four-year student indicated his intention of training as a teacher at the end of his degree course before entering the university, and grant was awarded on that basis. During his degree course the UDE exercised a degree of supervision over him and helped and advised him in connexion with his preparation for the post-graduate training course. The category of four-year student is, however, now being abolished and in future all university students in training will be one-year. Such students are not definitely marked down for teacher-training until near the time when it will be necessary for them to embark on the professional course.

One reason for the change is that it is held to be undesirable that university students should be marked down for the teaching profession too early. These young people often change their ideas and interests during their undergraduate years so that it is well to postpone the crucial decision as long as possible. Another reason for the change is that the four-year system is clearly open to abuse. A would-be university student who was not of high enough calibre to obtain an award such as a State scholarship or a university scholarship might announce his intention of becoming a teacher as the only way of obtaining a grant to enable him to go to the university, even though he might actually have little or no intention of teaching. Though it may be possible technically to put pressure on such a student to honour his declaration, it is far from easy to compel him in practice, nor would such a student be likely to become an adornment to the teaching profession.

A one-year student, in order to gain admission to a course of professional training, must be accepted by a UDE, though not necessarily the UDE of the university where he took his degree. In fact many students take their professional training at a university other than their parent university.

Boarding grants (in the case of resident students) and tuition grants are paid for these one-year students at an approved rate, and are assessed after allowing for the student's contribution.

TYPES OF TRAINING INSTITUTION

Training institutions, then, are divided into two main categories: non-graduate (mainly) training colleges, and university departments of education for graduates. The training colleges are again divided into LEA or provided colleges, and voluntary or non-provided colleges.

The normal length of the course in the training colleges is two years. It has long been recognized that this is insufficient, and all are now agreed that the course should be lengthened to three years as soon as possible, although present difficulties have made inevitable a further postponement of this desirable end. Some of these difficulties, partly financial, are related to the provision of adequate additional staff, accommodation and equipment. Another difficulty is that, during a period of urgent need for teachers, the sacrifice of one year's output from the colleges, which the change from two to three years would involve, can hardly be contemplated. The best hope is, perhaps, that a way will be found of introducing the three-year course gradually by stages, though the best way of doing this has still to be discovered.

Most of the colleges train teachers for the various sections of the whole age-range of children from five to fifteen years. Some colleges, however, specialize in training teachers for the primary schools, that is schools taking children up to 11 years of age and 'all-age' schools where these still exist. In such colleges provision is often made also for the training of teachers for nursery schools and classes for children under five. Other colleges specialize in the teaching of certain subjects or groups of subjects, for example the colleges of domestic science, handicraft, and physical education. Of these the colleges of domestic science and the women's colleges of physical education have already established three-year courses and may be regarded as the advance guard in the progress towards a three-year course for all.

There is one other group of colleges, which also has a long established three-year course, deserving special mention—those famous pioneers in the education of young children, the Froebel colleges. These specialize in the training of teachers for the primary schools, and until quite recently, formed an autonomous group. They are now being integrated, however, into the general system of training under the ATOs. Some of them have managed to retain their special characteristics, including the three-year course, but one or two, owing to the exigencies of finance and other circumstances, have been compelled to surrender their independence, and have been taken over by LEAs with a reduction of the three-year course to two years.

Experiments with different types of college are at present being tried on a limited scale. For example some intending teachers of domestic science are taking two years of their course in one institution and then passing on for their third year to another institution specially adapted to provide a finishing course. In another case a college has been set up with a special bias toward music, drama, and art.

Certain institutions training students to become teachers receive no grant from the Ministry, usually because they wish to retain their independence. If such an institution desires that its students should receive the status of 'qualified teacher' it must apply to the Ministry. If, after inspection by H.M. inspectors, the institution is regarded as satisfying the appropriate conditions it may be put on the list of 'recognized

efficient' colleges and its students recognized as qualified teachers at
the end of their course; but it is the general policy of the Ministry not
to give approval of this kind without the concurrence of the local ATO,
and the willingness of the latter to take over the general supervision
of the institution concerned.

BUILDINGS AND EQUIPMENT

The colleges differ widely from one another in the quality and quantity
of their buildings and equipment. Inevitably the voluntary colleges
suffer on the whole by comparison with the LEA colleges. They were
first in the field and have not the same financial resources behind them
as have the LEA colleges. Nevertheless some of the voluntary colleges
have admirable buildings, and great efforts have been, and are being,
made to keep up the standard.

The Ministry issues no official regulations governing the nature of
college buildings, but a considerable body of knowledge and opinion
in regard to this has gradually come into being and the help and advice
of the Ministry's officers is readily available to governing bodies of
colleges wishing to put up new buildings or to extend existing ones.

Certain points stand out specially in this context. One relates to
study-bedrooms for the students. The ideal is, of course, a study-bed-
room for each student and some colleges can provide this, but owing
to the rapidly increasing demands for teachers in recent years it has
not been possible to conform to this ideal everywhere, and in many
cases rooms are shared by two, three or even more students. Another
important point relates to the provision of teaching rooms. With the
gradual replacement of the full-dress lecture as the main instrument of
method by work in small tutorial groups, there is an urgent need for a
considerable number of relatively small rooms in addition to an adequate number of larger rooms, together with a hall of assembly where
the whole college can meet.

Other requirements are common and recreational rooms for the
students and suitable accommodation for the staff, including a staff
common room. A properly equipped sick-bay is essential, and the provision of good facilities for washing, baths, heating and sanitary purposes. Much progress has been made of late in these respects. Moreover, increasing attention is being given to making colleges dignified
and pleasant places in which to live.

In regard to equipment, apart from the provision of the necessary
standard equipment, the colleges are doing their best to keep pace
with the demands of modern educational methods, especially in regard

to teaching aids of various kinds such as those connected with visual aids and broadcasting. The success of the colleges in this respect varies with their circumstances, especially financial, though they are of course helped by grants from the Ministry where repair and maintenance are concerned.

What has been said about training colleges in regard to buildings and equipment is true also, *mutatis mutandis*, of university departments of education, but the history and background of these is different from that of the colleges and their circumstances are determined largely by the universities with which they are associated. Moreover some of the facilities and amenities provided by individual training colleges for their students are covered in the case of the UDE by the general provision made by the university.

GOVERNING BODIES OF TRAINING COLLEGES

The function of the governing body (GB) of a training college is the overall administration and supervision of the work and general running of the college. It is with the GB that the Ministry communicates officially, usually through the medium of the college principal. The principal attends meetings of the GB, in some cases as a full member, in other cases as an adviser without voting rights.

The status of the principal in relation to the GB is one of the questions under active consideration at the moment. Opinion about it is divided. In practice, of course, the day-to-day running of a college is left entirely in the hands of the principal in consultation with his staff, and principals thus rightly enjoy a very large measure of autonomy. But at intervals there are meetings of the GB to which the principal reports and at which current problems are discussed. The GB is naturally concerned particularly with questions of finance.

All of the foregoing applies whether the college is voluntary or LEA. In the case of LEA colleges, the GB is generally a sub-committee of the education committee of the LEA.

Although the professional training of graduates is conducted mainly in UDEs, certain training colleges accept a limited number of graduates, after they have taken their degree, for a year's professional training. This is valuable in view of the shortage of places in UDEs. One difficulty however is that smaller grants and allowances are paid for these students than for their fellows in the UDEs. The position is now being reviewed.

Some training colleges, in particular the men's colleges in London, also accept students wishing to take a degree. These students are given a three-year course during which they are prepared for the degree concurrently with their professional training, but they must have covered the first stages towards the degree before admission to college.

The training colleges and UDEs which have been described are the units forming the constituent members of ATOs. Other educational institutions may become 'associate members', but the degree to which the practice of associate membership is carried out, and the acceptance of institutions as associate members, depends on the individual ATO.

CHAPTER II

THE AREA TRAINING ORGANIZATIONS

GENERAL LAY-OUT

There are 17 area training organizations, associated with the Universities of Birmingham, Bristol, Cambridge, Durham, Exeter (University College of the South West), Hull (University College), Leeds, Leicester (University College), Liverpool, London, Manchester, Nottingham, Oxford, Reading, Sheffield, Southampton, and Wales.

There is wide variation in the number of training colleges associated with these ATOs, from London at one end of the scale, with its large assembly of colleges, to Oxford and the university colleges at the other end with only two or three colleges. The newly established University College of North Staffordshire has at present no training colleges associated with it. As mentioned before, only three of the ATOs—Cambridge, Liverpool and Reading—are C institutes of education. The remainder are A institutes, that is schools of education of their universities.

It is not yet possible to judge what will be the long-term effect on the institutes of such factors as their degree of association with the universities; but there seems no reason in principle why, given the goodwill of all concerned, the C institutes should not discharge their functions as effectively as the A institutes. In what follows a distinction will be made between the two only when the circumstances call for it.

The distribution of the training colleges among the various institutes is ultimately a matter for the Minister, and the original lay-out was planned by the Ministry in consultation with the other interests concerned. From time to time modifications in this may become necessary: already some adjustments have had to be made owing to the entry into the field of two latecomers, first Cambridge and then, within the last year, Oxford.

Although the association of a particular college with a particular ATO is a matter ultimately for the Minister, in practice a college has to be accepted by the ATO itself before becoming a constituent member of it. This acceptance is usually dependent on the results of some kind of 'visitation' by a panel appointed by the ATO. If it is not possible to arrange such a visitation at once, it is customary to admit a college provisionally pending a visitation, provided there is a clear *prima facie* case for admission.

The training course leading to the status of 'qualified teacher' (QT) is known as the 'initial training' of the teacher. In general the Minister will accept recommendations for QT status, whether for a graduate or for a non-graduate, only from an ATO. Exceptions to this rule are theoretically possible in very special circumstances but are regarded as undesirable in practice. In particular an extremely convincing case would have to be made before a college could remain independent of any ATO or, having once been a member of an ATO, afterwards leave it. On the other hand circumstances of various kinds, e.g. geographical, may exist or arise where there is clear advantage in the transfer of a college from one ATO to another, and this has already happened in a few cases.

CONSTITUTION

The council of the institute is the supreme authority within an ATO. Subject to the general powers of the Minister and, in the case of A institutes, to the governance of the university, it is concerned primarily with all questions affecting the initial training of teachers in its area and secondarily with certain supplementary activities (to be dealt with in a later section) which are directly or indirectly relevant to training.

In carrying out its work the council is advised by its main committee, the academic or professional board, which is again advised by sub-committees or panels dealing with the various subjects and phases of education and training. All the main educational interests are represented on the councils of the institutes—universities, training colleges, LEAs and practising teachers, and there is also appropriate representation of these interests on the academic boards. In addition, two assessors from the Ministry sit with the council, an administrative officer and an H.M. inspector, and two, both H.M. inspectors, with the academic board. These assessors are not members of the bodies concerned and have no voting powers, but they are available for information or advice when called upon, or they may intervene on their own initiative when such intervention is plainly desirable. In discharging their functions the Ministry's assessors are aided, not only by their knowledge of the Ministry itself, but also by the briefings they receive from time to time from their colleagues engaged in the inspection of training.

Two of the chief matters with which the institutes have to deal in their concern with the initial training of teachers are the courses of training and the examination and assessment of students. These will now be considered in turn.

COURSES OF TRAINING

Although as much freedom as possible is rightly allowed to the training colleges in planning their courses, the latter must fall within the framework of the general regulations laid down by the institute. The content of the courses will be considered in some detail in a later section. Here they will be discussed only in respect of their relation to the conditions laid down by institute regulations.

There is, of course, variation in detail, especially in the actual working of the regulations, from one institute to another; nevertheless the general pattern is strikingly similar in the different areas.

This is an interesting and significant fact reflecting, no doubt, coherence and general agreement in the recent developments of educational thought in regard to training. Although, during the discussions of the last few years on the planning of courses, there was in the early stages comparatively little interchange of ideas and opinions among the different institutes—so that their discussions were largely independent of one another—the results as they emerged showed a substantial measure of uniformity.

The training course falls broadly into three parts which may be termed professional, general, and semi-professional; which are, in practice, kept in appropriate relation to one another.

The professional section covers such subjects as principles and practice of education, including health education, some aspects of special method (e.g. in arithmetic and English), and educational psychology.

In the general section the student has to select a subject from a list set out in the regulations. In some cases a second subject is also compulsory; in other cases it is optional. The subjects are such as contribute to the general education of the student, who will also study special teaching method in the subject when it is one, as usually happens, that he intends or is likely to teach. Here, by way of illustration, is a typical list of subjects: art and/or craft, biology, chemistry, divinity, English, French, general science, geography, history, horticulture, mathematics, music, physical education, physics, rural science.

There are minor variations in the list from one area to another, the actual length and content of the list depending on the circumstances of the area and the nature of the colleges in it. Moreover particular colleges within an area may not be prepared to offer every subject in the general list for the area. This will depend partly on the size of the college and partly on the nature and degree of its specialization, if any.

A word should be said on the position of English. Every teacher is expected to have adequate command of his native language, to be able to teach its usage to the degree required by his particular job, and to have appropriate acquaintance with English literature. Provision for this is made in the professional course, and this is extended when English is chosen as a subject in the general section. Steps are taken by the institutes, through written examination or otherwise, to satisfy themselves of the students' proficiency in English.

As a rule no formal differentiation of standard is made within each subject, but there are one or two areas where subjects may be taken at a 'higher' or a 'lower' standard. Variation in standard is now being dealt with in a different way, related to the natural abilities and interests of the individual student, as we shall see in the sequel. Here, and in the treatment of the general section as a whole, there are substantial differences from the practice under the delegacies.

The third, or semi-professional, section of the course is largely new, and consists of grouped studies known by such names as 'combined' or 'integrated' courses, of which 'project' work is a particular example. In this section the students make a practical study of real situations involving those various aspects of life and nature which, in the study of the traditional subjects, are dealt with in comparative abstraction. The work is in part professional method and in part a contribution to general education, for the students carry it on both at their own level of age and maturity and at the level of the children they intend to teach. This work is particularly important in the training of primary teachers.

This is perhaps an appropriate place to make some reference to the distinction between the training of primary and the training of secondary teachers in England. There is in fact no rigid and clear-cut distinction. Although certain colleges specialize in the training of primary teachers, there is in general nothing in the way of separate system of training for primary and secondary. Such differences as exist are mainly in regard to method and to some extent, perhaps, in bias in the choice of general subjects. These differences will be considered in the section on courses of training. Incidentally, with the exception of one or two UDEs, no training institutions specialize solely on training for secondary work, though naturally most students from the UDEs go to teach in secondary schools. But of late years there has been an increasing tendency in UDEs to make some provision for any students who may wish to teach in primary schools.

There are sound reasons for this state of affairs. For example, in principles and practice of education there is a substantial common core which should be studied by all students in training, wherever they are going to teach. Even more important, all teachers should be well educated people, and those in the primary schools should not compare unfavourably in this respect with their fellows in the secondary modern schools. Moreover it is an excellent thing to have a leaven of graduates in the primary schools, some of them persons of academic distinction. This is good, not only for the primary schools themselves, but for the educational system generally. The basic principle is parity of status and esteem for all teachers, no matter whether they be teaching a class in an infant school or the sixth form in a grammar school. This principle is embodied in a common basic salary scale, although provision is made in this scale for special qualifications.

Apart from these reasons, it is all to the good if students preparing to teach in different types of school can be trained in the same institutions or, where this is not the case, can be brought into contact from time to time, so that they may benefit from an exchange of ideas and from discussions in which each student may become aware of the special problems or lines of approach of others intending to teach in schools of a type different from those for which he is himself preparing. Moreover where students are being trained to teach children of a certain age-range, it is customary to give them experience of the education of children in adjacent age-ranges, not only so that their own work may become more intelligible and purposeful, but so that if, when they leave college, they find it necessary, through circumstances beyond their control, to teach for a time children in an age-range somewhat different from that for which they have been specially trained, they may not be at a loss. This is particularly important at a time when conditions are continually changing, owing to the progress through the schools of the 'bulge' arising from the abnormally high birth-rate during the immediate post-war years. At present, and for some time past, there has been a great demand for primary teachers and it has been necessary for the training colleges, at the instance of the Ministry, to make special provision for this. Later on this demand will naturally change into one for secondary teachers.

Reference was made earlier to the question of standard in connexion with courses of training *vis-à-vis* the institutes. The basic principle here, in accordance with modern ideas, is that, apart from any fixed external standard, everything should be done to develop the latent potentialities of each student to the fullest possible extent, by helping and encouraging him to carry on his studies to a depth and at a pace determined by his own natural capacities and interests. A student is to be judged as far as possible not so much by whether he can surmount an examination hurdle the height of which has been more or less rigidly fixed by regulation, but by whether, during his course, he has developed his own potentialities to a degree which can be regarded as reasonable in

41

his case, and has not finished up below an acceptable minimum level of general education and professional competence.

As the institutes are still in the experimental period, there is naturally some variation between different areas in the way in which the colleges are left free to implement this principle. In particular there is some variation in the flexibility and latitude allowed by the two main methods of control exercised by the institutes, namely by approval of courses and by examination regulations. It is too early to say whether things will ultimately settle down into overall uniformity in this respect or whether there will always be some area differences; but signs point to the latter, and this is no doubt desirable in the interests of progress.

The institutes are fully aware of the importance of regarding training colleges as places where a student receives a good general education as well as instruction in professional studies, and all their thinking and planning is informed by this idea; they have made it their business to see that the colleges are afforded every opportunity of pursuing this twofold aim so far as limitations of time and circumstance permit.

EXAMINATION AND ASSESSMENT

The second main task of the institutes was the establishment of an effective and enlightened system of examination and assessment. The history of the examination of training college students up to the time it was taken over by the new ATOs has been dealt with briefly in the introduction and it is only necessary to add one point here, but it is an important point.

Up to about 15 years ago the examination of training college students was conducted entirely by means of written papers except for certain practical tests in such subjects as art, craft, and science, and most of the examination was held during a comparatively short period towards the end of the second and final year of the training course. The examination was in fact known as the 'final examination', and each student was judged by the results he could produce in it.

During the pre-war period, however, another method of estimating a student's calibre was being tentatively tried out in some of the delegacy areas. This was known as 'assessment by course work'. The college staff, ultimately in consultation with external examiners, scrutinized the work of the student throughout the course, or the relevant portions of the course, not so much to assess the value of particular pieces of work as to form an estimate of the student's calibre on the basis of his progress and the use he had made of the opportunities available to him in developing his potentialities. Particular attention was naturally given to the result finally achieved. The common practice was in awarding him appropriate marks, to combine the results of this assessment with the student's performance in the final examination.

The method of course assessment received a double stimulus from the circumstances obtaining during the war period. Most of the men students were unable to complete the training course and sit for the final examination before they were called up, and it was therefore necessary to judge them by assessment of their course work, while a second stimulus to this method was provided by the coming of the emergency training scheme. It was felt that anything in the nature of a final examination was inappropriate in the case of students such as those trained under the emergency scheme, and these students were accordingly assessed by the quality of their work in the course as a whole, the final assessment being carried out by the college staffs in consultation with H.M. inspectors. By the time the new institutes of education came into being, therefore, a considerable amount of experience had been gained in regard to the best ways of applying the method of course assessment. In particular it had become apparent that this method had certain advantages over the written examination and enabled examiners to make a fairer estimate in some respects of the quality of the student.

Accordingly the institutes embarked almost as a·matter of course on a combination of written papers and course work assessment as their normal method of examination, the main problem being that of finding the right balance between these two instruments of judgment and the best way of combining them.

In the result there is considerable diversity of practice. In the first place some institutes apply a uniform method of combination to all the colleges in their area, while others take into account the wishes of particular colleges and allow some variation. In the second place, practice varies from complete or almost complete reliance on assessment of course work alone to the giving of major weight to the written papers; but in no case is judgment based on written papers alone, course work assessment always plays an important part. Here again the work of the institutes is still in the experimental period. No doubt the extremes will tend to approach one another in course of time, but it seems likely that some variation in practice will persist. This is all to the good, not only in the interests of progress but because it is hardly to be expected that there is just one method of combining written examination and assessment which is markedly superior to all others.

Two other problems have been engaging the attention of the institutes. One is to find the right balance between unifomity in the conduct of the examination (hereafter this term will be used to cover both written papers and course work assessment) through control by regulation, and freedom for a degree of variation between individual colleges or small groups of colleges. The other, and not altogether unconnected, problem is to find the right combination of 'internal' and 'external' examination.

In both matters there are considerable differences of opinion, not only between institutes, but also within individual institutes. Hence there is some variation in practice. One point around which there has been energetic discussion is whether there should be at least some written papers compulsory for all students in all colleges, e.g. in certain aspects of the principles of education, or whether such uniformity should be required only within relatively small groups of colleges the members of which share certain common and salient features in the nature of their work. Some people indeed would like to see separate papers for each college in every field, devised to suit the special characteristics of that college.

It is not surprising that there has been keen discussion and wide difference of opinion in regard to such matters. The members of the councils and the academic boards of the institutes have a common interest in education and training, but they represent different interests in some respects and approach their work with different backgrounds of experience. In particular the universities have their own tradition of examination; the LEAs are anxious that there should be some guarantee of professional competence in trained teachers on which they can rely and which has universal currency; the practising teachers keep a careful watch on academic standards in the interests of the status of their profession; the training colleges naturally desire as much latitude and flexibility as possible in order that they may carry on their work along the lines which seem most suitable to them. It speaks well for all concerned that, for the most part, the business of the institutes is carried on so harmoniously and with so much tolerance and good sense in working out reasonable solutions to which all have contributed and which are therefore acceptable to all.

The examination and assessment of the students of a particular college is carried out partly by the college staff—'internal' examination—and partly by examiners appointed by the institute—'external' examination. Internal and external examiners work in close consultation with one another though, for the purposes of the institute, it is of course the external examiners who have the final word. The panels of external examiners are appointed by the institute on the recommendations of the academic board and the boards of studies, and are reviewed from time to time.

Not all external examiners come from within the ambit of the particular institute concerned. It has become the practice for an institute to look to other areas for some of its examiners. This has the advantage of pooling the experience of people coming from different parts of the country with different conditions. One hoped-for result is that a common standard in the awarding of the title of 'qualified teacher', on the basis of examination, will gradually be established, and a special word should be said about this.

The idea of a common standard, in any precise sense, is something of a chimera, not only because of the great difficulty of defining exact criteria to determine it, but also because of the great difficulty of applying such criteria in practice. Evidently one cannot define a common standard in terms of subjective judgments, while objective criteria that are practically applicable (e.g. in the form of percentages of passes and failures) though precise within their limits, are open to criticism on the grounds of possible variation in the calibre of students from one area to another, and almost inevitable variation in the standard of 'difficulty' of the different examinations. In fact this difficulty itself can be defined objectively only in terms of percentage of passes, so that we are left with a vicious circle. Perhaps the only possible solution to this problem lies in the gradual spreading of something approximating to what might be called a uniform 'climate' of judgment as the pooling of the ideas and experience of the different institutes continues to grow.

Reference should here be made to three points in connexion with the implications of the title of 'qualified teacher'. The first is that the title has significance only in relation to teaching in primary and secondary schools, and only in such of these schools as are grant-aided by the Ministry, though if a teacher in another kind of institution wishes to transfer to a grant-aided primary or secondary school account may be taken of his previous teaching experience in laying down the conditions which he must satisfy before he is accorded the title of 'qualified teacher'.

The second point is that a QT may teach in any grant-aided primary or secondary school and in any part of that school. So far as the Ministry's regulations are concerned, there is nothing to prevent a QT trained to teach infants from actually teaching in the sixth form of a grammar school. This looks extremely odd on the face of it; but the reason for this latitude is that the Ministry prefers to rely on the good sense of LEAs, governing bodies, and others in making their appointments rather than itself to lay down meticulous regulations as to where a particular teacher may or may not teach. There is no doubt that, with few exceptions, this policy of the Ministry justifies itself in practice.

The third point is that at present a graduate, or other person with qualifications deemed to be equivalent to a degree, is automatically accorded QT status even if he does not take a course of professional training. This practice is at present under review, and it is not unlikely that it may cease before long with the introduction of compulsory training for all desiring to become QTs. Apart from the question of the desirability of compulsory training for all, the practice gives rise to certain anomalies. In particular, what about the graduate who takes a course of professional training but is then held not to have completed that course satisfactorily? Can he then fall back on his degree? Up to the present the Ministry has taken the line that he cannot, but must be deemed to have failed to become a QT.

Apart from their main tasks of examination and the supervision of training courses the institutes have embarked on a number of ancillary lines of activity, and we may now pass on to a consideration of these.

ANCILLARY ACTIVITIES OF THE INSTITUTES

It was held by the McNair committee that one of the proper aims of an institute, whether of A or C type, was—becoming something more than a body for supervising the training of teachers—to provide an educational centre catering for all those working, or interested, in education in the area which it served. In spite of their preoccupation with their main task, the institutes have already embarked whole-heartedly on this project and although progress naturally varies with local conditions much has already been done.

The value of a centre evidently depends to a marked extent on ability to provide suitable accommodation to house it and to furnish and equip it adequately. It is in this respect particularly that progress has depended on local conditions. Such an educational centre can not only provide a pleasant and convenient place where people may meet and make use of such facilities as an educational reference library and, where accommodation is sufficient, offer rooms for lectures or discussion groups but it can also serve as a focus for other activities of the institute. The centre may actually be housed in the university buildings or, especially in the case of C institutes, it may be accommodated in a separate building.

One important activity of the institutes is the provision of courses mainly for practising teachers. These courses may be in the nature of 'refresher' courses of various kinds which are of comparatively short duration, though the institutes are now considering the possibility of establishing in addition something more substantial, namely courses at a relatively high level, and of considerable duration, through which practising teachers and other suitable candidates can proceed to an advanced qualification, possibly carrying with it a title of some kind. This project raises certain points on which there is a variety of opinion, and which are now being keenly discussed. In particular it has not been found easy to agree on what exactly should be the title associated with an advanced qualification of the kind envisaged.

There is another type of course in regard to which the institutes are working in close collaboration with the Ministry—the 'supplementary courses'. These will be considered in a later section and it is only necessary to say here that they are courses of one year's duration, following on the initial training course, which are taken by selected students. Each course deals with a particular subject, and it may be taken by the student immediately he finishes his initial training or after the lapse of an interval during which he is engaged in teaching.

Another activity which the institutes have taken up with enthusiasm is that of educational research. There is no doubt that they have a valuable part to play in this field for they have great resources, direct and indirect, at their command, and their work involves a multitude and variety of contacts. Many interesting investigations, some of them in collaboration with other bodies, have been carried out or are now in train.

There is, of course, a possible danger in all this. The main business and primary function of the ATOs is the initial training of teachers. Whatever else they may do it is essential that this part of their work should be carried out as effectively as possible. No enthusiasm, however commendable in itself, for other forms of activity should be allowed to interfere with, or to limit in any way, the performance of the primary function. There are bounds to the amount of time, energy and money which can be spent on the work of an institute as a whole, and it is important that a sense of proportion should be preserved. It is perhaps true to say that there is at present some variation in balance from one area to another and this is a matter which has to be kept under review. There is, of course, an ultimate financial sanction. It would never be applied except with great reluctance, but a brief word should be said about it here.

FINANCE

There are two methods of financing, according to the type of institute. The C institutes are financed by direct grant from the Ministry. The A institutes, being schools of the universities, are financed through the University Grants Committee (UGC). The financial estimates of the C institutes are reviewed anually by the Ministry and they receive a 100 per cent grant on current maintenance and capital expenditure. The estimates of the A institutes are reviewed quinquennially and it is usual for the UGC to obtain the comments of the Ministry on them before apportioning their share of the university grant. In making the reviews consideration is given to the way in which expenditure is distributed among the different parts of the institutes' work; this distribution is carefully scrutinized.

RECRUITMENT AND SELECTION OF STUDENTS

An important matter in which the ATOs are concerned, partly directly partly indirectly, is the recruitment and selection of students for training.

Some young people enter the teaching profession because they have a natural urge to do so. Others are influenced by family tradition: it is not uncommon for children of teachers to become teachers. Others again—and there are very many of them—while reaching a good level of general education may lack the special interests and aptitudes required for success in so many occupations, but teaching provides promising opportunities. In late years, however, owing to the great need for teachers and the increasing competition from other occupations, these traditional stimuli have not been sufficient to provide an adequate volume of recruitment, especially in the case of women teachers and teachers of such subjects as science and mathematics. It has therefore been necessary to resort to various methods of publicity and 'propaganda'. Leaflets and pamphlets of various kinds have been published giving information and guidance as to prospects in the teaching profession and the methods of gaining entry to it. From time to time special campaigns have been set on foot to meet urgent and immediate needs.

This has been effective up to a point in stimulating recruitment, but continual effort is needed in view of the great demand in our modern society for persons of high calibre in all walks of life. The needs of the teaching profession alone require that a large proportion of pupils staying on to complete the grammar school course in the sixth form should become teachers. Already two-thirds of the girls completing the course, but not going on to universities, are entering the training colleges each year. This indicates that one important way of increasing the supply of suitable people for teaching is by helping and encouraging all those pupils who are fit to do so to stay on in the grammar schools till the end of the course instead of leaving, as so many do, at the age of 16.

More will be said about the supply and requirements of the teaching profession in Chapter III. Here we will pass on to consider the way in which selection is made from the mass of applicants for entry to training colleges produced by the various stimuli to recruitment.

Each applicant for training prepares a short list of colleges in the order of his choice. He then sends an application form to the college of first choice, stating in it the names of the other colleges in his list. If he is accepted by the college of first choice that ends the matter subject to his passing the necessary medical examination. If the applicant is rejected by the college of his first choice that college sends on his papers to 'the college of second choice and the process begins again. If no college on his list is willing to admit the applicant, his papers are then referred to a 'clearing house' administered in London by the Association of Teachers in Colleges and Departments of Education (ATCDE), the professional body of the training world. The group of applicants available at any time, through rejection or otherwise, for consideration for admission to a college should a vacancy· occur, is known as 'the pool'. The clearing house, through its knowledge of the content of the pool at any time, acts as a liaison between would-be students and colleges in which vacancies occur. This is an important part of its business of keeping an eye on questions of supply and requirements generally.

The actual process of selection has been under review, but traditionally, and quite naturally, the chief part in it is played by the principal of the college to which application is made, and this continues to be so. The principal may be, and generally is, aided in his task by one or two other people, particularly by members of his staff, and the institutes themselves take a great interest in selection, sometimes appointing special officers to help and advise in this. Great care and trouble are taken. Information about each student is gathered from every available source including teachers, LEAs, and others who are acquainted with the applicant. After a scrutiny of this, all applicants who seem at all likely are interviewed personally. The college principals spare no effort in making their selection, often making long journeys about the country in order to interview applicants.

When all is said and done, however, recruitment to the teaching profession faces a basic dilemma. This arises from the fact that the total number of teachers required is primarily determined not by the number of persons in the community judged fit to be teachers according to some acceptable standard, but by the total number of children to be taught and the size of the classes in which it is desired to teach them.

There has been a great increase in the number of teachers during late years and, as we have seen, the demand continues to grow and must indeed do so if there is to be further reduction in the size of classes, agreed on all hands to be desirable. How then can the minimum intellectual and academic standards of entry to the teaching profession be maintained, let alone raised, especially in the face of strong competition?

If we are realistic, we must see that these standards cannot be maintained in every respect. But there is no reason for discouragement. Many other qualities beside academic standing are necessary to success as a teacher and we must look to the possession of a high degree of such qualities as some compensation for a certain amount of academic deficiency. In other words, in choosing a student for training we must have regard to his personality as a whole in order to decide whether the degree and balance of his qualities is such as to make it likely that, if a suitable post is found for him at the end of his training course, he will become a competent teacher.

This being so it is important that the net should be cast as widely as possible, in the attempt to catch suitable entrants to the teaching profession. Traditionally the latter have consisted mainly of pupils of grammar schools who have completed the full course satisfactorily, and the present regulations in regard to academic standing for admission to a training college are in terms particularly applicable to them. These regulations require that, in the examination for the General Certificate of Education (GCE), the applicant should have passed in (a) five subjects at the ordinary level; or (b) four subjects at the ordinary level and one other subject at the advanced level; or (c) two subjects at the ordinary level and two other subjects at the advanced level; or (d) three subjects at the advanced level, provided that there is evidence that other courses have been studied beyond the minimum age for entry to the examination.

On the other hand the regulations make provision for moderating these academic requirements in special circumstances, particularly where an applicant may be deemed to have other, compensating, qualities or experience. It is clearly important that full advantage should be taken of this moderation, not only in regard to older people who may wish to enter college at an age later than the normal entry age of 18, but also in regard to those who enter at the normal age. Thus we may look, for these younger special entrants, not only to some of the relatively weaker pupils in the grammar schools but also to some of the pupils of the secondary modern schools. For example, the latter may be encouraged to stay on at school after the statutory leaving age of 15 or, if they have already left school and later wish to become teachers, they may be encouraged to enter on one of the pre-training courses now being established which are designed not only as a preparation for subsequent training as a teacher but also to aid entry to other comparable occupations.

The first, and sometimes the only, step in the consideration of these special cases is taken by the college principal when application is made. If he is unwilling to accept the applicant, that ends the matter. On the other hand if he decides that the applicant is likely to make a competent teacher he must then secure the agreement of the ATO to the admission. No reference to the Ministry is required in the case of students entering at the normal age on the two-year training course.

This places a great burden of responsibility on the ATOs as the final decision rests with them. They have to ensure an adequate supply of teachers while doing everything possible to maintain academic standards and yet making suitable allowance for compensating qualities.

We cannot yet see clearly how the situation will develop. In particular the full impact of the new regulations in terms of GCE has yet to be felt. Many think that these regulations are too stiff and that, if they are adhered to too rigidly, it will be impossible to maintain an adequate supply of teachers. On the other hand many others feel that nothing less than the academic standard implied by the regulations should be regarded as acceptable in a teacher. Time alone can provide the outcome, and show whether or not some further moderation of the regulations will be necessary.

CENTRAL BODIES

There are two central bodies associated with the present training system, namely the National Advisory Council on the Training and Supply of Teachers (NAC) and the Standing Conference of Area Training Organizations (SCATO). The origin, status and functions of these two bodies are quite different.

The National Advisory Council has been an integral part of the new system from the beginning. It was set up, with due official status, to advise the Minister on all matters connected with the training and supply of teachers. It deals for the most part with the widest and most general questions of policy. It has two main committees: Standing Committee A, which deals with training, and Standing Committee B, which deals with supply. Its secretariat is provided by officials of the Ministry. All the main educational interests are represented on the NAC as on the councils of the ATOs, and the ATOs as such have representatives on it. Its 40 members are appointed by the Minister in consultation with the professional bodies associated with those interests. It issued its first report in 1951.

One of the first points to which the NAC had to direct its attention was that of the minimum examination qualifications for admission to training colleges. The results of this have already been described. By way of illustrating the kind of topics which come up for consideration it may be said that, among other matters, Standing Committee A is at present studying the question of the training of specialist teachers, and Standing Committee B the problems of requirements and supply generally, and especially the supply of specialist teachers. Sub-committees have been set up to deal with special aspects of these problems.

Another matter which has been reviewed recently is that of the relative proportions of men and women teachers with particular reference to the passage of the 'bulge' through the schools and the consequent need at present for a greater number of men to teach junior children. The appropriate proportions of men and women teachers required in the primary and the secondary schools respectively will, of course, change with the upward movement of the 'bulge'.

The Standing Conference of ATOs, on the other hand, did not come into existence until after the first ATOs had been established and were getting into their stride. The need soon became clear for some central body to discuss matters of common interest to the institutes and to co-ordinate opinions and experience in regard to these. Accordingly the Ministry took the initiative in setting up the body now known as SCATO, but, after the first stage, the running of this body was handed over to the ATOs as a whole, as an autonomous institution, though officers of the Ministry attend its meetings and continue to carry out most of the secretarial work. The same interests are represented on SCATO as on the NAC and the councils of the institutes, but this representation is effected indirectly, via the individual ATOs. Each of the latter sends representatives, the number of these depending on its size, and it is open to it to decide whether these are selected according to particular interests or in some other way.

The standing conference is specially concerned with questions regarding the desirable degree of uniformity and practice in various matters from one area to another. It has discussed certain aspects of school practice and also the provision of courses in connexion with post-initial training. In particular it has been considering the establishment, mentioned before, of substantial courses leading to an advanced qualification. In this matter difficulty has been found in agreeing on the title to be associated with such a qualification, whether, for example it should be 'certificate' or 'diploma', and the question is not yet settled.

Another matter which has been engaging the attention of SCATO is the nature of the certificate to be awarded to the student at the end of his initial training course and what should appear thereon. Such a certificate bears the imprimatur of the institute and, where appropriate, of the university under the aegis of which the particular student has been trained, and it is important that it should give adequate particulars, though with due economy of statement, of the course which the student has taken, especially in regard to the age-range of the children he has been specially trained to teach and the subjects in which he has reached a high degree of achievement. This question, again, has not been finally settled and there is accordingly still some variation in practice. In this connexion it has to be remembered that, apart from his certificate, each student takes with him, on leaving college, a letter from his principal setting out the main facts in regard to his character, interests, and achievements.

AREA TRAINING ORGANIZATIONS AND UNIVERSITY DEPARTMENTS OF EDUCATION

Both training colleges and university departments of education are constituent members of ATOs, but we have notably been referring mainly to the former, as they are more directly under the control of the ATOs. In concluding this chapter, therefore, a brief reference will be made to the relation of an institute to the UDEs among its constituent members.

It has been said earlier that, in general, the Minister will accept recommendations for the status of QT only from an ATO. In putting forward its students for recognition as QTs, therefore, a UDE can no longer send its list direct to the Ministry. It has first to receive the approval of the ATO—whether the ATO concerned is an A institute or a C institute.

Clearly a question at once arises as to the grounds on which the ATO can give this approval. Can it be expected to 'rubber-stamp' the UDE list without direct knowledge of the nature and content of the training courses and the effectiveness with which these are carried out? How far, and in what way, should an institute concern itself with these courses, and should it express opinions or criticisms in regard to them?

These are delicate matters, especially where C institutes are concerned. The university departments rightly attach great importance to their autonomy; on the other hand, it is asking a good deal of any institution to recommend to the Ministry approval of something about which it may not have adequate information. All that it is necessary to say further here is that this is again one of those matters which, in England, settle themselves satisfactorily in time—unless someone sets out to make trouble—through the gradual establishment of a procedure which everybody accepts without talking much about it.

This chapter has been concerned with the general organization and administration of the training of teachers. The remaining chapters will deal with more detailed aspects, beginning with a consideration of the students.

CHAPTER III

THE STUDENTS

The large majority of students in training are in the two-year (exceptionally three-year) training colleges which they entered at the normal age from the grammar schools; except where otherwise stated, the first part of this chapter will be mainly concerned with these. Other categories of students will be dealt with in the latter part of the chapter. But something must first be said about the size and quality of the student body as a whole.

QUANTITY

In 1938 about 5,000 students were admitted to training colleges, while about 1,800 graduates were admitted to professional training. There has been a large increase in these figures since the war. In 1950 about 10,500 students were admitted to training colleges and about 2,900 graduates to professional training.

Assuming that all available places in training institutions are filled it is likely that, from the time the students entering the two-year colleges this year complete their course in 1954, there will be an annual output of teachers from all sources of about 14,000 per annum. As the annual 'wastage' from all causes is about 10,000, we can after 1954 look forward with some confidence to an annual increase in the total number of teachers of about 4,000—to staff new schools built to meet the requirements of shifting populations and the increasing number of children entering the schools, and ultimately, if and when numbers become stable, to reduce the size of classes.

There are certain comments and reservations to be made in regard to this. Of the prospective annual output of 14,000 about 10,000 are likely to come from training colleges, 2,500 from UDES, and 1,500 from other sources such as the supply of untrained graduates and comparable specialist teachers.

Although there is at present much competition for places in the UDEs so that they are likely to remain full (even if extended somewhat) in the foreseeable future, it is by no means certain that it will be possible to fill all the available two-year places in the training colleges. In the case of the 1951 entry some vacancies, though not very many, were left unfilled in the woman's colleges, in spite of great efforts by all concerned. There is at present no difficulty in filling the places in the men's colleges.

The total number of teachers in the primary and secondary schools at the beginning of 1951 was about 216,000. This was some 4,000 more than was necessary to preserve the staffing standards obtaining in 1950. Owing to the increasing number of children in the schools, however, it is likely that, in 1953, in spite of the prospective annual increase in the total number of teachers, this number will be barely sufficient to maintain 1950 staffing standards; while, after 1953, staffing standards are likely to drop somewhat below the 1950 level. Not unless and until the number of children in the schools becomes stable will it be possible to recover the 1950 level and afterwards to improve upon it.

As regards graduates in particular, it seems that the present supply is sufficient to meet the effective demand, though, as stated before, more scientists and mathematicians are needed. If the number of the latter could be increased there is something to be said, in existing circumstances, for limiting the total number of trained graduates to its present figure. If the effective demand warranted it, this number could readily be increased at any future time.

QUALITY

What are we to say of the quality of the large mass of students now training as teachers? There is, of course, wide variation. So far as graduates are concerned it is a matter of opinion whether or not the general level of the students in the UDEs is above or below the general level of all graduates; but, although there are students of distinction training to become teachers, many, possibly most, graduates of the highest academic achievement go to professions other than teaching in the schools. This is again especially true of the scientists and mathematicians, who are naturally attracted by the alluring material prospects now offered in the fields of industry and technology and, more recently, medicine.

The students at the lower end of the UDE scale are many of them of modest academic attainment judged by university standards, but only an almost negligible number of them fail to achieve QT status. There seems no reason, indeed, why most of them should not become competent teachers if they get into the right sort of job.

The best students in the training colleges would undoubtedly have been capable of taking a good honours degree had desire and circumstance combined to lead them into the universities, while the weakest students who pass their examinations and become QTs are not so very much above the average calibre of the general population. This wide range gives additional point to the modern practice of concentration on the fitting of the training course to the needs and abilities of the individual. Moreover, it should be added that the above comparison relates mainly to intellectual calibre and academic achievement. Many of those concerned have other qualities which fit them admirably to become teachers in posts suitable to them. The large mass of training college students are intelligent young people who put up a good solid performance, professionally and academically, without marked brilliance.

The number of trained students who finally fail to become QTs, some of them after the period of teaching probation which will be described later, is a very small proportion of the whole, certainly not exceeding about 3 per cent. It is of course possible for a student who fails the examination at the end of his training course to begin teaching, though not as a QT, and subsequently to retrieve his failure through re-examination on not more than two subsequent occasions. The conditions of such re-examination vary somewhat from one ATO to another.

Some think the percentage of failures too low and that people are being admitted too easily to the teaching profession. It is important that the probable failures should be spotted as early as possible, preferably during the course of training, so that their course may be terminated before they have spent too much time in fruitless endeavour. If possible these students should be persuaded to turn to some other occupation, but in cases where the college principal and staff have become convinced of the student's unfitness to become a teacher though the student refuses to accept this, it may be necessary to terminate his course willy-nilly.

The responsibility for terminating a student's course of training rests squarely on the college principal. The latter may consult others with relevant knowledge but he must take the final decision himself. If he decides that the student's course must be terminated, he will naturally report the case to his governing body and he is also required to report it to the Ministry. The Ministry, however, takes no action unless the student appeals, either directly or through his parents or other accredited representatives. As the college principal and staff are in the best position to know the facts, in considering such appeals the Ministry is concerned, not so much with detail, as with the question whether the nature of the grounds on which the principal made his decision was reasonable and appropriate. Where the circumstances warrant it, therefore, principals should feel encouraged to exercise freely their power of terminating a student's course as soon as his unfitness becomes apparent, not only in the interests of the teaching profession and the training system as a whole, but also in the interests of the student himself.

MEN AND WOMEN STUDENTS

Just before the war rather more than three times as many women as men were entering the training colleges. Then, during the war, there was a large wastage of men students and teachers, and the emergency training scheme, to be described in a later chapter, was instituted mainly to make up for this wastage. In the permanent training colleges, however, there has been a steady increase in the proportion of women students since the end of the war. In 1950 the proportion of women to men students entering the colleges annually was not far short of four to one. The increasing need for women teachers has meant that most of the new permanent colleges established during the past few years— some of them were taken over from the emergency training scheme— have been for women, with a certain number of 'mixed' colleges taking both men and women.

The question of mixed colleges is an interesting one. Mixed colleges have long been included among the training institutions. They have usually been large, as colleges go, but there have not been many of them. During the last few decades, however, there has been a slow but steady trend throughout the English educational system in favour of co-education. The effect of this has naturally been felt mainly in the schools, but from time to time the question of the relative advantages and disadvantages of mixed and single-sex colleges has been raised.

The balance of opinion is in favour of associating men and women students in training, not only socially but also educationally and professionally. Apart from the establishment of mixed colleges, much has been, and is being, done in making contact between men's and women's colleges, especially when these are situated at a reasonable distance from one another.

What is the optimum size of a training college? Many people feel that a college of about 300 would be the most effective on general grounds. It would be large enough to make it possible to use the resources available with economy and efficiency, while it would not be so large that important personal contacts would be lost. At present colleges of this size are the exception rather than the rule, and experiments in this direction are limited, not only by immediate urgencies, but also by geographical conditions and by the fact that we are dealing not, as in the case of emergency training, with a system to be established *de novo*, but with a system of long standing the roots of which go very deep. Experiment must therefore wait upon opportunity and can only come gradually. So far as existing colleges are concerned there are many· to plead the advantages both of the small and of the large college, according to where their interests and affections lie.

So far we have been dealing mainly with the normal entrants to the training colleges. We may now go on to consider other categories of student which find their way into these colleges from time to time, beginning with the uncertificated teachers.

UNCERTIFICATED TEACHERS

This type of teacher is a legacy from a now rather distant past when the Board of Education issued certificates to teachers based on the results of an annual examination conducted by the Board. This examination was different from that held at the end of the training course, which was also then conducted by the Board, though it included a professional element, and it could be taken by a teacher even if he were untrained. A large number of teachers availed themselves of this opportunity of obtaining an accepted professional qualification.

The certificate examination came to an end about 1928, and many of those who tried to pass it and failed, thus continuing as 'uncertificated teachers', have disappeared from the schools in the natural course of events. But there are still for various reasons, a number of teachers in the schools who rank, in effect, as uncertificated teachers. Some of these were students who took a course of training but failed their final examination and have never retrieved their failure. Others have been taken into the schools from time to time as 'temporary assistants' to meet current shortages or for other special reasons.

The Ministry has now firmly adopted the policy that, except at present in the case of graduates, a professional qualification to teach in grant-aided primary and secondary schools can be obtained only as a result of a course of training, but a few years ago it came to the conclusion that something should be done to enable the 'uncertificated' type of teacher to obtain such a qualification by taking a training course of limited duration. It was decided that, if a teacher had been teaching as uncertificated in the schools for 20 years or more at a date fixed in 1950, and was regarded as a competent teacher by those in a position to judge, he might be granted QT status without further ado. For those who had been teaching more than five but less than 20 years special one-year training courses were provided the satisfactory completion of which would carry with it the status of QT.

These courses have been conducted in selected training colleges able to offer facilities for them. For the most part each of these colleges took a small group of the new students, though in one case a considerable number were concentrated in one college which took no other students during their period of training.

There have always been a few uncertificated teachers scattered about the training colleges, but these were people who, of their own initiative, had entered as students on the normal two-year training course in order to obtain professional status. It should be noted, in passing, that such people, by virtue of their teaching experience and greater maturity, usually made special and valuable contributions to the college life and work.

The new one-year scheme, however, presented new problems for in general it meant the training of a group of older students, through a one-year course, alongside young people taking the two-year course. The colleges coped with these problems admirably, and the scheme has fully justified itself in practice. It is now coming to an end, but, as by no means all those qualified to take advantage of this opportunity have done so, often no doubt through financial or domestic circumstances (although special grants were made to meet difficulties arising from these as far as possible), consideration is being given to the possibility of embarking on a further instalment of the scheme.

Another category of older student to be found in the training colleges is the 'mature student'.

MATURE STUDENTS

The great experiment in the training of what is officially known as the 'mature student' was, of course, the emergency training scheme and many lessons were learned, as we shall see later. Provision for training this type of student is now an integral part of the permanent training system.

The mature student is one who, for one reason or another, wishes to embark on a course of training as a teacher at an age considerably later than the normal age of entry to college. If he has a reasonably adequate educational background, and has had some responsible experience since leaving school, the results of which might be held to compensate for late entry to training, he may be admitted to a one-year course at a training college provided he is not less than 25 years old at the time of entry and is judged likely to become a competent teacher at the end of a course of only half the normal duration. Special grants are made for this purpose, adjusted according to the individual case, to preclude financial or domestic hardship. It is clearly important that the selection of these mature students for training should be a very careful one. The prime responsibility falls on the principal of the college to whom application is made. If the principal is willing to admit the applicant the approval, not only of the ATO, but also of the Ministry must be obtained.

An important point of principle, which is worth emphasizing, is illustrated here. If a principal wishes to admit a student for the normal two-year course in special circumstances, e.g. where there is some academic deficiency, it is only necessary for him to secure the approval of the ATO, but where it is a question of admission to a course of training shorter than the normal, the consent of the Ministry must, in general, also be secured.

In the case of some mature applicants it may be felt that, while a one-year training course would not be enough, they would probably become efficient teachers if they could take the full two-year course. In its recent report the National Advisory Council recommended the provision of two-year courses, with suitable grants, for such people. The Ministry has noted the recommendation, which remains a possibility for the future.

These mature entrants to teaching not only have a special contribution to make to the work and standing of the profession but, like the uncertificated teachers, they play a valuable part in college life during their course. Moreover they make a useful, if at present small, addition to the supply of teachers, and it is hoped, when circumstances permit, to extend this source of supply as far as possible.

POSTGRADUATE AND PRE-GRADUATE STUDENTS

These have already been mentioned. Owing mainly to the pressure on UDE provision—the demand is greater than the supply—some graduates take their year of training in training colleges, where the facilities available in the colleges permit.

These students have the advantage of training in an institution, usually larger than the average UDE, which specializes in professional training over a wide range. Hence they are brought in contact with a large variety of aspects of teaching and training, apart from that in which they are themselves specializing, and this has a valuable effect in developing their understanding of the place of their own work, and in stimulating breadth of vision. On the other hand, this class of student is at some disadvantage in the matter of grants as compared with their fellows in the UDEs, but this matter is now under review.

Some colleges, with suitable staff and equipment, admit students who wish to take a degree concurrently with their professional training and who, for one reason or another, are unable or unwilling to enter universities. The colleges in question make special provision for these during a three-year course. This practice raises some difficult questions and the officials of the Ministry have never felt quite satisfied about it. In particular there is doubt whether, without undue pressure, a training institution can make adequate provision for students both to complete a full course of training and, at the same time, to prepare for a degree during a period of not more than three years. It is for this reason that the stipulation has been made that the students concerned shall have completed the preliminary stages of the degree course before entering college or very shortly after.

In the result it is probably fair to say that the colleges in question are doing a good job with these students so far as the circumstances allow, sometimes co-operating with one another in pooling resources to this end where geographical conditions permit. Moreover the students form a useful addition to the supply of trained graduate teachers at a time of shortage in university provision.

Like the other categories of students, the pre-graduate and postgraduate students have their own contribution to make to the life and work of the colleges. In particular they introduce a leaven of academic distinction into the colleges and raise their standing in this respect. This provides a special kind of stimulus to the work, not only of the general run of students, but also of the staff. The colleges concerned would therefore be understandably reluctant to cease admitting students of this type and providing special courses for them.

NATIONAL SERVICE

The continuance of compulsory national service for men after the end of the war created problems both for the universities and for the training colleges. In the case of the training colleges the issue and its solution were clear. If the men took their training before national service they would have the advantage of continuing the educational process from school to college, but they would then have a break between training and teaching during which much of what they had learnt in college might grow rather dim. On the other hand, if they took their period of national service last, they would not only go subsequently from training to teaching direct, but they would have had the benefit of some experience of the outside world before entering college. These advantages far outweigh the disadvantage of a break in the normal educational process between school and college. It was therefore agreed by all concerned that the right course for a man student to pursue, was to take his period of national service before entering college, and this is now the general practice; for the time being, therefore, colleges are admitting a generation of young men of greater maturity than those entering college before the war.

COLLEGE ROUTINE AND DISCIPLINE

Of late years there has been a considerable increase in the part played by students in the general running of a training college. It has long been the practice for students to play a major part in the organization of games and other recreational pursuits as well as in the development of their general education through relatively informal methods, such as the formation of societies and discussion groups of various kinds, which enable them to pursue a wide range of intellectual and cultural interests and activities. Nowadays, however, the students also have a substantial share, through their representative council, in the general organization of college life and in the framing and enforcement of rules of discipline.

The Student's Council is normally affiliated to the national Union of Students, and it is common practice for the members of the council to be elected by the students themselves. The nature of the relations of the principal and staff to the council, and the degree of control which they exercise over it, varies in detail from college to college, but in general the students enjoy a considerable measure of freedom in carrying on the work of the council and in the application of this to college life.

On discipline something has been said already, and it is only necessary to repeat here that there is a steady tendency towards a more liberal and flexible practice in drawing up and administering the college rules. In fact the position of training college students in this respect is approximating more and more closely to that of university students.

In addition to the expansion of intellectual and cultural interests made possible by students' societies, the colleges themselves provide valuable contributions here. Outside lecturers on various topics are frequent visitors to college, as well as experts in music, drama and art. Moreover, wherever practicable, visits are arranged to museums and exhibitions of various kinds and also to plays and concerts, while in the colleges themselves dances and other entertainments have become a normal feature. Students of one college often visit another college for the latter. In particular when a dance is organized by a men's college the students from some not too distant women's college are invited, and vice versa.

In short it may be said that training college students now live a richer and more varied life than was the case even in the years immediately preceding the war. It is clear, however, that the full benefit of this cannot be secured unless the student is in residence. It is therefore held to be desirable that, except in special circumstances or to meet special needs, training should be residential. Residence is not however compulsory, for there are evidently cases in which, if residence were insisted upon, serious hardship would be caused, or, alternatively, the intending student would give up the idea of teaching; but everything possible is done to help and encourage the students to train in residence and the large majority do so. Many colleges, however, take some day students, the proportion of these naturally being greater when the college is situated in a heavily populated district, and for these the best provision is made that the limitations of non-residence allow. There is one women's college (in Manchester) for day students only.

FINANCIAL AID

The aid to students in training derived from the regular system of Ministry grants has already been described and it is only necessary to add here that, in order to qualify for such grants, the student must normally be a British subject resident in England or Wales who is willing to sign the declaration that, after completing the course of training, he intends to adopt and follow the profession of a teacher in a grant-aided school in England or Wales.

There are, however, expenses to which a student is liable other than those due to the provision of tuition, board and lodging by the college. For example there are expenses to cover the cost of books and material, travelling, and vacations. How far the student is able to meet these from his own resources will naturally depend on his particular circumstances, but application may be made to the LEA for the area from which the student comes for a grant towards such incidental expenses. If the case is a genuinely hard one the LEA is usually willing to help, though the readiness and degree of generosity with which LEAs make grants of this kind varies from one area to another. In any case when such a grant is made it counts as LEA expenditure ranking for grant from the Ministry.

STUDENT ATTITUDES AND OPINIONS

As might be expected, the widest variation of attitude and opinion on all kinds of subjects is to be found within the student body, and, subject to the requirements of a reasonable discipline, the students are allowed a great measure of freedom in discussing their opinions and beliefs among themselves and in acting in accordance with them.

In the case of religion, the voluntary colleges make special provision for students with firm religious beliefs who adhere to particular denominations. But, while a majority of the students in a denominational college will be members of the particular church concerned, there are many students in such colleges who either have no very definite religious convictions or, if they have, do not adhere to any particular sect. The proportion of these varies both with the college and with the denomination. They are made welcome and, indeed, their presence often acts as a challenge and a stimulus to their fellow students. Conversely, students with definite sectarian beliefs are frequently found in the LEA or other non-denominational colleges. The mixing of students in this way is an admirable and effective encouragement to thought and tolerance. It should be added that the Ministry's regulations lay down that any student who, when offered a place in a college, claims exemption on the conscientious ground of not belonging to the denomination of that college, must not be required, as a condition of entering or continuing in the college, to comply with any rule of the college as to attendance at religious worship or observance or instruction in religious subjects. Moreover in the selection of candidates for half the number of places vacant in the college no application may be rejected on religious or denominational grounds.

As for politics, keen discussion is common among training college students, the views expressed varying from the more conservative to the more radical; but it should be mentioned here that it is an accepted principle in England, a principle to which great weight is attached, that the actual courses in educational institutions should be non-political in all their aspects and should never be used in any way for the propagation of particular political beliefs. Some of the courses will, of their very nature, include the discussion of the various types of such belief, but this discussion is comparative and objective, and in no sense propaganda.

There is one matter in connexion with student opinion to which reference is rarely made though it is of considerable importance. That is the attitude of the students themselves towards the new organization in the system of training and the results as it affects them. So far no evidence has been collected systematically in regard to this, and it is therefore difficult to say just what is going on in the students' minds.

It is in any case somewhat early to attempt to form any conclusions in the matter, but there is one aspect of the new arrangements about which we already have an indication as to what students are feeling. As might have been expected this is in connexion with examination and assessment.

Most young adults are by nature practical minded, and training college students are no exception. They may or may not be impressed and stimulated by the closer association of their colleges with the universities. What each of them certainly does ask is 'Just how is all this going to affect me, and particularly my prospects of becoming a qualified teacher?' This of course involves at once the whole question of the examination system, especially the comparatively new combination of course assessment and written papers.

Student opinion appears to be divided in roughly equal proportions. It is largely a matter of temperament. Some students prefer to bank all on the verdict of a single written and practical examination at the end of the course. They feel that it gives them a chance of making up lost ground by intense work during the last stages of the course and that, so far as their weaknesses are concerned, they may get a lucky break since the examiners of the written papers may not, and generally will not, be acquainted with them personally and in any case are supposed to take account only of the written answers. Others feel that a fairer judgment of them will be made if all their work during the course is considered by, or in consultation with, people who have known them well over a substantial period of time, for most of which they will have been working free from the strain of examination conditions.

Whatever the differences of opinion, however, there has been a widespread uncertainty and apprehension on one point, arising from the fact that assessment of course work is now an established feature of the examination system. This tends to make students feel that they are under observation all the time, and that the results of every piece of work they do, good or bad, from the time they enter college will be recorded and totted up into some kind of grand total which will be put to their account when the final judgment is made on them at the end of the course. Some of those in a position to judge have come to the conclusion that this apprehension produces a sense of pressure, varying with the temperament of the student, which is at least as severe as that produced by the traditional method of assessment by a single final examination.

The students' fears are, however, mistaken, for they are based on a misunderstanding of the nature and operation of course work assessment. The purpose of the latter is, not to add up marks for individual pieces of work, but to look at a student's work as a whole, particularly as an indication of the rate and rhythm of his development and of his

65

ability to make progress by fostering his capacities and eliminating or minimizing his weaknesses. The significant thing is, not the sum of the student's work, but the progress he has made from first to last which, when considered in all its aspects, is an index of his personality.

It is of prime importance that all this should be explained to students by their tutors as soon as possible after they enter college. If they understand that the work they produce will be considered with sympathy and consideration, by people whose only aim is to give them the best help and guidance in becoming competent teachers, they will be confident of receiving a fair deal and any feeling of pressure, if it exists, will be greatly diminished.

CHAPTER IV

STAFF

The members of the staffs of university departments of education are members of the teaching bodies of their universities and, as such, are in every way comparable with their fellows in other university departments. They are appointed in the same way, their type of organization—usually with a professor at the head—is the same and, in their own field, they have a standing comparable with that of their colleagues in other fields. Their background of experience will of course be different, for the normal educational course does not ultimately lead so simply and naturally to a post in a department of education as to one in the traditional subject departments of the universities. Some of the members of UDE staffs have been appointed comparatively soon after taking their degrees, though during the interval they will generally have taken a postgraduate course in some subject such as psychology. Others have had teaching experience—sometimes considerable—before taking up their university posts.

Most of what follows will refer to the staffs of the training colleges. Judged by the usual criteria, these institutions enjoy a status somewhere between that of the universities and that of the schools. In regard to basic salary scales, to which more particular reference will be made later, they rank approximately with establishments for further education, such as technical and commercial colleges and institutes and art colleges, although the two sets of salary scales are dealt with by different committees.

QUANTITY

Regulations governing the size of training college staffs, comparable with those issued from time to time on the maximum sizes of classes in schools, have never been imposed either by the old Board of Education or by the present Ministry. As a general working rule a staff-ratio of about 11 students per full-time tutor has been regarded as adequate staffing.

On the whole the colleges at present conform fairly closely to this rule, though it is only a rough guide in the case of individual colleges. The suitable staff-ratio for a college depends on its particular circumstances, especially its size. A small college usually needs a more favourable staffing-ratio than a large one. Moreover, with the increased demands made on the colleges during recent years, a revision of the normal staff-ratio in the direction of providing more tutors for a given number of students, is indicated as soon as circumstances permit. Extension of the two-year course to three years would, of course, require a substantial increase in staff.

In calculating staff-ratio it is customary to include the deputy principal but not the principal, while part-time staff are allowed for at a proportionate rate. Every college, by the way, has a deputy principal. In the case of mixed colleges principal and deputy are of opposite sex. At present the principal of every mixed college is a man, and the deputy a woman.

There has lately been a great demand for women staff to meet the expansion of accommodation for training women made necessary by the increased requirements of the schools for women teachers. The market for male staff has not been so good. Not only are the present requirements for men not so great, except to make up for the shortage of women in the primary schools; but, with the closing of the emergency training colleges, which were mainly for men, a considerable number of male tutors wishing to continue to work in training institutions has become available.

One effect of the operation of these factors has been to increase the number of men on the staffs of women's colleges. There has long been a small number of men teaching in women's colleges, but this number is now increasing substantially. The shortage of women staff accounts for this in part, but also, where an emergency college for men has become a permanent college for women it has often been convenient and appropriate to retain some of those members of the male staff who wished to remain.

The presence of women on the staff of men's colleges is rarer, but is becoming commoner. This is due primarily to the need for staff to train the increased number of men preparing for work in the primary schools. Hitherto very few male tutors have been specially qualified to undertake this type of training.

Apart from the natural effects of demand, there is much to be said in favour of a 'mixed' staff for single-sex colleges. Not only is it of advantage in the social life of the college, but women have their own contribution to make on general questions of training so far as they affect men, and similarly for men in respect of the training of women. In colleges where there is a mixed staff, both men and women members of the staff prefer this to a staff of one sex only. In fact, other things being equal, there is now an increasing tendency, when a vacancy occurs on the staff of a single-sex college, to appoint the best applicant, whether man or woman.

Perhaps the most difficult type of post to fill satisfactorily on a training college staff is that concerned with the professional side of the work, particularly in regard to principles and practice of education and educational psychology. The educational system—school and university—produces in the natural course of events a reservoir of possible applicants for teaching posts in training colleges concerned with the subjects of general education. There is no such natural and obvious avenue of approach to the teaching of the professional subjects. Probably the best line of progress for one who wishes to teach these is to take a degree in one of the traditional general subjects followed by a postgraduate course in psychology or some allied field, with a subsequent period of teaching in the schools. To embark on this is a considerable undertaking, and the number of people who have done so is far fewer than those who are equipped to teach general subjects at training college level. Accordingly college principals usually find considerable difficulty in filling vacancies on the professional side. Not rarely one finds on this side tutors who, while teaching general subjects in college, have acquired an interest in the general professional subjects and taken such opportunities as were available to them to prepare themselves for work in this field to which they have subsequently transferred. Tentative steps are now being taken to increase the supply of tutors for the 'education' staff, in particular through the provision of special courses for abler teachers in the schools, some of whom wish to take up work in a training college.

One question relevant to the supply of training college staff is that of the possibility of a certain amount of interchange between the staffs of colleges and of schools. This would, of course, affect the mobility of staff rather than the total quantity. The McNair committee referred to the matter in their report, recommending that steps should be taken to make practicable the secondment of teachers from the schools for a period of work in training institutions. The committee was of the opinion that the staff of such institutions should always include a proportion of teachers from the schools.

In theory this idea has much to commend it. It would help to keep colleges and schools in touch with one another and would stimulate freshness of outlook in both. Its value would be enhanced if it became a genuinely two-way traffic, so that some at least of those whose main business was to teach in a training college went from time to time to teach for a while in the schools. In particular this would help to break down the tendency—fortunately a diminishing tendency—of training college staffs to remain static. In the past too large a proportion of college staff has consisted of persons who have remained in the same college for a very long time.

In practice, however, there are certain difficulties and disadvantages, and accordingly not very much has been done so far in the way of implementing the idea of staff interchange. The obstacles arise, not only from considerations of geography and of administration, but from the differences in status and salary scale between schools and colleges and the consequent necessity for making somewhat awkward and delicate adjustments to ensure that none of those concerned shall suffer detriment either financially or in any other way.

Evidently it is easiest to effect interchange of staff in areas where there are LEA colleges, as in such areas the staffs of both colleges and schools are employed by the LEA. Experiments are indeed being tried in some of these areas; but here again there are disadvantages arising from the danger of too much 'inbreeding'. At present, therefore, there is not much sign of enthusiasm for establishing systematic interchange on an extensive scale. It remains an idea which is attractive to many, but for which no really satisfactory method of implementation has yet been found.

QUALITY

There are, and always have been, many persons of high distinction teaching in training colleges; but, for the most part, the quality of staff is determined by the fact that the status of a training college is somewhere between that of a school and that of a college of a university. The average level of academic standing among the staff tends to adjust itself accordingly.

Apart from academic standing of the normal kind, however, there are many other special qualifications required of training college staff. In particular there is the ability to instruct in the principles and practice of education. The last point applies, not only to the staff of the education department of the college but also to the tutors concerned with the subjects of general education. An interesting and significant change has taken place in this connexion during the last 50 years. In earlier days teachers of general subjects in the colleges were supposed to confine themselves to giving instruction in the content of those subjects. They were rigidly excluded from giving instruction in teaching method which was dealt with, both in general and in regard to particular subjects, by a tutor known as the 'master (or mistress) of method'.

The defects in such an arrangement are fairly obvious. Not only is it impossible for one person to deal adequately with teaching method in the whole range of subjects but, as students, in addition to gaining knowledge of the general subjects they choose for study, are usually going to teach them and therefore mentally link the content of a subject with the teaching of it, it is absurd to have one person dealing solely with instruction in content and another solely with instruction in teaching method with little or no liaison between them. Nevertheless the post of master of method was a deeply rooted one, with a very long tradition supporting it, and it took many years to bring about its total abolition. In the colleges today the approved practice is for the members of the education staff, who may be dealing with different phases and age-ranges in education, to work closely with one another under the general guidance of the senior among them, while at the same time maintaining adequate contact and consultation with the tutors in the general subjects upon whom now falls the prime responsibility for giving instruction in the methods of teaching those subjects.

In most colleges there are a number of part-time tutors, usually but a small proportion of the whole staff. The particular posts filled by these will vary with the circumstances. For example the college may be able to take advantage of local resources such as the presence of teachers or others of suitable, and perhaps distinguished, qualifications in neighbouring schools or other institutions. Such persons may be able to make a part-time contribution to the work of the college.

The relative proportions of resident and non-resident staff vary from college to college. It is regarded as important that every tutor should spend at least part of his time in residence so that he may play as full a part as possible in the college life while also taking his fair share of responsibility in the running of the college. On the other hand it is important, especially in the case of full-time resident staff, that every tutor should get away from college for adequate periods, during term as well as vacation, so that he may keep in sufficient contact with the outside world.

Part of the college staff work mainly in the academic field while part work mainly in such practical subjects as art, craft, physical education, and gardening. The presence in one institution of persons in close association but working in these different fields plays a significant role in developing breadth and integration of outlook, and it may be said that the staffs of the training colleges are, in general, fully adequate to cope with the work on which they are engaged. Not only so but the average level of quality among them has been steadily rising.

SALARIES

A specially appointed committee exists to deal with salary scales. It is usually known as the 'Pelham committee' from the name of its original chairman. It consists of 32 members. Twenty of these form what is known as the 'authorities and governors' panel' representing the LEAs and other governing bodies. The remaining 12 members form the 'teaching staff panel', representing the Association of Teachers in Colleges and Departments of Education.

The present position in regard to salaries may be summarized as follows: lecturer (man), minimum of £550 rising by annual increments of £25 to maximum of £850; lecturer (woman), minimum of £500 rising by annual increments of £25 to maximum of £750; senior lecturer (man), minimum of £800 rising by annual increments of £25 to maximum of £1,050; senior lecturer (woman), minimum of £700 rising by annual increments of £25 to maximum of £950; deputy principal, receives in addition to salary as lecturer or senior lecturer an allowance, approved by the Minister, of not less than £50 per annum and, in general, not more than £200 per annum.

Provision is made for increasing the deputy principal's special allowance beyond the limit of £200 in certain circumstances, e.g. in the case of a mixed college.

The salaries of principals are reviewed and adjusted from time to time by the LEAs and other governing bodies in agreement with the Minister. There are no published scales. Roughly average salaries are a minimum of £1,200 rising by annual increments of £50 to a maximum of £1,500 for men principals, and a minimum of about £1,050 rising to a maximum of £1,300 for women principals. There are variations above and below this according to size of college or special circumstances. In addition a principal generally has emoluments in connexion with board and residence often including a principal's house.

Lecturers, senior lecturers, and deputy principals serving in a defined 'London area' receive an additional payment of £36 per annum which is increased to £48 per annum after the person concerned has completed 16 years of full-time service in the 'London area' or elsewhere, or has attained the age of 37 years.

The present scales will continue in operation until 31 March 1954, and thereafter from year to year unless either panel should give to the other panel not less than one year's notice in writing to terminate the operation of the scales on 31 March in any year.

To conclude this chapter it may be pointed out that the principals of training colleges are appointed by the governing bodies concerned, generally by selection from a short list compiled from the applications received as a result of advertisement or through other means. The size and nature of the assistant staff of a college is determined by the GB in consultation with the principal. Appointments to the staff are technically made by the GB as they are the employers; but the principal naturally plays a major part in the making of such appointments, and, in normal circumstances, his selection stands.

CHAPTER V

TRAINING COURSES

The general character of the courses of training has been described in Chapter II, with especial reference to those features which all such courses have in common. In this chapter the courses will be discussed in somewhat greater detail with especial reference to the differentiation between them in regard to the age-range of children the student is being trained to teach.

There is great variety in college courses with innumerable variation in detail. It is therefore not possible to deal with these courses in any way exhaustively. The method adopted will be that of describing typical courses for training college students intending to teach younger children, for those intending to teach older children, and for students in the university departments of education.

As regards the general subjects of education, particularly so far as they contribute to the education of the student himself, there is little more to be said in a non-specialist study of this kind. The syllabuses in these subjects follow the usual lines and are adjusted to the level of training college students, that is somewhat below the level of university undergraduates. Some reference will be made to teaching method in this field; but we shall be mainly concerned with the more general professional work.

THE TRAINING COURSE FOR TEACHERS IN PRIMARY SCHOOLS

The teacher in the nursery or infant school is faced with a particularly important and difficult task, as the children who come under her charge will be entering upon a process of systematic education for the first time. They come to school already deeply influenced and moulded in character and temperament by the conditions of their home life and by the effects of their social and material environment. It is natural, therefore, that the training course relating to the earlier stages of primary education should pay great attention to the foundations of character and to the establishment of desirable personal and social habits. In the first stages the most obvious emphasis is perhaps on the physical health and habits of the child, though this is continually accompanied by direct and indirect training in appropriate methods of securing sound mental development which is, of course, greatly affected by, and indeed inseparable from, the child's physical condition.

Students receive instruction in the child's bodily development. Special attention is also given to the growth of language ability and to ways of fostering this through conversation, story and poetry. Methods are considered of bringing the child into suitable contact with nature and of developing his social sense and practice in the simple beginnings of social service through association, in play and otherwise, with other children of the same age. Attention is given to the appropriate daily routine for young children, through which they come to habits of orderliness and begin to acquire the right attitude towards authority.

Special consideration is given to the ways in which children learn during these early years and particularly to the close linkage of intellectual and practical development at this stage. Already individual differences, both physical and mental, are clearly apparent, and it is of the first importance that the student should understand how these are estimated and dealt with, and what her mode of approach should be in providing for the needs and capacities of the individual child. In this she will be in the line of a great tradition, for the major pioneer work in individual methods of education was carried out in the field of the education of young children.

In her study of the development of children as they pass through the infant school the student is instructed in a number of topics. These include the increased control of bodily movement which the children gain through various kinds of physical activity and through the natural demands of everyday practical life; the transition from solitariness to the beginnings of social development, co-operation with others, and the recognition and acceptance of simple duties and responsibilities; the enrichment of vocabulary and correctness in its use: the gain in physical co-ordination and control and in intellectual development through play and through simple project activities; and the development of the knowledge of number with the best methods of fostering this.

It will be clear from the foregoing that the so-called 'combined' or 'integrated' courses, to which reference was made in Chapter II, play a particularly important part in the training of the student who intends to teach young children. These children do not learn in compartments. For them, far more than for older children who have acquired some power of abstraction, the fields of language, number, art, craft, music, drama, and nature are aspects of an experience which is for them a unity. The task of the primary school teacher is not to teach 'subjects' in the traditional sense, except to some extent in the later stages of the junior school, but to foster, and create the conditions for, sound and healthy development of the child-personality as a whole.

As one corollary of this, special attention is given in the training course to the importance of balanced and harmonious emotional development in young children, and to the best ways of securing this and of avoiding its opposite. A study is made of home influence in this respect, both before and after the child comes to school, and consideration is given to the importance of contact between the teacher and the child's parents and to the most tactful ways of developing this so that the teacher's help and guidance may be acceptable to the parents and a ground for confidence.

A study is also made of the influence of the child's social environment, including that of the school itself, and of the causes which tend to set up anti-social attitudes in the child or mental conflicts and frustration. At the same time the students are warned that, when such traits have become strongly marked in children only properly qualified persons are competent to deal with them. Accordingly attention is given to the methods of working of such institutions as child guidance clinics which may be called in to help and advise when the matter is too grave to be dealt with by teachers and parents alone.

Evidently knowledge about the topics just mentioned is of importance to all students, no matter what the age-range of the children they intend to teach, but particularly important to those preparing to teach younger children. Another matter which is of importance to all teachers but especially so to those teaching younger children is the keeping of records for individual children. These records should refer not only to intellectual characteristics and to the progress the child is making in educational attainment, but also to social and temperamental qualities. They are of use not only to the child's teacher herself, but as the basis of helpful reports to be passed on when the child transfers to a school for older children. The students are instructed in the most effective way of devising and filling in such records, and they are given plenty of practice in observing the behaviour of children in different situations, known as 'child study', as a result of which they can draw up their own records describing the children they have studied.

During these parts of the course the great importance to little children of persons and personal relationships is impressed on the students, and they are instructed in the establishment of a happy and confident child-teacher relationship, and in the adjustment of the child to the various other types of personal relations in which he finds himself.

The special importance of physical health in the case of young children is stressed throughout the whole of the training course. In this connexion particular attention is given to the more or less organized activity known as 'physical education' through the medium of games, dance, and elementary gymnastics, and to the development of the skills required in these.

As the child approaches the age of 7, problems concerned with the transfer to the junior school begin to present themselves more urgently. In most cases the mould in which the child's personality is cast will by then have taken firm and coherent shape, while he will have achieved some degree of proficiency in the basic skills. Accordingly the students preparing to teach infants are instructed in the most effective ways of achieving smooth transfer and ready adjustment of the child to his new surroundings, so far as it is in the power of the infant teacher to deal with this. Attention is given to the opportunities arising from the stimulus due to entry into a new environment, and the corresponding difficulties arising from unfamiliarity, and to the importance of securing, with the help of the teachers in the junior schools, conditions favourable to continuity in development. This is one of the reasons why, both in theory and in school practice (a matter which will be dealt with in a later section), intending teachers of infants make a study of the lower ranges of the junior school.

The nature of the course for those students who are preparing to teach in junior schools is determined largely by the fact that these schools cover an age-range during which the child is in process of transition from one crucial period of life to another, from the period of infancy and early childhood to that of pre-adolescence and puberty.

During his passage through the nursery and infant stage the child has enjoyed a large measure of freedom to experiment and try out his powers in dealing with the world around him. At the same time his school education has preserved as far as possible a unity related to the development of his whole personality. It is fresh from these conditions that he comes to the junior school.

On the other hand when the child passes on from the junior school to the secondary phase of education he is entering upon a stage of growth during which he will be subjected to more definite kinds of discipline and during which he will acquire knowledge and skill in a far more specialized and, as it were, compartmentalized manner than in the past. It is the main task of the junior school to ensure smooth and effective transition from the earlier to the later stage and, through ministering to the needs and capacities of the child as he is at the moment, to build upon the former while preparing for the latter.

The training course centres upon the consideration of this transitional process in the junior school and on the problems which it raises. The students are instructed in methods of easing the path of the young children at entry to the junior school and during the earlier stages in it, while at the same time effecting a measure of consolidation in regard to the knowledge and skill which the child has acquired in the infant school. For the junior stage is not only one of transition but also one of consolidation during which threads are brought together and woven into coherent patterns to serve as a basis in which knowledge and skill may be firmly grounded. This dual process of stabilizing the results of earlier education while at the same time preparing for the transition to more formalized work is the hallmark of the junior school, and it is upon it that the attention of students in training is focused.

It is at this point that the study of the general subjects by students assumes a special importance. It has already been pointed out that, so far as they contribute to their personal education, the students intending to teach infants and juniors study these subjects in the same way, and with the same ends in view, as their fellows who are going to teach older children. But teaching method in the general subjects presents special problems, especially for those students who are likely for the most part to teach children in the later stages of the junior school, and the nature of these problems varies from one subject to another.

On the one hand there are subjects such as English, mathematics, and some aspects of science, geography and nature study, which are natural parts of the education of a child from a comparatively early age. During the later part of the junior stage the earlier free and inter-related development of these has to be guided into more clearly defined channels corresponding to the division of the subjects which the child will meet when he passes to the secondary stage. On the other hand there are subjects such as history, civics, and social studies, as well as some aspects of, for example, geography and the physical and biological sciences, which are fitting subjects of study only for the more mature mind. Nevertheless the teacher in the junior school has to consider how best to prepare the ground so that when the child, at the appropriate time in the secondary stage, is introduced to the serious study of the subjects mentioned, he may enter upon this with interest and without undue difficulty.

Again subjects such as music, art, the crafts, and physical education all present their special problems. In the infant and early junior stages they are related as aspects of the child's experience which contribute naturally to his growth and development. At the secondary stage, when the child's special interests and aptitudes are becoming increasingly apparent, these subjects require different treatment, not only in regard to their customary separation from one another in the school curriculum, but also in regard to the proportionate emphasis laid on each of them in the education of the individual child. The student who is going to teach the older children in the junior school must know how to prepare his pupils for this change of treatment which they are shortly going to meet.

Enough has perhaps been said to indicate the main themes determining the content of the training course for students intending to teach in junior schools. During the course the students will be given opportunities of studying the work both of the infant schools and of the secondary schools. It must not, of course, be thought that the junior schools are merely subsidiary. They have an important life of their own, and in their passage through them the children exhibit the characteristics peculiar to their stage of development. All this forms a subject of study during the training course for, when they become teachers, the students must know how to adapt their methods to the child as he is, for only thus can they foster his natural development, let alone prepare him for the future. Nevertheless the part played in the educational system by the junior school in linking the infant and the secondary stages is a specially vital one.

THE TRAINING COURSE FOR TEACHERS IN SECONDARY MODERN SCHOOLS

With the exception of a certain number of specialists in such subjects as handicraft, domestic science, and physical education, the large majority of training college students trained to teach children at the secondary stage find themselves entering the secondary modern schools. The training course is planned accordingly.

The teacher in the modern school (this will be used as an abbreviation of secondary modern school) is generally called upon to lend a hand in the teaching of some subjects other than those of which he has made a special study. These may include any such subjects as English, arithmetic, religious instruction, and, perhaps, history and geography. Where possible, arrangements are made for the teacher to spend as much time as possible in the teaching of the subject or subjects in which he is particularly competent and specialists in such fields as handicraft, domestic science, and physical education will generally be engaged all or most of their time in their special fields. The degree to which the work of any particular teacher is spread over subjects other than those special to him will depend on the size of the school in which he is teaching and the composition of its staff, particularly in regard to the proportion of graduates included in the latter. In smaller schools where there may be no graduate members of staff the non-graduate trained teacher may well find himself in charge of some such subject as mathematics, science, history or geography. Where there are graduates to teach these, he will be more likely to play the part of an assistant in such share as he may take in the teaching of the subjects in the school concerned.

The training course is framed to meet this situation. The student receives instruction in the professional part of the course in method of English and arithmetic teaching. As regards the teaching of other subjects he makes a special study of method in the teaching of the subject or subjects which he has selected from the general list, while opportunities are provided for him to take short subsidiary courses which will help him if he is called upon to play some part in the teaching of the other subjects already mentioned. Religious instruction is a special case which will be referred to in a later section.

One matter which receives special attention during the secondary training course is that of the use of books, with particular reference to school and public libraries and the educational opportunities which these provide. At the same time the student is instructed in the use of other teaching aids such as films, filmstrips, the gramophone, and the radio, and in the application of techniques of comparatively recent development, such as the project method.

In addition to his instruction in the more formal side of school life, the student training for modern school teaching will make a study of the characteristics, both personal and social, of children at the secondary stage. At this stage individual differences have become more marked and the student is instructed in adequate methods of coping with these differences, both inside and outside the classroom. He also considers the community life of the school and the part that can be played by the pupils in the organization of school life, in the maintenance of discipline, and in the running of clubs or groups of various kinds in connexion with games and other activities. This part of the course may be linked with the study of the teaching of civics and social subjects.

Towards the end of the secondary stage, questions of vocational guidance and selection become of increasing importance. The student is therefore introduced to the preparation and use of school records appropriate for this stage, not only as aids in the educational process within the school itself but also as providing valuable information in regard to suitable occupations for the pupils when they leave school. In this connexion consideration is given to the important part which the schools can play in collaboration with the Juvenile Employment Service.

A reference, unavoidably brief, should be made in this section to the training course in the specialist colleges such, for example, as the colleges of domestic science. The aim of these, as of all other, colleges is to turn out teachers who are educated persons as well as competent professional workers. The students are instructed in the general principles and practice of teaching, while particular attention is given to method in the teaching of English. Each student also chooses a special subject of study from the general field. The main difference between the specialist colleges and the others is that, in the former, all the work is coloured by the particulàr field of education in which the college specializes, while the subjects chosen by the students for study are in general related to, or considered in their possible relation to, this field.

SCHOOL PRACTICE

The student activities grouped under this heading fall into two fairly well defined parts: visits to schools for purposes of observation either of the general running of the school and the behaviour of the children, or of 'demonstration lessons'; and visits during which the student actually plays a part in the teaching, taking over charge of a class for a substantial portion of time.

During observation visits the students will become acquainted with the organization and administration of the school and with the nature of the routine tasks which fall upon the head and assistant staff. These tasks will include not only the clerical and purely administrative work but matters concerned with the grouping of the children in classes and otherwise for their various educational and recreational activities, the preparation of syllabuses, the making of records, and the carrying out of tests and examinations.

In addition the visits may be the occasion of valuable opportunities for the students in their work on child study. The type of schools visited by particular students will depend on the age-range of the children they intend to teach, but it is now common practice, for reasons already given, to arrange some visits for students to schools dealing with age-ranges outside those with which the students in question may be specially concerned.

Observation visits are usually introduced early in the training course and renewed from time to time throughout the course. Systematic teaching practice, on the other hand, occurs generally in two stages: a preliminary practice during the first year of the course, and a final practice, on which teaching work assessments are made, during the latter part of the second year.

The duration of school practice was formerly laid down by regulation. In normal circumstances a total of 12 weeks practice was required. The Ministry, however, no longer lays down precise requirements in this respect. The period of practice must be adequate, but the prime responsibility for ensuring this falls on the colleges acting under the supervision of their area training organization.

It was formerly the custom for college supervision of teaching practice to be left mainly, or solely, in the hands of the education staff, headed, in earlier days, by the master or mistress of method. Nowadays, however, practically all the members of the college staff play some part in the supervision of school practice, paying frequent visits to the schools while the practice is going on, in order to observe and help their students and at the same time to discuss the progress of the practice with the heads and staffs of the schools.

It will be clear that the schools themselves play a vital part in all this. They are, in fact, co-partners with the colleges in providing a supply for competent teachers. It has long been their statutory duty to make provision for students carrying out teaching practice, but the way in which they perform this duty depends on the attitude of the head teacher and his staff and on the nature of their relations with the training colleges. Of recent years definite steps have been taken, often by the colleges themselves, to impress on the schools the importance of the part they play in the training of teachers. At the same time the colleges have paid increasing attention to the fostering of good relations with the schools, not only by individual personal contacts, but through the arrangement of educational and social occasions on which members of school and college staffs can meet together and discuss questions of common concern.

This matter is of great importance, for the burden placed on the schools by teaching practice is a heavy one and has been steadily increasing with the growth of the output of students from the colleges. The arrangements for the practice can no longer be left to individual colleges, LEAs, and schools working out a plan between them by mutual agreement. The pressure is now too great, and it has been found necessary to organize practice regionally by sharing out the schools among the colleges on the basis of zones decided upon by special committees representing all the interests concerned and acting under the aegis of the various ATOs.

In concluding this section it may be remarked that the McNair committee was of the opinion that, when circumstances permitted, part of a student's period of teaching practice should consist of about a term spent as a member of a staff of a school. They noted, however, that this suggestion could not be regarded as coming within the field of practical possibility until the training course had been lengthened to three years.

Some colleges, though not very many, have schools adjacent to them which are closely associated with them and are used for practice and demonstration. This has certain obvious advantages, especially in connexion with the teaching of very young children. The schools in question are readily accessible and have become used to working in close collaboration with the nearby colleges. On the other hand there are certain disadvantages. Too much reliance may come to be placed on the demonstration schools, with consequent lack of variety for the students in gaining experience, while it is arguable that the use of a school as a kind of experimental laboratory with a continual stream of visitors coming and going may not be good for the education of the children in it. It may be said that, on the whole, the balance of opinion has turned against the 'practising school' and it seems unlikely that any new colleges will be built with such schools attached, with the possible exception of nursery schools in conjunction with colleges some of the students in which are training to teach the youngest children.

Before going on to consider the courses for students in university departments of education, there are a number of topics of general interest in connexion with training college courses of which some brief mention will be made in the section which follows.

GENERAL

The professional section of the training course includes a study of educational history. This falls broadly into two parts: the history of the growth and organization of the educational system and the history of the development of educational ideas. The two are, of course, interconnected closely and the study of the relations between them and the degree to which the progress of the system lags behind the movement of educational thought is itself an interesting part of the training course. It leads naturally to a consideration of the educational system as it now is, in all its aspects, not only in regard to the more directly educational work but also in regard to services ancillary to education such as the school medical service, the school meals service, and all the many agencies which minister, directly or indirectly, to the needs of the children.

As for educational psychology, an interesting and significant change in the method of approach to this has taken place during the last 30 years. Formerly the study of it in the training colleges was of an extremely abstract and academic nature, stemming no doubt from that traditional linking of philosophy and psychology, from the bonds of which the latter was, at the beginning of this century, only just beginning to shake itself free. The establishment of psychology as an independent science during the last few decades has been paralleled in the training colleges by the development of a quite different method of dealing with the subject of educational psychology. This subject is the basic science on which the art of teaching is founded, and it permeates the whole of the professional side of the training course.

It is now the common practice in training colleges to approach the study of educational psychology not so much from general principles as from a consideration of the concrete problems raised by the various kinds of situation in which the student will find himself when he begins to teach. From a consideration of these situations the relevant general principles emerge naturally and thereafter theory and practice are studied in close relation to one another.

The degree to which certain aspects of psychological study are formalized varies from area to area and from college to college. Among the topics treated in the more formal work are growth, with the influence on it of heredity, environment and the basic human needs; learning, with the motivation for this, attention, memory, imagination and reasoning; social development and the part played in this by the influence of various groups and agencies; and the general question of the integration of personality.

Among the most important of the topics studied in this field is that of individual differences and the methods of measuring and recording these. In this connexion the students are instructed in the elementary theory of tests of various kinds, and in the application of these tests.

A particularly difficult problem for the teacher is that of the backward child. The student's attention is drawn to the difference between the child who, though reasonably intelligent, is backward because of circumstances due to absence from school through sickness or other causes, or to the emotional effects of such things as unhappy or unsatisfactory family life, and the child who is backward because of sub-average intelligence.

The last topic raises some points of special importance. A distinction must be made between children who, though sub-average and perhaps low in IQ (intelligence quotient) are nevertheless quite normal specimens of humanity, being merely in the lower ranges of the scale of normal biological and psychological variation, and those children who are so afflicted by mental or physical handicaps as to be, in effect, pathological cases.

The teachers in the ordinary schools—as distinct from the 'special schools' for severely handicapped children—and therefore the general run of training college students, are concerned with normal children over the whole range of intelligence. The portions of the training course in educational psychology which deal with the normal but sub-average child are therefore of great importance. The student is instructed in methods of enabling these children to live a full and satisfying life in the development of their capacities to the fullest extent which their natural limitations permit, and in the importance of creating in them a sense of pride and interest in what they are able to accomplish free so far as possible from the feelings of inferiority, inadequacy and frustration which have so often characterized these children in the past.

The student is also informed as to the ways in which children, especially young children, suffering from defects not immediately apparent may be distinguished. Here faults in vision and hearing call for particular consideration. But the education of children suffering from the more extreme mental and physical defects is not regarded as part of the normal work of the teacher in the ordinary schools, though such children are not infrequently found in these schools owing to lack of accommodation in the special institutions which exist for their care and education or to other circumstances. It is important that teachers should bring to the notice of the authorities concerned the presence of such children in the schools, and this is impressed upon the students in training.

There are no institutions specializing solely in the training of teachers for the special schools for handicapped children. These teachers get their training for this work mainly through special one-year courses laid on for them in certain institutions such, for example, as the London Institute of Education (not the ATO but the Training Department), and the Manchester University Department of Education. There are also short 'refresher' courses of two or three weeks which the special school teachers can attend from time to time. In most, but not all, cases a teacher will have put in a period of service in an ordinary school after leaving college before taking up work in a special school. The whole question of the supply and training of teachers of handicapped children is at present under consideration by the National Advisory Council.

It was said earlier that special problems arise in connexion with religious instruction or divinity. This subject is now compulsorily included, under certain specified conditions, in the curriculum of all grant-aided primary and secondary schools so that a considerable number of teachers are required to deal with it. Any teacher may in fact be asked, though he cannot be compelled, to teach divinity. The position is put clearly before students in training. Many of them wish to teach divinity and may choose it as a special subject of study; but, in addition to the special courses in the subject, subsidiary optional courses are arranged which may be taken advantage of by any student willing to take a share in religious instruction in the school in which he will teach.

Another question of some difficulty is that of sex instruction. This is of particular importance to students preparing to teach in secondary schools. A remarkable degree of ignorance and confusion on sexual matters is observed in students even at the age when they enter college. The first task to which the college staff have therefore to address themselves in this field is that of putting the students themselves right in the matter. The subsequent treatment of the subject of sex instruction in the schools to which the students will go is governed, in general, by the following considerations: (a) increasing attention is being given to the provision of adequate sex instruction in the schools; (b) it is rightly unlikely that a student fresh from college will be given a responsible part in specific sex instruction in a school; but nevertheless, (c) it is important that students should have adequate knowledge in this field so that they may understand the problems and difficulties of the children they teach and may be prepared, when time has brought greater experience and maturity, to play their part when necessary in specific sex instruction.

Another point, closely related to this, which is of importance particularly to students preparing to teach in the secondary schools, is that of the sex-differences between boys and girls in regard to their various interests, aptitudes, and activities. These differences will determine educational method in certain respects and some attention is given to this during the training course, as the students of today, both male and female, may find themselves teaching in any type of school, boys', girls', or mixed.

Reference has already been made to the existence in the training colleges of subsidiary courses, which may be of comparatively short duration, and some of the topics dealt with in this section are treated in such courses. The number and character of the courses vary considerably from college to college. Moreover they may be entirely optional, or the student may be required to take one or more of them, though it is open to him to choose which particular ones he will take.

A matter which has not so far been specifically mentioned, though much attention is given to it during the training course, is that of speech training. Here again one of the first things that has to be done is to deal with the generally rather poor speech habits of the students themselves. Modern methods of recording and reproducing speech are proving of great assistance, while in addition to set exercises in the oral use of language good speech is fostered in the students through the opportunities provided by such activities as drama and debate. Methods of speech training applied in the teaching of children form an integral part of the professional course in English.

Finally some points of general interest should be mentioned in regard to the specialist colleges. There are 14 colleges of housecraft or domestic science, while some of the general colleges run special courses in this subject, the third year of which may be taken at another institution. There are seven colleges of physical education for women while one college (Loughborough) makes special provision in physical education for men. Two colleges (Shoreditch and Loughborough) make special provision for men interested in handicraft, while this subject can be taken as a main course in most of the general colleges for men. One college (Bretton Hall) makes special provision for intending teachers of art and music.

Up to the present, it has not been the policy to earmark individual students in training specifically for urban or for rural schools. Some colleges however run courses with a rural bias, while the students themselves will naturally choose for their special studies those subjects (e.g. biology and gardening in connexion with rural studies) which are allied to their individual interests and to the circumstances of the kind of school in which they hope to teach.⌋

THE TRAINING COURSE FOR UNIVERSITY GRADUATES

The university departments of education are the normal source of supply of teachers for the secondary grammar schools. With the exception of specialists in certain fields such as handicrafts, art, domestic science, and physical education, practically all the teachers in grammar schools are graduates. On the other hand, except, in the case of Oxford, Cambridge, and London, by no means all, or nearly all, trained graduates go to teach in grammar schools or the few secondary technical schools which now exist. A very substantial proportion of the students go into secondary modern schools. Some indeed go to junior and infant schools, mainly women.

The training course in the UDE is adjusted to this situation. Not only do the students make a study of all types of secondary school, but they carry out part of their teaching practice in modern as well as grammar or technical schools.

The proportions of time spent during school practice in the various types of school depends on the prospects of the individual student, but even those students who, because of academic level and their own wishes, are almost certain to teach in grammar schools, spend part of their period of practice in modern schools, and this applies, though to a somewhat less extent, to the three exceptions mentioned, namely Oxford, Cambridge and London.

It is not uncommon, indeed, for UDE students to visit junior schools. The reason for this breadth and variety of school practice is that it is desirable that all students intending to teach should have some contact with all or most of the range of school education, for only thus can they hope to attain the breadth of vision essential to the understanding of the nature and problems of the educational process in general and of the purpose of universal secondary education in particular.

On the more theoretical side, the main purpose of the training course for graduates is threefold: To enable the student to keep up the study of the special subject in which he took his degree, to instruct him in educational philosophy and psychology and in the principles of teaching, and to extend his knowledge and skill, though over a rather narrower range than in the case of non-graduate students, to other school

86

subjects or activities in which he may be called upon to play a part as a member of a corporate school staff.

Much of the ground covered during the graduate course is similar in nature to, though in some respects at a higher level than, that covered during the training course for non-graduates. Graduate students in training may also carry out simple research work and special inquiries in connexion with educational topics to illustrate and illuminate their studies in the main body of the course.

As already implied, some of the women students, and there are among them women of academic distinction, deliberately choose to go into junior or infant schools. The quality and amount of provision made for these students varies from one university to another, but the presence of such women in the primary schools is now recognized to be of great importance, and increasing attention is being given to the need for providing them with adequate and suitable facilities and opportunities during their training course.

Apart from QT status the qualification accorded to graduate students on the satisfactory completion of their training course is known as the teachers' certificate or the teachers' diploma according to the university concerned or the level at which the course is taken. When the student, whether graduate or non-graduate, has, in the judgment of the examiners, satisfactorily completed his course of training he is given the status of 'qualified teacher'; but he still has to serve a probationary period.

PROBATION

In the case of students from the permanent, as distinct from the emergency, training colleges the normal length of the period of probation is one year. Until quite recently the recommendation for confirmation of QT status after the satisfactory completion of the probationary year had to be signed jointly by the LEA and H.M. inspector on lists including the names of all teachers on probation during the year in question. In cases of doubt the probationary period was extended for a specified period, e.g. six months, and only in very rare and extreme cases was a teacher finally banned from QT status without such an extension. In any case the number of teachers so banned, even after extension, was and is a very small proportion of the whole.

Different arrangements have now been made. At the expiry of the probationary year the status of QT is automatically confirmed, except in doubtful cases. In these cases the responsibility for recommending the appropriate action, e.g. extension of probation, rests on the LEA, though an H.M. inspector is, always available for consultation by the latter and will also generally be consulted by the Ministry when the LEA reports the case.

Clearly it is of great importance that the new teacher should be put in a suitable post when first appointed, so that he may be given a fair trial during his probationary year. In cases where doubts arise consideration is given to all the circumstances, and it may be regarded as desirable to transfer the teacher concerned to another school for the remainder of his probation, to see if he makes a better showing there. Care is therefore taken to spot the doubtful cases as early in the probationary year as possible; those concerned, especially the heads of the schools where the teachers in question are serving, should bring the matter to the attention of the LEA as soon as they feel doubts about a probationer's competence as a practising teacher.

CHAPTER VI

POST-INITIAL TRAINING

Post-initial training now falls broadly into three categories namely supplementary courses, special courses for experienced serving teachers, and short refresher courses. The first of these takes the place of what, before the war, were known as 'third-year courses'.

SUPPLEMENTARY COURSES

These courses, which normally last one year, are meant to enable the student or practising teacher to increase his knowledge and teaching competence in a subject in which he is specially interested and able. They cover, in principle, much the same range as the general subjects of study in the initial training course, but the particular courses in operation in any one year depend on the special needs of the schools and the financial circumstances of the Ministry at the time. The programme of supplementary courses is reviewed annually by officers of the Ministry, while the area training organizations are being brought more and more into consultation in the drawing up of the programme for the coming year.

In their general nature the supplementary courses are similar to the old third year courses and, as in the case of the latter, they may be 'continuous' or 'deferred', that is the student may take such a course immediately after finishing his initial training course or he may put in a period of teaching first. The courses are intended for non-graduates, though a few graduates may be admitted to them in exceptional circumstances.

There is, however, one important difference between the old and the new. Third-year courses were carried on mainly in training colleges, though a student often took such a course in a college other than that which gave him his initial training and which might not have facilities for running a third-year course in his special subject. But the present policy in the case of the supplementary courses is to lay on such courses as far as possible in educational institutions other than training colleges. This has the double advantage of helping to keep free the much needed accommodation in these colleges for their main business of initial training, while taking advantage of the special facilities available in such institutions, as colleges of art or music, facilities which few training colleges possess to any extent. Nevertheless a substantial number of supplementary courses are still held in training colleges.

Selection of students for supplementary courses is extremely careful. In the initial stages students are advised by their training college tutors, but, in the final stages, the last word in selection rests with the institution running the course. H.M. inspectors are available for consultation when desired and, through them, the Ministry exercises general supervision over the running of the supplementary courses.

Students with the status of qualified teacher are approved by the Minister for supplementary courses and the Minister will pay grant according to the circumstances of the student and the nature of the institution in which the course is being held.

SPECIAL COURSES FOR SERVING TEACHERS

Courses of this kind are a comparatively recent innovation and at present exist only on a small scale. Their main purpose is to meet special needs of the schools or the training institutions while at the same time enabling a limited number of practising teachers to raise their professional qualifications to a substantially more advanced level should they wish to do so. For example the great need for teachers of young children has created a problem not only for the schools but also for the training institutions, as an increase in staff with appropriate qualifications is required to train the additional number of students preparing to teach young children. Special courses have been established to meet this situation. Regulation requires them to be of not more than one year's duration.

Any experienced serving teacher may apply for admission to a special course. Those selected from the batch of applicants by the institution running the course may then, with the approval of the Minister, be admitted to the course. The Minister will pay to, or in respect of, any experienced serving teacher admitted as a recognized student to such a course a grant for tuition and maintenance of an approved amount at the rate of not more than £300 a year.

Some of the teachers taking these courses may afterwards go on to training colleges; others may go back into the schools where their presence acts as a valuable stimulus. There is little doubt that the courses are justifying themselves and one purpose they may serve is to provide a contribution to the education staff of training colleges, the shortage in which has been mentioned previously. How far and in what way the courses will be extended in the future depends on the needs of educational institutions, the demand from the teachers themselves, the facilities available, and the financial circumstances at the time.

SHORT REFRESHER COURSES

These are mainly for practising teachers, most of whom will naturally come from the schools, though many of the courses are open also to members of the staffs of other educational institutions, such as training colleges, who have been attending them in increasing numbers. The courses exist in great profusion and variety. They vary in length, but a typical duration is from about 10 days to a fortnight. The chief agencies in running them are the Ministry, the LEAs, and, more recently, the ATOs.

The Ministry's short courses are of very long standing. They were originally entirely 'national' in character, that is the entrants to them were drawn from all over the country. They were of a purely 'subject' character, that is they were concerned with the general subjects of education but not with the teaching of those subjects. In the first instance they were intended as a contribution to the personal education of teachers in rural schools who had not the same educational opportunities open to them as their fellows in the towns and cities.

All this has changed. At the present time some of the Ministry's courses are national, others are regional: the courses may deal with subjects or phases of education, or with professional method, or with both: the teachers attending them come from both town and country. No tuition fee is charged, but the members of the course pay for board and residence. The Ministry pays third class travelling expenses in excess of 10 shillings. The LEAs may give some financial assistance to their teachers, individually considered, to enable them to attend the courses.

The courses run by LEAs are naturally local in character. They are laid on *ad hoc* to meet some current need or demand. They have been increasing in number, with the encouragement of the Ministry, and they may be wholly or partly residential (i.e. some of the teachers coming from a distance in a large area may have to stay away from home for the course), or non-residential.

The area training organizations, once they had established as a going concern their main business of supervising initial training, soon began to plan programmes of short refresher courses for practising teachers, and many such courses have already been held. They cover much the same field as the courses run by the Ministry and the LEAs, though approached from the ATO angle and staffed by tutors from the constituent colleges and departments of the institute concerned and other suitable persons invited by the council of the institute on the recommendation of the academic board. The scope of the existing programmes of the ATO courses varies from one institute to another. Some have preferred to give proportionately more attention to this ancillary aspect of their work than others; but these courses are now widespread and flourishing.

Within limits, it is all to the good that these various agencies should be making their contributions to the provision of refresher courses for practising teachers. But a position has perhaps now been reached—or soon will be reached when all the parties concerned might well come together and, in consultation with the teachers' professional associations—who run their own courses on a considerable scale—survey the situation. They might then be able to frame some kind of joint plan, in which all would play their appropriate parts, to bring into being a system of courses that would operate with the maximum scope and effectiveness, yet without unnecessary overlapping. Much might be gained by tidying up the present state of affairs.

The opportunities for post-initial training described in the foregoing are through courses the level of which is not for the most part greatly in advance of that reached by the abler students at the end of their initial course, though, where practising teachers of considerable experience are concerned, extensions are added in other dimensions. Facilities already exist for obtaining qualifications at more advanced levels through the various degrees and diplomas in education offered by the universities. Many practising teachers, however, are not in a position to satisfy the conditions preliminary to entering upon courses of study for these university titles. It is partly for this reason that ways and means are now being studied, in particular by the Standing Conference of Area Training Organizations, of bringing some measure of uniformity into the existing field of advanced qualifications and at the same time establishing new types of qualification which may be more readily accessible to teachers of sufficiently high calibre. Discussions on this matter have not, however, advanced much beyond the preliminary stages.

It will be seen that the possibilities for post-initial training are already considerable and are steadily increasing. This is the more important at the present time in view of the short duration of the initial training course.

THE TRAINING OF TECHNICAL TEACHERS

This study is concerned almost entirely with the training of teachers for primary and secondary schools. No account of the training of teachers in England and Wales would be complete, however, without at least a brief reference to an interesting and significant development which has come into being within the last few years. This is the training of technical teachers.

Before the war there were in existence no arrangements for the systematic training of teachers in technical institutions. The McNair committee gave a considerable amount of attention to this matter and their recommendations provided a stimulus to the establishment of the system which now exists. That system began as an offshoot of the emergency training scheme during its later stages, and was in fact then conducted in accordance with principles and regulations analogous to those governing the main scheme for the training of primary and secondary teachers. The technical training courses were short, running to a duration of not more than six to nine months.

The training of technical teachers has now, however, become an established part of the permanent training system. There are three technical colleges in which courses of one year's duration are being held, the Bolton Technical College, the Huddersfield Technical College, and the London North-West Polytechnic.

The courses are intended mainly for teachers in technical institutions who wish to take a course of professional training and for persons with experience in industrial and other technical occupations who wish to take up teaching. The course does not lead to the status of 'qualified teacher' as this has significance only in the primary and secondary field and there is at present no corresponding titled status in the technical field. Nevertheless a proportion of those who have taken the technical training course may later wish to transfer to a secondary school, usually a secondary technical or a secondary modern school. The agreed principle provisionally governing such transfers is that—although a teacher entering the primary or secondary field must, by regulation, serve a probationary period before being recognized as a QT—in determining the nature and duration of this service in the case of teachers transferring from the technical field account will be taken of the fact that a training course has been followed and of any teaching experience already gained in the technical field. Each case is, in fact, considered on its own merits in laying down the conditions which the teacher in question must satisfy before being accorded QT status.

In comparison with the provision available there is a very large demand for admission to technical training courses. In 1951–52, for example, there were some 4,000 applicants though the actual intake to the courses was only 250. Drastic selection is therefore possible. On the whole the placing in suitable posts of those who have taken the course is satisfactory, the great majority of those trained securing teaching appointments within a reasonable time.

A relatively small proportion (which has been decreasing since the inception of the scheme) of those trained in the technical course, take, as their first appointment after training, a post in a secondary school. The majority go, as intended, to teach in institutions of further education, particularly in the technical fields of buildings, commerce, and engineering.

The London and Huddersfield Colleges put on courses for those intending to teach in county colleges. The number thus being trained is small, as there are at present few county colleges or their equivalent in existence, and the provision of such colleges on a large scale is postponed, mainly for financial reasons, to what may be a somewhat distant future.

The content of the training course is mainly concerned with principles of education and the theory and practice of teaching with particular reference, in the case of each group of students, to teaching method in the technical field with which that group is concerned. Teaching practice is carried out in technical institutions, but generally includes also some practice in secondary schools, technical and modern. Educational visits of various kinds are arranged and student social activities are developed.

The National Advisory Council has been considering the training of technical teachers, and development in this has followed the general lines of their preliminary recommendations. These were to the effect that, while full-time teacher training for teachers in technical colleges should not be made compulsory, it was highly desirable that one-year full time training courses should be established on the lines of the emergency courses; that each technical training college should be associated with an ATO which would award an appropriate certificate and could recommend for QT status students who had successfully completed the one-year full-time training course and subsequently took posts in secondary schools; and that more part-time courses should be provided for part-time technical teachers. These recommendations are being implemented with the approval of the Minister.

94

With regard to the last recommendation, about 40 short courses have been provided by LEAs and from 1,500 to 2,000 part-time teachers have been enrolled. The regional advisory councils for technical education have considered the possibility of providing courses for serving full-time teachers in technical institutions of various kinds, and it is likely that such courses will be provided in several large centres of population.

Altogether, then, the training of technical teachers has got off to a good start. As the numbers involved are small it will never in actual size form more than a small, though very important, part of the training system, and it is unlikely to be made compulsory, at least in the foreseeable future; but that the advantages it offers are widely appreciated is indicated by the large number of applicants in proportion to the training places available.

CHAPTER VIII

STATUS AND PROSPECTS OF THE TEACHER

The status and the salary scale of any occupation interact in a complex and subtle way. The esteem in which the occupation is generally held is an important factor in determining the salary scale which those who follow that occupation can secure: on the other hand, once a salary scale is established it is itself a factor in determining the degree of esteem in which the occupation is held. This circular inter-action proceeds in combination with, though in part independently of, the operation of the normal laws of supply and demand. Something will be said in the latter part of this chapter about the status of the teaching profession in so far as this arises from the esteem in which the profession is held by the general public; but the question of salary will be considered first.

SALARY

It is a matter of general agreement that, having regard to the vital nature of its work, the teaching profession has, until comparatively recent times, been grossly underpaid. It was only with the setting up of the Burnham committees that the profession began to receive a financial reward more commensurate with the importance of its work. The general principle now operative is that, in any field of education, e.g. that of primary and secondary schools, there is a basic scale which applies whatever the particular school, or type of school, in which a teacher is working. Differentiation is made by additions to the basic scale for special qualifications.

The main points relating to salaries are summarized hereunder. Full details are set out in the reports of the Burnham committees. To all the figures given, the recently agreed flat rate allowances of £40 for every man teacher and £32 for every woman teacher should be added.

SALARIES FOR TEACHERS IN PRIMARY AND SECONDARY SCHOOLS

There are three main categories of teacher to be considered in these schools: qualified, unqualified, and temporary. Qualified teachers are those with QT status: unqualified teachers are those who, though permanent members of the teaching profession have, for one reason or another, not achieved QT status: temporary teachers are those who, at the time considered, are not permanent members of the profession but are employed temporarily for some particular reason or to meet some particular current need.

Temporary teachers fall into two groups, those who are so employed prior to admission to a recognized course of training, and those who are unable or do not intend to enter upon such a course. The former are paid in accordance with the scale for unqualified teachers: the latter have a special scale of their own.

The basic salary scales for primary and secondary school assistant teachers are now as follows:

MEN

Qualified. Minimum of £375 rising by annual increments of £18 to a maximum of £630 after 14 completed years of service, the final increment being £21.

Unqualified. Minimum of £225 rising by annual increments of £15 to a maximum of £375 after 10 completed years of service.

Temporary. Minimum of £225 rising by annual increments of £15 to a maximum of £285 after four completed years of service.

WOMEN

Qualified. Minimum of £338 rising by annual increments of £15 to a maximum of £504 after 11 completed years of service, the final increment being £16.

Unqualified. Minimum of £202 rising by annual increments of £12 to a maximum of £338 after 12 completed years of service, the final increment being £4.

Temporary. Minimum of £202 rising by annual increments of £12 to a maximum of £250 after four completed years of service.

Various additions may be made to the basic scale in respect of special qualifications.

There is an addition for training, other than normal initial training, up to a maximum of three annual increments, for those who have taken an approved course of training or certain approved courses of study of not less than three years duration. Another addition of £60 for men and £48 for women is made for graduates or their recognized equivalents. For teachers employed in special schools for handicapped children there are additions of £36 for men and £30 for women.

There are also additions to the minimum of the scale in respect of certain approved types of experience, e.g. in long service as an unqualified teacher or in certain other types of occupation in the professional, business or industrial world, gained prior to the date on which the teacher concerned is deemed to have obtained the qualifications by which he or she is approved as a qualified teacher.

A qualified teacher may be eligible for any one or more of the additions which have been described. There are also certain additions to the scale for unqualified teachers.

The additions in respect of the teaching of special classes for partially deaf or partially sighted children in ordinary schools, and in respect of work in special schools, other than those for the teaching of the blind or the deaf, where a special qualification is required, apply to unqualified teachers, the additions in either case being £30 for men and £24 for women. Unqualified teachers satisfying the conditions of teaching in special schools for the blind or the deaf receive a further addition of £24 in the case of men and £18 in the case of women.

Unqualified teachers who have had previous experience as supplementary teachers (an old and now obsolescent category of teachers in rural schools) receive as an addition to the minimum of the appropriate scale £15 in the case of men and £12 in the case of women in respect of each period of three years of such experience gained after the age of 18 years. Temporary teachers receive additions equal to those provided for unqualified teachers working in similar circumstances.

Apart from additions of the kind we have been considering, teachers in the defined 'London area' receive an additional allowance of £36 per annum which is increased to £48 when the teacher has completed 16 years of full time service, in the 'London area' or elsewhere, or has attained the age of 37 years.

HEAD TEACHERS

A head teacher receives the basic salary of an assistant teacher in similar circumstances, plus any of the additions for which he may be eligible, together with a special 'head teacher allowance'.

Qualified head teachers receive allowances assessed on the basis of the number of pupils on the roll of the school, classified by ages, except in the case of special schools, where the allowances are assessed according to the type of special educational treatment provided by the school. Men head teachers in ordinary schools receive an allowance varying from £55 per annum in the case of the smallest schools to £900 in the case of the largest, while the corresponding allowance for women varies from £50 to £790. (The largest schools here envisaged, with over 3,000 pupils on the roll, are at the moment only a possibility for the future.)

The qualified head teacher allowances in the case of special schools vary from £80 to £370 in the case of men, and from £75 to £330 in the case of women. The allowance for unqualified head teachers of ordinary schools is, in all cases, £55 for men and £50 for women, while for unqualified head teachers of special schools it is, in all cases, £80 for men and £75 for women. Finally there is a system of 'special allowances'. These may be paid to assistant teachers for specially responsible or specially advanced work or other appropriate reasons. No such allowance may be at a rate of less than £40 per annum.

The total amount of special allowances permissible in a particular school depends on the size of the school, but, over and above the allowances for individual schools, there is a fund available in the area of each LEA, known as the 'area pool', from which special allowances may be paid to any teachers in the area who qualify for them. The size of the area pool depends on the total numbers of pupils enrolled on the registers of the schools in the area. Special allowances to assistant teachers in special schools are all paid from the area pool.

All special allowances are subject to the over-riding condition that they shall not be granted in such manner as would effect a general alteration in the operation of the salary scales.

SALARIES FOR TEACHERS IN ESTABLISHMENTS FOR FURTHER EDUCATION

Establishments for further education include technical and commercial colleges and institutes, and art colleges and schools. The main points regarding the salary scales applicable in such establishments will be briefly summarized. There are three categories of assistant staff: 'assistant' (Grade A and Grade B), 'lecturer', and 'senior lecturer'. At the higher levels there are heads of departments, vice-principals, and principals.

ASSISTANTS

Grade A

Men. Minimum £375 per annum rising by annual increments of £18 and one final increment of £21 to a maximum of £630 per annum.
Women. Minimum £338 per annum rising by annual increments of £15 and one final increment of £16 to a maximum of £504 per annum.

Grade B

Men. Minimum £450 per annum rising by annual increments of £25 to a maximum of £725 per annum.
Women. Minimum £405 per annum rising by annual increments of £20 and one final increment of £15 to a maximum of £580 per annum.
Additional payments to assistants may be made for training, up to a maximum of three increments each of £18 in the case of men and £15 in the case of women, and for a degree or its equivalent of £60 in the case of men and £48 in the case of women.

LECTURERS

Men. Minimum £900 per annum rising by annual increments of £25 to a maximum of £1,000 per annum.
Women. Minimum £720 per annum rising by annual increments of £20 to a maximum of £800 per annum.

SENIOR LECTURERS

Men. Minimum £1,000 per annum rising by annual increments of £25 to a maximum of £1,150 per annum.
Women. Minimum £800 per annum rising by annual increments of £20 to a maximum of £920 per annum.

HEADS OF DEPARTMENTS

Salary depends on the grade of the department. For the lowest grade there is, for men, a minimum salary of £900 per annum rising by annual increments of £25 to a maximum of £1,000, and, for women, a minimum of £720 per annum rising by annual increments of £20 to a maximum of £800 per annum. For the highest grade there is, for men, a minimum salary of £1,450 per annum rising by annual increments of £25 to a maximum of £1,600 and, for women, a minimum of £1,160 rising by annual increments of £20 to a maximum of £1,280 per annum.

In special circumstances the LEA may, in agreement with the Minister, pay such higher salary as it deems appropriate.

VICE-PRINCIPALS

Where a head of department is appointed by the LEA as vice-principal he receives, in addition to the salary otherwise payable to him, an allowance of not less than £50 and not more than £200 per annum. Where the LEA appoints a vice-principal other than a head of department, his rate of salary is determined in agreement with the Minister.

PRINCIPALS

The salaries or scales of salaries of principals are reviewed and adjusted at appropriate times by LEAs in agreement with the Minister. In making such review and adjustment LEAs have regard to the guidance afforded by the scales for other posts and to the volume of full-time and part-time work, the importance and standard of the work, and the number and type of staff for which the principal is responsible.

As in the case of teachers in primary and secondary schools additional payments are made to further education teachers in the 'London area' at the rate of £36 per annum increasing to £48 when the teacher has completed 16 years of full-time service or has attained the age of 37 years.

Some teachers make up full-time work by combining service in establishments for further education and service in primary and secondary schools. When full-time service of each type would be remunerated at different rates, teachers who devote one-half or more of their time to the more highly paid service are paid at the higher rate for all work, but in other cases payment is made at the lower rate for all work.

PENSIONS AND RETIREMENT

Teachers' pensions and gratuities are governed by the Superannuation Acts, 1925 to 1946. Provision is made for pensions at the age of 60 (or on retirement after that age), pensions or gratuities on retirement on permanent incapacity due to infirmity, and gratuities on death.

When the appropriate qualifying period of service has been worked and the other conditions of the Acts are satisfied, benefits are payable on pensionable service, which is defined as full-time service between the ages of 18 and 65; (a) as a teacher in grant-aided schools and establishments and in certain other recognized schools, institutions and centres; or (b) as an educational organizer or adviser under a LEA in work approved by the Minister and preceded by three years approved teaching service; or (c) as an educational adviser or organizer under a grant-aided voluntary association in service of a kind approved by the Minister.

There are four methods of qualifying for an age pension payable at the age of 60 or on retirement if later. They are:

1. A teacher may qualify by doing 30 years of service, either pensionable service or other educational service approved for the purpose and called 'qualifying service', of which at least 10 must be pensionable and of which a certain proportion must have been after 31 March 1919. The qualifying period of 30 years is reduced in the case of a married woman by the number of years (not exceeding 10), of her absence from service while married (but not during widowhood). It should be noted that 'qualifying service' does not count in the calculation of the amount of the pension.

2. A late entrant into pensionable service may qualify for a pension by doing pensionable service amounting to two-thirds of the number of years between the date of entry into pensionable service and his sixty-fifth birthday, subject to a minimum of 10 years.

3. A teacher who returns to pensionable service after an interval may qualify by doing pensionable service, during the period between the date of any re-entry into pensionable service and his sixty-fifth birthday, amounting to two-thirds of that period, subject to a minimum of 10 years. Any pensionable service done before the relevant date of re-entry does not count towards the qualifying period under this provision, but if qualification for pension is achieved it counts in the calculation of pension.

4. A teacher who on 1 April 1919, was a certificated teacher subject to the Elementary School Teachers (Superannuation) Act, 1898, may qualify on a total of pensionable service equal to one-half of the period between the date of certification and his sixty-fifth birthday.

'Qualifying service' does not count towards the periods at (2); (3) or (4).

Certain teaching service and public service in the British Dominions at home or overseas (including service in a university), if it is pensionable otherwise than under the Teachers (Superannuation) Acts, may be treated as 'approved external service'. Approved external service counts as if it were contributory service for the purpose of the qualifying periods for benefits and in some cases for the purpose of calculating average salary, but it does not count otherwise in the calculation of pension.

Provision has been made for dealing with the pensions of persons who move between pensionable teaching service and the following employments: (a) established service in the civil service; (b) pensionable local government service; (c) pensionable employment under certain public boards, (d) national health service, and (e) employment on the staff of the Central Council for Health Education.

Special arrangements exist for the payment of infirmity pensions or gratuities, and death gratuities, subject to certain defined conditions.

Pensions, whether for age or infirmity, are calculated on the total amount of pensionable service and on the 'average salary', i.e. the average amount of salary for the last five years of pensionable service. For each year of pensionable service there is normally granted (a) an annual life pension of one-eightieth of the average salary (up to forty-eightieths), and (b) a lump sum of one-thirtieth of the average salary (up to forty-five-thirtieths).

Certain modifications and reductions may be made in the age-pension as a consequence of, and in relation to, pension benefits received under the National Insurance Act.

Where a teacher qualified for an annual pension dies, and the total of the sums paid by way of pension and lump sum is less than his average salary, the difference is paid as a 'supplementary death gratuity'. A teacher of good health may, subject to certain conditions, surrender part of an annual allowance in return for actuarially equivalent benefits for a wife or husband or a dependant.

Arrangements for the payments described are based on contributions paid by the teachers and their employers. A teacher in pensionable service pays, normally by deduction from salary, five per cent of his or her salary with appropriate reductions where the teacher is subject to the Acts as modified in consequence of national insurance. Equivalent contributions are payable by employers for which they are, generally speaking, partially reimbursed by grant from the Ministry. If a teacher receives a gross salary from which a deduction is made for board and lodging, the gross salary is the salary on which contributions are based.

Where given conditions are satisfied, arrangements are made for repayments to be made in the case of teachers who, for certain reasons such as death or departure from pensionable service, are unable to obtain benefits under the Act.

Finally provision is made, under stated conditions, for the application of the Act to teachers in schools not aided with grant from the Ministry but approved under the special arrangements for such schools.

STATUS OF THE TEACHER

The status of the individual teacher has two aspects, his status within the teaching profession and the status of that profession as a whole. We will consider the latter first.

The status in the community of any given occupation depends on the social importance of that occupation, the demand for its products, and the amount and nature of the supply of persons suitably trained to turn out the products to meet the existing demand. All these factors, the operation of which is deeply influenced by tradition, combine in determining the status of the teaching profession. In the opinion of the writer however, there is a far deeper and more subtle influence at work affecting the esteem, and therefore the status, accorded to those engaged in the work of education. This is the nature of the relations existing between teachers and children and the consequent attitudes of children towards teachers and towards the process of education itself. The children of one generation become the adults of the next, and their attitudes as adults are largely determined by their experiences as children.

There is no doubt that, until comparatively recent times, the nature of the relations between teachers and children was far from satisfactory. This was the fault of nobody in particular. It arose from general ignorance of the true nature of children, and therefore of the most effective ways of educating them, not only to produce well-balanced and socially valuable adults, but so that they might find interest and enjoyment in their education and desire to continue it for its own sake. Ignorance was particularly marked as to the nature and effect of the differences between individual children in regard to their natural interests, abilities and aptitudes, and as to the general circumstances of their lives. Discipline was rigid and unenlightened, and punishment severe and often inappropriate.

As a result the attitude of children towards their teachers was too often a mixture of fear and contempt, and school became a place to escape from as soon as possible. This attitude was carried forward into adult life. In the process, fear tended to become a kind of awe, tinged with the suspicion of the less knowledgeable for the more knowledgeable, to which contempt was a defensive reaction tending to create a climate of opinion in which teachers were regarded as a race apart and generally to be avoided as much as possible. Their status as a whole in the community, though with many marked individual exceptions, was therefore low.

The emergency training scheme provided some striking illustrations of this. For most of those trained under this scheme systematic continuous education had ceased many years before when they left school.

There was noticeable in many cases among them an apprehension arising from a sense of inadequacy in their capacity for education and a revulsion from particular subjects of the curriculum. This could be traced to the nature of their experiences during school life particularly in regard to the way in which they had been taught and their relations with their teachers. Marked improvement in rate of progress was noted when these apprehensions had been dissolved.

This unfortunate situation has been steadily changing for the better during the last 30 years. With the developments in the study of general and educational psychology, and the consequent greater understanding of children and of their relations to one another and to adults, modern educational methods are leading to a happier atmosphere in the schools and to far better and more sympathetic relations between teachers and children. Most children and young people will probably always look forward to the time when they leave school for this is a natural step in their growth towards full manhood or womanhood, but they are coming to look upon the end of their school days less as an escape from an unpleasant ordeal and more as the completion of a happy and enjoyable period in their lives which has served its purpose and from which they are passing to a wider freedom and a greater personal responsibility. This change of attitude is having a profound effect on the esteem in which the teaching profession is held by the general public, though, in the nature of things, increase in this esteem lags something like a generation behind the causes which produce it.

What of the status of the individual teacher within the profession? Before the Education Act of 1944 the system of compulsory education was divided into elementary and secondary and the majority of children spent the whole of their school life in elementary schools. Traditionally there was a tendency to regard teachers in these schools as being of a status inferior to that of teachers in secondary schools and there were definite if intangible barriers between the two sections of the profession.

Apart from social distinctions, this difference of attitude towards elementary and secondary teachers was largely due to the fact that the latter dealt with education at the higher levels for which special study and special academic qualifications were required. Nevertheless the elementary teachers had a place of their own in the community. In some ways they were nearer to the heart of the mass of the people than were the teachers in the secondary schools. The teacher in the elementary school, especially the head teacher, was often the guide, philosopher and friend of the people living in the neighbourhood of the school. This was notably the case in rural areas.

It has gradually come to be realized that, whatever the age of the children taught, and whatever the school, the teacher is doing work of vital importance and of considerable difficulty. Moreover each part of the educational system depends on the other parts for its satisfactory working and constant contact is essential. Already before 1944 the barriers to personal and social contact between the elementary and secondary worlds were beginning to break down and teachers were coming together to try to understand one another's problems and to discuss matters of mutual concern.

This change in the climate of thought was given statutory recognition in the Act of 1944. The old distinction between elementary and secondary was abolished and replaced by that of primary education up to the age of 11 + and secondary education, in different types of school, after that age. The principle embodied in the Act was that of parity of esteem, not only as between the different types of secondary school, but also as between primary and secondary, together with recognition of the fact that longer periods of preparation and special courses of study were required for some kinds of teaching post. This principle was implemented in the basic salary scale with additions for special qualifications.

The general public has not yet fully accepted the spirit of the Act the purpose of which was to secure for every child the type of education most suited to him. There is still intense competition for places in the secondary grammar school, regardless of the fact that it is worse than useless to put a child in such a school if he is not suited to the type of education which it provides. Snobbery survives and, more important, the higher level of vocational opportunity afforded by the grammar school is a great attraction, though again it is useless to place a child in such a school if he is not of a calibre to take advantage of the vocational opportunities it provides. There is no reason for discouragement here. Great changes of the kind we have been considering require time to be understood and accepted; if soundly based, they prevail in the end.

Whatever may be thought of the adequacy of the present salary scales in existing economic circumstances, the general prospects for the teacher are now good. There is little difficulty in obtaining employment, especially in the case of women, and where some difficulty exists, it is usually due to extraneous circumstances such as housing conditions or ties which keep the teacher concerned from moving freely from one area to another.

Promotion prospects are by no means unfavourable. Seniority, general efficiency, and ability in organization and leadership are the main bases of promotion; but, other things being equal, account may be taken of special qualifications and of efforts to improve teaching efficiency and academic standing and to keep abreast of educational thought. Where possible, though this is far from easy at the present time, special provision is made for teachers working in unusually difficult circumstances, for example in remote rural areas or in areas where housing conditions are very bad.

As such things go, teachers possess security of tenure in comparatively high degree. Short of gross inefficiency or gross misconduct, a teacher is safe in the profession. The teachers' professional organizations are large and powerful and are always available in the interests of the individual. They exercise their power wisely and in fruitful collaboration with those upon whom the welfare of their members depends. They hold no brief for inefficiency or for conduct unbecoming to the profession. On the contrary they act always in the interests of academic standing and professional competence in the widest sense.

This concludes our survey of the permanent system of teacher training in England and Wales and of the general conditions under which the teacher works. It only remains to consider that remarkable achievement of the immediate post-war years, the emergency training scheme.

CHAPTER IX

THE EMERGENCY TRAINING SCHEME

With the beginning of the turn of the tide of war in 1942, when it became possible to think of the needs of the future and to make plans to meet them, one point demanding urgent attention was the necessity of taking steps to meet the shortage of teachers, especially men teachers, which would arise from the wastage of war and ancillary causes. Later on, when the preliminaries to the subsequent Education Act were under discussion, the need for more teachers was increased by the prospective raising of the school leaving age by at least one year, to 15, and by the possible effects of the policy of 'secondary education for all', together with a hoped for progressive reduction in the size of classes.

It was estimated that about 70,000 new teachers would have to be recruited and trained during the immediate post-war years. The normal training agencies, even if expanded, would not be able to cope with this task, and it was held that special measures would have to be taken to provide about 30,000 new teachers as soon as possible after the end of the war. The plan embodying these measures became known as the 'Emergency Training Scheme'.[1]

It may be of interest to record at once that, in the event, about 19,600 men and 9,400 women successfully completed the emergency training course from first to last. At the peak period, early in 1948, 55 emergency colleges were in operation. The selection of students for the colleges was made from among the 82,000 men and 42,500 women who actually applied for training under the scheme.

FIRST STEPS

The first steps taken to bring the scheme into being were rather in the nature of a crusade by officers of the Ministry, or rather the Board of Education as it was then. The scheme could have no hope of success

---

[1] A very full and detailed account of the scheme is given in *Challenge and Response*, published in 1950 by Her Majesty's Stationery Office. The present chapter is a summary, for reference, of the history and main feature of the scheme, and the lessons to be learned from it.

without the active faith and co-operation of the Local Education Authorities, the practising teachers and their professional organizations, and the existing training institutions. The new colleges could be administered effectively only by LEAs, and it was essential that the LEAs in general should be ready to accept the products of the colleges for appointment to their schools. The goodwill of teachers was necessary, not only to help staff the colleges, but to welcome and advise the new entrants to their profession. The staffs of the existing training institutions would be able to make an invaluable contribution from their great wealth of experience and by providing, so far as they could be spared, a leaven of tutors, already experienced in training, as members of the staffs of the emergency colleges.

Accordingly a small group of officials toured the country, calling meetings of all the interests concerned to explain to them the purpose and provisional nature of the scheme, to invoke their aid, and to discuss with them the initial problems involved in getting the scheme under way. These efforts met with a generous response and it therefore became possible to set about systematic plans for putting the scheme into operation. At the same time the help of the Ministry of Works was sought in making the necessary adaptations to the buildings which would house the colleges, and in furnishing and equipping the latter. This help was readily given and played a vital part in the success of the scheme.

An advisory committee was set up, consisting of LEA officers, teachers representing schools and training institutions, H.M. inspectors and other officials of the Board. This committee recommended an intensive one-year training course of 48 weeks, with most careful selection from the available candidates, followed by a course of part-time study lasting two years after entry into the schools. The committee discussed in detail the administration and lay-out of the course, and their recommendations were accepted and published in Circular 1652 dated 15 May 1944.

It was essential that the scheme should be ready to come into operation as soon as general demobilization began, but a number of possible candidates for training were already available before this stage was reached. It was therefore decided to run a small 'pilot' course. For this purpose the help of Goldsmiths' College was enlisted and, with the ready co-operation of the principal and his staff, a group of 28 students, selected by the college authorities, began training late in 1944. A second course was run in 1945–46. These preliminary experiments were of great value, shedding light on some of the problems likely to arise under the new scheme.

Meantime everything possible was being done to discover and secure premises likely to be adaptable for the scheme. At the same time the Ministry began to appoint the first batch of principals for the new colleges before it could be known to what particular college a principal would go, and when. It was essential, however, that the principals should be ready, and should have collected at least a nucleus of staff, by the time the colleges were in a position to come into operation.

All this involved a great deal of publicity in order to stimulate applications for posts on the staffs of the colleges, and, at the same time, applications for training from potential candidates. Steps were taken to enable intending candidates still in military or other national service (this service being a condition of eligibility) to make their applications.

The whole venture called for a high degree of faith. It was impossible to foresee whether enough suitable premises would be available or whether an adequate number of tutors and of students of suitable quality would come forward. It was uncertain whether the training course would prove to be long enough for its purpose—for it was a cardinal principle of the scheme, that the men and women trained under it were not to be regarded as mere stop-gaps rushed into the schools to meet an immediate crisis, but as potential teachers in the fullest sense. It was hoped to go far towards meeting the last point by making the course an intensive one, lasting in time actually spent in college about half the duration of the normal training course, and by adding the condition that an approved part-time course of study lasting two years should be followed after the student had begun to teach.

It seems fair to say that, in the result, the scheme justified the highest hopes and expectations. Not only did it produce competent teachers capable of making a unique kind of contribution to the work of the schools: it also exercised a valuable influence on education and training in ways which will be considered later.

FINANCE

The whole cost of the emergency scheme was met, directly or indirectly, by the exchequer through expenditure by the Ministry of Education, about half of which was by way of reimbursing LEAs, and by the Ministry of Works. The total cost was somewhat over £20,500,000, of which the Ministry of Education bore more than four-fifths.

The running cost of the colleges averaged about £220 per annum for a resident student and about £120 per annum for a day student. The average maintenance allowances for the main categories of student were: men—day £320, resident £220; women—day £200, resident £130. About half the men students were married and about half of these had children. Allowances were paid for dependants up to £110 per annum for a wife, and £40 per annum for each child.

The cost of converting and equipping the colleges averaged rather more than £100 per student place.

BUILDINGS AND EQUIPMENT

The colleges varied widely in size. The largest accommodated rather over 400 students, the smallest under 200. Most of the colleges were for men, though there were some mixed as well as women's colleges. The colleges were spread over most of the country and the buildings housing them included country mansions, industrial hostels, former schools and colleges of various kinds, office buildings, hotel premises, and hutted hospitals. Most of the colleges were residential, and this had obvious advantages; but some day colleges were required, especially because many of the married men students asked to be allotted to a day college so that they could live at home while training.

Apart from the suitability of the premises, one of the main points to be considered was the availability in the neighbourhood of adequate facilities for the school practice which played a large part in the training course. The problem of providing school practice became increasingly difficult with the growth in the number of colleges in operation, and special measures had to be taken to deal with it in the later stages.

Great difficulty was experienced in getting the colleges ready for occupation and work owing to the shortage of labour and materials. In many cases colleges opened although much still remained to be done on them. Both staff and students accepted the situation cheerfully, preferring to start in makeshift conditions of considerable difficulty and discomfort rather than to accept a longer period of waiting.

The Ministry had drawn up a schedule of accommodation for emergency colleges, not because it was thought, nor did it indeed prove, that colleges could conform closely to the schedule, but to serve as a basis for planning and a norm to be approached as nearly as circumstances permitted. The schedule was based on modern ideas of training, with due regard to the needs of these older and more mature students, and on the experience of the permanent training colleges. In working to the schedule each type of building presented its own peculiar difficulties and problems.

A standard schedule of furniture and equipment was also drawn up, flexible enough to be adapted to the various sizes and types of colleges and college buildings. Furnishing was plain and economical. Suitable provision was made for the use of visual and auditory devices including one sound and one silent 16-mm. film projector and a main radio receiving set with two or more separate loud speakers. Assembly halls with stages and suitable arrangements for dramatic work were also provided.

An important feature of the scheme was the provision of college libraries, a matter of great difficulty owing to the acute shortage of books. A system of central purchase through H.M. Stationery Office was introduced combining a standard nucleus of books, to be supplied to all colleges, with a selection of additional books by principals and staffs which ultimately constituted the bulk of the library. The nucleus comprised 400 books of various kinds and a limit was placed on the number of additional books permitted, varying from 2,000 for the smallest colleges to 5,000 for the largest.

STAFF

Immediately after the issue of Circular 1652 the Board of Education invited applications from teachers in schools and training colleges for posts in emergency colleges. The response was generous and highly encouraging.

In the first stage, before the colleges had actually come into being, a pool was formed of selected applicants both for principal and assistant posts. From this pool a suitable staff allocation was made to each college when it was ready to start work. Each principal had already gathered round him a nucleus of staff ready to go into action as soon as circumstances permitted. At a later stage, when a considerable number of colleges were fully established, posts were advertised in the normal way, application being made direct to the LEA administering the college concerned. In the selection of assistant staff the LEA was advised and assisted by H.M. inspector, but only in the case of the appointment of principals was the agreement of the Ministry essential.

It was made quite clear from the outset that all posts in emergency colleges were of a temporary nature; all LEAs and other bodies employing teachers who took up posts in the colleges were urged to make arrangements as far as possible to regard the transfer to colleges as a secondment from posts which would be kept open, or an equivalent provided, against the return of staff when the emergency scheme ended. Again the response was generous.

The normal staffing ratio adopted was that of one tutor to 11 students. Taking a college of 200 as 'standard' size, though there were wide variations, the staff would be the equivalent of 18 full-time tutors, excluding the principal. In larger colleges the proportion of tutors was rather less, in smaller colleges rather more. It was decided that the number of senior lectureships should not normally exceed half the total full-time teaching staff including the principal. With a few exceptions, rates of salary were in accordance with the salary scales laid down by the Pelham committee for permanent training college staff.

The total staff of 1,211 tutors and principals when the emergency scheme was in full operation was made up as follows: from training colleges, 60; secondary grammar schools, 577; secondary modern schools, 314; primary schools, 172; miscellaneous, 88. The last category was made up mainly of local inspectors of schools, county organizers, and technical teachers. The mixing of staff from different types of educational institution was itself of great value. Praise is due to all who contributed to the successful staffing of the colleges: first to the teachers who came forward, often at considerable personal sacrifice—usually it meant at the least a complete uprooting of established life and a by no means certain future—to answer the call to meet an urgent national need; secondly to the employing bodies, LEAs and others, who readily released their best teachers at a time of staffing difficulty. In the result magnificent work was done in the colleges by a devoted body of men and women.

STUDENTS AND THEIR SELECTION

The students selected from the mass of applicants for emergency training came originally from a diversity of civilian occupations too wide to be listed here. Their ages ranged from 22 to 48 or even more. This diversity itself proved a major factor in the success of the scheme. The community life of men and women of such different interests and backgrounds, and with such different beliefs and opinions, fostered a spirit of tolerance, and a growth in understanding and breadth of view.

The success of the scheme depended on the effectiveness of the system of selection. After clearly impossible candidates, and those who failed to satisfy the conditions of admission to the scheme, had been weeded out at the Ministry, the remaining applicants were sent forward for interview by special boards set up throughout the country.

An interviewing board consisted normally of a teacher, a person experienced in local administration, and another with experience in the training of teachers. An officer of the Ministry, usually one of H.M. inspectors, presided. The board had before it all relevant information, including any examination successes, e.g. in school certificate.

Attention was given to the personal qualities required in a teacher and to the steps a candidate had taken to maintain his interests in reading and general culture. Any applicant who had not passed the school certificate or some similar examination was required to write a passage on some topic related to his experience, and his script was laid before the board at the time of interview.

In addition to accepting or rejecting an applicant for the emergency training course the interviewing board was empowered, alternatively, to recommend a two-year training course, or even a university course, where one of these was thought to be more suitable in the particular case. In the early stages of the scheme a number of boards were sent overseas to interview applicants still serving in the forces, so that these might not be handicapped in any way.

The quality of those selected, and the small proportion of failures in college, bore witness to the highly successful work of the interviewing boards without which the scheme would have been doomed to failure.

Candidates were medically examined at the time of interview, the resulting pressure on civilian doctors being relieved by arrangements with the Service departments to obtain, with the candidates' consent, the demobilization medical reports on ex-Service candidates, which were accepted in lieu of a subsequent report by a civilian doctor.

When an applicant had been accepted for admission to the scheme his name was entered on a 'waiting list'. Allocation of students to the colleges as they came into being were made in the order of this list with suitable modifications to avoid hardship to Service candidates. An accepted student might be allocated to any college according to conditions at the time, but, wherever possible, consideration was given to the circumstances of the individual.

The waiting period after acceptance was considerable and at one time rose to about a year. The Ministry therefore allowed men and women accepted for the scheme to take posts as 'temporary teachers' in schools while they were waiting, and at the same time asked LEAs to get in touch with waiting candidates in their areas and help them in any possible way to prepare for their training course. The Ministry also published to waiting candidates a list of books suitable for preparatory reading, while each candidate as he was accepted received a bulletin of information and advice kept up to date by supplements.

The general quality of the students admitted to training through the selection process reached the highest expectations. For most of them success in the training course was vital, for they were of an age when personal and domestic responsibilities were already heavy upon them, and their work was accordingly marked by concentration and seriousness of purpose. This was especially true of the first batch of entrants to the colleges, as these consisted largely of men and women who felt a genuine urge to teach, though no opportunity for this had previously come their way, and they had therefore made teaching their first choice in deciding upon a post-war occupation.

The students exhibited a wide range of talents and accomplishments and thus were able to make substantial contributions both to the professional work and to the general life of the colleges. They learnt much from one another. More interesting and significant still, a very large number of them were found to possess hitherto unsuspected aptitudes which they developed to a really surprising degree during the year. This was, perhaps, particularly true in the field of art and craft.

It was perhaps to be expected that these comparatively mature people would have the desire and ability to organize their community life to a large extent themselves and this indeed proved to be the case. Able and acceptable leaders soon showed themselves and, under their guidance, and through the establishment of college committees or councils, the student bodies disciplined themselves for the most part with a high sense of responsibility. Appropriate relationships between staff and students in their respective contributions to the general running of the colleges were established without difficulty, and problems of discipline were extremely rare.

It was inevitable that, in the case of the mixed colleges, difficult sex problems should arise from time to time in the relations of the men and women students, but these problems never reached serious dimensions owing to the enlightenment and sympathetic understanding with which they were handled as they arose by all concerned.

THE TRAINING COURSE

For initial guidance a suggested plan for the general layout of the course was included in Circular 1652. It was emphasized that this should be regarded only as a basis on which to start. Initiative and experiment were encouraged. In the early stages of the emergency scheme the suggested layout was, in fact, followed fairly closely, but as time went on and experience showed where modifications and developments were desirable, departures from it became increasingly marked, though the general pattern maintained its form to the end.

The course was divided into four parts: a preparatory stage of about six weeks and a main course in three stages, Part I of about four weeks, Part II of about 12 weeks, and Part III of about 14 weeks. In addition there were to be two periods of teaching practice one of three weeks following Part I of the main course and another of nine weeks immediately after a period of two weeks vacation following Part II of the main course. There were two other vacations of one week each after the two periods of teaching practice.

One of the first things to become apparent was that the amount of vacation allowed was insufficient in view of the intensive strain on both students and staff, and of the necessity for allowing enough time between sessions for the staff to recuperate and prepare for the next entry of students. Early in 1946, therefore, it was laid down that the working time of the session should cover some 38 weeks while provision was made for a total of four to eight weeks vacation during the session and a vacation of seven weeks between sessions, or more if less than eight weeks was taken during the session.

During the preparatory stage, steps were taken to accustom the students to their new way of life and prospective occupations. Visits of observation to schools played an important part, but it was generally found that the six-week period originally suggested as the duration of this stage was too long. The students tended to be impatient and naturally anxious to 'get on with the job' by settling down to the main course. In the event the duration of the preparatory stage was cut down to from two to four weeks. In this and other ways modifications in the originally suggested layout of the session were introduced in the light of experience, each college adapting the scheme in ways which seemed most suitable to its particular circumstances.

A student's time was divided between lectures, tutorials, and private study, and it was important to find the most suitable balance between these. Generally speaking about half the time was given to lectures and tutorials with the main emphasis on the latter, carried out in small groups, and about half to private study some of which was 'directed' by the tutors and some left entirely to the discretion of the student. Difficulties were experienced at first in stimulating students to take their due part in question and discussion and in instilling into them confidence and judgment in planning their private work, but these difficulties diminished as the course proceeded.

The provision of adequate facilities for teaching practice was a problem. The influx into the schools of the students from the emergency colleges in addition to those from the permanent colleges tripled the load on the schools as compared with the pre-war period. In some congested areas, e.g. London and south-west Lancashire, the difficulties were particularly acute.

Although everything was done by various organizational means to meet the problem, the fact remains that the high degree of success which marked its solution was due to the individual and co-operative efforts of all the people involved. The heads and staffs of the schools, many of which were having their first experience of this kind of work, did all in their power to make the students welcome and to help and advise them, often in extremely difficult conditions. The students themselves brought a new and, as it proved, generally acceptable element into school life.

In the main course every student was required to take principles and practice of education, health education, and English usage. Apart from this every student was free to choose, with the approval of the college principal, whatever combination of subjects seemed most appropriate for him personally in relation to the opportunities provided by the circumstances of his college.

All the emphasis, therefore, was on freedom and initiative; but, as a basis for consideration, fairly detailed suggestions in regard to courses in the various subjects were drawn up by panels of H.M. inspectors at an early stage and made available to principals. The governing principle throughout was that courses should be such that, at the conclusion of their training course and subsequent two-year period of continued study, emergency trained teachers should be entitled to full recognition and regarded as equals with teachers who had entered the profession through the normal channels.

Early in 1946 the position was reviewed at a conference of college principals, which was also attended by some of H.M. inspectors. The following decisions were made:

1. When considering courses appropriate to the needs of students desiring to work in different types of school these age-ranges should be borne in mind: 2–6, 7–12, 9–15, 11–15, and the courses planned accordingly. In this way a student's course, though it rightly had particular reference to a certain age-range, would not be too narrowly conceived.

2. In addition to the three compulsory subjects already mentioned, a student might choose from the following list: English literature, Welsh language and literature, history, geography, religious knowledge, French, German, mathematics, general science, physics, chemistry, biology, rural science and gardening, music, art, art and light craft, handicraft (woodwork and/or metalwork), housecraft, needlecraft, physical education, social studies, combined courses and individual study.

3. As a rule a student should take not more than three and not less than two of the above-mentioned subjects, though he might, and generally would, take various short professional courses of varying length during his training year.

On being accepted for the scheme, students were invited to state the two main optional subjects they wished to study, and the age-range for which they wished to train. This was of considerable help to the Ministry in allocating a student to the college most suitable for him, although these preliminary choices by the student not infrequently proved to be based on uncertain grounds and were changed after admission to college. The final choice was made, as soon as possible after admission to college, by the student in consultation with principal and tutors and according to the circumstances of the college. It was for the principal to give final approval.

The Ministry provided facilities for additional study for a limited number of students, after the conclusion of their year's course, in order that they might extend to a more advanced level their knowledge of a particular subject. Such facilities were provided in the case of house-craft, needlecraft, art and crafts, handicraft, music, and physical education. These special courses were taken during the student's probationary period and counted as part of his two years of further study. They were held in permanent training colleges and other suit-ably equipped educational institutions and varied in length from 35 weeks for housecraft to one academic term for needlecraft, handicraft, and physical education. The courses might be taken immediately after the conclusion of the emergency course or, where circumstances war-ranted it (and this was more usual), after an intervening period spent in teaching.

Towards the end of the emergency course the principal prepared a list of students recommended for special courses, the basis of his recommendation being that, while the student was likely to complete the general course successfully and showed promise in his special subject, he required further instruction if he were to do really good work in the latter. The list was considered by H.M. inspectors who were specialists in the subjects concerned, and approved by them, with any necessary modifications, after visits to the college, to see the students concerned and their work, and consultation with the principal. The approved list was then forwarded to the Ministry.

ASSESSMENT

It was felt from the outset that anything in the nature of a formal 'external' examination at the end of the course, with all the elaborate machinery necessary to operate it, was inappropriate in the case of the emergency scheme, and this view was expressed in Circular 1652. Students of the kind trained under the scheme would undoubtedly have found the prospect of such an examination irksome and oppres-sive: it would probably have led to the evils of 'cramming' in an in-tensive form, and in any case time was too short to allow of concen-tration on the long and complicated business of establishing a formal system of examination.

Accordingly a method of cumulative assessment of students by college staffs was adopted, similar in character to that which has already been considered in some detail in connexion with the permanent training system. The work and conduct of each student was kept under sympathetic and skilled observation in order that a final judgment of his fitness to become a teacher might be made at the appropriate time. The way in which this was done varied in detail from college to college, while steps were taken to ensure that the students understood the nature and purpose of the process without feeling themselves to be under the strain of constant surveillance.

In order to check the college assessments, and to preserve something in the nature of a national standard, an external element was provided by H.M. inspectors. The inspector for the college concerned kept in touch with the work during the session, and, together with some colleagues, considered a representative sample of it, including teaching practice, near the end of the session. The student assessments were then discussed with the principal and staff and an agreed assessment list drawn up. This method of assessment fully justified itself in practice. College staffs regarded it as helpful and effective and most of the students felt it to be just.

As soon as it became apparent that any student was unlikely to complete the course satisfactorily, opportunity was provided for him to withdraw, of which he usually availed himself. There were, however, a number of appeals by rejected students to the Minister whose decision in such cases was final. In the result less than 4 per cent of the men and less than 10 per cent of the women were failed.

At the end of the course each student who had satisfactorily completed it received from his principal a certificate stating the subjects of study he had pursued and the age-range of children with which his professional work had been mainly concerned. This certificate could be accepted by employing bodies as indicating that the student would be recognized as a qualified teacher, pending formal notification from the Ministry.

PROBATION AND CONTINUED STUDY

So far as probation as a practical teacher was concerned, emergency trained teachers were in much the same position as those trained in the normal way except that their period of probation lasted two years instead of one; but they had in addition to pursue a definite course of continued study during their probation. Each student, before leaving college, discussed with his tutors the most profitable form which this course might take, and a provisional plan of study was drawn up. Armed with this he approached the LEA which had agreed to appoint

him and upon which—alone or in collaboration with other authorities—rested the responsibility for providing facilities for continued
study.

The provision of such opportunities for continued study, and the
supervision of this, presented serious difficulties at the beginning when
emergency trained teachers were few and far between; but as the number of these teachers in the schools increased, and group arrangements
became possible, these difficulties diminished considerably.

Each area of employment had its own problems and each employing
authority, or group of authorities, had its own way of dealing with
these problems, but one thing found to be essential to the establishment of an effective system of continued study was the appointment
by the LEA concerned of an officer specially charged to look after the
interests of the emergency trained teachers fresh from college, to help
them when necessary, and to advise on the provision of suitable facilities. In particular it was important to ensure that the course of study,
in combination with the various difficulties of adjustment to a new life
in the early stages of teaching—difficulties in some ways more acute
than those facing the probationer from a two-year college—should not
press too hardly on the individual.

There seems little doubt that, in general, the results achieved in this
field were quite as sucessful as could have been expected in the particularly difficult circumstances, and this view is confirmed by inquiries
which were made from past students after they had been teaching for
a while.

The two-year period of probation has provided an indication of the
probable degree of success in the schools of emergency trained teachers.
In the vast majority of cases they have been well received, and accepted
as making a valuable contribution in the field of education. In spite of
inevitable deficiences arising from the nature of their background and
comparatively short period of training, they are in general enthusiastic
for their work, get on well with children and colleagues, and command
respect for their personal qualities. They are industrious and play a
large part in out-of-school activities. More, if as much, could not have
been hoped for.

MAIN LESSONS FROM THE EMERGENCY SCHEME

Perhaps the most important fact learned from the operation of the
emergency scheme is that there exists in the population a large reservoir
constituting a potential source of recruitment for the teaching profession. This reservoir consists of men and women who, through force of

circumstance or lack of opportunity, have never realized that they have a latent capacity for teaching, or, if they have realized it, have been denied the chance of fulfilment. Moreover not only have these people, though generally lacking in academic achievement, a latent capacity for practical teaching, but a large number of them also have latent capacities of a practical or intellectual nature in various fields which have not hitherto been brought out.

Another interesting point, which was brought out as the result of a special inquiry, is that although the proportion of really good practical teachers was greatest among those students of higher intellectual and academic standing, the total number of such teachers provided by the lower intellectual groups among the students was substantially greater than the total number provided by the higher groups. This has an important bearing on the necessity, already referred to, in present conditions of shortage, of taking full account of those qualities necessary to practical success in teaching other than high intellectual calibre and high academic attainment.

A complementary point which stands out is the absolute necessity of a most careful and thorough system of selection of candidates for training as teachers, especially in abnormal circumstances such as those in which the emergency scheme was operated.

Another fact which has emerged is that an occasional and exceptional influx into the schools and the profession of a body of older and more mature teachers—trained under a system which starts practically *de novo* and which, though it lacks the benefits of established routine and tradition, is also free from their hampering effects, and works out its problems with a marked freshness of approach—may well provide a novel stimulus not only to the schools but also to the permanent system of training. The contacts between permanent and emergency college staffs, in which some tutors from permanent colleges took posts in emergency colleges while many tutors from the latter have remained in training work in the permanent colleges, has proved of inestimable value.

In the more detailed aspects, much has been learnt about the most effective ways of handling various subjects of study, theoretical and practical, professional and general, and about methods of assessment which, when due allowance has been made for the type of student in training, provides a new and valuable kind of contribution to the art and science of teacher training.

In summary it may be said that there has been shown to exist in the community the will and the power to meet an urgent need requiring rapid, drastic and complex measures, and that, with all the risks and difficulties inherent in it, an operation such as that of emergency training may not only prove sufficient to meet the immediate need but may carry in its train a number of consequences of lasting benefit.

CONCLUSION

This survey of the training of teachers in England and Wales is now completed. There seems little doubt that, in all fundamentals, the way in which the system of training is now developing is that best calculated to serve the purposes for which it is designed. Such relatively strong or relatively weak points of detail in it have been indicated, implicitly or explicitly, in the foregoing. In the opinion of the writer, however, there is one potential source of danger which should be kept in mind. This is inherent in the present close relation between the universities and training.

The traditional business of the universities is learning and research. Accordingly there has in the past been a tendency in university circles to regard the subject of 'education', if indeed such a subject exists, as not among the proper concerns of a university. At the same time there has been a suspicion of the need for, or the value of, teacher training. It was in this atmosphere that the university departments of education had to struggle for a firm foothold and then fight hard to establish themselves on an equal footing in esteem with other university departments.

At the same time, even when the need for teacher training was accepted, some members of university staffs, other than those in the education departments, while in comparative ignorance of much that was being done in training institutions, yet had definite opinions about what *ought* to be done in such institutions.

In these circumstances, remembering the great power and prestige of the universities and their present close association with training, everything depends on the way in which they exercise the profound influence they can now bring to bear on the training institutions. If they attempt to make conditions—in a field which is in many ways very different from that of the university proper—conform too rigidly to the pattern of university routine, tradition and convention, and if too great a weight is given to the opinion of those who are insufficiently informed, the training institutions may find that they have acquired a closer relationship with the universities at too great a price in terms of their freedom. But if the universities use their power discreetly, and with a full realization of the repository of knowledge and experience which exists in the training institutions and in the teaching profession, then the future is indeed hopeful.

Although it is perhaps too early yet to judge the final outcome all the signs are that, in general, the universities will exert their influence wisely, considerately, and with high regard to the prime importance of the contributions coming from the other parties to the common venture. The omens are good.

BIBLIOGRAPHY

OFFICIAL PUBLICATIONS

Great Britain. Board of Education. Committee to consider the supply, recruitment and training of teachers and youth leaders. *Teachers and Youth Leaders.* London, H.M.S.O., 1944. 176 pp. (also known as the McNair Report).
——. Ministry of Education. *Challenge and Response; an Account of the Emergency Scheme for the Training of Teachers.* (Pamphlet no. 17.) London, H.M.S.O., 1950. 164 pp.
——.——. *Education 1900–1950. The Report of the Ministry of Education and the Statistics of Public Education for England and Wales for the Year 1950.* London, H.M.S.O., 1951. 250 pp.
——.——. *Education in 1951. Being the Report of the Ministry of Education and the Statistics of Public Education for England and Wales.* London, H.M.S.O., 1952. 199 pp.
——.——. *Report of the Committee ... on Scales of Salaries for the Teaching Staff of Training Colleges, England and Wales, 1951.* London, H.M.S.O., 1951. 10 pp.
——.——. *Report of the Working Party on the Supply of Women Teachers.* London, H.M.S.O., 1949. 18 pp.
——.——. *Training Colleges in England and Wales recognised by the Minister.* London, H.M.S.O., 1951. 27 pp.
——.——. Burnham Main Committee. *Report ... on Scales of Salaries for Teachers in Primary and Secondary Schools Maintained by Local Education Authorities, England and Wales, 1951.* London, H.M.S.O., 1951. 38 pp.
——.——. Burnham Technical Committee. *Report ... on Scales of Salaries for Teachers in Establishments of Further Education, including Technical and Commercial Colleges and Institutes, Art Colleges and Schools Maintained by Local Education Authorities, England and Wales, 1948.* London, H.M.S.O., 1948, 39 pp.
——.——. *Report ... on Scales of Salaries for Teachers in Technical Colleges and Institutes, Art Colleges and Schools maintained by Local Education Authorities, England and Wales, August, 1945.* London, H.M.S.O., 1945. 24 pp.

124

——.——. National Advisory Council on the Training and Supply of Teachers. *First Report, covering the Period July 1949 to February 1950.* London, H.M.S.O., 1951. 26 pp.

BOOKS

BARNARD, H.C. *An Introduction to Teaching.* London, University of London Press, 1952. 256 pp.

CAMPBELL-STEWART, W.A. *Philosophy, Psychology and Sociology in the Training of Teachers.* Ledbury, Herefordshire, Le Play House Press, 1950. 35 pp.

DENT, H.C. *To be a Teacher.* London, University of London Press, 1947. 115 pp.

International Bureau of Education. *Primary Teacher Training; from Information Supplied by the Ministries of Education.* (Publication no. 117.) Paris, Unesco; Geneva, IBE; 1950. 253 pp. 'United Kingdom', pp. 232–41. Published also in French.

Joint Standing Committee of the Training College Association and Council of Principals. *The Training of Teachers.* London, University of London Press [1939], 74 pp.

London University. Goldsmith's College. *Teachers from the Forces; an Experimental Short Course of Training at Goldsmith's College; ed. by M.M. Lewis.* London, Harrap, 1946. 146 pp.

MARTIN, Loveday. *Into the Breach; the Emergency Training Scheme for Teachers.* London, Turnstile Press, 1949. 65 pp.

OLIVER, R.A.C. *The Training of Teachers in Universities.* London, University of London Press, 1943. 59 pp.

Oxford University. Nuffield College. *The Teaching Profession Today and Tomorrow.* London, Oxford University Press, 1944. 47 pp.

PETERSON, A.B.C. *A Hundred Years of Education.* London, Duckworth, 1952.

RICH, R.W. *The Teacher in a Planned Society.* London, University of London Press, 1950. 120 pp.

RICHMOND, W. Kenneth. *An Apology for Education.* London, Redman, 1952. 180 pp.

SMITH, W.O. Lester. *Compulsory Education in England. 'Studies on Compulsory Education' – VI.* Paris, Unesco, 1951. 63 pp.

JOURNAL ARTICLES

HILL, Alfred T. 'The Emergency Training Scheme for Teachers in England.' *The Educational Record,* vol. XXXII, no. 2, pp. 205–16, April 1951. New York, American Council on Education.

KYTE, C. 'Selective Teacher Recruitment in Britain.' *Phi Delta Kappan*, vol. 33, pp. 145–48, November 1951. Homewood, Ill., Phi Delta Kappa.

OLIVER, R.A.C. 'Institutes of Education.' *Universities Quarterly*, vol. 5, no. 4, pp. 359–65, August 1951; vol. 6, no. 1, pp. 48–53, November, 1951. London, Turnstile Press.

SIMMS, T.H. 'Further Education of the Experienced Teacher.' *Journal of Education*, vol. 83, pp. 318–20, 379–81, June, July 1951. London, Journal of Education, Amen House, Warwick Square.

PART II

THE TRAINING OF TEACHERS IN FRANCE

by Hélène Brûlé

FOREWORD

In France, the laws on compulsory education affect over 5,000,000 children, and nearly 200,000 men and women teachers are engaged in catering for their needs.

The selection and qualification of these primary teachers is, rightly, a matter of concern alike to the State and to the children's families. The State authorities and private organizations each provide for the training of those who are to teach in their respective schools. During the past 75 years, considerable efforts have been made in France to organize teachers' training and adapt it to the country's needs.

The administrative aspects, the duties and rewards of the profession of primary teacher are clearly defined. The circumstances in which the teachers work differ according to geographical and demographical conditions, and the age or special characteristics of the children in their care, but the powerful bonds of common educational interests, of devotion to children, and of identical aims, confer on them a powerful corporate feeling. This is evidenced, as regards both moral and material issues, in the activities of their professional associations. Anyone thoroughly familiar with the life of France knows the importance and value of the contribution made by her school teachers.

CHAPTER I

ORIGIN AND DEVELOPMENT OF THE TRAINING OF PRIMARY TEACHERS

In 1881, the Third Republic took over public education. It decided to provide French children with free and secular (i.e. undenominational) education, compulsory from 6 to 13 years. The enforcement of this law gave rise to tremendous problems.

The first was a financial one. Jules Ferry proclaimed the 'golden rule' that one-sixth of the State's total budget was to be allocated to public education.

Next, there were the problems of school buildings, organization, allocation of expenses and responsibilities, inspection and examinations. These matters were dealt with in the organic law and regulations of 1886 and 1887 and the law of 19 July 1889.

Another problem, no less vital, was that of the training of teachers; even before submitting the great educational laws to Parliament, Jules Ferry had succeeded in persuading the authorities of the necessity of opening teachers' training colleges. The law of 9 August 1879 laid down that 'every department should have two primary teachers' training colleges, one for men and one for women, capable of training a sufficient number of men and women teachers for its communal schools'.

What was the origin of these colleges for the training of primary school teachers? What was to be their later development? How much remains today of Jules Ferry's legislation on this subject?

BEFORE 1879

Just as there were no primary schools maintained by the State before 1879, there was no training of primary teachers by the Ministry of Education. Such government projects as existed remained a dead letter; at the most there was some sporadic action by private bodies or local communities.

As early as the seventeenth century, a Lyons priest by the name of Démia, whose mission it was to educate poor children, conceived the idea of organizing a training—a sort of special noviciate—for school teachers, for he considered that 'such a saintly vocation requires apprenticeship, far more than do the other arts'. He founded the small St. Charles' Seminary at Lyons, 'a kind of teachers' training college, where he received young men without means intending to enter the priesthood; the latter, in return for the free education which they obtained, were required to go out twice a day to the different schools for the poor to give lessons'.

Some years later, Jean-Baptiste de La Salle opened a seminary for school teachers at Rheims and devoted all his time and resources to it. Despite endless difficulties, he succeeded in his lifetime in establishing 22 schools of the Brothers of the Christian Schools, which provided free education. Teachers intended for 'the little schools" were given moral training and were initiated in the methods and procedures laid down in the *Conduite des Ecoles Chrétiennes* (Conduct of Christian Schools). They introduced the simultaneous form of teaching and taught without remuneration.

During the Revolution, efforts were made to spread education and train the people as good citizens of the Republic. In the third year of the Republic, the Convention issued a decree, sponsored by Lakanal, establishing in Paris 'a teachers' training college where citizens from all parts of the Republic, already versed in the useful sciences, shall learn the art of teaching from the most skilled members of the teaching profession. 1,400 students—a proportion of one for every 20,000 inhabitants—appointed by district administrators, shall follow a four-months' course; they shall then return to their respective districts and open teachers' training colleges in the three chief towns of the departmental sub-division, as designated by the administration. In these colleges, their aim shall be to communicate the teaching methods which they have learnt at the teachers' training college in Paris to all men and women citizens wishing to devote their lives to public education'.

This new project, bold in its simplicity as it was, nevertheless remained a dream: the Convention had neither the time nor the funds to carry it into practice. The teachers' training college in Paris soon had to close down and the plan to open district colleges was abandoned.

On 17 March 1808, the Empire ordained 'that the university shall take steps to ensure that reading, writing and elementary arithmetic shall henceforth be taught in primary schools only by such teachers as are sufficiently educated to communicate this essential, basic knowledge easily and efficiently. To this end, one or more classes for the training of primary teachers shall be established in every educational division (*académie*) and in *collèges* and *lycées* (municipal and State secondary schools). Student teachers shall there be shown the best methods for improving the teaching of reading, writing and arithmetic'. A further decree of 15 November 1811 stipulated that 'the authorities shall ensure that primary school teachers do not exceed those limits in their teaching'.

The government was too absorbed by other tasks to carry out this programme, modest though it was; and the Congregation of Brothers of the Christian Doctrine, recognized and approved by the university, continued to train teachers for poor children.

In one part of France, however, the combined efforts of the prefect and the divisional director of education (*recteur d'académie*) did, in fact, lead to the establishment of a primary teachers' training college—the first—at Strasbourg, in 1810.

This college was designed to take in 60 scholarship holders from 16 to 30 years of age, and an unlimited number of other boarders. Districts and departments contributed to the payment of the scholarships. The original four-year course of study was soon reduced to three. The course included French and German, penmanship, drawing, singing, music, arithmetic, elementary physics and agriculture, gymnastics and, finally, a study of the best educational methods.

The work of the college was so successful that, in 1833, Guizot stated in his report on public education in France: 'The superiority, from all points of view, of the schools for the working classes in the educational division of Strasbourg is striking; the view that this is owing to the existence of the primary teachers' training college is as widespread as it is correct.' Neighbouring departments followed the example of the Bas-Rhin; the department of the Moselle opened a primary teachers' training college at Heldefange, and that of the Meuse at Bar-le-Duc. Others followed suit, so that in 1830 there were 13 or 14 teachers' training colleges in France; between 1830 and 1833, 34 others were established. All these colleges were set up either by private associations or by local communities. They differed considerably from one another in character, administration and syllabus. Some were independent, others attached to a secondary school; some were secular and others directed by religious congregations; the length of the course was usually two years, but in some cases it was only one, and in others three. The colleges admitted young people from 18 up to 30 or even 35 years. They were open to teachers already employed in primary schools who felt the need to improve their knowledge, and particularly their methods, and could follow the courses during their school holidays.

Parallel to these colleges, the Society for Elementary Education, founded in 1815, had opened two establishments in Paris 'especially designed to promote the wider use of the mutual education method'.

With the Guizot ministry, the government took over the organization of teachers' training colleges. The regulations of 14 December 1832 brought them under the authority of the State, but without severing their links with the departments. The Ministry of Education became responsible for their administration, determined their syllabuses and fixed the length of the course everywhere at two years. The law of 28 June 1833 stipulated that 'every department, either by itself or in co-operation with one or more neighbouring departments, shall maintain a primary teachers' training college'. The movement continued to grow and 29 other departments soon opened their respective colleges for the training of primary teachers. Future women teachers followed primary 'training courses' organized in some girls' schools, the majority of them being under the direction of religious congregations. For those wishing to teach in nursery schools, Carnot set up, in Paris, in 1848, a specialized training college which was for 25 years directed by Mrs. Pape-Carpentier. Here the student teachers were taught how to care for very young children.

In certain quarters, however, some anxiety was expressed concerning the development of teachers' training colleges. They were accused (already!) of being over-ambitious, undermining moral and religious traditions, encouraging a tendency to claim rights and fostering a dangerous ferment of ideas. Some contended that they were responsible for the social and political unrest brought about by the industrial revolution and the far-reaching social changes introduced under the July Monarchy. In 1838, the Academy of Moral and Political Sciences held a competitive examination on the following subject: 'What improvements could be introduced into teachers' training colleges, from the point of view of their bearing on the moral education of children?' Further, the philosopher Jouffroy, in his report on the paper which won the prize, protested against the social danger constituted by 'the arrogant pseudo-scholarship and sharpened, misplaced ambition of that host of primary teachers, so unwisely accustomed in our training colleges to an unnecessarily high standard of education and over-refined habits'.

These criticisms, this anxiety caused by the popular movement towards an improved social order, were to result in the Falloux Law of 1850. Article 35 of this law stipulated that 'every department shall provide for the recruitment of local school teachers, by arranging for student teachers to be trained either in primary schools designated by the divisional council or in the teachers' training college set up for the purpose by the department. Teachers' training colleges may be abolished by order of the departmental general council, or by the Minister, in the higher council of education, on the advice of the divisional council'.

The regulations of 24 March 1851 omitted nothing that could stifle what remained of the teachers' training colleges; syllabuses were curtailed,[1] a strict limitation was imposed upon the number of texts to be used by the young trainees, the teaching staff was reduced to two, at a poor salary and under almost monastic living conditions, while the powers of the supervisory board were extended. Students were no longer recruited by competitive examination, but selected by

---

[1] *De l'Instruction Publique en France dans le Passé et dans le Présent* (Past and Present Public Education in France), Paris, Durand, 1864.

the divisional director of education, from a list of approved candidates drawn up, after an enquiry into their conduct and morals, by the supervisory board. Students were forbidden to take leave or to go on any private outings, and their holidays were in no circumstances to exceed a fortnight.

Everything possible was done to discredit and stamp out this dreaded institution, and the *Ami de la Religion* declared: 'Teachers' training colleges, which are so dangerous, such powerful forces of evil, and have so deplorably distorted the character and mission of primary teachers, have been abolished.'

Yet they did not disappear; no minister used his prerogative to abolish them and only two departmental councils did so. From 1856 onwards, their situation improved. Rouland, as minister, authorized the establishment of a third teachers' post in colleges where there was a recognized need for it, and granted an installation allowance of 100 francs to all teachers taking up an appointment in public primary schools and student teachers leaving college. It was chiefly Duruy, however, who broadened the syllabuses, lowered the age for admission to 16 years and provided for a competitive entrance examination. 'When Duruy left the ministry in 1869, almost all departments possessed a primary teachers' training college for men, but very few, indeed only 19, had established such colleges for women. In most other departments, future women teachers received some sort of instruction, generally inadequate, at what were known as teachers' training courses. These courses were organized in certain girls' schools, usually church schools, where both the instruction and the teachers' training given left much to be desired. The law of 8 August 1879 put an end to this situation. By this law, Jules Ferry made it compulsory for all departments to establish, within a specified time, a primary teachers' training college for women.'[1]

FROM 1879 TO THE PRESENT DAY

A period of organization, productive of results, followed the Jules Ferry ministry. From 1879 to 1940, teachers' training colleges developed steadily, equipping their laboratories, adding to their libraries, organizing their annexed and demonstration schools and enjoying the advantages of a competent teaching staff trained at the higher teachers' training colleges of Saint-Cloud and Fontenay-aux-Roses. During

---

[1] Ministry of Education, *Rapport sur l'Organisation et la Situation de l'Enseignement Primaire Public en France* (Report on the Organization and Conditions of Public Primary Education in France), Paris, Imprimerie Nationale, 1900.

these 60 years, the only noteworthy events were changes in the system of studies and internal discipline.

In 1905 and again in 1920, the Ministry of Education introduced changes into the syllabuses. Up to 1905, the qualifying examination for which student teachers worked was the primary teachers' higher certificate, which was originally taken at the end of three years' study. In 1905, it was decided that the higher certificate examination, a test of academic capabilities, should be taken at the end of the second year, and that the third year should be reserved for professional training in a broad sense. The ministerial circular of August 1905 stated: 'It appears to us that the most important task of our teachers' training colleges is not so much to turn out teachers who have obtained their higher certificate, as to provide a special training for the future educators of a democratic nation. An experiment conducted successfully over several years and gradually extended to 20 of our colleges has proved that a two-year period of study, especially with revised and shorter syllabuses, is sufficient to enable students to obtain their higher certificate; and that the third year, when they are no longer too exclusively concerned with an examination which, like all examinations, is always fraught with uncertainty, should be entirely devoted, firstly, to more disinterested studies with a more direct bearing on the social aspect of education and not culminating in any examination, and, secondly, to the acquisition of a fuller and more thorough knowledge of educational processes and methods through more varied and extensive practical experience of teaching.'

When the system was reformed in 1920, however, the higher certificate examination was put back to the end of the third year, but the various parts of it were spaced over the three years. From the time of entering the training college, students were brought into contact with the children in the school annexed to it, being required at first to give them short, infrequent lessons, which gradually grew longer and more frequent as their training proceeded.

For reasons unrelated to their functional value, teachers' training colleges became, once again, a target for criticisms and attacks. Of what were they accused? It was said that they were communities apart—'secular seminaries', as it were—where the students had no contact with young people of their own age studying at *collèges* or *lycées* (municipal or State secondary schools); that the knowledge which they imparted was at once imperfect and over-dogmatic; that they placed emphasis on scientific disciplines and dared to tackle the social sciences (the inclusion of sociology in the 1920 syllabus gave rise to much controversy in the press). Lastly, conservative public opinion was more than once alarmed by the agenda of the annual congresses of the Primary Teachers' Union and the motions adopted at those meetings. The Union was accused of dealing ostentatiously with all

problems of concern to citizens, of passing harsh judgments and proposing rash solutions. After the disaster of 1940, those who acceded to
power hoped to right this state of affairs. They abolished all primary
teachers' professional associations and training colleges. Analysing the
influences to which student teachers were subject, one of the severest
critics of the system wrote: 'Teachers' training colleges provide them
with indifferent general culture, all the more harmful in that it gives
them the impression of being very knowledgeable. The result is that,
on leaving college, they are convinced socialists, trade-unionists and
anti-clerical. However, their period at the training college has taught
them understanding of their profession and pride in it.'

The abolition of teachers' training colleges, which was one of the
first acts of the Vichy government, looked very much like a political
measure. The law of 18 September 1940 stipulated that: 'primary
teachers' training colleges shall be abolished as from 8 October 1941'.
Hurriedly, and unfounded on previous experience, a new system of
primary teachers' training was introduced; candidates, recruited, as
in the past, by a competitive examination, entered a *lycée* (State
secondary school), where they worked for the *baccalauréat* (secondary
school leaving certificate); they then took a one-year course of teachers'
training at a professional training institute. The school year was in
fact divided into three-monthly periods, occupied respectively by the
transition from school to institute, practical teaching experience in
primary schools, and agricultural or technical training. Directors and
teachers in these institutes hardly knew their pupils and could not
exercise any lasting influence over their educational development.

Teachers' training colleges were destined to reappear at the Liberation. By order of 9 August 1944, the so-called law of 18 September
1940 relating to their abolition was annulled. Not until the beginning
of the school year in October 1945, however, were 60 primary teachers'
training colleges for men and 60 for women reopened. Of the alleged
reform introduced by the Vichy government, nothing remained but
the substitution of the *baccalauréat* for the higher certificate (*brevet
supérieur*). The length of the training course was extended from three
to four years. It was decided that the two training colleges per department should be reopened; in many cases, this was done in the three
years that followed; at present, almost all teachers' training colleges
have resumed their activities.

While the ruthless abolition of teachers' training colleges had been
put into immediate effect, their reconstitution often proved a long and
difficult task. In its anxiety to ensure the rapid disappearance of
teachers' training colleges, the Vichy government had scattered libraries and scientific equipment, handed premises over to other establishments and assigned administrative and teaching staff to other posts.
War damage and looting added to the confusion. To restore the former

buildings or find new ones, to re-equip them and, especially, to re-constitute their teaching staffs, requires time and money and calls for a variety of measures. Most departments have voted large sums for the re-establishment of teachers' training colleges and, thanks to a collective effort in which the Ministry of Education has taken part, almost the whole country is now equipped with restored training colleges, fitted for their new tasks.

THE PRESENT POSITION

Since the Liberation, a new conception of primary teachers' training has tended to develop. Administrators responsible for defining and enforcing the new system already have some basis for their work, since the Third Republic—and even the July Monarchy—laid down the principles; they realized the essential problems and endeavoured to solve them.

The present system of primary teachers' training, therefore, is the outcome of experiments and vicissitudes in which both historical events and a constant desire to achieve perfection have played their part. Thus, State teachers' training colleges have inherited a tradition and a sense of what can and cannot be achieved, while at the same time they are striking out in new directions. For they have to meet educational needs which, owing to world events, the speeding up of economic development, population trends in contemporary France and the prolongation of compulsory school attendance, are growing daily more dissimilar to those of the last century.

In our country, with its tradition of freedom, private colleges co-exist with State institutions at all levels of the teaching system. They are inspired by different principles and seek their own solutions, but they are faced with the same problem of adapting themselves to the general conditions existing in the modern world and to the special requirements of the teaching profession.

Whether Catholic, Protestant, Jewish or undenominational, these colleges also have their traditions and continue with their experiments. The authorities to whom they are responsible are anxious to organize, as far as their resources and duties permit, the best possible training for their teachers.

Teachers' training courses, institutes or educational study centres pass on to each other techniques which they have proved to be effective or they give assistance where their own particular situation enables them to do so. Although in many ways very different from State teachers' training colleges, they sometimes model themselves upon the latter, and both often share a common heritage.

CHAPTER II

TRAINING OF PRIMARY TEACHERS AT THE PRESENT TIME

TRAINING OF PUBLIC PRIMARY SCHOOL TEACHERS

EQUIPMENT AND ADMINISTRATION OF TEACHERS' TRAINING COLLEGES

'Every department shall be provided with two primary teachers' training colleges, one for men and one for women, capable of training a sufficient number of men and women teachers for its communal schools. At the recommendation of the Higher Council for National Education, two departments may be authorized, by decree, jointly to establish and maintain, on the basis of equally shared expenditure, either one or the other, or both, of their teachers' training colleges.' Such was the law of 9 August 1879, which remained in force until 18 September 1940.

When this law was passed there were 79 primary teachers' training colleges for men, 3 of them being run by religious orders, and 29 primary teachers' training colleges for women, 9 of them run by religious orders. In 1939, on the eve of their suppression, there were, on the same territory: 82 primary teachers' training colleges for men and 83 for women, without counting 6 teachers' training colleges in Alsace-Lorraine, 5 in Algeria, 2 in Tunisia, 3 in Indochina and 1 in Syria.

At present, that is to say eight years after the official reopening of teachers' training colleges, the number of scholarship holders to be recruited by competitive examination and the sum to be granted to each training college are determined by order of the Ministry of Education for each of the 90 departments of France.

Of the four new departments (Guadeloupe, Martinique, Guyane and Réunion), the first three come under the authority of the educational division of Bordeaux, and the fourth under that of the educational division of Aix. These departments have no teachers' training colleges; their student teachers do their studies at *lycées* and may, if they so desire, take a course of professional training at the teachers' training colleges in metropolitan France.

The departments of Alsace and Lorraine continue to maintain denominational (Roman Catholic) teachers' training colleges, in addition to other colleges, which are either undenominational or open to students of various religions.

In the territory of Belfort, student teachers attend the teachers' training colleges of the Doubs; the department of the Nièvre sends some to the Allier and others to the Yonne; that of the Hautes-Pyrénées sends them to Auch (Gers).

The departments of the Basses-Alpes and the Vaucluse have agreed to keep up only one teachers' training college for boys, at Avignon, and one for girls, at Digne; the same arrangement has been made by the departments of the Lot and the Tarn-et-Garonne (boys at Montauban and girls at Cahors). Boys of the department of the Haute-Marne go to Troyes; those of the Tarn to Toulouse, those of the Hautes-Alpes to the *lycée* at Gap to work for their *baccalauréat* and afterwards to the teachers' training college at Valence; those of the Corrèze go to the *lycée* at Tulle and then to the teachers' training college at Guéret.

Girls of the department of the Hautes-Alpes first attend the *lycée* at Gap and then follow teachers' training classes at Valence; those of the Haute-Savoie go to the *lycée* at Annecy and then to the teachers' training college at Chambéry; those at Aurillac and Tulle attend the *lycées* in their respective towns. All girls in the Dordogne are allowed to attend the teachers' training college at La Rochelle. Lastly, the towns of Perpignan, Agen, Mende and Foix share a single teacher's training college for both boys and girls.

This shows that the uniformity which might be assumed from the official texts does not in fact obtain. Owing to lack of buildings or money, provisional solutions have had to be adopted in many cases; however, they do enable experiments to be made, and time will prove whether or not they are satisfactory.

Equipment and Maintenance Costs

Teachers' training colleges are still responsible, as instituted by Guizot's regulations in 1832, to two different authorities. They are dependent upon the Ministry of Education for the appointment and remuneration of their teaching and administrative staff, the organization of their entrance examinations, their time-tables and syllabuses, and the general conditions governing their operation. They are dependent upon their respective departments, whose communal schools they supply with men and women primary teachers, for the acquisition, maintenance and enlargement of buildings, the installation and upkeep of furniture and equipment for their boarding houses, offices, classrooms, laboratories, sports grounds, etc. Buildings, furniture and equipment are the property of the departments concerned, which are usually careful to ensure that their teachers' training colleges are well equipped. Most of these institutions are spacious, well equipped and surrounded by parks and gardens, which are not only useful for agricultural and horticultural activities, but provide a pleasant and healthy environment for the students.

This dependence of the teachers' training colleges on two separate authorities is evident in their budgets, their funds coming both from the State and the respective departments; it is shown also in their governing boards, which consist both of members of the educational division's administration or representatives appointed by it, and of members of the general council which is the departmental assembly.

The proportion of the cost of teachers' training colleges contributed by the State and by the departments, of course, varies; it depends on the size of the colleges, the condition of the buildings and the extent to which they need to be enlarged or modernized; it also depends upon the importance which departmental councils attach to primary teachers' training.

In 1950, out of a total of 87,535 million francs obligated for primary education—i.e. 7.8 per cent of France's general budget—teachers' training colleges absorbed 4,268 million francs, i.e. 4.8 per cent of the total spent on primary education. This sum was expended as follows:[1] salaries of principals and teaching staff, 1,038 million; salaries of bursars, agents and management costs, 417 million; salaries and scholarships for 5,400 students, 1,166 million; maintenance grants for 12,055 students, 771 million; teaching material and costs, 222 million; building repairs, 654 million.

This last item represents subventions granted to departments which are making an especially valiant effort to restore their college buildings.

Administration of Teachers' Training Colleges

Teachers' training colleges are public State institutions with legal status and financial autonomy (decree of 24 April 1948). They are responsible to the divisional director of education under the authority of the Minister of Education. Every college is administered by a man or woman principal and a governing board. A bursar (*intendant* or *économe*) is responsible for keeping the cash and store records. There is no difference, either in operation or organization, between teachers' training colleges for men and those for women.

The principal is the head of the college; he represents it in all actions at law and for all legal and contractual purposes. He prepares the budgets and concludes contracts, agreements or commercial trans-

---

[1] Debiesse, Jean. *Compulsory Education in France.* '*Studies on Compulsory Education*',–II, Paris, Unesco, 1951, p. 49.

actions. He presents the bursar's accounts to the governing board. He issues authorizations to the bursar to collect college dues. He appropriates funds, settles accounts and authorizes payments within the limits of the college's regular budget. He keeps administrative accounts of the authorizations to collect dues and of the postal orders which he issues. He supervises and keeps a check on all parts of the bursar's service, but is not empowered to interfere with the keeping of the cash and store records.

The governing board is composed of: the divisional director of education (chairman); the divisional inspector (vice-chairman); four members, of whom one is the principal of the college, appointed by the divisional director of education; two members of the departmental council, elected by their colleagues. The bursar attends meetings of the board in an advisory capacity, as do also the architect and doctor when matters within their competence arise.

The functions of the governing board are to discuss the administering of the college's resources and income, purchases, transfers, exchanges of land, and loans; the college's budgets and accounts, additional and exceptional requests for funds; in general, all receipts and expenditure; procedure and conditions for the effecting of commercial transactions; the scrapping of worn-out furniture; work plans for buildings, fittings, extensive repairs and demolitions; donations and requests; legal proceedings and transactions.

Budgets and accounts are submitted for approval to the Minister of Education; specifications and commercial transactions have to be approved by the divisional director of education.

The decree of 24 April 1948 governing the administration of teachers' training colleges also explains in detail how bursarships are to be administered and lays down directives for budgeting and accounting. It gives a list of allowances in kind to which those living in a college are entitled; it lays down the conditions for admission to the common dining-room; and it defines the respective contributions of any two departments to the cost of maintaining a joint teachers' training college. It is compulsory for departments to bear the cost of establishing and maintaining teachers' training colleges; and, if necessary, the Ministry of Education can request the Ministry of the Interior to have recourse to the procedure of obliging a defaulting department to include the necessary sum in its budget.

Provisions relating to the administration and management of teachers' training colleges have been drafted with all the scrupulous care involved in the management of public funds. Additional explanations regarding the responsibilities of college principals and bursars are given in the order of 18 May 1948.

TABLE 1. Statistics on recruitment for teachers' training colleges

Before the Second World War

Year	Number of primary teachers' training colleges		Number of student teachers		
	For men	For women	Men	Women	Total
1900	86	84	3 897	4 094	7 991
1910	85	84	4 424	5 026	9 450
1920[1]	83	83	4 617	5 135	9 752
1925[1]	83	85	4 904	5 463	10 367
1930[2]	87	86	6 433	6 692	13 125
1935[1]	83	84	4 789	4 589	9 478
1936[1]	83	84	5 487	5 518	11 005
1937[1]	83	84	4 440	4 397	8 837

[1] Excluding Alsace-Lorraine and Algeria.
[2] Including colleges in Alsace-Lorraine.

Since the Liberation

Year	Candidates applying		Candidates admitted	
	Men	Women	Men	Women
1946	1 676	3 251	803	1 712
1947	1 780	3 536	871	1 680
1948	3 770	6 654	1 616	2 129
1949	4 175	7 931	1 986	2 130
1950	4 477	7 966	1 991	2 154
1951	5 952	10 204		

Total number of student teachers following courses in 1951–52: Men, 7,453; women, 8,714.

Number of former men and women student teachers who have given up teaching since the Liberation: 1946, 404; 1947, 290; 1948, 180; 1949, 90; 1950, 155.

ADMISSION TO TEACHERS' TRAINING COLLEGES (FIRST-YEAR CLASS)

The majority of student teachers enter teachers' training colleges for the first-year class. Every year, the educational authorities inform each department of the number of men and women students to be admitted to its training colleges.

The procedure is as follows: the departmental council is consulted as to how many men and women student teachers should be admitted at the beginning of the following academic year. It takes into account both the accommodation available in the teachers' training college, whose students are usually boarders, and the number of primary teachers required by the department. It is for the divisional inspector to estimate the number of primary teachers likely to be at his disposal four years later, that is to say, when the batch of students to be recruited are ready to take up their first posts. He has to take account, for example, of the number of primary teachers who will be leaving because they have reached retirement age, and must calculate, on the basis of birth statistics, the number of children who will at that time have attained school age.

The report of the departmental council is communicated to the divisional director of education, who forwards it, with his proposals, to the Minister of Education. At the beginning of July, the Minister announces the total number of scholarship holders to be recruited for the whole country, at the next competitive examination, stating how many scholarships are to be allocated to each teachers' training college. In calculating the number of scholarship holders, he aims at a compromise between requests received and actual funds made available by the Ministry of Finance.

During 1952, a total number of 3,906 scholarships were granted, 1,896 of them for men and 2,010 for women. The departments which received the largest allocations of student teachers were the following: Seine, 110 male, 110 female; Seine-et-Oise, 85 male, 65 female; Nord, 55 male, 55 female. Every training college, throughout the country, admits an average of 20 students a year.

It sometimes happens that a teachers' training college is unable to recruit, through the competitive examination in July, the total number of students to which it is entitled; in that case, a second examination is held in the autumn to fill the vacancies.[1]

Candidates

Candidates must enter their names at the divisional inspector's office at least one month before the date fixed for the competitive examination. They must be at least 15 and not more than 17 years of age, and must be of French nationality. They are required to produce:

A birth certificate.

An application for admission to the examination, stating the school or schools which they have attended since the age of 12 years.

---

[1] In 1952, all primary teachers' training colleges for women were able to recruit their full number of students by means of the competitive examination in July, whereas 278 vacancies remained in primary teachers' training colleges for men (41 in the Seine, 31 in the Seine-et-Oise and 17 in the Bouches-du-Rhône).

A certified copy of the secondary first cycle certificate (they must have obtained this certificate in order to sit for the competitive examination).

An undertaking to teach in public schools for ten years (this paper must be accompanied by a signed statement whereby the candidate's father or guardian authorizes the candidate to enter into this obligation and undertakes to reimburse the college fees of his child or ward should the latter leave the college of his own accord or be expelled from it, as in the case of refusal to complete the compulsory ten years' service).

Male candidates must, in addition, undertake to request the military authorities to defer their military service in cases where they will reach military age before completing their training.

The divisional inspector makes enquiries, in the schools which candidates have attended, regarding their capabilities, suitability for the teaching profession, and conduct; he then draws up a list of candidates to be admitted to the competitive examination.

The latter may come from various educational establishments (secondary schools, continuation courses, private courses) and from all departments of metropolitan France or the French overseas territories. From the time of their admission to the training college, they are destined to teach in the department in which that college is situated.

Tests covered by the Competitive Examination

Medical Examination. Teaching is tiring work; it requires, in particular, sound vocal organs and lungs and a strong nervous system. Since young people passing through teachers' training colleges are dedicated to public service, it is the duty of the responsible authorities to reject those liable to require periods of sick leave or disability pensions, which are a heavy drain on public funds. Therefore, even before their intellectual abilities are tested, young people have to go before a special committee of three doctors, i.e., two general practitioners (one of whom must be the school health officer, assistant to the divisional inspector) and a qualified phthisiologist; the principal of the training college must be present at the interview. The committee studies the candidates' medical files; it examines their lungs and sensory organs with particular care.[1] It may pass or reject candidates or postpone their admission. Before they are finally admitted to the training college, successful candidates have, in addition, to undergo an X-ray examination of their lungs.

---

1 Constitutional defects and infirmities disqualifying those wishing to enter the teaching profession are listed in the ministerial circular of 17 May 1951.

Academic Examination. This examination takes place at the training college, the examiners being members of a committee of which the divisional inspector is chairman and the principal of the college, vice-chairman. Candidates are examined on a curriculum published at the beginning of the school year, the standard being equivalent to that of the third class[1] in secondary schools (*lycées* and *collèges*).

The examination is in two parts, the first being written and consisting of the following papers:

1. A spelling test, consisting of twenty lines of dictation followed by four questions, two of them on vocabulary and phraseology, and two on grammar. In judging the dictation, handwriting is taken into account; candidates are allowed thirty minutes in which to reply to the questions and read through what they have written. Weighting factor: total 3, i.e. 1 for dictation, 1 ½ for the questions and ½ for handwriting.
2. Comments on a French text. Time allowed: 2 hours. Weighting factor: 2.
3. Mathematics: working out of two problems, showing how the solutions were reached—one geometry problem, and the other a problem in arithmetic or algebra or one covering both these subjects. Time allowed: 2 hours. Weighting factor: 2.
4. Modern languages: a translation into French. Time allowed: 2 hours. Weighting factor: 2.

The subjects are selected by the divisional director of education in consultation with the committee of divisional inspectors under his authority. Subjects may be selected by the Minister.

The second part of the examination, which is oral and practical, consists of:

1. Reading of a French text, followed by questions on its meaning. Time allowed: 20 minutes for each candidate. Weighting factor: 3.
2. Mathematics. Time allowed: 20 minutes. Weighting factor: 3.
3. Written report on a half-hour talk given to the candidates on a literary or scientific subject. The report has to be drawn up immediately and handed in together with the notes taken by the candidate during the talk. Time allowed for drafting of report: 1 hour. Weighting factor: 3.
4. A free-hand drawing test. Weighting factor: 1.
5. A music test, consisting of a simple sol-fa exercise and the singing of a song selected from a list drawn up by the educational division. Weighting factor: 1.
6. A handicraft test for boys and a needlework test for girls, including, in each case, the drawing of a preliminary sketch. Weighting factor: 1.

---

[1] Pupils beginning secondary school enter the 'sixth class' and reach the 'third class' in their fourth year of successful study.

7. A physical education test. Weighting factor: 1.
Each test is marked from 0 to 20.

A list of candidates qualified to take the second part of the examination is drawn up in alphabetical order. No candidate is allowed to take it who has not obtained at least the average mark for the papers in the first part as a whole. A candidate having obtained, for any paper, a nought which is confirmed after discussion by the board of examiners, is eliminated. When the second part of the examination has been taken, the committee draws up a list of candidates, in order of merit, to be proposed to the divisional director of education for appointment as student teachers.

It will be seen that the tests have been selected with the twofold aim of discovering the knowledge possessed by candidates and their particular abilities. For example, commenting on a text and reporting on a talk are especially conclusive tests of the candidate's culture, sensibility and mental alertness.

ADMISSION TO TEACHERS' TRAINING COLLEGES (THIRD-YEAR CLASS)

The present tendency in public education is to reserve posts in primary schools for young teachers who have been trained at a teachers' training college.

Some young people who have their *baccalauréat* decide to go in for elementary teaching only after they have completed their studies at a secondary school (*lycée* or *collège*); others who may have failed to gain admission to a training college through the competitive examination for recruitment for the first-year class, have nevertheless not given up hope of becoming primary teachers. There are two ways open to them of entering a teachers' training college for professional training: the competitive examination for holders of the secondary school leaving certificate (*baccalauréat*), or a course for training as replacement teachers.

Competitive Examination for Holders of the Baccalauréat

This examination is a normal way of preparing for a career as a primary teacher. The regulations governing the competitive examination for admission to a teachers' training college for the first-year class also lay down the terms of admission for the third-year class for those who have passed the *baccalauréat*.

This provision, which did not exist in pre-war legislation, makes it possible to extend the benefits of professional training to young people who have not had the advantage of preparing for their *baccalauréat* at a teachers' training college. As soon as they enter such a college, these

147

young people who have passed the *baccalauréat* are treated in identically the same way as other student teachers; like the latter, they receive a salary, and are subject to the same administrative regulations; they undertake to teach for 10 years and, when they leave college, should have obtained their teachers' training certificate. They are guaranteed a post upon completion of their training, and are included in the single classified list of all students terminating their training in that particular year.

Their admission is governed by the following clauses of the decree of 6 June 1946:

'Article 59. The course shall be reduced to two years' professional training for students who have passed the *baccalauréat* and have been recruited by a special competitive examination, the conditions of which are set out in Article 70 of the present decree.

'Article 70. Every candidate must: (a) Be of French nationality. (b) Be over 17 and under 19 years of age on 1 January of the year in which he is a candidate for the competitive examination for the third-year class. This rule shall be strictly applied. (c) Have passed the *baccalauréat*.'

There follow the clauses relating to the medical examination, the ten years' compulsory service and, for men, the application for deferment of military service, which are exactly the same as those governing admission to the competitive examination for the first-year class.

'Article 90. The competitive examination for admission to a primary teachers' training college for the third-year class consists of two series of examinations. Those of the first series are: (a) An essay, which also serves as a spelling and handwriting test. Weighting factor of 3 for the essay, 2 for spelling, 1 for handwriting. (b) Written account of a talk on a scientific subject including experiments and observations. Weighting factor: 3. Those of the second series are: (a) Explanation of a text. Weighting factor: 4. (b) A statement to be made by the candidate on a general subject, drawn by lot. Time allowed for preparation: 1 hour. Weighting factor: 4. (c) A drawing or explanatory diagram of a simple mechanism which the candidate has before him. Weighting factor: 2.'

Articles 91, 92 and 93, governing the place of the examination, the choice of subjects, the marking of papers, and the admissibility and admission of candidates, cover both competitive examinations.

The idea of allowing *baccalauréat* holders wishing to become primary teachers to enter professional training colleges has proved to be a fortunate one, and there would be a great many candidates every year if training colleges could accommodate them. Unfortunately, in many colleges lack of space or money has prevented them from putting the above clauses into practice, and the competitive examination for the first-year class is still the only way of gaining access to them.

During 1952, the funds allocated under the Appropriation Bill enabled 261 *baccalauréat* holders to enter teachers' training colleges. These scholarship holders (133 young men and 128 girls) were divided among 23 men's colleges and 24 women's colleges; the greatest number of fellowships were allocated to departments with a large population: Seine: 28 men, 22 women; Nord: 15 men, 11 women; Pas-de-Calais: 11 men, 11 women.

Training of Replacement Teachers for Primary Schools

It has never been possible to fill all posts in elementary schools with teachers who have studied at a teachers' training college. Temporary and other vacancies occurring as a result of sick and maternity leave, for example, and unforeseeable events such as the mobilization of teachers and increased establishments due to a rise in the birth-rate, make it necessary to recruit replacement teachers of both sexes. For a long time the latter were obliged to learn by experience, with no proper training; they were guided mainly by advice given by headmasters or headmistresses, by colleagues, and by school inspectors. Now, fortunately, these beginners can also enjoy the benefits of professional training.

Every year, some 2,000 *baccalauréat* holders, i.e. 50 per cent of the student teachers, enter their profession as replacement teachers. Article 60 of the decree of 6 June 1946 stipulates that: 'As from 1 January 1951, male and female replacement or temporary primary teachers holding the *baccalauréat* certificate or higher certificate may not occupy an established post until they have received professional training in a teachers' training college...

'They must have served at least two years and must satisfy the conditions set out in paragraphs 1, 3, 4 and 5 of Article 70 of the present decree. Moreover, they shall not be admitted to a teachers' training college if they are more than 25 years of age on 1 January of the year in which they request admission.

'Recommendations for admission shall be made by a committee consisting of the divisional inspector (chairman), the principals (male and female) of teachers' training colleges, primary school and nursery school inspectors (male and female), a primary teachers' representative on the departmental council, a male primary teacher for boys, and a female primary teacher for girls.

'The right to admission shall be decided by the divisional director of education.

'The time during which such teachers have taught in public schools before entering the teachers' training college shall be counted as part of their ten years' compulsory teaching service.'

It has not been easy, for various reasons, to ensure the satisfactory execution of the above regulations at one stroke; they came into force in 1946, but are still in an experimental stage which has called for various slight alterations. The law of 8 May 1951 gives a definition of the status of replacement teachers in primary schools. Under the decree of 28 October 1952, the professional training of replacement teachers is organized as follows:

'Article 6. The professional training course for replacement teachers shall last for two years; this period may, however, be extended by ministerial decision. It shall begin with the first term following the inclusion of the names of the candidates concerned in the departmental list.

'It shall consist, during the first year, of theoretical and practical training in teachers' training colleges and attached schools, and, during the second year, of replacements organized and supervised by departmental nursery school inspectresses and primary school inspectors, together with courses of instruction given by those officials and by men and women principals and teachers of teachers' training colleges.

'Should any replacement primary teacher refuse to go through the various stages of the training and follow the courses referred to above, he shall, unless he can supply a valid excuse, be struck off the list of replacement primary teachers by the divisional inspector, on the advice of the joint administrative commission. Any such replacement primary teacher whose excuse has been accepted must later undergo the parts of the training from which he has been absolved.

'Article 7. Replacement primary teachers shall be admitted to teachers' training colleges as boarders; in some cases, however, particularly if they are married, they may be day-boarders or live out.

'Their remuneration during their stay at the teachers' training college shall be equal to the basic salary of fourth-year student-teachers.

'Article 8. At the end of the first year following their inclusion in the departmental list of replacement primary teachers, those who have obtained a general average of marks calculated in accordance with the directives of an order issued by the Ministry of Education, and not less than the average fixed by that ministry, shall be included in the list for the following year.

'Replacement primary teachers having failed to obtain their qualifying certificate after five years of inclusion in the departmental list may not be re-entered on the list for a sixth time, unless they can produce a valid excuse for having failed to obtain the certificate.

'Article 9. Replacement primary teachers who, through their own fault or owing to disciplinary action taken against them, do not complete the compulsory five years' service in primary schools to which they pledged themselves under Article 4 of the law of 8 May 1951, shall reimburse to the State the total expenditure incurred by the latter for their maintenance and remuneration during their training in the teachers' training colleges and attached schools.

'Article 10. While awaiting employment, replacement primary teachers shall complete their professional training in a school in their own locality or in a locality near their home. Conditions for the payment of a transport allowance to teachers obliged to travel to a neighbouring locality shall be laid down in a joint order issued by the Ministry of Education and the Ministry of Finance.'

STUDENT TEACHERS

Successful candidates at the competitive examination are granted State fellowships for their four-year course of training. In some cases they spend two years preparing for the *baccalauréat* and two years doing professional training; in others, three years are spent on preparing for the *baccalauréat* and one on professional training. A general definition of their status in teachers' training colleges has been given in the decree of 18 January 1887, that of 6 June 1946, the order of 7 June 1946 and the order of 18 May 1948. Teachers' training colleges are boarding establishments; day boarders or day students may be admitted as an exceptional measure.

Internal Administration

Sundays, public holidays and Thursday afternoons are the regular holidays. In training colleges for women teachers, not until they enter the professional training class are students free to go out except to their parents or to a friend *in loco parentis*. These restrictions do not exist for men.

Men and women student teachers are given every facility for practising their religion. They may belong to professional organizations and, from the time when they enter the professional training class, may become members of the departmental branches of purely trade-union organizations, may receive the official national and departmental publications of such organizations, and may attend their meetings on regular holidays.

They may not, however, form themselves into political or denominational associations, nor may they receive any propaganda publications.

The college's administrative regulations are laid down at a meeting of the teachers' committee and are submitted to the divisional director of education for approval. Whenever he deems it necessary, the principal convenes the teachers and the bursar of the training college, as well as the headmaster or mistress of the attached school, in committee to discuss any questions relating to college teaching and discipline. At least once a quarter, assistant teachers and students' representatives (the latter being elected one from each year) are admitted to these meetings in an advisory capacity.

Students are liable to the following punishments only: (a) Detention imposed by the principal. (b) A warning given by the principal. (c) A reprimand before the teachers' committee, administered either by the principal or by the divisional inspector, according to the gravity of the offence. (d) Temporary expulsion for a period not exceeding a fortnight, imposed by the divisional inspector. (e) Transfer to another teachers' training college within the same jurisdiction, imposed by the divisional director of education. (f) Permanent expulsion imposed by the Minister of Education.

Any student found guilty of a serious offence may be sent back immediately to his family by the principal.

These clauses relating to discipline may at first sight appear unduly severe, but they are fully justified when one considers, firstly, the youth of the students and, secondly, the standard of behaviour and work which it is right to expect of young people who are all benefiting from State fellowships. In any case, the official rules are enforced in a very paternal manner; the administrative regulations leave the students a good deal of freedom, and it is very unusual for a principal to have to resort to the official punishments.

The time-table drawn up by the teachers' committee and submitted for approval to the divisional director of education is so arranged that at least eight hours are allowed for sleep at all times of the year; approximately five hours a day are reserved for personal hygiene, meals, recreation, games, domestic duties and physical exercise in training colleges for men, and five-and-a-half hours in colleges for women teachers.

At least five of the working hours each day are devoted to personal work, reading, the preparation of lessons, and teaching practice in elementary or nursery schools.

The subjects taught are so arranged that, in principle, not more than four hours a day are spent in class, not counting the time devoted to singing, physical training, handwork and drawing.

The men and women student teachers themselves are held responsible, under the supervision of the principal, the bursar and the assistant teachers, for maintaining law and order in the college. For example, students help to keep the house and garden tidy, run the library and supervise evening studies; the supervisory service is very small, being composed of young men or women primary teachers not following the ordinary course, but generally proceeding with certain studies while providing the training college with this service. By participating in the maintenance of law and order in the college, students share the administrators' responsibilities and receive practical training in self-government.

Scholarships and Salaries

Since 1879, students in teachers' training colleges have always had all their expenses covered by State scholarships; at the present time, the Ministry of Education includes in the budget of a teachers' training college a sum equivalent to the total cost of food, laundry, and standard supplies for each pupil in the class preparing for the *baccalauréat*. For 1952, these sums were respectively 66,150 francs for food, 4,590 francs for laundry and 5,760 francs for educational costs, which amounted to a total of 76,500 francs for each student teacher. To this must be added an annual outfit allowance paid to families to help them to meet the cost of clothing, dormitory kit, sporting equipment, books, etc. This sum is at present 13,500 francs.

In some cases a departmental grant may also be made, either to particularly needy students only, or, as in the Seine, to all student teachers without distinction.

Since 1947, students have received a salary as soon as they enter the professional training class. The principle of paying a modest salary to these young people whose studies enable them to render public service has been justified by the very real services which young men and women students have rendered as teachers during their professional training. The granting of this salary has certainly helped to improve the general conditions of recruitment for teachers' training colleges, both as regards enrolment for the first year class and the admission of students holding the *baccalauréat*.

In 1952, this salary was as follows:

In the first-year class of professional training (in the case of a two-year course) the salary index is 110, corresponding to a basic salary of 166,000 francs a year, i.e. 13,887 francs a month.

In the second-year class of professional training (in the case of a two-year course) and for students taking the one-year course, the salary index is 175, corresponding to a basic salary of 282,000 francs a year, i.e. 22,634 francs a month.

Out of this salary, students pay back to the college bursar a sum equivalent to the cost of their food, laundry and standard supplies, together with their contribution to general expenses, which amounts to 650 francs a month.

They receive a monthly payment of 4,000 francs for small current expenses; the bursar gives them the rest when they leave college, in the form of a provident fund, intended to help them to meet their initial installation expenses. In the course of a year, however, the principal may authorize the payment of advances from the provident fund to cover essential expenditure, such as purchases of equipment needed when students go out to gain practical teaching experience—for example, purchases of warm clothes, a bicycle, basic works to be added to their own store of books.... Such advances may not exceed 50 per cent of the total amount of the student's provident fund.

TEACHING STAFF IN TEACHERS' TRAINING COLLEGES

The staff of a teachers' training college is composed of the principal, the bursar, teachers, assistant teachers, and sometimes monitors (instructors). In training colleges for women, all the administrative posts and, in principle, all the teaching posts are filled by women.

In addition to his or her administrative duties, the principal may give classes and lectures on ethics, the principles of education, and psychology; he is further responsible for supervising teaching in the college and directing the students' professional training. Most principals are former members of the staff of a teachers' training college; they are all holders of the qualifying certificate for primary inspectors and principals of teachers' training colleges[1] and must have served as primary inspectors for at least two years. They continue to inspect the primary teachers in the attached or demonstration schools. Their duties are thus difficult and manifold; they are responsible for the practical management and the moral standards of their college, they teach and also supervise teaching in the elementary or nursery schools where student teachers gain their practical experience; lastly, they have a part to play in the administration of primary education in their department, for they are members of the departmental council and joint commissions.

Teachers must hold the qualifying certificate for teachers in teachers' training colleges or the qualifying certificate for teachers in secondary schools (*lycées* and *collèges*), and in some cases they are *agrégés* (teachers who have passed the *agrégation* examination). Their number varies according to the number of student teachers; in an average-sized teachers' training college, i.e., one with 60 to 80 students, the teaching services are as follows: one-and-a-half for physics and natural sciences, one each for philosophy, humanities, history and geography, mathematics, and physical training.

Modern languages, drawing, music and handicrafts are taught by specialists who usually divide their time between several institutions in the same town.

---

[1] *Programme des Conditions d'Obtention du Certificat d'Aptitude à l'Inspection Primaire et à la Direction des Ecoles Normales* (List of Conditions for obtaining the Qualifying Certificate for Primary School Inspectors and Principals of Teachers' Training Colleges), Paris, Librairie Vuibert.

Instruction in agriculture and domestic science is given by specialist teachers, with the co-operation of the departmental directorate of agricultural services. Subject to the minister's approval, auxiliary teachers or instructresses may be employed in teachers' training colleges to give instruction in manual work or domestic science.

In principle, and according to the decree of 6 June 1946, professional training, or at least training in educational theory, must be given by teachers selected by the minister from among primary school inspectors who have had at least two years' experience and hold the qualifying certificate for teachers in primary teachers' training colleges or secondary schools (*lycées* and *collèges*), or a degree. Such teachers retain their status and salary as primary inspectors. In actual fact, it has been impossible to entrust all teaching in the professional training classes to primary inspectors, and often it is the college teachers who not only prepare students for the *baccalauréat* but also teach the theory of education and supervise teaching practice in their own subjects.

When Jules Ferry undertook to organize popular education in France, he created, on the whole, a very sound and well-knit system. Even before ordering the establishment of elementary primary schools, he made it compulsory to set up the teachers' training colleges which were to train teachers for those schools. He also realized the importance of providing training of a high standard for future teachers in teachers' training colleges. He therefore founded the two higher training colleges for primary teachers; the first of these to be established, by decree of 13 July 1880, was the women's training college at Fontenay-aux-Roses. The reasons for its foundation given in the ministerial report were the following:

'As the law of 9 August 1879 has made it compulsory for all departments to equip themselves, within four years, with a primary teachers' training college for women, and as the decree of 5 June 1880 has stipulated that, in order to qualify for posts as principals and teachers in such colleges, women candidates must pass an examination calling for specialized knowledge, the administration has had to devise means of providing a large number of qualified teachers within a very short time.' Félix Pécaut was appointed director of all the academic activities of the college, which swiftly proved such a brilliant success that a higher teachers' training college for men was opened at St. Cloud on 30 December 1882.

Up till 1940, these two senior primary teachers' training colleges supplied the whole of France with very competent teachers; further, each college included a special section for the preparation of candidates, selected by the administration, for the qualifying certificate for primary school inspectors and principals of teachers' training colleges. The colleges at Fontenay-aux-Roses and St. Cloud have therefore played a predominantly important part in training teachers for primary schools.

In 1940, however, with the disappearance of teachers' training colleges they in their turn were to undergo a period of change. When, at the Liberation, future primary teachers were required to have passed the *baccalauréat*, it meant that their training, from the standpoint of general culture, came close to that of *lycéens* (secondary school pupils). Consequently, teachers, instead of having to take a special diploma, such as the former qualifying certificate for teachers in teachers' training colleges, have now to take the qualifying certificate for secondary school teachers (teachers in *lycées* and *collèges*); many of them sit for the *agrégation* examination and quite often they pass extremely well.

Thus the dividing line between teachers in teachers' training colleges and those in *lycées* or *collèges* no longer exists; whether or not this innovation will assist the recruitment of training college staff remains to be seen. Will the most brilliant teachers, holders of an *agrégation*, who intended to teach in primary teachers' training colleges, remain true to their original purpose, or will they prefer to teach in *lycées*? Teachers' training colleges offer them the same salary and, with the same weekly time-table of classes, but often a smaller number of pupils, greater possibilities of carrying out research on their own, particularly in the field of child psychology. Young teachers today will no doubt be influenced in their choice by the facilities available in training colleges, such as their laboratory equipment and libraries, and by their situation, i.e. whether or not they are placed in pleasant and intellectually stimulating surroundings.

The career of a teacher in a teachers' training college is, broadly speaking, the same as that of a teacher in a *lycée* or *collège;* in either case, the teacher's grading is fixed according to his diploma, qualifying certificate or *agrégation*. Promotion from the first to the ninth 'steps' takes place according to the same standards by seniority or selection. The retirement age, pensions, various allowances and overtime rates have been standardized.

The division of work between the various teachers is outlined at the beginning of the academic year by the principal, in consultation with the teachers' committee, and is submitted to the divisional director of education for final approval.

The inspection of staff in teachers' training colleges is as complex as the teaching itself, for some students are being prepared for the *baccalauréat* while others are being trained for actual teaching in elementary or nursery schools. The divisional director of education and the divisional inspector inspect all the teaching staff coming under their respective purviews. General inspectors, however, have very clearly defined duties as regards teachers' training colleges: secondary school inspectors visit staff teaching their particular subject in the classes working for the *baccalauréat;* primary school inspectors visit the teachers in charge of professional training. In addition, inspectors of administrative services inspect the bursar's service, the accounts, and the organization and operation of all the administrative services. In primary teachers' training colleges for women, general inspectresses of nursery schools are responsible for inspecting the boarding establishment.

Appointments, promotions and transfers of staff come under the jurisdiction of the directorate of primary education at the Ministry of Education. The director of primary education, with the assistance of the appropriate joint administrative commission, plans all movements, promotions, etc. of personnel, whether it be a question of principals, bursars or teachers.

SYLLABUSES AT TEACHERS' TRAINING COLLEGES

Teachers' training colleges have a two-fold character, for they are both cultural institutions and schools for professional training.

Successful candidates at the competitive entrance examination receive a study grant for four years. During that time, they have to pass the secondary school leaving certificate (the *baccalauréat*) and follow a course of professional training in preparation for the qualifying examination that is held at the end of the course. As a rule, students spend two years preparing for each of the two tests. It often happens, however, that students enrolled through the competitive entrance examination are not sufficiently advanced to follow the lessons of the first class which lead up to the first part of the *baccalauréat*. In that case, they enter the second class of the teachers' training college, and spend three years working for the certificate that caps their general education, thereafter taking only a one-year course of professional training.

How do the authorities decide in which class to place them?

If, in the school which the students attended previously, they have already passed through the second class, if their school report shows that their work has been satisfactory, and if they obtain a high enough place in the competitive entrance examination, they are immediately placed in the class preparing for the *baccalauréat*. If not, they enter the second class.

General Education—The Baccalauréat (*Secondary School Leaving Certificate*)

For the first part of the *baccalauréat*, all student teachers take the modern section with only one modern language. They have to take the following papers: Essay in French, weighting factor 3; other modern language, weighting factor 2; Physics, weighting factor 2; Mathematics, weighting factor 2. The time allowed for each paper is three hours.

The oral part of the examination consists of the explanation of or commenting upon two texts, one in French and one in a foreign language, and questions on history and geography, mathematics and physics. Further, candidates can gain additional marks on certain optional subjects: for boys, physical training, music or drawing; for girls, physical training or domestic science, music or drawing.

Those who pass the first part of the *baccalauréat* qualify for the experimental science class, where they work for the second part. The Minister of Education decided that it was unsuitable for student teachers, who would have to teach their classes arithmetic and science as well as French, to take the *baccalauréat* either in philosophy and humanities or in elementary mathematics.

They are therefore obliged to take the experimental sciences section, which consists of the following written papers: philosophical essay (time allowed 4 hours), weighting factor 4; physics (2 hours), weighting factor 2; natural sciences (2 hours), weighting factor 2.

The oral part of the examination consists of questions on philosophy, history and geography, mathematics, physics and natural sciences, and the explanation of a text in a foreign language. Candidates can gain additional marks by taking certain optional subjects, which are the same as those in the first part of the *baccalauréat*.

In some cases, however, student teachers are exceptionally gifted in literary or scientific subjects. For the benefit of those who wish to carry out advanced studies and cannot any longer defer specialization, special classes have been established for the preparation of the *baccalauréat* in philosophy and humanities or elementary mathematics. There is generally a class of this kind in every educational division. Pupils who have obtained good marks during the school year and in the examination which they have just taken may be enrolled in this class, on the recommendation of their headmaster and teachers. These classes are reserved for students intending to take the competitive examination which leads to secondary school teaching, and are not open to future teachers in primary schools who are expected to aim, during their period at a teachers' training college, not so much at making progress in the subjects at which they are most brilliant, as at learning to teach all the subjects in the curriculum to children of 6 to 14 years of age.

The curriculum for the experimental science class is extremely lengthy and comprehensive, calling for a considerable effort of memory, particularly in the natural sciences; at the same time it introduces pupils, through lessons on philosophy, to new methods and a whole realm of thought hitherto unknown to them. The experimental science year is thus one of intense effort; indeed it is sometimes to be feared that, in exhausting pupils with so much work, it blunts their intellectual curiosity. Fortunately however, during their years of professional training, they have many opportunities of developing in accordance with their own tastes and of choosing activities which appeal to them from among those offered.

The official time-table drawn up by the Minister (order of 28 August 1946) for *baccalauréat* classes in teachers' training colleges is as follows:

TABLE 2. Official time-table

Subject	1st year (second class)	2nd year (first class)	Experimenta sciences
	hours	hours	hours
Philosophy	—	—	5
Humanities	—	—	1
French	5	5	—
Modern languages (one only)	5	5	1½
History	2	2	2
Geography	1½	2	2
Mathematics	4	4	4
Physics	4½	4½	5
Natural sciences	1	1	4
Physical training	3	3	3
Drawing	3	2½	1½
Music	2	2	1
Handicrafts and horticulture	2	2	2
Practical exercises and psychology (in the attached school)	—	1	1
TOTAL	33	34	33

It will be observed that the fact that pupils are training to become primary school teachers is constantly borne in mind: whereas drawing, music and handicrafts are optional subjects at a *lycée*, here they are compulsory;[1] immediately they enter the first class, students come into contact with the children in the attached school by watching classes, upon which one of their teachers, generally the philosophy teacher, comments. During the first and second years, in addition to following the secondary school curriculum, students are given lessons in nature study, designed to familiarize them with plant and animal life, a subject which is rightly given a very important place in rural schools.

The results are usually satisfactory. A high percentage of successes can be expected, in view of the fact that the student teachers have been

[1] The curricula for *baccalauréat* classes are given in: *Enseignement du Second Degré: Horaires et Programmes* (Secondary Schools: Time-tables and Curricula). Paris, Vuibert.

selected by means of a competitive entrance examination, that they take everything connected with their studies and future career extremely seriously, and that the working conditions in teachers' training colleges are very favourable. Among students who are obliged to pass the *baccalauréat* if they are to take up the career they have chosen, this percentage should be 100 per cent. Repeated failures to pass the *baccalauréat* may have consequences for them which will be described later on.

Professional Training—Primary Teachers' Qualifying Certificate

Once they have passed the *baccalauréat*, student teachers embark upon a period of professional training which may last either one or two years, according to circumstances. Their time is divided between theoretical classes in the college and practical teaching exercises in the attached and demonstration schools; close contact is maintained between the training college and the classes where students practise teaching; principals and teachers frequently visit their students in the schools and join the official teachers in giving them advice. When not engaged in teaching practice, groups of students are often taken by their master into a classroom, where they watch the children being taught and become familiar with the methods used by the teacher. They attend model lessons given by primary teachers selected for their outstanding professional ability. Test lessons are given by students in front of their teachers and fellow-students. Often, also, groups of children come to the training college to see a film or a play, to use some domestic science equipment or workshop better than those possessed by their elementary school, to do gardening or nature study in the park, or to serve as subjects for psychology tests and observations. The attached school is usually in the college grounds and, whenever possible, the demonstration school[1] is next-door to the college. Article 61 of the decree of 6 June 1946 stipulates that: 'Men and women student teachers shall acquire a practical knowledge of teaching in: (a) Schools, specially set up for the purpose, attached to teachers' training colleges as permanent centres for experimentation in teaching; (b) Demonstration classes—chosen by the divisional inspector in the departmental schools—where the various courses in professional training shall be organized.'

---

1 Attached schools are primary or nursery schools annexed to a teachers' training college for men or women; in these schools, student teachers acquire a practical knowledge of teaching. They are established by decision of the Minister of Education, at the proposal of the divisional director of education, who has previously consulted the departmental council. The number of classes is proposed by the divisional director of education and fixed by the minister. Such schools come under the jurisdiction of the principal of the training college to which they are attached. They may take boarders. The establishment and maintenance costs of such schools are borne by departments. Certain operational expenditure may be charged to the State. All income and expenditure connected with the running of an attached school are added to those of the training college to which it is annexed and are included in the same budget.

Primary teachers in attached and demonstration schools, who are appointed by the divisional director of education at the proposal of the divisional inspector, are selected with the utmost care, for their proved ability as teachers and the good example which they can set student teachers. They form an *élite* and may be appointed, at their request, to posts outside their own department; those teaching in attached schools are directly responsible to the Ministry of Education, while those in demonstration schools are responsible to the divisional directorate of education. Irrespective of the category of school in which they teach, they belong to a single association which, since 26 May 1951, has been called the Syndicat Autonome du Personnel des Ecoles Annexes et des Ecoles d'Application de France et de l'Union Française (Independent Union of Teachers in Attached and Demonstration Schools of France and the French Union).

The practical teaching courses are spaced out over the school year; they are generally held in October, January and the month following the Easter holidays. At the end of the course, the class teacher and the headmaster of the school draw up a report on the student teacher whom they have had in their charge; marks are given for each course.

Student teachers usually take a keen interest in these practical training courses and prepare their lessons with great care; they are anxious to collect information and to apply the advice given them, to experiment with new methods and master those which have already proved effective.

Studies carried out at college during the years of professional training, although intended to improve students' general education, are particularly designed to prepare them for the teaching profession; hence the importance attached to child psychology, knowledge of educational theories and methods, and information on the development of educational institutions and current achievements in France and abroad.

The scope of the training given to student teachers is further broadened by the attention given to social conditions and by bringing students into personal contact with workers and all those who, in various capacities, have to do with children; visits are organized to workshops, laboratories, hospitals, day-nurseries and co-operative shops. Students are given every opportunity to go to plays and lectures and visit exhibitions in the town in which they are residing and elsewhere. Travel is arranged for them, in France or abroad. In encouraging such activities, principals are helped by the arrangement of the syllabus. In accordance with the official regulations governing the activities of professional training classes, studies are spaced out over two years. When the course has to be reduced to one year, the principal, in consultation with the teachers' committee, proposes a revised syllabus to the divisional director of education.

The professional training curricula[1] appear to be extremely full, but it is rather a question of drawing ideas from them than of trying to cover all their contents, particularly when the course is limited to one year, three months of which must be spent on practical teaching exercises.

The training college leaving certificate for which student teachers sit at the end of their professional training is awarded on marks obtained during the training period following the passing of the *baccalauréat* and at the final examination.

Marks obtained during training. Work and conduct: weighting factor 1. Practical teaching exercises: weighting factor 2. (Marking is done by the teachers' committee with the headmasters or headmistresses of the attached and demonstration schools.) General average of marks obtained in the various subjects: weighting factor 2. (In order to calculate this general average, the teachers' committee decides upon appropriate weighting factors for each subject, including physical training.)

Marks obtained at the final examination. For this examination, the board of examiners consists of the divisional inspector (chairman), the principal of the teachers' training college (vice-chairman), one or more primary inspectors, teachers of the professional training classes, and a small number of primary teachers, two of whom must be the headmasters or headmistresses of the attached and demonstration schools.

The tests set are as follows:

1. Essay on general pedagogy: weighting factor 2 (time allowed: 3 hours).
2. Essay on special pedagogy: weighting factor 2 (time allowed: 3 hours).

The subjects for these written papers are selected by a committee presided over by the divisional director of education and composed of the divisional inspectors, principals of teachers' training colleges, and one primary school inspector of the area.

3. Oral statement on professional ethics or school legislation or the history of education: weighting factor 1.
4. Oral statement on child psychology: account of observations or experiments: weighting factor 1.

For each of the above oral tests, candidates have a choice of two subjects and are allowed one hour for preparing their statements. Each statement must last at least a quarter of an hour and should show a candidate's ability to make a good and clear oral statement of facts; the candidate may afterwards be subjected to short questioning.

---

[1] Circular of 15 November 1947, reproduced in *Compulsory Education in France*, by Jean Debiesse, Paris, Unesco, 1950, pp. 123–35.

5. Questions on personal work accomplished during the training: weighting factor 1 (time allowed: 15 minutes).

The certificate is awarded to candidates who have obtained, for all the tests put together, the general average mark. Those who have obtained an average of at least 12, 14 or 16 marks are passed and noted as 'Fair', 'Good' or 'Very Good'. Holders of this certificate are exempted from the written and oral tests of the examination for the primary teachers' qualifying certificate, and have therefore only to take the practical tests.

'Personal work accomplished during the training' is a thesis on a subject selected by each student teacher in agreement with the teacher who will have given him guidance in such work throughout the year. Students are allowed great freedom in choosing their subjects; many of them show interest in current events, discoveries and inventions, problems of organized labour, or artistic and technical matters. They carry out individual research, which leads them to use libraries and museums, conduct enquiries, travel in order to obtain the necessary information, or correspond with people living at a distance. Considerable taste is often shown in the presentation and illustration of their work.

On the basis of the marks and distinctions entered on their college leaving certificate, student teachers are classified with a view to their appointment to primary teachers' posts vacant in the department. Student teachers who fail to secure the certificate are obliged, like auxiliary primary teachers (who have not studied at a teachers' training college), to take the written part of the examination for the primary teachers' qualifying certificate, which delays their appointment as teachers; but failure is rare except in a very small minority of cases.

ACTIVITIES DESIGNED TO HELP TEACHERS ALREADY IN EMPLOYMENT TO BRING THEIR KNOWLEDGE AND METHODS UP TO DATE

There is no profession in the world in which a man can go through the same movements and resort to the same expedients throughout his lifetime; technological progress, changes in the raw material on which he works, and the need to adjust production to the customers' requirements, all force him to make a constant effort to adapt himself to changing circumstances.

Teaching is more exacting in this respect than almost any other profession; teachers must be able to adapt themselves not only incessantly, but to a great many different things. Their teaching must be realistic, yet they must prepare for the future; they must base themselves on general principles, but discover how to vary their

163

application in countless different ways, so as to suit each individual child's personality.

Primary teachers cannot overlook trends of ideas and the progress of knowledge; techniques, like printing and films, which can be of assistance to them in school, may on the other hand undermine their teaching, as in the case of cinemas and theatres, the radio at home, and so forth. No views as to childhood, on new educational methods or ideas, should escape them.

Their keenness to keep themselves up to date and carry out experiments is intensified by their eager interest in everything, and because, being constantly in children's company, they have retained their desire to make new discoveries and their capacity to be struck by new facts and ideas. They are assisted by the authorities of the educational division, by professional or educational associations and by the output of publishing firms.

To enable them to improve their methods and broaden their culture, the administration has organized inspections, pedagogical conferences, training courses and school visits, and has set up the National Centre of Educational Documentation, as well as local educational libraries.

Functions of Inspectors

The primary teacher's immediate superior, who knows all about his work, family conditions and the people among whom he is teaching, is the primary school inspector. The latter is a former secondary school or primary school teacher who, in order to become an inspector, has had to pass a very difficult competitive examination, which was a test of his general education, knowledge of school legislation, and ability to form a valid judgment on the management of a class and the educational value of the lessons given. The same competitive examination serves for the recruitment of principals of teachers' training colleges and elementary school inspectors. There is a special competitive examination for women, by means of which female principals of teachers' training colleges and secondary and primary school teachers can become departmental inspectresses of nursery schools.

A primary school inspector heads a division comprising some 300 primary teachers. He visits them all at least once every two years, concentrating upon beginners or teachers who, for various reasons, have not been very successful. He is familiar with their activities in school and outside it, and with the attitudes of the townspeople towards them; he is in contact with municipalities, local personalities and parents' associations. He does not confine himself merely to judging a teacher's worth and giving him the mark he deserves. He weighs many factors, such as the efforts made, the results achieved and the working conditions. He encourages, gives advice, and draws attention to useful documentation and methods which have proved successful in other classes. He has a very definite influence on the pedagogical development of primary teachers who are anxious to improve in their profession.

Some countries have given up using the term 'inspector', on the ground that it may suggest a severe fault-finder or a somewhat implacable judge; and have substituted that of 'adviser'. Our inspectors and inspectresses encourage reflection as to methods, spread a knowledge of useful new departures, and show how work in schools can be made more effective. Their concern is to be constructive and creative rather than to concentrate on their purely administrative duties or to exercise harsh and nearly always discouraging supervision.

Pedagogical Conferences

These conferences, which were first started in 1837 and subsequently discontinued, were reinstituted in 1880 and reorganized in 1925. They are held at the beginning of the school year, under the chairmanship of the divisional director of education or, in his absence, the primary school inspector, and are attended by all the primary teachers in each *canton* (departmental district sub-division). They deal with theoretical and practical teaching questions. It is essential for all public primary school teachers to attend these conferences. The divisional director of education decides upon the number, date and place of the meetings. The ministerial circular of 5 June 1880 explains that: 'It is desirable that members of pedagogical conferences should consider questions mainly from the practical point of view. Educational problems too often give rise to vague declarations. Impractical plans, ambitious and empty theories have often impeded, rather than advanced, our progress. Our primary teachers must be convinced that the science of teaching is a positive science, based on experience. I should therefore like the practice of holding pedagogical conferences in schools themselves to be followed more generally; such conferences should consist of a real class in school, taken by a primary teacher in front of his colleagues, and followed by a discussion in which every teacher comments on points that he has noted. To pool daily school experiences, keep each other informed of small practical discoveries made in each class, and discuss, not learned systems, but real facts as they exist in primary schools—such is the true aim of these conferences, and the reason for their well-deserved popularity.'

The main topic for discussion at these autumn conferences is selected by the Minister and communicated to all teachers several months before the meeting.[1] Primary teachers thus have ample time to think about

---

[1] The following topics have been discussed at pedagogical conferences during the last few years: In 1947, 'The teaching of reading in primary schools. Traditional and new methods. Results

the subject and to forward their report and comments to the primary inspector. During the meeting, the inspector takes note of their recommendations concerning topics to be selected for the following years. together with their views, and in some cases their vote, on the inclusion of new works in the list of school textbooks to be used.

A special conference of teachers in nursery schools (kindergartens and classes for small children) is also held. The choice of subject is generally left to the departmental inspectress, who presides over the meeting. The topic selected bears on some particular aspect of nursery school teaching, such as knowledge of children from 2 to 6, or the social functions of nursery schools. When women primary teachers are thus gathered together, the opportunity is generally taken to show them exhibitions of practical work done.

Training Courses and Visits

There are other ways in which administrators can help teachers to improve their professional capabilities; for example, inspectors and inspectresses can organize, for their respective divisions, 'teachers' days' which, without partaking of the official nature of the autumn conferences, have a general cultural character and provide an opportunity for exchanges of views. Sometimes distinguished lecturers come to give talks, or debates are organized or visits to exhibitions, monuments, sites, etc. arranged.

It is not unusual for an inspector to arrange, for a newly appointed primary teacher, a training course for a few days in a class that the inspector knows is well taught; or he may take a group of teachers to visit demonstration classes or schools whose equipment and methods can serve as examples.

There are also specialized training courses organized either by the administration or by the Centres d'Entrainement aux Méthodes d'Education Active (CEMEA) (Centres for Training in Active Educational Methods). These training courses are growing increasingly popular with young primary teachers; they enable them to discover in themselves unexpected gifts, and show them fields in which they might engage in specialization. Such courses last from eight to ten days, and are optional. There are, for example, courses in art education,

achieved during the school year 1946–47.' In 1948, 'Curricula and examinations in elementary primary schools. The ideas underlying them. Nature of each subject in the different courses. The resulting pedagogical organization problems.' In 1949, 'The teaching of grammar: nomenclature, parsing, individual words, groups of words; syntax.' In 1950, (1) 'Results of surveys and experiments on grammar teaching conducted during the school year as a follow-up to the pedagogical conferences held in 1949. Progress made in grammar teaching in primary schools'; (2) 'Educational and pedagogical advantages of co-operation in school.' In 1951, 'Teaching pupils to express themselves both orally and in writing. Appropriate exercises: reading, writing, speaking. Part played by grammar in adding to the value of language and style.' In 1952, 'Written expression: composition exercises.'

plastic arts, singing, pipe-playing, puppets, and folk crafts; courses in active methods; courses for public libraries; courses in the study of environment and in out-door manual work; courses in the methods of obtaining and using educational films; physical training courses.

The National Centre for Educational Documentation: the Educational Museum and its Library

In 1817, the writer Marc-Antoine Jullien de Paris, the forerunner of comparative education,[1] recommended the creation of a special commission on education 'composed of men responsible for assembling, by their own means and through carefully chosen correspondents, material for a general work containing comparative data on the educational establishments and teaching methods of the various European countries'. The first attempt to carry out this recommendation was made in 1879, when the Educational Museum was established by the decree of 17 May of that year. This museum, which was modified in 1903, 1936 and again in 1950,[2] is now known as the National Centre for Educational Documentation.

The National Centre for Educational Documentation serves various purposes: it is a repository for documentation, an information and research centre, and a liaison agency; it also supplies educational equipment. Its aims and resources are as follows:

1. It encourages educational research and the improvement of teaching methods by facilitating comparisons of experiments, the diffusion of information on educational activities in France and abroad, and the trying out of new teaching and educational techniques and methods.

2. It assists secondary and primary school teachers in their studies (preparation for tests and competitive examinations for university appointments), teaching (preparation of courses, classes, and lectures for students who have left school), research and practical work, and the improvement of their general culture (by supplying them with equipment such as books, gramophone records, films, etc., organizing exchanges of information, and encouraging intellectual and practical co-operation among teachers).

3. It supplies primary teachers and parents with information on schools and careers, in order to ensure more effective educational and vocational guidance for young people; it organizes educational and professional training by means of correspondence and radio

1 *La Pédagogie Comparée—Un Précurseur: Marc-Antoine Jullien de Paris* (Comparative Education—A Forerunner: Marc-Antoine Jullien de Paris), Paris (13, rue du Four), S.E.V.P.E.N., and *Forerunners of the International Bureau of Education*, by P. Rossello, London (Russell Square), Evans Bros. Ltd., 1944, pp. 11–19.
2 Order of 7 October 1950.

courses; and it furthers the operation and development of supplementary out-of-school projects.

For these purposes the centre brings together official services and private groups or associations of teachers or people interested in education, who are allowed to hold their meetings at the Educational Museum and co-operate in its activities.

At present, it is still the museum's task to preserve, classify and exhibit objects, works and documents useful to teachers (specimens of school furniture, teaching materials, work done by selected pupils, etc.). It is not only an educational museum, but a centre for education, pedagogical research and primary teachers' training. It presents exhibitions of objects or documents characteristic of university and other intellectual activities in France and other countries. After being shown in Paris, these exhibitions are usually transported to the principal towns of various educational divisions, and then to foreign capitals. The museum was responsible for preparing, in its own building, the first International Exhibition on Education, organized by Unesco. It is also responsible for renewing and maintaining the French stand in the International Exhibition on Public Education at Geneva.[1]

The centre's library has an educational section equipped with 200,000 volumes and 2,000 collections of French and foreign periodicals; it lends or sends them free of charge to all teachers employed in public schools, and to school and teachers' libraries.

The centre also has a film library and a record library, and a service for the study and production of audio-visual aids.

In some educational divisions, regional educational documentation centres, operating under the authority of the divisional director of education, fulfil the same functions, at the regional level, as the museum in Paris.

In addition, in every department and primary education division there are teachers' libraries, which supply primary teachers with the books and publications that they need for their general culture. There is no postal charge for books or documents circulating between the library and the localities where the teachers reside.

Professional Associations

Teachers' associations make it their task to protect the moral and material interests of their members, to ensure the pooling of their professional experience, and to seek for ways of improving educational methods.

For example, in each departmental branch of the National Primary Teachers' Union there is a pedagogical committee that studies methods,

---

[1] At the headquarters of the International Bureau of Education at Geneva.

issues recommendations, collects bibliography, shows films and col-
laborates with the administration in preparing curricula. This trade
union publishes a lengthy weekly review entitled *L'École Libératrice*
(Freedom through Schools); in it a great deal of space is devoted to
children's problems and educational information of all kinds, broad in
scope and regularly kept up to date.

The General Teachers' Union, affiliated to the Confederation of
Christian Workers, publishes a fortnightly bulletin entitled *École et
Education* (Schools and Education), dealing mainly with cultural
questions, school legislation and matters of interest to teachers.

The Association of Women Primary Teachers in Nursery Schools,
the Association of Primary Teachers in Attached and Demonstration
Schools, the Association of Public School Headmasters and Headmistresses and the French section of the World Organization for Early
Childhood Education—to name only a few such bodies—include in
their publications information relevant to their own fields and likely
to help their members to improve their professional capabilities.

Primary teachers of all categories belong to other organizations
whose principal aim is to bring about a better knowledge of children
and of educational methods and techniques. Among such organizations
are the French section of the New Education Fellowship, which counts
among its members secondary school teachers in private and public
schools, psychologists and parents; the French Pedagogical Society;
and the French Modern School, founded by C. Freinet, a primary
teacher who played an important part in helping to introduce into the
schools methods of printing, free composition, individual work and the
classification of information on index-cards.

Publications

Publishing firms interested in education not only publish handbooks,
which are often excellent and are constantly brought up to date, or
produce teaching materials; many of them also publish educational
works which are extremely useful to serving teachers.

The list of these works gives an idea of France's richness in educational publications. From the standpoint of the quality of the paper
and the number of photographs they contain, they would probably
fall below the publications of wealthier countries. However, one
cannot fail to be struck by the variety and current interest of the
problems dealt with and by the accuracy of the information, continuously brought up to date and admirably adapted to school needs.
Most of these publications make a considerable contribution to the
improvement of teachers' professional capabilities.

The Ministry of Education itself provides primary teachers with
educational information and discussion matter and encourages them

to collaborate as closely as possible with it, by means of a supplement to its weekly review *L'Education Nationale* (National Education) which it publishes under the title of *L'Ecole Publique* (Public Schools).

TRAINING OF PRIVATE PRIMARY SCHOOL TEACHERS

As distinct from the public schools, the law of 30 October 1886 recognized the existence of private schools, founded and maintained by private individuals or associations.

Wherever there are normally at least three children, belonging to two different families, gathered together for instruction, that constitutes a school. Day-nurseries, crèches, sewing, etc. workrooms, church clubs and orphanages are not regarded as schools, unless one of the courses of instruction included in the elementary school curriculum is given there.

As in the case of public education, the law recognizes the existence of nursery schools, elementary schools and continuation courses. It defines the status of private primary school teachers, whose pupils, while they may take private school examinations, are obliged to take State examinations if they wish to obtain the certificates and rights which these latter examinations confer. Thus private education is organized more or less on public school lines, but is completely in-dependent from the teaching point of view. For reasons of public security which can easily be imagined, the national education author-ities exercise supervision over private schools, but only as regards morals, health, sanitation and the discharging of the obligations laid upon them by the law. The actual education provided in such schools is supervised only with a view to ensuring that it is not contrary to good morals, the Constitution and the laws.

Private primary school pupils attend—in descending order of num-bers—elementary schools, nursery schools (these have greatly decreased in number since before the war), and continuation courses (attended by scarcely 10 per cent of the total number of pupils). For a long time now, the number of primary schools has varied little. The number of pupils has also remained relatively stationary, being generally about 900,000 (the only time it rose to over a million was during the last years of the Occupation). This figure shows the importance of private primary education; indeed in some areas (Ille-et-Vilaine, Loire-Infé-rieure, Maine-et-Loire, Mayenne, Vendée and, generally speaking, all the western departments), the number of children attending private schools exceeds that of those in public schools.

There are in France private denominational schools (Roman Catho-lic, Protestant and Jewish) and private secular schools. The majority of them are Roman Catholic schools, maintained by associations; there are, however, also undenominational schools, run by individuals, and usually these are boarding-schools.

Teachers in Roman Catholic schools may be either lay or religious. Under the law of 1901, teaching by members of religious orders was subject to prior authorization by the Ministry of Education; then, under the law of 7 July 1904, such teaching was forbidden altogether and a time-limit of 10 years was laid down for the complete enforcement of this measure. However, the 1914 war, special measures involved by the return to France of Alsace-Lorraine and, at a later period, the policy of the Vichy Government, caused full implementation of the prohibition to be deferred.

The principal teaching orders are the Brethren of the Christian Doctrine (authorized by Napoleon I) and a few others authorized by Louis XVIII or Charles X (Brethren of St. Gabriel), whose training centre is at St. Laurent-sur-Sèvre in the Vendée; the Marist Brethren of Bordeaux; the Ploërmel Brethren; the Brethren of the Sacred Heart at Paradis-lès-le-Puy, and the Brethren of St. Viateur, at Les Ternes (Cantal).

By reason of their well-defined aim and the hierarchy upon which they depend, Roman Catholic schools present a certain uniformity and show an increasing tendency to build up a body of teachers, together with a sincere desire to provide proper training for primary teachers. However, such training is neither centralized nor standardized; there are variations, contingent upon the nature of the staff (secular or members of religious orders), the diocese to which the schools belong, and the different approaches to the problem of education. One finds survivals of the past, but also schools that experiment with new educational methods and conduct child psychology tests.

Among the various forms of primary teacher training, there are teachers' training colleges, teachers' training sections in other establishments, institutions for the training of women educators, pedagogical institutes and centres for the study of educational theory.

Teachers' training colleges have been established in some dioceses and student teachers are sometimes recruited from more than one diocese. We may mention, for example, the colleges in the departments of the Rhône, the Aveyron, the Vendée, the Sarthe, the Maine-et-Loire and the Loiret.

Where it has been impossible to open an establishment purely for teacher training, there are often teachers' training sections annexed to full-time secondary schools. This is the case in the Seine, the Indre-et-Loire, the Bouches-du-Rhône, the Mayenne, the Loire-Inférieure, the Seine-et-Oise, etc. Most of the classes here are followed by all the pupils in the school, but students in the teachers' training section receive additional instruction (especially in educational psychology and applied psychology), and do a course of practical teaching exercises in primary schools.

Women educators intending to teach children under compulsory school age are trained in colleges or by means of special courses that are identified by the name of *écoles normales sociales* (social teachers' training colleges) or *écoles d'éducatrices* (colleges for women educators). The social teachers' training colleges have set up an association which awards a certificate for teachers in private nursery schools.[1]

In large towns such as Paris, Lyons, Lille, Strasbourg, Marseilles and Rouen, there are private courses for women teachers in kindergartens. Those who obtain their certificates at the end of these courses can serve both in kindergartens annexed to private schools and in those attached to industrial or commercial establishments.

The College for Women Educators in Paris, which is under the authority of the *Centre d'études pédagogiques* (Centre for Educational Research), trains women to teach children from 3 to 10 years of age. The studies cover two years and consist of: (a) four afternoons a week of practical teaching experience with the children, a weekly course of training in physical education, eurythmics and educational games; (b) five classes a week: general principles of teaching and teaching methods; didactics (ages 3 to 10 years); physical training (lesson and personal training); general culture focused on the science of teaching; arts and handicrafts (modelling, painting, cutting-out); (c) weekly report on practical experience; (d) one month's training course in a holiday camp or children's village.

The conditions for admission are the following: minimum age 18 years; a satisfactory standard of general education, with possession, if possible, of the *baccalauréat* (only teachers holding this certificate or the lower certificate may teach children of over 6 years of age); and the payment of educational fees amounting to 30,000 francs a year. Lastly, candidates must produce good references and, if possible, should take a short trial course at the college before their enrolment.

Teachers in Roman Catholic schools who are members of religious orders are trained in the educational institutes and colleges of their respective orders (theological colleges and noviciates' training colleges); in some cases, several diocesan orders arrange for their recruits to take their teachers' training course together. After a few years' service in the teaching profession, young members of religious orders generally come back to the training college to take a third-year course there.

Private teachers' training colleges do not issue a certificate at the end of the course; but there is a private teachers' qualifying certificate, which is a *sine qua non* for establishment, and all primary teachers

---

[1] There is no official certificate for those teaching in this field; women primary teachers serving in nursery schools and kindergartens are on the same roll as all other primary teachers.

wishing to do so may also sit for the public primary teachers' qualifying certificate.

Students in private teachers' training colleges are usually boarders. Their expenses may be borne by their parents, or they may be awarded scholarships by the diocesan director of private schools; in the latter case, parents are required to pay the family allowances which they obtain in respect of the students. Scholarship holders have to sign a contract with the diocese, pledging themselves to serve in its schools for a certain number of years.

Young primary teachers who are not recruited from teachers' training colleges or sections can take a professional training course while they are actually serving as teachers. They are placed in the charge of experienced men or women principals and must follow the training course under the supervision of the diocesan director of education and diocesan inspectors. The course may consist of classes on Thurdays or of lessons by correspondence; such instruction is supplemented by educational 'days' organized at the district level, or diocesan 'days' for teachers.

The tests for the teacher's qualifying certificate are the following:
1. In the first year, three exercises during the year (one each term) and a written examination at the end of the year, which qualify the student who has also obtained satisfactory marks from the inspectors and for regular attendance to take the second year of the course;
2. In the second year, three written exercises and a written examination which, if the requisite number of marks is obtained, qualify the student to take the pedagogical examination in the candidate's class before a board of examiners (composed of the director of education, an inspector and the principal of a training college), as well as the oral examination.

Finally, holiday training courses, usually lasting one week, are arranged for teachers. They may be planned on the diocesan, inter-diocesan or, as in the case of those organized by the 'Christian Teachers', on the national level.

To whatever level of education they belong, primary teachers wishing to improve their general culture may, if they have enough spare time, study further at the pedagogical institutes attached to the five Roman Catholic Institutes in Paris, Lyons, Lille, Angers and Toulouse, or at the Paris Centre for Educational Research. The centre collects useful national and international documentation and compares results achieved; also, with a view to facilitating the work of all teachers' training colleges, it disseminates studies and research carried out by specialists. The centre publishes a monthly review entitled *Education*. It has its own primary teachers' training school and demonstration school, and organizes courses for secondary and primary teachers.

CHAPTER III

PROFESSIONAL STATUS OF PRIMARY TEACHERS

STATUS OF PUBLIC PRIMARY SCHOOL TEACHERS

ORGANIZATION OF PRIMARY EDUCATION

The public primary school teacher is a civil servant or, in other words, the holder of a permanent post in the government service, occupying a recognized place in the hierarchy of a central government department.

The French civil servant is subject to the following conditions: He must be a Frenchman and entitled to exercise his civil rights. He must have fulfilled his obligations under the laws relating to service in the army.

He must be physically fit for his position.

Deductions are made from his salary for pension purposes.

He is forbidden to engage in any other form of paid activity.

Officials in certain posts, particularly those employed in the education service, are prohibited from holding certain other posts.

Civil servants may engage in trade union activities.

Primary teachers, like all other civil servants, are subject to the provisions relating to the status of the public service, laid down in the law of 19 October 1946. The provisions governing their particular status may, subject to the views of the Higher Council for the Public Service, differ from certain provisions relating to the status of civil servants in general which are incompatible with the special requirements of their work. At present, these special provisions are still under consideration.

The regulations governing the organization of the teaching profession define the respective functions of the administrative authorities and the councils with which the staff are associated.

The Administrative Authorities

The authorities exercising control over primary teachers may be listed as follows, in descending order of administrative seniority:
(a) The Minister of Education.

(b) The Director-General of Primary Education, in the Ministry, who, in co-operation with the Higher Council for Education and the Council for Primary Education, prepares the laws, decrees and departmental orders governing public and private education and submits them to the Minister for approval, lays down provisions concerning the running of the schools and the position of the teachers, and publishes those provisions in his executive circulars. Nearly 160,000 public primary school teachers come under his control, through the divisional inspectors (inspecteurs d'académie).

(c) The inspectors-general of primary education (eight of them inspect elementary schools and continuation courses—*cours complémentaires*) and the inspectresses-general of nursery schools (six in number) who are responsible for general inspection under the authority of the director-general of primary education. Each of them is allotted each year an inspector's district (circonscription d'inspection générale), which is both a geographical and an administrative division of the country.

(d) The divisional director of education (recteur d'académie), who at the divisional level is in charge of all types of education and may inspect all educational establishments. He appoints student teachers and approves their promotion from one grade to the next. Since 1945, he has, on the proposal of the divisional inspector, appointed established primary teachers and teachers employed in continuation courses.[1]

(e) The divisional inspectors. Each divisional inspector resides in the chief town of his department and is in charge of all that department's educational services. He is entitled to inspect all the educational establishments coming under his control; he appoints replacement teachers, probationers and temporary teachers; he makes proposals to the divisional director regarding the appointment and transfer of primary teachers and serious disciplinary measures against them. He may himself reprimand, censure or temporarily suspend teachers. He is the vice-chairman of the departmental council, and chairman of the Joint Administrative Commission and the Joint Technical Committee. He considers plans for school building and appoints the boards to examine candidates for the teacher's qualifying certificate (*certificat d'aptitude pédagogique*).

(f) The primary school inspectors and the departmental inspectresses of nursery schools, who inspect both public and private schools in their districts. They assess the work and the merits of public primary teachers and advise on appointments, transfers, awards for good service, or disciplinary action. They approve the educational

---

1 Previously such appointments were made by the Prefect, as the representative of the Government.

arrangements in force in the schools and act as chairmen of the boards of examiners for the teacher's qualifying certificate and the primary school-leaving certificate.

The foregoing are the administrative superiors controlling public primary school teachers at the national, regional, departmental and local levels.

Besides these administrative officials, whose powers are clearly defined and whose authority has behind it the prestige of a long-established tradition, there are various councils, some set up long ago and others more recently created.

Primary Education Councils

Under the Fourth Republic, a number of new councils have, as a consequence of the new provisions regarding the status of civil servants, been set up in addition to those already in existence. The provisions in question recognize the following general principle: at the various levels of the administrative hierarchy and on all important questions, the administrative authorities consult what are known as joint assemblies, half of whose members are elected representatives of the staff and half representatives appointed by the administration. Some of these (joint administrative commissions) deal with staff questions and others (joint technical committees) with technical matters. The following list shows the organization of these assemblies.

In Paris. The Higher Council for Education, established by the law of 27 February 1880, which was amended in 1933 and 1946, has the Minister as its chairman and includes *ex officio* members, members appointed by ministerial decree, and elected members (including representatives of public and representatives of private primary schools). The Higher Council holds ordinary sessions twice a year, and the Minister may convene extraordinary sessions. It is the highest national authority in matters relating to curricula, teaching methods, the organization of examinations, and the approval or proscription of school textbooks; it also has various functions connected with discipline, legal questions and matters for arbitration.

The Council for Primary Education established by the law of 18 May 1946 and consisting of the director-general of primary education and the director of education for the department of the Seine, nine members appointed by the Minister and 21 delegates of all types of teachers, advises on all questions relating to primary education.

The functions of the National Joint Commission and the National Joint Technical Committees will be defined only when the special provisions governing the status of primary teachers are published.

At the Departmental Level. There is a similar association of an old assembly with new assemblies.

The Departmental Council, set up by the law of 30 October 1886, which was amended by the law of 14 July 1901, has played a complex and important part ever since the public educational system was begun. Its chairman is the Prefect, and its membership consists of the divisional inspector of education (vice-chairman), the principals of the training colleges for men and women teachers, two primary school inspectors appointed by the Minister, four members of the general council (a departmental assembly elected by universal suffrage) elected by their colleagues and two men and two women public primary school teachers elected by their colleagues, and two private primary school teachers (men or women) likewise elected by their colleagues.

As the Prefect is the chairman of the Departmental Council, and as its membership includes representatives of the general council and of private schools, its competence is wider than that of the purely professional assemblies. Its decisions therefore carry great weight in all matters concerning the municipalities and the administration of private schools.

The functions of the Departmental Council cover educational and administrative questions (it draws up the lists of the men and women primary teachers who are to be established or promoted, and periodically reviews the distribution of schools throughout the department), as well as disciplinary, legal and arbitration matters.

The Departmental Joint Administrative Commission, established by the law of 18 May 1946, consists of: the divisional inspector of education (chairman), the principal of either the men's or the women's training college for teachers, three primary school inspectors and five representatives of serving teachers.[1]

Pending the fixing of the special status of teachers, it remains, like the Departmental Joint Technical Committee, an informal advisory body: even as it is, however, it exercises a very definite influence, and its decisions pave the way for those of the Departmental Council. But it has not taken the latter's place, and cannot legally do so. Only the Departmental Council, by virtue of its broader membership, is competent to deal with certain questions, such as those relating to the duties of municipalities with regard to the allowance payable in lieu of living accommodation.

The Rating Schedule. The joint administrative commission is particularly concerned with questions of promotion and transfer. A ministerial circular of 22 May 1946 requested the divisional inspectors of education to draw up, in co-operation with the advisory committee (now replaced

---

[1] In the Department of the Seine, the membership is larger.

by the joint administrative commission), a schedule for the purpose of comparing the merits of the various candidates for promotion or transfer. The 'schedule' is the name given to a method of candidate classification based on the award of marks representing a wide variety of factors: professional competence, seniority, family responsibilities, university degrees, etc. After multiplication, where necessary, by a suitable weighting factor, these marks are added together to give the rating in the schedule.

As a guide, the ministerial circular gave a specimen schedule in which the mark for professional competence, ranging from 0 to 20, was given a weighting factor of two.

The mark for seniority was calculated on the basis of one point a year for the first 10 years and half a point a year for the next 20 years—maximum: 20 points.

Under family responsibilities, one point was allotted for each child, with a maximum of five points.

One point was also allotted for each year that a husband and wife had been obliged to live apart, with a maximum of five points.

Graduates of a teachers' training college were awarded two points.

Those holding the higher certificate (*brevet supérieur*) or secondary school leaving certificate (*baccalauréat*) were awarded two points.

Lastly, service in positions involving special difficulties (isolation, poor communications, dilapidated school buildings, keen competition from private schools, etc.) might also entitle a candidate to the award of a maximum of five additional points.

Slightly different calculations, in which the mark for professional competence was given more weight, were used to draw up the schedule for teachers in continuation courses and for headmasters and headmistresses.

Schedules, differing in greater or less degree from the specimen given above, have been drawn up in each department, and are used in preparing recommendations for promotion or transfer for submission to the departmental council and the divisional director of education.

A staff council operates in all schools in which there are several classes. Its functions were defined in a ministerial circular of 15 January 1908. It is responsible for drawing up rules for the internal administration of the school, in conformity with the regulations laid down by the departmental council; for dividing the pupils among the classes and deciding which teacher shall take which class; for forming opinions on the conduct and behaviour of the pupils and, where necessary, for taking disciplinary action. The council has certain educational responsibilities in such matters as the choice of textbooks and teaching methods, and the co-ordination of time-tables and of the application of curricula.

POSITION OF PRIMARY TEACHERS

The teaching profession, like the rest of the public service, is subject to definite regulations concerning establishment, promotion, salaries, pensions, leave, etc.

A Teacher's Career

Let us take the case of a young teacher leaving his training college and embarking on his career (what applies to him applies equally to a young woman teacher, as there is complete equality of rights between men and women in the teaching profession).

He will be appointed to a post prior to the beginning of the school year in October, and outgoing students of the teachers' training colleges take precedence over any other non-established teachers. The new teacher will serve for three months as a probationer in the post to which he has been assigned and, before the end of December, will take the practical tests for the teacher's qualifying certificate (*certificat d'aptitude pédagogique*), which involve his taking a class for three hours (including lessons in physical training and singing) before a committee of three, consisting of the inspector of primary education (chairman), assisted by a headmaster and a secondary teacher or an experienced primary teacher; after this, he has to reply to questions about school administration.

Promotion

He will be established on the following 1 January and, from that time on, will be eligible for regular promotion in his profession. His salary will improve each time he moves from one grade to another, there being six 'classified' grades and a higher 'unclassified' grade of teachers. He will remain four years in the sixth and fifth grades and five years in the fourth, third and second grades if his career follows the normal course. If he proves to be of exceptional ability, he will be eligible for 'selective promotion' which will reduce his time in each grade by one year, or even for 'preferential promotion' which will reduce his time in the fourth, third or second grades to three years. Admission to the 'unclassified' grade is always by selection, generally after five years' service in the first grade.

Selective promotion, though the most substantial, is not the only advantage for which the best primary teachers are eligible; they may also be awarded distinctions and honours. The distinctions open to them are honourable mention, the bronze medal and the silver medal. The honours are the title of *Officier d'Académie* or *Officier de l'Instruction Publique*, with the insignia of the *palmes académiques*.

Administrative measures may be taken against a primary teacher who fails in his duties. The person concerned must be informed of such action and is entitled to ask to see his file; he may present a defence to the departmental council, the Minister or the higher council, as appropriate. The administrative measures in question are:

1. Disciplinary measures: deferment of promotion by seniority for one year; compulsory transfer; temporary suspension.
2. Disciplinary penalties: reprimand by the divisional inspector of education; censure by the divisional inspector of education, after consultation with the departmental council; reduction to a lower grade or post, on the authority of the divisional director of education; suspension without pay for a maximum of one year, on the authority of the divisional director of education; dismissal on the authority of the divisional director of education (a teacher against whom such action is taken may appeal to the Minister); prohibition from teaching for a time or for life, on a decision of the departmental council.

Transfers are another important feature in the professional life of a primary teacher. There may be many things to make one post more desirable than another, such as the size of the school, the amenities of the locality or the accommodation and opportunities for family life (especially for the education of children). On the other hand, places badly served by communications or without any particular advantages attract no applicants and are generally allotted to beginners.

Proposals regarding transfers are prepared by the divisional inspector of education in consultation with the joint commission for primary education. In the framing of the proposals, account is taken of professional competence, qualifications and family responsibilities, all of which are numerically rated in a table from which arithmetical comparisons can be made. The decision rests with the divisional director of education.

Departmental Organization

In most cases, a primary teacher spends his whole life in the same department. He is regarded as a member of the staff of that department from the time he enters the teachers' training college; in order to leave it to serve in another department, he is required to apply for an *exeat* (acceptance by the divisional inspector of education of the department to which he wishes to move, and authorization by his official superior to leave his original department). There are special regulations regarding admission to the Department of the Seine, to which many teachers (particularly women teachers) are attracted, very often so that husband and wife can live together.

It is well to emphasize the importance of the departmental form of organization. It helps to moderate the rigid uniformity which might result from the centralization of the French administrative system. At his training college the prospective teacher has been prepared for work in a particular part of France, and equipped to deal with the needs of a town or country population or of people living by the sea or in the mountains. In the demonstration classes which he has attended, he has seen how school work is adapted to the type of country and type of people characteristic of that particular locality. His training is not standardized, but is adjusted to living conditions in the place where he will have to work.

The divisonal inspector of education, who is in charge of all the department's primary teachers, may have anything from 1,200 to 1,500 teachers under him. If he spends a fairly long time in the same place, he gets to know the teachers in his district and is acquainted with their merits, any original work they have done, and their past history in the profession. He can judge whether they are suitable for a particular post, and can thus avoid serious errors. The departmental form of organization makes it possible for there to be a certain measure of elasticity that takes the individual human factor into account and prevents it from being thought that all posts of the same nature can be filled by any and every official of the same status.

The departmental form of organization may have the disadvantage of separating the teaching profession into compartments, so that some departments (Seine, Bouches-du-Rhône and those in the Pyrénées) have too many teachers while others (Vendée, Manche and Nord) cannot recruit enough. Where there are too many teachers, it is not always possible for temporary teachers to achieve established status as soon as they normally should.

Salaries

The teaching profession was for a long time one of the least remunerative in France. Security was good and promotion regular, but the pay was not high. The public authorities were disturbed by the recruitment crisis which became acute immediately after the war, and agreed to the principle of a reclassification of the teaching profession; a scale of indices was drawn up which improved the position of teachers in relation to that of other public officials and of people in the private professions. Budgetary difficulties were later brought up and have delayed the full implementation of the promises made in 1948. The following table shows the present indices and corresponding basic salaries in francs:[1]

---

[1] Exchange rate: U.S. $1 = 350 French francs.

TABLE 3. Indices and basic salaries

Grade	Index	Basic Annual Salary
Probationers	185	299 000
Grade 6	218	360 000
Grade 5	240	403 000
Grade 4	262	446 000
Grade 3	284	490 000
Grade 2	306	533 000
Grade 1	328	576 000
Unclassified	360	640 000

One-twelfth of the salary is payable at the end of each month, with a deduction of six per cent for pension purposes and a further deduction for social security.

These indices put the primary teacher, from the salary point of view, on a level with *secrétaires d'administration* in a Ministry, *rédacteurs* in a Prefecture, and army officers of the rank of sub-lieutenant to captain.

The annual salary may be increased by various allowances attaching to the post occupied, the place of residence, or family responsibilities—such as allowances for administrative responsibilities, service in continuation classes, demonstration classes or schools attached to training colleges; residence allowances, varying according to the 'salary zone' in which the person concerned is serving; travel allowance in the Paris area; allowance for exceptionally difficult living conditions in certain regions which suffered particularly heavily during the war; and various family allowances (for cases where only one member of the family is earning, children's allowances, family housing allowances, etc.).

Finally, the municipality is obliged to provide its primary teachers with suitable living accommodation; if it is unable to do so, it pays them a housing allowance by way of compensation, the amount of which varies according to the locality. The factors entering into the fixing of these allowances are complex; account is taken of the post occupied (principal or assistant teacher) and of family responsibilities.

Pensions

Throughout his working life, a deduction of six per cent is made from an official's salary as a contribution to the pension fund.

Primary teachers may retire on pension at the age of 55, provided they have then been in service for 25 years. The age of retirement may be lowered for the mothers of families (at the rate of one year for each child, to a maximum of five years), for ex-service men, for teachers who have served outside Europe, and for people who have been invalided out of service.

The upper age-limit for retirement is 58; it may, however, be deferred for two years at the request of the person concerned, and for a maximum of three years if he still has dependent children to provide for.

The pension is 60 per cent of the salary payable to the grade to which the teacher belonged during his last six months in service. Various increases may also be payable, but the total must not exceed 75 per cent of salary. Such increases may be granted for years of service in excess of the regulation 25 years, for active military service, for service outside Europe and for children brought up to the age of 16.

The widow of a civil servant is entitled to half her husband's pension; a retired woman primary school teacher may add this half-pension to her own retirement pension. Orphans under the age of 21 may receive part of the pension which would have been payable to their father or mother.

A disability pension may be awarded by decision of a disability board.

Prohibitions on the Concurrent Exercise of Professions

All civil servants are prohibited from exercising any profession in commerce or industry, from occupying a salaried private post, from engaging in private work for payment (with the exception of literary, scientific or artistic creation) and from simultaneously occupying two salaried positions in the service of the State, a department or a commune.

Primary teachers are prohibited from holding paid or unpaid positions in the service of any religious denomination, from serving on a jury, and from holding any administrative post, even if unpaid, with the exception of the post of *secrétaire de mairie* (clerk to the local council) in a commune with less than 2,000 inhabitants.

Leave Entitlements of Teachers

These are, in principle, the same as those of other civil servants, i.e. sick leave, maternity leave, long leave and compassionate leave. Established teachers are entitled to three month's sick leave on full pay and three months on half pay during any period of 12 months. The total length of maternity leave is 14 weeks for established and replacement teachers. Teachers suffering from tuberculosis, cancer or mental illness are granted leave for successive periods of six months up to a total of three or five years, according to circumstances. Successive periods of compassionate leave, without pay, may be granted up to a maximum of three or five years, according to cases.

In addition, primary schools have a free day on Thursday as well as on Sundays; this free time is allowed in order to enable children to fulfil their religious duties without ill-effects on their school work.

The school holidays were fixed as follows by a ministerial order of 11 February 1939: 1, 2 and 11 November; 14 July; Christmas and New Year—from the evening of 23 December to 2 January inclusive; Shrove Tuesday—Sunday to Thursday inclusive, if Palm Sunday falls in April; if it does not, no leave is granted; Easter—a week before and a week after Easter Sunday; Whitsun—Sunday to Thursday inclusive, if there has been no holiday for Shrove Tuesday (Whit Monday and 1 May are always public holidays): Summer holiday—evening of 13 July to 30 September inclusive.

General Conditions of Teachers' Work

The teacher's work is regulated by the following provisions. He has a working week of 30 hours divided over five days—three hours in the morning and three in the afternoon. The syllabuses for each course are drawn up by the higher council for education and are published with instructions, which it is advisable for teachers to study carefully. The syllabuses and instructions at present in force are contained in the decree of 15 July 1921 for nursery schools, and in the ministerial orders of 17 October 1945 and 24 July 1947 for elementary schools. The divisional inspector of education, with the technical committee, may make adjustments to adapt the syllabuses to local conditions and to facilitate the work of teachers responsible for schools which have only one class.

The time-table and the subjects to be dealt with each month, as approved by the inspector of primary education or by the departmental inspectress of nursery schools, must be posted up in the class room.

At the end of the elementary primary school course, an examination is held for the primary leaving certificate (*certificat d'études primaires*), and is taken by children who will be 14 years old on 31 December of the year in which the examination takes place. This certificate, which is awarded to some 250,000 children each year, is highly valued by the people in general, particularly in country districts.

The teacher is left completely free to choose his own methods and textbooks, within the very broad limits of the approved list. The administrative authorities rely on his educational background, conscientiousness and personal gifts to enable him to choose efficient methods suitable for the type of class with which he is entrusted.

WOMEN AS MEMBERS OF THE TEACHING PROFESSION

The laws of France recognize full equality of rights as between men and women in the teaching profession. At one time, a woman primary or secondary teacher was paid a salary lower than that of a man doing similar work; since 1919, however, thanks in particular to the energetic action of the teachers' associations, this difference has been removed. Salaries, time-tables, leave entitlements and the certificates, etc. required are exactly the same for both sexes.

All types of posts in elementary schools are open to women. Posts in nursery schools or kindergartens are reserved for them. They are given preference in appointments to co-educational schools. In 1950, 15,131 of the 24,459 public co-educational schools had headmistresses. Women may hold important administrative posts in special schools for girls, and may serve as teachers or principals in continuation courses.

The regulations specify the cases in which a woman may work in a boys' school (when she is the wife, sister or a close relation of the head-master of the school) and the class to be placed in her charge (the preparatory class, taking children between the ages of 6 and 7). In certain circumstances, it may be necessary to appoint women to other posts normally reserved for men; for instance, if the masters in boys' schools are called up, they have to be replaced by auxiliary women teachers; and when economic conditions, as in the post-war period, attract men to more lucrative or more adventurous professions, they can generally be replaced fairly easily by women. A woman teacher in a boys' school is, however, always regarded as temporary and her position is insecure; as soon as circumstances permit, the authorities arrange for her to be replaced by a man teacher.

There are not, in fact, twice as many women as men in the primary schools. In 1950, out of a total of 158,603 primary teachers in France, 56,812 were men and 101,791 women. These figures are worth em-phasizing; in some countries, elementary teaching is regarded almost exclusively as a woman's province. Possibly because the salary seems poor in comparison with the opportunities available in industry and commerce, or because the lower salaries paid to women encourage local administrative authorities, for reasons of economy, to recruit women rather than men teachers, or again because it may be generally thought that the education of young children is not a suitable type of work for men, male staff is so rare that only administrative and direct-ing posts are given to men and, even so, not in all cases.

The French practice has definite advantages. It keeps a masculine influence in the profession, which often proves necessary when dealing with boys of 12, 14 or 16; it ensures a useful point of contact, in par-ticular with the country people, who are glad if the primary teacher makes a good clerk to the local council and knows something about agriculture; and it gives the teachers' associations more force. There is more chance of claims being pressed successfully when the negotiations are conducted by men teachers, who are more accustomed than women to political and trade union affairs. Whenever great things have been achieved or new advances made in the history of public education, men teachers have played a decisive part in building up the prestige and authority of the teaching profession, in educational and professional matters alike.

Married Women

Women are not obliged to give up their work when they marry and become mothers. This sometimes surprises nations that are against women remaining in the public service after their marriage. The French point of view is sympathetic to the individual and at the same time realistic. Why should a young woman who has spent years in studying, and who has a vocation for teaching, give up her work simply because she has embarked upon family life? It would involve both injustice and a waste of effort and ability to compel her to choose between her profession and her personal happiness. The additional expense which may be entailed by the need to employ replacement teachers during maternity leave is surely balanced—though in a sphere other than that of finance—by the increased affection for and understanding of children and adolescents that motherhood develops. A teacher who is also a mother of a family is surely likely to be one of the best people to educate children.

The French laws are particularly considerate towards a mother in the civil service. Their provisions allow for a total of 14 weeks' maternity leave, two weeks at least being taken before the date of confinement. Maternity leave is not counted in the sick leave to which a woman teacher is entitled; nor, incidentally, is leave for quarantine purposes.[1]

A 10 per cent increase in the retirement pension is awarded to mothers of families who have brought up three children to the age of 16; and the length of service necessary to qualify for the pension is reduced by one year, to a maximum of five, for each child a woman has had.

Lastly, a law of 30 December 1921, known as the *Loi Roustan*, makes it easier for a husband and wife residing in different departments to obtain posts in the same area. This law provides that 25 per cent of the vacancies in each department during a year shall be set aside for women living outside the department who are married to officials serving within the department or to persons who have been resident in the department for at least a year. This provision makes it possible to end the long separations which are sometimes unavoidable when husband and wife are both working. It may be added that the administrative authorities, whenever there is a suitable opportunity without detriment

---

[1] Women teachers whose children are suffering from a contagious disease are required, in the interests of the school, to stay away from work.

to the rights of any other official, offer a husband and wife who are both civil servants either two appointments in the same commune or two appointments in contiguous communes.

Husband and Wife both Teachers

The above provisions are of great help to a man and wife who are both teachers—a situation which deserves some further consideration, for it is quite commonly met with in French educational life. It often happens that similarity of background and way of living, and the fact that they are brought together in the course of their work, lead two young teachers to marry. One provincial department, for instance, has a total of 1,224 men and women teachers which includes 207 married couples. A man and wife who are both teaching in the same school often spend their youth, if not their whole life, in a country district. The needs of their own children's education and the desire to save them, if possible, from having to board may one day induce them to move closer to a town where there is a secondary school; but for several years they will have been associated with the life of a rural community. The husband often acts as secretary to the local council, which gives him added importance in the eyes of the municipal authorities. The wife may be able to advise the local girls and mothers and to bring the benefits of modern civilization to their homes. Both partners are able to explain the provisions of social and family legislation to workers and heads of families. A satisfactory standard of living, the prestige they enjoy, and their fondness for the village in which they have settled are all stabilizing factors in their life. They are in a position to exercise a deep and lasting influence on children and grown-ups alike. In some cases, a 'teaching' couple has been able to change the mentality of the people of a whole district, making them more aware of their civic responsibilities, more open to progress and more prosperous. Due recognition must be given to the part often played in the past, and still played today, in French country life by the respected and influential married couple teaching in the village school.

Co-education

'When a commune or a group of communes has a population of 500 or more, it shall be provided with at least one special school for girls, unless the departmental council gives authority for the establishment of a co-educational school in its place.'

At the request of the municipal council and subject to the agreement of the departmental council, the Minister may authorize the temporary conversion of girls' schools into co-educational schools with one or two classes.

As a general rule, the teachers employed in co-educational schools are women; but the departmental council may, as a temporary measure, authorize a man teacher to take charge of a co-educational school provided that he has the assistance of a woman teacher of sewing (law of 30 October 1886).

Co-education is still rather uncommon in French elementary schools. It is, of course, necessary in small communes with less than 500 inhabitants, and there may be co-educational schools in communes which have asked for such a school instead of two separate schools, for boys and girls; but the change is never regarded as very permanent. The co-educational system is unusual in the case of schools with three classes or more. Teachers are often in favour of a measure which makes it easier to organize teaching on more satisfactory lines and, where the experiment has been made, the population has generally been satisfied.

It may be mentioned, in conclusion, that France has already put into practice the measures for promoting educational opportunities for women suggested by the Fifteenth International Conference on Public Education (Geneva, July 1952) in its Recommendation No. 34 addressed to Ministries of Education.

SPECIALIZATION

Men and women teachers together constitute a homogeneous group, trained in the same colleges, subject to the same rules concerning recruitment and promotion, and accustomed to the same alternation of work and holidays. Keenly aware of its own unity, the primary teaching profession is quick to react to anything touching its honour as a whole, is proud of its unquestioned professional competence, and is anxious to maintain its high standards.

But this unity is not synonymous with uniformity; and anyone closely acquainted with the life of primary teachers is surprised at the diversity of activities and talents they display. Many teachers engage in local historical or archaeological research; others are keenly interested in scientific subjects, such as astronomy or mechanics; some of them are poets or novelists, painters or specialist photographers; and some contribute to periodicals or write school textbooks. The taste for further study leads many of them to think of specializing in their professional activities. What opportunities are open to them in such cases?

Nursery schools and kindergartens attract women teachers who are particularly interested in young children. They are not required to take any specialized course of study; the training they were originally given was as thorough as that of any of their colleagues. Though the methods they use are often different, their intellectual training has been quite as comprehensive. Teachers dealing with very young children are never regarded in France as occupying a secondary position, or as nurses rather than as teachers proper. Their own tastes and the requirements of their profession generally lead them to enquire specially into the psychology and health of young children, in which they are helped by the books and periodicals made available to them by the local branch of the Association of Nursery School Teachers, the material circulated by the World Organization for Early Childhood Education and the talks published by the organization known as the 'School for Parents'. They keep themselves informed of the methods used in France and abroad, and have made a very considerable contribution to the development and success of the so-called 'active' methods of education. Many of them devise educational materials and evolve ingenious methods of carrying out their work. Any woman teacher may be appointed an assistant in a nursery school if she applies for such a post and is regarded by her superiors as likely to succeed in this branch of education. For appointment as head of a nursery school, candidates must have served for five years in nursery schools or infants' classes.

At the other end of a child's school life there are the continuation courses in which children between the ages of 10 or 12 and 15 or 16 are given a short course of secondary education. In the age of their pupils and the standard of the subjects taught, they correspond more or less to what are known in other countries as 'intermediate schools' or 'junior high schools'. These schools are attached to primary schools and the teachers serving in them are chosen from among the primary teachers. Candidates for appointment to a continuation course must be at least 25 years old and must have been employed in an established post for not less than five years. A teacher who achieves good results in a continuation course may be confirmed in his position with the title of 'continuation course teacher' (*professeur de cours complémentaire*); he has a higher salary than other primary teachers (maximum index 400) and his weekly hours of work are reduced from 30 to 25. He must have a wide general knowledge and may specialize in the humanities, science or modern languages; he must also be interested in understanding adolescents and in the methods which are likely to prove successful in dealing with them.

The continuation course teachers also have their own association, which defends the interests of the profession and helps to extend the educational knowledge of its members, especially by means of their monthly bulletin.

Primary teachers may be particularly gifted for singing, drawing or physical education; they may then have the opportunity to specialize in such teaching wherever the district in which they work is large enough to allow of their dividing their time among a group of schools.

The Department of the Seine has developed a complete system of specialized appointments for domestic science, cutting-out and dress-making, tailoring, singing, handwork and technical subjects, geometrical and mechanical drawing, and free-hand drawing, all of which are open to primary teachers with special gifts or knowledge in these different branches.

Some teachers turn to the education of the deaf and dumb or the blind; to work in an institution of the 'approved school' type (*établissement d'éducation surveillée*); or to the teaching of general subjects in an apprenticeship school. They are then seconded from their original department and come under the control of the Ministry of Public Health, the Ministry of Justice or the Directorate of Technical Education, as the case may be.

Without ceasing to be considered as primary teachers, men and women may specialize in one of the forms of education provided for backward children, in work in open-air schools, or in agricultural instruction. All these offer opportunities of exercising special interests, earning higher salaries, and belonging to a national rather than a departmental establishment. Applicants for posts in these specialized branches of teaching are required to present the following qualifying certificates:

1. The qualifying certificate for the teaching of backward children (*certificat d'aptitude à l'enseignement des enfants arriérés*), which may be awarded to teachers who are at least 21 years old and can show that they have successfully completed a year's teaching in an adjustment class or have taken a special practical course. There are courses of training for this certificate at the education centre in Beaumont-sur-Oise and at the institute of Asnières. The examination covers elementary physiology, school health, psychology and education of dull and backward children.

2. The diploma for teaching in open-air schools (*certificat d'aptitude à l'enseignement dans les écoles de plein air*), which may be awarded to teachers who are at least 21 years old, hold the teacher's qualifying certificate and have served for a year in an open-air school. The examination, which includes written, oral and practical tests, requires a knowledge of psychology, educational theory, hygiene, physical education and singing. Courses of training for this diploma are being organized.

3. The teacher's diploma in agricultural instruction, which in the case of men teachers is known as the *certificat d'aptitude à l'enseignement post-scolaire agricole* (diploma in post-school agricultural instruction) and, in the case of women, as the *certificat d'aptitude à l'enseignement post-scolaire agricole-ménager* (diploma in post-school instruction in rural domestic science). This form of instruction is provided in special courses, seasonal schools and continuation courses, and is

compulsory for boys and girls between the ages of 14 and 17 who are not pursuing other courses of study and whose parents are engaged in agricultural work. Men and women teachers who wish to specialize in this branch may sit for the diploma on condition that they have served as established teachers for at least three years. The examination includes written papers and practical tests. That for men covers plant cultivation, animal husbandry, gardening, poultry-keeping and farming in general. That for women includes domestic hygiene and child-care in addition to agricultural subjects. Teachers holding these diplomas may be appointed travelling teachers, serving several communes.

Teaching in the elementary classes of secondary schools (*lycées* or *collèges*) is not regarded as specialization; teachers appointed to such classes belong to the same establishment as primary teachers serving in the local schools, are paid the same salaries, and have the same leave. Generally speaking, the only difference is in the type of children attending the two institutions.

PRIMARY TEACHERS' ASSOCIATIONS

The law of 19 October 1946, defining the status of public servants recognizes the right of teachers to engage in trade union activities.

Prior to 1946, there was in fact a trade union movement among teachers in the form of societies or associations for the defence of common interests. In 1924, the teachers' unions were recognized by the administration, and their representatives were later authorized to take part in the work of the departmental advisory commissions. It was not, however, until 1946 that the unions were given a status in law and that co-operation between the staff and the official sides ceased to be informal or to depend on the goodwill of the administrative authorities, and became legal and compulsory.

Primary teachers may be members of the National Primary Teachers' Union (Syndicat national des Instituteurs) or of the General Teachers' Union (Syndicat général de l'Enseignement).

The National Primary Teachers' Union (SNI)

This organization, which was the successor of the old departmental associations and of the first trade unions (against which proceedings were taken, in the early days, for illegality), was set up as a national union in 1920. The basis of the system is the departmental branch, which is regarded as a local union, is very active, and has a large measure of independence within the framework of the SNI's constitution. These branches reach their own decisions on the questions included in the agenda of the national councils or congresses; and put forward their nominees for positions on representative departmental bodies, such as the departmental council, the joint administrative commission and the joint technical committee.

The aims of the SNI are defined in its constitution as follows:

Article 1. A union is hereby established among the men and women teachers employed in the public primary schools and acceding to this constitution, under the title of Syndicat National des Institutrices et Instituteurs Publics de France et de l'Union Française (National Union of Men and Women Public Primary School Teachers in France and the French Union).

Article 2. The purposes of the union are:

(a) To draw closer the bonds of fellowship between its members.
(b) To work for their greater professional competence and for the improvement of educational and teaching methods and curricula.
(c) To protect the moral and material interests of primary teachers, both individually and collectively, in relation to public opinion, their official superiors, the public authorities and the courts.
(d) To defend the interests, both material and moral, of the secular school, and to work for its development and for the spread of its influence.
(e) To co-operate with organized labour in general.

The SNI occupies an important place in the French trade union movement. It is a unit in which the various tendencies of trade unionism—realist, revolutionary, or typical of the Confédération Générale du Travail—are all represented. It is an independent union; since the split of 1946, it has belonged neither to the Confédération Générale du Travail nor to Force Ouvrière, and its desire is that the workers as a whole should once more be united in a single movement.

The union is a member of the National Education Federation (Fédération de l'Education Nationale), which is also an independent organization and covers all unions of teachers in all types of school; the SNI is the largest body represented in the federation and carries great weight in it.

It maintains contact with international organizations and, in particular, with the International Federation of Teachers' Associations, in which Georges Lapierre (who died in Dachau during the war) played such an important part in the campaign carried on between the two world wars for the revision in all countries of textbooks of an aggressively nationalist character.

It also has contacts with the various international teachers' associations through the Joint Committee of International Teachers' Federations, which was founded in November 1948.

The national union at present has 143,500 members; in most cases the members rely on the union to represent them on the joint commissions and committees for which provision is made in the organization of the public service.

The union publishes a weekly review, *L'Ecole libératrice*, dealing with its activities in the interests of the profession and giving news and information on educational topics for the benefit of its members.

The union carries on a number of prosperous public works. These include co-operative undertakings such as the important SUDEL publishing business (Société Universitaire d'Edition et de Librairie), which brings out textbooks, background information on educational topics, and works on professional matters of interest to teachers; and undertakings for mutual benefit, such as the Mutuelle générale de l'Enseignement National (which administers social security for civil servants employed by the department of education and provides supplementary benefits, owning sanatoria, nursing, convalescent and rest homes and clinics) or the Mutuelle Assurance Automobile des Instituteurs de France (car insurance, fire insurance, purchasing co-operative, and mutual aid fund). Finally, the union works in consultation with the Ligue Française de l'Enseignement, both organizations being members of the Confédération Générale des Œuvres Laïques.

Syndicat Général de l'Education Nationale

This union was established in 1936 and is a member of the French Confederation of Christian Workers (Confédération Française des Travailleurs Chrétiens).

The aims set forth in its constitution include the following: the union states that, in its professional activities, it is guided by 'the academic tradition which declines to make the recruitment and promotion of teachers dependent upon acceptance of any state doctrine; ...the conviction that public education can help in training the citizens of the future by developing energies in the young which will be put freely at the service of the public weal, rather than by imposing any given doctrine upon young people.'

Realizing the bonds of fellowship between its members and other civil servants and wage-earners as a whole, which necessitate permanent contacts with organizations employing the same methods, the union fully supports the French Federation of Civil Servants' Unions and the French Confederation of Christian Workers. These affiliations in no way alter the principles guiding its professional activities set forth above.

The SGEN includes, in addition to primary teachers, teachers serving in all grades of school. At the departmental level, its organization includes separate branches for primary teachers, secondary teachers and technical teachers, each of which has its own officers and holds its own meetings. At least once a year a joint meeting takes place.

193

At the level of the educational division, the SGEN has a group of officers, who are elected annually at a divisional congress, and a divisional secretary elected by this group, and acting on behalf of all teachers employed in the public schools.

At the national level, there are national officers elected annually by the national committee, the latter being elected by the congress.

The SGEN is represented on the national committees and at the departmental union congresses of the French Confederation of Christian Workers. A representative of the SGEN is an elected member of the bureau of the confederation, in which he exercises a considerable influence.

The SGEN issues a fortnightly publication, *Ecole et Education;* in addition bulletins are published by branches in a number of educational divisions.

At the national and departmental levels, the SGEN makes use of all the services of the French Confederation of Christian Workers, such as training courses, leisure-time activities, co-operatives, etc. It remains entirely independent, however, in professional matters.

The SNI and the SGEN often take concerted action to secure improvement of the status of teachers.

STATUS OF PRIVATE PRIMARY SCHOOL TEACHERS

Teachers employed in private schools are subject to certain obligations laid down by law; they are also required to satisfy the conditions stipulated by the particular authorities under whose control they come and, in certain cases, to fulfil special obligations under the rules of the association or community which maintains the school.

The organization of private schools is not uniform throughout France. The secular private schools are linked up by a conference of the heads of secular private educational establishments (Chambre Syndicale des Chefs d'Institutions d'Enseignement Laïc Libre). For Catholic schools, there is a diocesan directorate of private education, corresponding to the system of divisional inspectors of education in the public schools. 'Christian teachers come under the authority of the Church. No school can call itself Christian if it has not been established or approved by the Church and is not under its supervision.'

'The bishop is thus the head of all teaching staff, whether secular, monastic or under the direction of religious orders, and teachers are required to receive his representatives and accept their instructions. From this point of view, it makes no difference whether a school has been founded or is run by the parish priest, by an association, by a single owner or by the teacher himself.

'In most dioceses, a diocesan director is responsible for the administration of Christian schools, which are supervised by an ecclesiastical or secular inspector; there are regulations laying down the duties of teaching staff.

'Parish priests always have both the right and the duty to visit Christian schools and supervise the intellectual and moral training of the pupils.'[1]

The conditions for employment laid down by the law are as follows:

Applicants must be of French nationality.

They must be at least 18 years old for appointment as a primary teacher, 21 years old for appointment as the head of a school, and 25 years old for appointment as the head of a boarding school.

They must hold a certificate qualifying them to teach in a primary school (*brevet élémentaire* or *brevet supérieur*), or the *baccalauréat* or *diplôme complémentaire d'études secondaires*.

They must undergo a medical examination.

They must not have been convicted for any crime or misdemeanour or any act contrary to public morals.

They must not have been deprived, by judicial decision, of all or any of the rights mentioned in article 42 of the Penal Code.

No absolute prohibition from teaching must have been pronounced against them.

They must not be either active ministers of religion (vicars, curates, etc.) or public primary school teachers.

Provision is made for inspection by the official authorities to secure observation of the regulations regarding health and hygiene and the moral conduct and qualifications of the teachers.

The teachers are subject to the provisions of a joint convention applying to each of the various grades of school. The director of education is not the contractual employer of the staff. The signatories to the contract are the teacher himself and the legal employer under the terms of the joint convention.

Appointments are made by engagement. The applicant must be approved by the diocesan director, after which the engagement is completed by an exchange of letters between the applicant and the authority responsible for the school. Letters of engagement must include:

The date on which the engagement takes effect.

The status of the teacher engaged (probationer or established teacher, assistant or head teacher).

---

[1] Laude, *Manuel Pratique des Ecoles Libres.*

Mention of the grade held, in the case of established teachers and head teachers.

The amount of salary and, where appropriate, allowances granted in money or in kind, possibly subject to charges during the year.

An undertaking by both parties, to observe the foregoing conditions regarding status, which the applicant must acknowledge having read.

Engagements are signed for one year, from 1 October to 30 September. They are subject to renewal by tacit agreement.

The salaries paid in Catholic private primary schools are fixed according to a regional or local scale; they must not be below the recognized basic wage. The low salaries paid to teachers in private schools have been cited as one of the main reasons in favour of grants-in-aid to private schools, and article 1 of the law of 28 September 1951 stipulates that the sums allocated to the funds of the parents' associations shall be used, as a matter of priority, to increase the salaries of teachers in private schools.

Salaries are payable in 12 instalments, at the end of each month. Remuneration in kind, such as accommodation, heating, lighting and gardens, may also be provided, and the value of such remuneration is taken into account in calculating the salary.

The lenght of time spent in class work is 30 hours a week: two further hours may be devoted to the general needs of the school and to the supervision of religious observances. Payment is made for extra time spent in teaching or in supervising study.

The provisions regarding sick leave and maternity leave are similar to those in force in the public schools. The disciplinary action which may be taken by the authority responsible for the school, at the request of the diocesan director, includes: written warning; reprimand; appearance before the disciplinary council; compulsory transfer; dismissal.

Promotion is by seniority or by selection. There are five grades and one 'unclassified' grade of established teacher, and teachers serve in each grade for five years. Transfers may be arranged where necessary or (where proper reasons are given) at the request of the person concerned. A husband and wife serving in the same district must always be transferred together.

The right of private school teachers to engage in trade union activities is recognized.

Several dioceses have already joined a pension scheme—organized by the General Institute of Pensions for Salaried Employees (Institut Général de Retraites pour Salariés)—which is financed by deductions from salaries, in order to provide pensions for their retired teachers. The pension is payable at the age of 65.

The provisions quoted above, which are now being applied in

Catholic schools, relate—so far as transfers, establishment, salary and joint conventions are concerned—only to the salaried lay staff. Teachers who are priests or members of religious orders are subject to special regulations regarding their conditions of employment, promotion and cessation of service.

Private schools are left entirely free to choose their own methods, syllabuses and textbooks. except for works which are proscribed by the Higher Council for Education as being contrary to morality, the constitution or the laws of the country. They are also free to fix their annual holidays, and the place accorded to religious instruction in the daily and weekly time-table.

In 1946, there were about one million pupils being educated in 11,337 private schools, divided between different categories as follows: nursery schools, 201; boys' schools with continuation courses, 280; boys' schools without continuation courses, 2,793; girls' schools with continuation courses, 1,156; girls' schools without continuation courses, 6,210; co-educational schools in the charge of men teachers, 33; co-educational schools in the charge of women teachers, 659; schools, other than full-time, 5.

Table 4 shows the variations in the number of educational establishments over the last 12 years.

TABLE 4. Number of private nursery and primary schools[1]

| School year | Nursery schools | Primary schools | | | | | | | Co-educational | Miscellaneous | Total No. of primary schools |
| | | Boys | | | Girls | | | | | |
		With conti-nuation course	Without conti-nuation course	Total	With conti-nuation course	Without conti-nuation course	Total			
1939–40	310	169	2 555	2 724	917	6 696	7 603	661	4	10 992
1940–41	263	191	2 567	2 758	949	6 722	7 671	631	3	11 063
1941–42	—	—	—	—	—	—	—	—	—	—
1942–43	225	256	2 802	3 058	1 101	6 649	7 750	699	4	11 511
1943–44	217	272	2 851	3 123	1 112	6 714	7 826	755	8	11 712
1944–45	199	281	2 763	3 044	1 106	6 424	7 530	734	17	11 325
1945–46	200	312	2 750	3 062	1 178	6 332	7 510	695	3	11 270
1946–47	201	280	2 793	3 073	1 156	6 210	7 366	692	5	11 337
1947–48	185	312	2 769	3 081	1 155	6 042	7 197	721	4	11 003
1948–49	217	317	2 754	3 071	1 120	5 985	7 105	749	7	10 932
1949–50	188	334	2 758	3 092	1 140	5 979	7 119	807	10	11 028
1950–51	198	342	2 788	3 130	1 128	5 816	6 939	882	31	10 982

[1] The statistics for the Strasbourg Educational Division for the years from 1939–40 to 1944–45 are not included.

Table 5 shows the number of classes during the same period.

TABLE 5. Number of classes in private nursery and primary schools[1]

School year	Number of classes					Grand total
	Continuation courses	Elementary	Infants	Nursery school	Miscellaneous	
1939–40	1 973	23 764	4 162	120	—	30 019
1940–41	2 209	23 467	4 250	444	—	30 370
1941–42	—	—	—	—	—	—
1942–43	2 779	31 533		354	—	34 666
1943–44	—	—	—	—	—	—
1944–45	2 794	29 923		259	28	33 004
1945–46	3 035	25 949	4 812	274	16	34 086
1946–47	3 066	25 267	4 654	261	8	33 256
1947–48	3 093	25 166	4 103	244	17	32 623
1948–49	2 998	24 766	4 263	397	96	32 520
1949–50	3 060	25 305	4 323	266	334	33 288
1950–51	3 137	25 102	4 528	292	250	33 309

1 Statistics for the Strasbourg Educational Division for the years from 1939–40 to 1944–45 are not included.

A very large number of private primary school teachers hold only the *brevet élémentaire;* but the responsible authorities are endeavouring, to an increasing degree, to obtain the services of young people holding the *baccalauréat.*

CHAPTER IV

SPECIAL PROBLEMS INVOLVED IN THE TRAINING OF TEACHERS

In the course of this study we have called attention to the various problems involved in organizing the training of teachers. Some of them are specific to France, others seem to be quite general; some go back to the time when the teachers' training colleges were established and, despite changes made in the system or in the courses of study, have not been fully solved, while others are now arising as a result of present circumstances.

Whether they are of general or national interest, and whether they are of a continuing or a temporary nature, these problems throw light on the questions to which the spread of education gives rise, and the solutions which have been found for them may often suggest ways of solving other problems.

THE GENERAL EDUCATION OF THE PRIMARY TEACHER

Primary teachers have sometimes been criticized for knowing too much and sometimes for not carrying their studies far enough. We have seen how anxious Napoleon was to limit the scope of their teaching; their 'pretentious sciolism' has often been brought up against them.

Since the teachers' training colleges were established, the authorities of the Ministry of Education have constantly tried to improve the general education of primary teachers. One must have a complete grasp of one's subject to be able to teach clearly and convincingly. One must be able to follow contemporary discoveries, ideas and events in order to develop in children an understanding of the world in which they are to live. One must also know much about the past in order to be able to help them to understand and love the natural and human environment in which they are placed.

Although it has not proved better suited to the needs of elementary teaching than the old *brevet supérieur*, the *baccalauréat* enjoys high prestige and puts the school teacher's qualifications on a par with those which open the way to the liberal professions, so that it is possibly more likely to give the general public a good opinion of the primary teacher's general educational background.

What is the place given, respectively, to general education and to professional training, and how are the two combined? On this point experience has varied, the examination in general educational subjects being sometimes held only at the end of the course at the training college, and sometimes earlier in order to leave one or two years free, in which greater emphasis can be placed on professional subjects. In actual fact, the importance attached to giving additional general knowledge irrespective of the needs of examinations, is evident in the syllabus for the post-*baccalauréat* years; and, in the same way, the desire to give student teachers an early opportunity for contact with their future pupils through psychological observation or work in connexion with after-school and out-of-school activities has the result that they are, from the moment they arrive at the training college, interested in knowing and understanding children.

The studies pursued by the primary teacher help to determine his place in the social scale and to enable a comparison to be made between his qualifications and those of other public servants or of people privately employed. While the nineteenth-century law-makers recommended that teachers should be poor and respected, modern ideas take better account of the length and difficulty of the studies involved by the profession, of what is due to it, and of the part it plays in society. To determine the teacher's place in the hierarchy of the public service, he should be compared with other officials who have done two years' specialized study after the *baccalauréat*.

The fact is sometimes deplored that the classics occupy so little place in the teacher's training. This is to forget, however, that the teacher must above all explain the modern world and see that the rising generation is equipped to take its place in that world. This leads, not to neglecting the legacy of the past and the lessons to be learnt from it, but to giving them a place corresponding to their continuing influence in modern life.

The Vichy Government, eager to pronounce the official abolition of the teachers' training colleges, said that they were 'intellectual insulators' because their students had no academic contacts and no links of friendship with young people going in for other professions; this was said to breed in student teachers feelings compounded of an inferiority complex, a certain arrogance, and rebellion.

The reform tried out under the occupation, whereby student teachers were sent to secondary schools (*lycées*), did not prove successful in bringing them fully into line with the students traditionally attending these institutions. At the present time, student teachers are given the same general education as all the other *lycée* and *collège* secondary school pupils who, in increasing numbers, are working for the *baccalauréat* in science, i.e. the doctors, chemists and agricultural experts of the future. They often meet on the games field and the sports ground, where friendly contacts are established. At the same time, the training they are given in methods of popular education and the practical study of social phenomena, give them opportunities for useful contacts with the working world. The collection of material for the thesis they are required to write at the end of their course opens up many avenues to them and makes them aware of many important practical and human problems.

Nor is it correct to say that primary teacher training leads to nothing; it is a form of training adapted to a specific profession, but we have seen what a wide variety of activities is open to anyone wishing to specialize in a direction offering scope for the development of his or her particular gifts. Those who embark on further study, whether or not they have in mind the *baccalauréat* in philosophy or in elementary mathematics, can easily, when encouraged by their teachers and outstandingly successful in their examinations, go on to take a *licence*, the certificate qualifying them to teach in certain secondary schools (*collèges*) or even the *agrégation*. Any student teacher who gets 'bien' (corresponding to an average of 14 out of 20) for one of the two parts of the *baccalauréat* or 'assez bien' (corresponding to an average of 12 out of 20) for both is more or less certain, if his candidature is supported, to be awarded a continuation scholarship which will enable him to work for the competitive entrance examination for the Ecole normale supérieure at St. Cloud for men, or at Fontenay-aux-Roses for women. If the student prefers to start teaching immediately and applies for appointment to a primary school, he or she may, and often does, spend his or her free time working for degree certificates, possession of the *baccalauréat* qualifying for matriculation in a university faculty. Lastly, the student may apply to be seconded as assistant teacher in a training college, where he will act as a supervisor; such an appointment, which may be extended for two or even three years, enables him to complete his work for his examinations in helpful circumstances.

There are thus many reliable ways by which really gifted student teachers who are fond of study may advance their education and qualify for the positions for which higher education fits them.

CONTACTS WITH CHILDREN

Future teachers need a knowledge and a love of children quite as much as a diploma. We have already drawn attention to the care

  型

evidenced, in curricula, to bring students into contact with children from the beginning of their course at the training college. For this purpose, such means as observation classes, after-school and out-of-school activities, and helping with school functions, the church clubs where children meet on Thursdays, and holidays camps, are used.

A reading of the syllabus for the classes in professional subjects makes clear how great is the attention devoted to instruction in child psychology.[1] Life in a teachers' training college does, in fact, offer many contacts with children of school age—among them, practical teaching experience in schools, in a town or in the country, and constant interchange between the training college and the demonstration schools, particularly with the school attached to the college and housed on its premises, which, like the college, is maintained out of departmental funds and truly shares its life. The children attending the school attached to the college may be boarders; they may be allowed to take their midday meal in the dining hall, where the student teachers keep a friendly eye upon them and thus learn more about their health, their rest, their games, and their conversation than they can do when they are simply in charge of a class.

Everything likely to familiarize young people with the various aspects of the problems of handicapped, unhappy or maladjusted children has its place in their final years of training—sociological studies, short periods of practical work in adjustment schools, and visits to open-air schools or institutions for the rehabilitation of young delinquents. The student teacher's elementary knowledge of the theory of education is not purely academic but is based on actual fact. The special practical courses (in dramatic art, puppet-show, pipe-playing and folk dancing) for student teachers, which are sometimes organized in the school itself, develop their gifts and open up forms of expression which will often win them the trust and friendship of the children.

THE NON-SCHOLASTIC ASPECTS OF EDUCATION

The high intellectual qualifications which France requires of her public primary school teachers must not cause us to overlook the wide variety of abilities which are also necessary. Candidates for the teacher's qualifying certificate must take a class in physical education and in singing practice before the board of examiners. Special practical courses taken during their training at the college or when they are in service

---

[1] Reproduced in *Compulsory Education in France* by Jean Debiesse, Paris, Unesco, 1951, pp. 124–27.

foster creative and artistic activities among primary teachers. There are opportunities for passing on to the children the benefits derived from these courses, both in and out of school. Drawing, singing, handwork and projects all gain from the contributions the teacher is able to make in the shape of new methods and a richer repertory of songs, dances or games. Character training profits by the practice of sustained endeavour and the enthusiasm of creative effort. Out of the classroom, in the evenings or on Thursdays, and during the summer holidays, children and adolescents will gladly congregate around the teacher who brings them such pleasures. There is an enormous variety to be seen in the different types of after-school and out-of-school activities by which the school's influence is spread; the earliest of these were adult education courses, men and women being driven by the need for instruction to come back to school to learn the general or practical rudiments of agriculture and domestic economy. These activities are now being adapted to our contemporary tastes and offer, as the case may be, a better use of leisure time (reading, plays, etc., arts and crafts) or escape from routine (holidays and travel).

The scout movement, church clubs and various forms of school co-operation give opportunities for making friends and promote the development of individual talents. The various undertakings carried on in association with the Confédération des Œuvres Laïques or under the auspices of the Ligue de l'Enseignement, founded by Jean Macé in 1866, are developing more and more educational contacts between teachers, adolescents and adults. All primary teachers and all those interested in school activities are familiar with the various branches of these organizations known as UFOLEP (for physical training), UPOCEL (for educational films), UFOLEA (for art education) and UFOVAL (for holiday camps), as well as the CLAP (for amateur flying) and the CLTC (for cultural holiday travel).

OBLIGATION TOWARDS THE STATE

Prospective primary teachers enjoy a number of substantial advantages, such as the full maintenance scholarships awarded to student teachers preparing for the *baccalauréat*, the salary paid to those undergoing their professional training, or the various facilities available to young people anxious to go on to higher education. In this respect, the Fourth Republic has continued and indeed improved on what was done by the Third Republic.

The State, undertaking to see that all French children receive the necessary elementary education, looks upon teaching as a public service. It has to provide qualified staff for all its classes and, for this purpose, maintains schools where the courses of study are adapted to the specific aim in view and where the State bears the whole cost of training teachers. It is only reasonable that it should, in return, require a certain minimum of service from the teachers so trained. This accounts for the undertaking to serve for 10 years in the public schools, which must be given by any student teacher on entry into a training college.

Breach of the 10-year undertaking entails the obligation to repay the whole or part of the expenses arising out of the student's attendance at the training college. Such breaches may occur in the early years of service, as in the case of girls who give up their profession when they marry. It may likewise happen that the undertaking is broken before the end of the training course, either by the student's leaving or by his expulsion for unsatisfactory conduct. A student may also be compelled to leave for academic failure; failure to pass the *baccalauréat* in a specified time entails loss of the status of student teacher. The special characteristics of the teachers' training colleges necessarily impose a limit on the opportunities for taking any class a second time. Permission to take a class again must be given by the Minister, within the limits of the funds available. In theory, such permission may be given to 10 per cent at most of the students in any year, and only to the students nominated by principals and teachers as most deserving. In practice, it is sometimes possible to go slightly above the stated maximum, as the official instructions are applied most sympathetically. Moreover, students who are compelled to leave as a result of repeated failures in the *baccalauréat* may return to the training college if they succeed, within a specified time, in preparing for the examination by their own endeavours. After the expiry of this time-limit, it is still open to them to become teachers, once they have achieved the *baccalauréat*, by serving as replacement teachers; but in this contingency they lose the advantages of the status of student-teacher.

It is understandable that the prospect of failure, with the accompanying danger of loss of status and possibly of having to repay the cost of the course, which means heavy expense for students and their families, is regarded as an extremely serious matter. The mutual obligation thus entered into by the State and the prospective teacher is a distinctive feature of teachers' training. The system presupposes the early revelation of a vocation for teaching which does not afterwards prove to be false; it also presupposes ability to complete the course of study leading to the *baccalauréat*, and the competitive entrance examination is intended to test this ability. It is better to restrict the list of successful candidates than to open the doors of the training college to young people who cannot profitably pursue their studies in the later years of the course and in whom the short-lived hope of entering the teaching profession will give way, after fruitless efforts, to the bitterness of failure, and the hard necessity of repaying considerable sums.

INCREASE IN SCHOOL ATTENDANCE

Since the Liberation, there has been a rise in the birth-rate in France, which affects school problems at many points. The influx of pupils into nursery schools since 1948, and into primary schools since 1951, necessitates adjustments in the school position. New schools and classes are needed, and premises must be built, converted or enlarged to accommodate all these children. Teachers must also be provided for them. The shortage of premises and teachers was one of the reasons advanced in 1951 in favour of the allotment of grants-in-aid to private education; if the State was unable to provide the education, which it had itself made obligatory for all French children, how could it refuse to assist establishments which might be able to make up for its own shortcomings? The help for which provision was made by the law of 28 September 1951[1] is regarded as temporary, and the Ministry of Education is considering a vast educational equipment programme designed to make good what is at present lacking in its school system as a whole. In the conclusions of the committee on school, university, scientific and artistic equipment, which has recently finished its work, it is recommended that consideration be given to a five-year plan calling for a financial outlay in the neighbourhood of a thousand million francs. The increase in the number of children and the destruction or unsuitability of many school premises would justify the opening of more than 10,000 new elementary classes and more than 4,000 nursery classes.

The recruitment of teachers is also giving rise to urgent problems. If these are to be solved, it is necessary that the number of student teacher scholarships awarded each year for the whole territory should be commensurate with the country's need of teachers, and that the teaching profession should enjoy such prestige and advantages as to make it attract young people and appear worth while to their families.

The undoubted merits and devoted work of French primary teachers have always earned a good report in public opinion; generally speaking, people also value the security of the profession. But teaching cannot compete with the other public or private professions, at a time

---

[1] Law No. 51–1140, published in the *Journal Officiel* of 30 September 1951, and decree No. 51–1395 of 5 December 1951, published in the *Journal Officiel* of 6 December 1951.

when the struggle to make ends meet has become a very serious pre-occupation, unless reasonable salaries are paid. The grant of a salary to students undergoing professional training, and the reclassification of teachers' grades, have certainly helped to improve recruitment to the training colleges. Further efforts still seem to be necessary, particularly in the large towns, where there are so many opportunities open to intelligent and industrious young people.

The admission of holders of the *baccalauréat* in the third year of the course and, above all, the new type of training available to replacement teachers, will certainly help to solve this recruitment problem. Some departments, however, are already finding difficulty in securing men replacements; not all the problems arising out of the present large number of children of school age have yet been solved.

CONCLUSION

The character of every people is revealed in its institutions; and the French have put their stamp upon those governing the recruitment, training and status of primary teachers.

The whole system is characterized by the democratic spirit and by liberal tradition. Not only is primary education provided free of charge for all children of school age, but persons who intend to devote their lives to this work of education are almost entirely supported by the State. The maintenance scholarships awarded during the first years at a teachers' training college, and the salary paid during professional training, enable intelligent young people in very modest circumstances to embark on the studies which will qualify them as school teachers. We thus have a teaching profession made up of vigorous and energetic individuals who appreciate the responsibilities of the work they have to do and the part they play in society.

The fact that both private and public schools exist in France is a sign of its liberalism. The State schools have no official views in matters of belief, but leave it to the families to decide what religious instruction shall be given their children and to make the necessary arrangements; the school confines itself to giving the children one free day a week (Thursday) which they may devote to religious observances; in addition, the State leaves parents free to choose between its own schools and those provided by individuals or associations. Freedom of conscience and recognition of the rights of families have been constantly in the minds of our law-makers.

Emphasis must be placed upon the high intellectual qualifications that France requires of all her teachers, whether they propose to work with infants in nursery schools, maladjusted children, or adolescents in continuation courses. Artistic ability, quick sympathies, and a sound character are also looked for, and we have seen what care is, at the moment, devoted to their development. The primary teacher, however, is first and foremost responsible for handing on knowledge, and the dictum of the Emperor Charlemagne, who founded numerous schools in the ninth century, is still true: 'Although to do good is better than to have much knowledge, yet knowledge is necessary for the doing of good.'

A master who teaches a peasant boy in the remotest of our villages is the equal of those teaching in the schools of the capital; a master who teaches children in a poor suburban district is not inferior in knowledge and professional competence to a teacher serving in the elementary classes of the most famous secondary school. One of the conditions conducive to equality among men is thus secured and, at the same time, the individuality of the country districts, and the prosperity and independence of the people living in them, are safeguarded. In a country where half the population lives outside the great towns and cities and where a third of the teachers exercise their office in schools with one or two classes, the merits of the country school teachers are properly appreciated. Devoting themselves wholeheartedly to their work, respected and influential in the village, they have for several generations exercised a far-reaching influence and have, in many cases, helped to bring the new advances of civilization to the people.

The identical cultural background, status and professional standing, which constitute the deep unity of the teaching profession, make an appeal to the French mind, with its love of clarity, and help to check the drift of everything worth while to the great towns. The vitality and balance of the country districts are thus safeguarded. The identical conditions we have mentioned are one of the consequences of the administrative centralization to be noted in the determination of school curricula, the organization of examinations, the administrative hierarchy and the composition of the various assemblies, and in the rules governing the promotion of teachers. A close examination of our institutions, however, soon reveals a number of variations, special cases, survivals from the past, and new experiments in which the future is perhaps already beginning to take shape. French rationalism, though attached to fine panoramas in which the eye can easily take in a whole system, does not underestimate the complexity of things. This rationalism can be seen in the clear design and simple structure of our school system; in the positive nature of the knowledge inculcated at school; in the attention devoted to a systematic sequence in the acquisition of knowledge, and in the underlying spirit of our teaching, which is concerned with reality rather than with mere words. It is a rationalism, however, that accepts the lessons of the past and appreciates the value of experience, making systematic use of the help these can afford.

A foreign statesman used to say: 'The French system is a sound one because it has been built up slowly'. This is true of the system of primary education, which has proved its worth over the past 75 years and is still undergoing improvement.

BIBLIOGRAPHY

BOOKS AND OFFICIAL PUBLICATIONS

ANSCOMBRE, J. *Le Tout en un de l'Instituteur.* Port Marly (Seine-et-Oise), chez l'auteur, 1950. 425 pp.

AURIAC, Oscar. *L'École Exemplaire, Initiatives et Suggestions.* Paris, A. Colin, 1948. 330 pp.

CAVALIER, Marie-Louise. *L'École Publique et ses Maîtres*, Paris, S.E.V.P.E.N. (13, rue du Four), 1953. 96 pp.

CHARRIER, Ch. and OZOUF, R. *Pédagogie vécue.* Paris, Fernand Nathan, 1948. 656 pp. 'La Préparation Professionnelle', chap. XXXVI.

COUSINET, Roger. *La Formation de l'Éducateur.* Paris, Presses Universitaires de France, 1952. 144 pp.

DEBIESSE, Jean. *Compulsory Education in France.* (*Studies on Compulsory Education*—II.) Paris, Unesco, 1950. 149 pp. Published also in French.

'*Encyclopédie Française*', Vol XV, *Education et Instruction.* Paris, Société de Gestion de l'Encyclopédie française, 1939.

France. Bureau Universitaire de Statistique et de Documentation Scolaires et Professionnelles. *L'Instituteur; Formation, Profession.* Paris, 1950. 88 pp.

———. Centre National de Documentation Pédagogique. *L'Organisation de l'Enseignement en France.* Paris, La Documentation Française, 1951. 116 pp.

———. Direction de l'Enseignement du Second Degré. *Concours d'Admission aux Centres Pédagogiques Régionaux. Certificat d'Aptitude au Professorat de l'Enseignement du Second Degré (C.A.P.E.S.—Nouveau Régime).* (Brochure No. 58/C/Sd.) Paris, Centre National de Documentation Pédagogique (1952) 17 pp.

———. Ministère de l'Éducation Nationale. *La Réforme de l'Enseignement. Projet Soumis à M. le Ministre de l'Education Nationale par la Commission Ministérielle d'Étude* (Paris, 1947). 47 pp.

GAL, Roger. *La Réforme de l'Enseignement et les Classes Nouvelles.* Paris, Les Presses d'Ile-de-France, 1946. 63 pp.

GLATIGNY, Michel. *Histoire de l'Enseignement en France.* Paris, Presses Universitaires, 1949. 128 pp.

GRIMAULD, L. *Histoire de la Liberté de l'Enseignement en France.* Grenoble, Arthaud, 1944. 2 vols.

International Bureau of Education. *Primary Teacher Training; from Information supplied by the Ministries of Education.* (Publication No. 117.) Paris, Unesco; Geneva, IBE, 1950. 253 pp. 'France', pp. 110–17.

KABAT, Georges Jule. *The Preparation of Teachers in France.* (College Park, Maryland) 1947. 236 leaves.

LETERRIER, Louis. *Programmes, Instructions, Répartitions Mensuelles et Hebdomadaires,* 1945–47. *Textes Officiels, Répartitions, Emplois du Temps. Examens, Réglements Scolaires.* Paris, Hachette, 1948. 548 pp.

Programme de l'Examen du Certificat d'Études Primaires. Paris, Vuibert, 1951. 36 pp.

Programme du Certificat d'Aptitude à l'Inspection Primaire et à la Direction des Écoles Normales et du Certificat d'Aptitude à l'Inspection des Écoles Maternelles. Paris, Vuibert, 1950. 32 pp.

Programme du Concours d'Admission aux Écoles Normales Primaires. Paris, Vuibert, 1952. 16 pp.

Programme du Concours d'Admission aux Écoles Normales Supérieures et des Bourses de Licence. Paris, Vuibert, 1951. 40 pp.

Programme du Certificat d'Aptitude à l'Enseignement des Enfants Arriérés et des Écoles de Plein Air. Paris, Vuibert, 1939. 16 pp.

SOLEIL, J. *Code Soleil. Le Livre des Instituteurs. Morale Professionnelle; Administration, Législation et Jurisprudence; la Nouvelle Organisation de l'Enseignement.* Paris, H. Le Soudier, 1947. 325 pp.

UNESCO. *World Handbook of Educational Organization and Statistics.* Paris, 1951. 469 pp. 'France', pp. 162–69.

WALLON, H. *De l'Enseignement et de son Organisation en France.* Paris, Cornon, 1948.

JOURNAL ARTICLES

'Les Carrières de l'Enseignement.' *Avenirs,* revue mensuelle, Nos. 41–42, November–December 1951. Paris, Musée Pédagogique. 100 pp.

HEMERY, R. 'Le Statut des Écoles Normales.' *L'École Émancipée,* 35e année, No. 9, January 1951. pp. 66–68. Marseille, Coopérative Ouvrière des Amis de l'École Émancipée.

LAFON, R. 'Les Écoles de Formation des Principaux Techniciens de l'Enfance Inadaptée.' *Sauvegarde de l'Enfance,* 6e année. No. spécial 2–3, February–March 1951. pp. 258–65. Paris, Union Nationale des Associations Régionales pour la Sauvegarde de l'Enfance et de l'Adolescence.

MAUNOURY, H. 'La Formation des Maîtres dans le Cadre de la Réforme de l'Enseignement,' *Enseignement Public,* 6e année, No. 7, April 1951. pp. 12–13. Paris, Fédération de l'Éducation Nationale.

——. 'Rapport sur la Formation des Maîtres dans le Cadre de la Réforme de l'Enseignement, Adopté à l'Unanimité.' *Enseignement Public*, 7e année, No. 1, October 1951. pp. 16–17. Paris, Fédération de l'Éducation Nationale.

POUILLARD, G. 'Réforme des Écoles Normales; l'Expérience Française et ses Enseignements.' *Education; Tribune Libre d'Information et de Discussions Pédagogiques*, No. 2, June 1952. pp. 17–22. Woluwe-Saint Lambert (Belgique).

SCHILTZ, Raymond. 'La Formation Professionnelle des Futures Maîtres et l'Expérience du Stage.' *Cahiers Pédagogiques pour l'Enseignement de Second Degré*, 8e année, No. 1, September 1952. pp. 65–67. Paris, Association Nationale des Educateurs des Classes Nouvelles de l'Enseignement du Second Degré.

SECLET-RIOU, F. 'La Formation des Maîtres.' *Pour l'Ère Nouvelle, Revue Internationale d'Éducation Nouvelle*, No. 7, April-May 1950. pp. 20–26. Paris, Musée Pédagogique.

THE EDUCATION OF TEACHERS FOR THE PUBLIC SCHOOLS OF THE UNITED STATES

Edited by Harold E. Snyder

FOREWORD

The preparation of this report has been a co-operative endeavour involving the efforts of many persons.

The basic manuscripts upon which the final report was based were prepared by two writing teams. The three chapters on the education of teachers in the United States were drafted by three members of the faculty at Teachers College, Columbia University, working under the general guidance of Karl W. Bigelow, professor of education. The chapter on the status of teachers was largely based upon materials prepared by three members of the staff of the research division of the National Education Association, working under the guidance of Dr. Frank Hubbard, director of the division. These six authors are:

Dr. Lawrence A. Cremin, Assistant Professor of Education, Teachers College, Columbia University (Backgrounds of Teacher Education in the United States).

Dr. Thad E. Hungate, Controller and Professor of Education, Teachers College, Columbia University (Control and Finance of Teacher Education).

Dr. Margaret E. Lindsey, Associate Professor of Education, Teachers College, Columbia University (Some Trends in Curriculum and Instruction in Teacher Education).

Dr. Hazel Davis, Research Assistant, National Education Association (Economic Status of Teachers).

Miss Beatrice Crump, Research Assistant, National Education Association (Social and Political Status of Teachers).

Dr. Ray C. Maul, Assistant Director of Research Division, National Education Association (Professional Qualifications of Teachers).

The Introduction was prepared by Karl W. Bigelow and Harold E. Snyder. The latter also assumed responsibility for revising and editing the entire report.

In addition to the persons mentioned above, many others made helpful suggestions and criticisms. Among those who contributed particularly were: Dr. W. Earl Armstrong, Chief for Teacher Education, United States Office of Education; Dr. William G. Carr, Executive Secretary, National Education Association; Dr. Ruth F. McMurry, Foreign Affairs Officer, Unesco Relations Staff, Department of State.

For their able assistance in preparing the manuscript, the editor is deeply indebted to two members of the staff of the Washington seminar, Miss Anne Carpenter, formerly of the School Affiliation Service, American Friends Service Committee, and Miss Rudi Walton, formerly of the staff of the Friends International Center in Paris.

INTRODUCTION

SPECIAL CHARACTERISTICS OF PUBLIC EDUCATION IN THE UNITED STATES[1]

Any educational system is a reflection of the particular culture of which it is a part. It is hence not easily understood by those who have grown up in other parts of the world. But visitors to the United States experience a special difficulty in comprehending its educational character because of the extraordinary diversity of American educational institutions and practices. The fact of this diversity, the reasons for it, and why it nevertheless does not constitute complete chaos—these are things that the observer from abroad needs to grasp at the very outset.

Why is there so much variety in the American educational scene? Why are some schools so 'traditional' and others so 'progressive'? Why do some give an impression of offering courses of study so broad as to verge on the superficial, while others seem to be dedicated to ensuring intense but narrow specialization? Why do American teachers vary so much in the character of their preparation? Why do they vary so widely in the salaries they are paid and the degree of respect they are accorded in their communities?

The answers to most of these questions are to be found largely in American history. The 13 colonies that combined in 1789 to become the United States of America had up to that time been separate political units. They had consequently developed their own separate educational ideas and arrangements suited to frontier conditions, and devised as an amalgam of the diverse educational views held by colonists from many lands. Moreover, when they formed the Union they were unwilling to assign to the new Federal Government more authority than was absolutely necessary. So they reserved many powers to the several states. Among these was power relating to education.

From the very beginning American education has been decentralized as regards control and financial support. The Federal Government in Washington has never exercised more than a very indirect influence

---

[1] From a manuscript prepared by Karl W. Bigelow and Harold E. Snyder.

on educational developments anywhere in the United States. But this is not all. There early developed within the states themselves a strong tradition of local community responsibility for the schools and a corresponding tradition of limited use of the powers of the state governments in educational affairs. Not only were the people of Massachusetts, for example, free to make their own educational decisions without any necessary consideration of what was being done in New Hampshire or New York, to say nothing of such remoter states as South Carolina or (eventually) California, but the people of Boston accepted major responsibility for providing schooling for Boston's children, and the people of other Massachusetts cities and towns did the same for theirs. Though the states came increasingly to contribute to the support of education within their boundaries and to establish certain minimum standards that every community must respect, the immediate control of the public schools still remains in the hands of local bodies that enjoy wide freedom to make their own decisions. These bodies, known as school boards, are made up of men and women elected—in all but a small proportion of cases—by their fellow-citizens. There are over 80,000 such boards with a combined membership of over 400,000 citizens.

In these circumstances the diversity already emphasized was made possible. It was made inevitable by the variations that distinguish American localities and states—variations in educational convictions and vision, in wealth, and in other respects. Thus in 1939–40 the average expenditure per classroom unit throughout the whole United States was $1,600 a year.[1] But one state, New York, averaged $4,100, and another, Mississippi, only $400. When local school systems within the several states were compared the range was found to be from $6,000 to less than $100. Obviously the character of educational provisions must be greatly affected by such differences in expenditure. But comparison of systems operating at almost identical cost would reveal many differences, too.

No informed American is likely to argue that this situation is without disadvantages. It makes for unequal educational opportunity, difficulty of transfer from one school system to another, and creates other problems. Yet there is a very deep general conviction that local control of education is highly desirable. It focuses responsibility where it is conceived to belong, in the people close to the children for whom education is being provided. It protects the schools from risk of domination by any central political power. It permits the adaptation of education to varying social needs and to the range of personal needs represented by the particular children of particular communities.

Among the disadvantages an obvious one is the risk that diversity

---

[1] American Council on Education. *Unfinished Business in American Education.* Washington, 1946.

will become chaos. This risk, however, has been avoided by the development of devices to assure a degree of order. Each state uses its legal authority to establish minimum standards within its borders. This is done through state constitutional provisions, legislative enactments, and the regulations set up by state boards of education—usually composed of private citizens, elected or appointed by the Governor—and by the state departments of education, under their control and administered by a state superintendent of schools. These state departments also supervise the distribution of supplementary state funds usually provided to the local school authorities, and offer professional advice and assistance to local school systems.

The Federal Office of Education exercises an influence, too, despite its lack of any formal authority. Headed by the United States Commissioner of Education, this office engages in statistical and other forms of fact-finding, disseminates information, calls national conferences on special educational matters, and offers advice and assistance on educational matters to those who desire this. In addition, it has, from time to time, responsibility for dispensing funds for special emergency purposes and for administering programmes designed to meet urgent, temporary needs beyond the capacity or responsibility of the several states. The office is also responsible for allotting to the states a special federal fund for agricultural and vocational education. In view of the inequality of wealth among the states, there is a strong movement toward establishment of a substantial programme of federal assistance to permit equalizing of educational opportunity. This responsibility would, if such funds should be provided by Congress, doubtless be vested in the U.S. Office of Education.

Possibly the most important of the devices operating in the direction of maintaining a degree of national educational uniformity are the voluntary professional associations, particularly those whose membership is national. There are many of these in the United States. Their members may be individuals, or educational institutions, or other associations, who have freely joined together on the basis of some shared interests and who support the agency they have created by the payment of dues. Such associations are the American Council on Education, composed of over 1,000 educational associations, colleges and universities, state departments of education, and public school systems, and the National Education Association, whose membership comprises more than half of all American teachers, and the American Federation of Teachers, affiliated with the labour movements. These agencies wield an enormous influence, as do the six voluntary regional associations of colleges and secondary schools which together cover the country.

These bodies, and many others similar to them, exert unifying pressures in several ways. Through their annual (or more frequently) national and regional meetings, as well as through their periodical publications, they provide for the exchange and discussion of facts and ideas, keeping educational workers everywhere in touch with new developments. Through their special committees and commissions they arrange for the intensive study of particular issues, leading to the issuance of reports and recommendations that are usually widely and respectfully considered. To their influence may be traced not a little legislative and other response in many states and localities.

Of particular importance is the system of accreditation developed by a considerable number of national and regional voluntary associations. Under this scheme an agency, composed of educational experts in the type or level of education to be accredited, publicly declares that it has satisfied itself that particular secondary schools, colleges, or university divisions (e.g. schools of education, medical schools, or schools of business administration) meet the association's minimum standards of excellence. Being thus accredited is often a matter of great importance to an educational institution. Hence ideas as to what constitutes presumptive evidence of a minimum excellence—ideas established not by law or political administrative authority, but by a voluntary association of professional educators—exercise a powerful national influence. The American courts have, in fact, recognized the right of these voluntary bodies to withhold or withdraw accredited status, and the proliferation of accrediting agencies has also resulted in a current effort on the part of the colleges and universities to control and simplify the accrediting movement. The better accrediting agencies seek to develop standards that are sufficiently flexible to permit desirable variations from any norm and, indeed, they deliberately encourage educational experimentation and above all the efforts of particular schools and colleges to surpass current minima. Perhaps it would be fair to say that American education is constantly seeking a balance between stability and adaptability to changing conditions. This balance is particularly important in view of the exceptional mobility of the people of the United States, which means that many American children attend schools in two or more communities owing to change of residence by their parents.

Against the background of analysis that has been provided it now becomes possible to call attention to certain practices that are characteristic of American education in all—or nearly all—the 48 states. First is the universal provision of free public schooling. Everywhere schools are available to every child, offering at least 12 (in a few states 11) years of formal educational opportunity. The elementary schools, beginning with a first grade customarily entered at the age of 6, are organized in units of eight or six grades. In the former case, the secondary school unit (high school) offers four years of work; in the latter there are two secondary school units, the junior high school (three years) and the senior high school (three years). Many communities provide a kindergarten for the year preceding first grade and a few have introduced nursery schools for even younger children. In a few parts of the country, moreover, free public junior colleges have been set up by localities, offering two years of free or inexpensive education beyond graduation from high school. Some of the states have also established junior colleges, and most of them support a state university, state teachers colleges and state colleges.

In American educational parlance a college is an institution that admits selected high-school graduates and offers them at least four years of instruction leading to the award of a bachelor's degree. A university combines several colleges, specializing in different fields of training—e.g., arts and sciences, education, engineering—and also offering programmes leading to the master's degree (one or, occasionally, two years beyond the bachelor's) and the doctor's degree (ordinarily two years beyond the master's). A few undergraduate (i.e. pre-bachelor's degree) institutions call themselves universities, and some graduate divisions of universities call themselves colleges.

Only a minority of such institutions of higher education are publicly supported and controlled. However, public higher institutions enrol slightly more than half of all the college and university students. They customarily charge lower tuition fees to students than those charged by the private or church-related institutions which also, however, receive support from income on philanthropic endowment and annual private gifts. Since the war both categories of institutions have received support indirectly from the Federal Government which has given veterans funds with which to pay tuition costs.

Private elementary and secondary schools also exist in the United States but they are attended by only about one child out of 10. Except when subsidized by religious or other bodies, they must necessarily charge relatively heavy tuition fees. Their appeal is to pupils of particular religious convictions (notably Roman Catholics), or to those requiring special or highly individualized instruction of a sort not generally offered in public schools, or desiring to participate in 'experimental' educational programmes. Usually the private schools are required by the state authorities to maintain the same minimum standards as those publicly provided.

School attendance is compulsory throughout the United States, usually between the ages of 6 and 16. Co-education, i.e., the schooling of boys and girls together, is universal in the public elementary schools, and virtually so in the public high schools, colleges, and universities. Most private high schools, on the other hand, and nearly half of the private institutions of higher education serve only one sex.

Characteristically the public schools are unspecialized as to the courses of study provided, although at the high-school level opportunities for specialization within the school are ordinarily available and in some large cities will be found vocational and other special types of secondary institutions. But the dominant American belief is that it is desirable for all the children of all the people to go to school together. And there is resistance to any arrangement that is calculated to force a child at any particular point to make a final choice between educational or career prospects. Even college entrance requirements are remarkably flexible—although varying a good deal from institution to institution. Indeed it is probably safe to say that no high-school graduate, if sufficiently motivated, could fail to find some college somewhere that would admit him—although many would (and do) find it impossible to complete the college course successfully.

Such emphases on 'equality of opportunity' have both advantages and disadvantages. In many schools and some colleges they doubtless result in lower—or at least different—standards from those held in, say, the countries of Europe. And this may offer a certain handicap to the more intellectually gifted young people. But an acute British observer, D. W. Brogan, has called attention to other values implicit in the American concept of education: 'If these millions of boys and girls are to be judged by their academic accomplishments', he writes, 'they will be judged harshly (in comparison with the academic standards of a good English, French, or German school).' 'But', he continues, 'they are not to be so judged, for their schools are doing far more than instruct them; they are letting them instruct each other in how to live in America.'[1]

There is one important exception to the general American practice of having all the children of a community attend the same schools. That is the dual school system, maintained in 16 of the southern and 'border' states, whereby separate schools are provided for white and for Negro children. This kind of segregation has its roots in pre-Civil War slavery days. However, under the Constitution of the United States as interpreted by the Supreme Court, the same standards and levels of opportunity must be provided in each type of school. Moreover the whole system is now under legal attack. Already qualified Negroes have been admitted to the graduate and professional schools of many Southern universities and suits now before the Supreme Court are attacking the theory that schools of any sort that are 'separate' can ever be 'equal'.

Another important characteristic of American public education is its non-sectarian—even secular—character. This stems from the American doctrine of separation of church and state, a doctrine given practical support by the difficulties that would attend any effort to introduce religious instruction into the schools of a country the people of which vary so widely in their religious convictions. This situation, is,

---

1 Brogan, Denis W. *The American Character.* New York, Alfred A. Knopf, Inc., 1944, p. 135.

of course, unsatisfactory to some religious leaders and is the subject of considerable current discussion. There is, however, little prospect of any marked change in the near future. Religious denominations are, of course, free to maintain their own schools which children may attend in place of the public schools. These church schools usually meet the same educational standards as the public schools, but are free to offer religious instruction. Such church and other private schools are for the most part privately financed, although the possibility of their sharing in funds derived from public taxation is currently under discussion.

Exceptional breadth and variation of curriculum is necessarily customary in such schools as have here been described. If extended educational opportunity is to be provided for all children attention to individual differences becomes essential. It is, as a matter of fact, generally considered in the United States that the school has the responsibility of adapting its offerings and methods, so far as possible, to the capacities and needs of each individual child. While there is stress on providing a common core of general education, a wide variety of special subjects suited to the interests and prospects of different types of boys and girls is available at the high school level and beyond. In the secondary schools, courses preparatory to entrance into colleges of liberal arts are accompanied by those designed to help fit students for vocations—trades, commercial pursuits, agriculture, home-making, and the arts. Both the academic and vocational offerings are usually to be found in the same high school.

The general education component in the high school programmes of all students usually includes courses in history, American government, English (language and literature), mathematics, natural science, health and physical education. Foreign languages will be required of the college-preparatory group and available as electives to others. In the elementary schools the basic skills of reading, writing, and arithmetic are developed, though with less emphasis, perhaps, than in European countries. The natural sciences are also customarily included, not as academic subjects alone, but as 'laboratory' subjects in which the pupils play an active role as participants. But what is most striking to the visitor from abroad is the relatively heavy stress upon the so-called social studies. These are designed to give the child an awareness of the community, the nation, and the world, of which he is a part, and to develop his capacity for citizenship in a democratic society.

The emphasis upon democratic citizenship has implications not only for the content, but also for the method of instruction. It accounts for the emphasis upon discussion techniques, and so-called 'direct learning', or learning through actual observation and experience outside the classroom. It helps to explain the deliberate informality which prevails between pupil and teacher, school administrator and parents, teacher and administrator. It is also reflected in the stress upon student self-government and upon student organizations.

The curriculum of the secondary school, and to a lesser extent of the elementary schools is, as just mentioned, supplemented by numerous extra-curricular activities now increasingly called co-curricular activities. Each school supports a programme of sports, clubs, excursions, student government, music, dramatic and other artistic activities in which pupils are encouraged to participate.

Another characteristic of American education is the heavy emphasis upon educational and vocational guidance. This is made necessary by the effort to keep all children in school for the entire 12-year period of public education and the wide variety of courses offered. The responsibility for guidance rests largely with the individual teacher, but larger schools may employ specially trained advisers, counsellors, or 'deans of students'. Guidance is not designed to tell the child what courses to select or what occupation to enter. Rather it helps both children and parents assess as objectively as possible the pupil's special qualifications and limitations in relation to the wide range of vocational and educational opportunities available. Aptitude and intelligence tests are commonly used, but they are only a small part of the guidance effort. The individual is assisted and encouraged to come to his own decisions with the teacher or guidance official helping him to obtain all relevant information and assisting him in applying this information to his own needs, capacities and interests.

One of the most striking differences between American and European education is the relatively small part played by the formal test or examination in determining student progress in particular studies. Examinations are always used, but other evidences of student development are given equal stress in most schools. Even upon the completion of secondary school, comprehensive examinations are rarely the sole determining factor in judging readiness to graduate, although some colleges require such examinations as a basis for entrance.

Many of the characteristics cited above are of course to be found in other countries as well. But in combination they present a distinctive educational pattern, unlike that of other countries. These differences in underlying assumptions, educational offerings, methods and administration naturally imply a difference in the preparation and status of teachers. The sections which follow elaborate the background and characteristics of public teacher education in the United States and the professional, economic and social status of the teaching profession.

BACKGROUNDS OF TEACHER EDUCATION FOR U.S. PUBLIC SCHOOLS[1]

The history of teacher education in the United States seen against the development of American education in general, may be divided into four chronological periods. The first of these is the Colonial period (1600–1789) during which there was little interest in popular education and almost no interest in teacher education *per se*. A second period embraces the years between 1789 and 1860 when Americans laid the foundations of their state public school systems—particularly at the elementary level—and established the first normal schools to meet the growing need for trained teachers. A third period covers the years from 1860 to 1910, a period when the vast expansion of elementary and secondary education was reflected in the increase of normal schools, the early evolution of the teachers college, the introduction of teacher training into liberal arts colleges and universities, and the development of supplementary educational programmes for teachers already in service. The fourth period covers the years since 1910 when rising enrolments, expanding curricula, and the growing efforts of state agencies and professional groups have raised the standards of every phase of teacher education.

AMERICAN EDUCATION BEFORE 1789

American education before 1789 was characterized by vast differences in availability, organization, and quality. Generally, as was the case in Europe, there were three kinds of school: elementary schools which devoted most of their time to reading, writing, and religion; secondary —or grammar—schools which had as their primary function the preparation of young men for college (the academy, a new kind of private secondary school which provided a more practical education, not necessarily followed by college attendance, was already in evidence by 1789, but its influence was still minor), and colleges which taught

---

1 From a manuscript prepared by Lawrence A. Cremin.

the traditional 'liberal arts', emphasizing languages, mathematics, and the classics.

Because the several regions had been settled by men of different religious and economic backgrounds, educational variations developed early. In Calvinist New England, there had been a strong school consciousness from the first; and many of the towns of Massachusetts, for example, had maintained publicly supported schools since the early 1640's. The middle and southern states, on the other hand, had tended to perpetuate the English pattern of private and philanthropic education. Relatively few people went to school at all anywhere in the colonies, and many of those who did went for brief and irregular periods.

The teachers who taught in colonial schools showed great differences in their preparation. Some could hardly muster the simplest ability to read and write; others had achieved the master of arts degree, representing usually two years of study beyond the college, including a written thesis. As a rule, the teachers of the best grammar or secondary schools and some of the new academies had received their training in one of the American colleges, or in the universities of England or Scotland. Other secondary school teachers had had but one or two years at college, and many only a grammar school education. As for elementary school teachers, while a few were college trained, the education of most was limited to work in a secondary school or even, in many cases, mere completion of the elementary course itself. In many sections of the country, the prime requisite of an elementary teacher was the ability to preserve order and discipline in the classroom. Higher standards prevailed in a few sections. In general, it was thought that the acquisition of knowledge was itself the best preparation of a teacher, and that the more knowledge a teacher had, the better he would teach.

THE BEGINNINGS OF
AMERICAN TEACHER EDUCATION: 1789–1860

The picture described above changed markedly during the first decades of the republic. Rooted in such fundamental social movements as the extension of the suffrage, the widening of candidacy for public office, the growth of industrialism, the rise of the labour movement, and the emergence of nationalism, the public school idea made rapid headway—particularly in the northern, middle, and mid-western states. Leaders in all parts of the country argued that if every citizen was to take part in the affairs of state, every citizen should be given at least the rudiments of an education. Their arguments soon achieved results in state legislatures. Massachusetts, having displayed a long interest in public schools, made elementary schooling free to all in the law of 1827. New York, which boasted few schools in 1789, had achieved a thriving educational system by 1860. By that same date, some states like Ohio, hardly settled in 1789, had placed schools within walking distance of virtually every child. There was a truly phenomenal expansion by mid-century, the public school systems of some of the leading states enrolling by this time over three-quarters of the children of elementary school age (approximately 6 to 13). It was clearly out of this movement that the first important demands for teacher education emerged.

THE DEMAND FOR TRAINED TEACHERS

As early as 1789, a writer in a leading Massachusetts periodical suggested that each county in that state establish a school 'to fit young gentlemen for college and school keeping'. While no action was taken on this recommendation, similar demands reappeared sporadically during the next decades, and were given great impetus by the expansion of public schools discussed above. They reached an important peak in the work of James G. Carter who turned the attention of leaders in Massachusetts to the fundamental relationship between teacher education and school improvement.

During the early 1820's, Carter wrote several articles pointing to teacher incompetence as a serious problem of the elementary schools; and in 1824–25, he published a series of essays in a Boston newspaper, the *Patriot*, which outlined a plan to correct this inadequacy.[1] In his essays, Carter proposed the establishment of a public 'normal school' to prepare trained teachers for the common schools. His school would give attention both to the subject matter to be taught and to methods of teaching; and ideally, there would also be a practice school where teaching principles might be demonstrated in action. Carter made no proposal as to the length of the course, but the assumption seems to have been that instruction would go on at the secondary level for one or two years. Carter's essays attracted widespread attention, receiving notice in the leading journals of many states. Moreover, similar proposals soon appeared in New York, Connecticut, and Pennsylvania.

Ideas such as these had enjoyed, of course, currency in Europe long before the nineteenth century. Some of Carter's proposals resembled those of the Brothers of the Christian Schools who late in the seventeenth century had developed their teacher training school at Rheims.

---

[1] Cf. Carter, James G. *Essays upon Popular Education*. Boston, Bowles and Dearborn, 1826. 60 pp.

Some of the early American conceptions of teacher education were also similar to August Herman Francke's as shown in his *Seminarium Praeceptorium* of the early eighteenth century, and to those of Francke's student, Julius Hecker, who founded, in 1784, a private *Lehrerseminar* in Berlin, later converted into a royal school and given a subsidy by Frederick the Great. At least half a dozen similar schools, opened in other German states during the next 20 years, influenced American thinking. France, too, had experimented with a normal school (from *norma*, Latin for 'rule') under the Lakanal law in 1794 and later under a more permanent scheme endorsed by Napoleon.

The fact that these European forms antedate the first American normal schools has led to considerable speculation over possible influences—particularly from Prussian sources—on American teacher education. It is, indeed, clear that a number of early normal-school enthusiasts patterned their proposals after the Prussian seminaries, which were visited by several leading American educators. Using this evidence, some American historians have argued the case for direct and fundamental European influence. On the other hand, it is equally evident that some of the most ardent American proponents of improved preparation of teachers knew little if anything about the European institutions. Thus, other educational historians have tended to root the American normal school far more in its predecessor and contemporary, the academy, and have in this way cast it as an indigenous American institution. As in many such cases, a fair resolution of the issue seems to rest in viewing the normal school as stemming both from native and European sources.

THE FIRST NORMAL SCHOOLS IN THE UNITED STATES

Before 1865, most Americans continued to believe that good secondary teachers could best be trained in existing secondary schools and colleges. Therefore, most of the demands for the special education of prospective teachers referred to the preparation of elementary teachers. The demands soon bore fruit. In 1823, Samuel R. Hall (whose *Lectures on School Keeping* proved an early best seller in the field of teacher education) opened at Concord, Vermont, the first American school for teachers. In 1830, he accepted the headship of a teachers' seminary opened in connexion with the Phillips Andover Academy, a private school in Massachusetts. This represented an early example of a pattern soon to become fairly common; that is, for regular academic secondary schools to introduce teacher training courses. (Actually, New York State subsidized with state funds the 'normal departments' of academies between 1834 and 1844.) In 1834, James G. Carter, whose proposals have been discussed above, founded a private teachers' seminary at Lancaster, Massachusetts, in concert with a group of interested local citizens.

These beginnings take on added interest as steps to the first state-sponsored normal schools. Carter had followed up his early essays with a memorial to the Massachusetts Legislature in 1827 proposing a teacher education seminary. The proposal missed passage in the Senate by one vote. He continued his efforts while conducting his private classes for teachers, and was one of the figures instrumental in organizing the American Institute of Instruction in 1830. This group, one of the earlist American teacher associations, pressed the Massachusetts legislature for normal schools. Much support came from reports published by observers of Prussian teacher training. Action finally came in 1838 when a member of the Massachusetts Board of Education offered 10,000 dollars toward the establishment of a state normal school if the legislature would match his grant. Shortly thereafter, the legislature did so; and the first public normal school in the United States was opened at Lexington, Massachusetts, in July 1839.

The character of this first institution set a pattern generally followed up to 1860. The student body of the school itself varied between 30 and 40 during the first few years, with some 30 children in the 'practice school'. For much of the early period, the school had only one staff member, while the teachers-in-training taught in the model or practice school. Candidates for admission had to be 17 years old if male, 16 years old if female. They had to declare their intention to be teachers, to take an entrance examination in elementary school subjects, and to submit evidence of good moral character. The minimum course was one year, and included six basic areas: (a) a thorough review of the common subjects—spelling, reading, writing, geography, and arithmetic; (b) some secondary school academic subjects (e.g. geometry, algebra, philosophy, etc.—but no ancient languages); (c) the physical, mental, and moral development of children; (d) the principles and methods of teaching the common subjects; (e) the art of school government; and (f) practice teaching. Candidates who completed the one-year course were awarded a certificate to teach in the district elementary schools of Massachusetts.[1]

Once the Lexington school had been established, others soon followed in its pattern. Massachusetts founded three more in 1839, 1840, and 1854 respectively. New York, Connecticut, Rhode Island, New Jersey, and Illinois had similar normal schools by 1860. Moreover, a number of cities, also pressed for teachers, soon became interested in the idea. Numerous schools and classes to prepare teachers and for teachers already in service were supported by municipal funds before the Civil

---

[1] Peirce, Cyrus and Lamson, Mary (Swift). *The First State Normal School in America*. Cambridge, Harvard University Press, 1926. 299 pp.

War. Thus, by 1860, at least three kinds of normal school were carrying on the work of training teachers for elementary schools: private, state, and municipal institutions.

The founding of these normal schools and the normal departments of some academies did not, however, appreciably affect the flow of teachers from the former sources. Thus, grammar schools, regular academies, and newly established public high schools continued to supply elementary teachers as before—prepared for teaching entirely with knowledge of advanced subject matter. Similarly, these institutions as well as the liberal arts colleges and the state universities which were beginning to appear continued as before to prepare teachers for the secondary schools.

Thus the years before 1860 saw the early development of new institutions to educate elementary teachers as well as the continuance of traditional means of preparing teachers at all levels. While the normal schools represented in many ways a remarkable achievement, their grave inadequacies were clearly evident. They only educated a small fraction of those who taught and did so at a relatively low level. Moreover, many who did attend stayed but a few weeks, devoting much of their time simply to reviewing elementary subjects with emphasis on school problems. To a great extent, these institutions were more notable for what they were to become than for what they actually were in 1860.

CONFLICTING CONCEPTIONS OF TEACHER EDUCATION TO 1860

Even though the movement to develop teacher education was relatively young in 1860, at least four different positions concerning the proper ingredients of a good programme were already distinguishable by that date. A first, held principally by leaders in secondary schools and colleges, maintained that completion of secondary education and, if possible, higher education would guarantee command of elementary subject matter and, moreover, ensure the ability to teach it effectively. This position also had some strong proponents within the normal school movement who felt that the rigorous instruction received in liberal arts courses was the best possible preparation for teaching.[1] A second group, closely related to this first, argued the need for a brief review of elementary subjects followed by more advanced secondary studies. The only attention to method they proposed was in the form

---

[1] In terms of actual practice Nicholas Tillinghast, first principal of the Bridgewater Normal School, seems to have held this position. See letter, N. Tillinghast to Henry Barnard in: Barnard, Henry. *Normal Schools and Other Institutions, Agencies and Means Designed for the Professional Education of Teachers.* Hartford, Case, Tiffany and Company, 1851. Part I, pp. 70–80; also: Edwards, Richard. *Memoir of Nicholas Tillinghast.* Boston, J. Robinson & Co., 1857. 23 pp. (Reprinted from Barnard's *American Journal of Education.* Dec. 1856.)

of 'helpful hints regarding teaching' rather than through any vigorous study of principles.[1]

The remaining positions placed more emphasis on the systematic treatment of teaching method. The third saw the need for subject matter, but only elementary school subject matter. This would be combined in the normal course with an extensive treatment of the theoretical principles of teaching.[2] The fourth position saw the job of the normal school as one of developing 'the art of teaching' in a much more practical sense, and therefore assigned first place to method. What subject matter was introduced entered in its 'professionalized' form, that is, as the substantive content which the student was learning to teach.[3]

Needless to say, the different emphases reflected in these positions implied different lengths of time for teacher-training. Thus, while those who held the first position—on the 'subject matter' and of the continuum—were seeking at least the completion of secondary school, those in group four—with emphasis on 'method'—were often willing to settle for one year of normal school studies following an elementary school course. Leaders in this latter group were fond of pointing out that the need for elementary teachers had assumed emergency proportions, and that their programme was realistic, while any longer requirement would be at best utopian and ineffective.

THE EXPANSION OF
AMERICAN TEACHER EDUCATION: 1860–1910

The years following the Civil War witnessed a vast expansion of every phase of American education. The elementary school population continued to follow the trend clearly indicated in 1860, and by 1910, there were over 18 million children enrolled in kindergarten and elementary schools—a number which came quite close to the total population between the ages of 5 and 13 inclusive, reported by the census of 1910.[4] It was in the realm of secondary education, however, that the expansion was really phenomenal. During the years before 1860, the private academy had been the dominant form of secondary

---

[1] Cf. Page, David P. *Theory and Practice of Teaching*. New York, Barnes & Burr, 1847.

[2] Cf. Boyden, Albert G. *History and Alumni Record of the State Normal School, Bridgewater, Massachusetts*. Boston, Noyes & Snow, 1876.

[3] This practice was indicated as the ideal by Calvin Stowe in 1839 and was generally followed by Cyrus Peirce, principal of Lexington State Normal School. See: Stowe, Calvin. 'Normal Schools and Teachers' Seminaries', in: Barnard, Henry. *Normal Schools*. Op. cit., pp. 123–42; Letter, Cyrus Peirce to Henry Barnard, Ibid. pp. 73–77.

[4] U.S. Bureau of the Census. *Statistical Abstract of the United States, 1933*. Washington, Govt. Print. Off., 1933. pp. 39, 104.

education. However, beginning in 1820, the idea of the free public high school began slowly to gain acceptance, and by 1860, there were already several hundred such institutions distributed through the New England, Middle Atlantic, and Middle Western States. The legality of free secondary education was, indeed, challenged in the courts in a number of taxpayer actions during the 1870's; but the courts forcefully sustained the legality of the institution. During the 1870's and 1880's, secondary enrolments began to rise significantly, and after 1890, they accelerated to the point where they practically doubled every decade. By 1910, the figure had passed 1,000,000, or close to 15 per cent of the total American population from 14 to 17 years of age, inclusive.[1]

Needless to say, these increases in enrolment intensified the fundamental need for well prepared teachers. Orator after orator echoed the view that the quality of the teacher is the quality of the school. It was largely to the normal school that Americans turned in the effort to secure well prepared elementary teachers. More and more, however, they held that the need was to devise new ways of training competent secondary teachers. While some felt that the normal schools should take on the task, others believed that colleges and universities were the only institutions equipped to do so. By 1910, the various ways in which teachers could be prepared had already clearly assumed much of their modern form.

NEW FORMS OF TEACHER EDUCATION

Factors Stimulating Change

A number of factors during the last decades of the nineteenth century served to stimulate a growing conception of post-secondary teacher education. One was undoubtedly the rapid growth of the high school population. This not only presented a need for trained teachers in the secondary schools—and it has already been pointed out that many believed that a normal school which was itself on the secondary school level could not meet this need—but also served to produce an increasing pool of high school graduates able to meet more rigorous entrance requirements for teacher-training. Another was the development of state universities. While the private liberal arts college could resist the demand that it introduce professional programmes, the state university was more sensitive to the needs and desires of the community, and thus less resistant to the introduction of teacher education.

A third factor lay in the expansion of the professional, normal school

[1] Ibid. p. 104.

curriculum itself. This was particularly true as the content of the new discipline known as 'education' was developed and elaborated. Finally, as will be pointed out below, there was growing pressure from increasingly powerful groups of colleges and secondary schools which were looking more and more into standards for teachers as criteria for accrediting given institutions. And the states and localities were themselves beginning to establish educational requirements for admission to teaching, and to institute administrative machinery to enforce such requirements through a process of certification.

The Normal School becomes the Teachers College

With all its shortcomings, the normal school after 1860 was fairly generally accepted as the proper institution to prepare elementary teachers. This is perhaps best illustrated in the rapid increase in the number of normal schools by 1910. By that year, the United States Office of Education reported a total of 264 normal schools enrolling roughly 132,000 students. Of these, 151, enrolling some 94,000 students, were reported as state normal schools; 40, enrolling some 17,000 students, were reported as city and county normal schools; and 73, enrolling over 21,000 students, were listed as private normal schools.[1]

As might be expected from the wide variations in educational interest among the states, there was considerable qualitative difference among these normal schools. Undoubtedly some, particularly in the poorer states of the South, still gave one-year courses strongly resembling that of 1840. On the other hand, others were offering four-year programmes at the post-secondary school level before the turn of the century. In Massachusetts, for example, applicants to the state normal schools were generally required to have completed secondary school or an equivalent education. The normal course for elementary teachers was two years in length, embracing history, psychology, and principles of education, teaching methods, school organization, and observation in the model school and in other public schools. Interestingly, the normal school at Bridgewater, Massachusetts, also offered a four-year course directed primarily toward those preparing to be high school teachers and elementary school principals. The additional subject matter in the extra two years was largely academic.

This development of a four-year course provides the key to one conception of the preparation of secondary teachers. Many within the normal schools believed that their institutions should train secondary as well as elementary teachers. Nevertheless, they had to take into account a general sentiment that secondary teachers should have a

---

[1] U.S. Office of Education. *Biennial Survey of Education in the United States, 1916–1918*. Washington, Govt. Print. Off., 1921, Part. IV, pp. 10–17.

bachelor's degree. Gradually, institutions whose programmes had without planning lengthened to four years began to give attention to the problem of reorganization and re-design. During the course of such reviews, considerable general—as opposed to purely professional—education was added to the curriculum. The first New York normal school, founded at Albany in 1844, was reorganized as the New York State Normal College and given authority to grant pedagogical degrees in 1890; but the first normal school to become a teachers college in the modern sense seems to have been Michigan State Normal College at Ypsilanti. In 1897, recognizing that the school was actually giving college-level instruction, the Michigan legislature designated it a normal college. By further action of the legislature in 1903, the State Board of Education organized courses leading to the bachelor of arts degree; and the first such degree was granted in 1905. Michigan's action started a slow but steady movement which began to accelerate after 1920.[1]

College and University Study of Education

This growing interest in the training of secondary teachers led also to another development which spread rapidly after 1870: the introduction of education as a subject of study in universities and liberal arts colleges. Although the faculty of Amherst College in Massachusetts had discussed the matter in the late 1820's, the first college department of education seems to have been the one established at Washington College, Pennsylvania, in 1831. During the following year, New York University established a chair in education to instruct 'teachers of common schools'; but there is no evidence as to whether or not the proposed lectures were ever given. In 1850, Brown University founded a normal department which was suspended four years later when a Rhode Island Normal School was established in Providence. It seems clear that the normal school idea was powerful enough in the East to enable the normal schools to bear the principal burden of teacher education.

It was rather in the mid-western states that the advanced study of education first took root—particularly in the new state universities. The growing need for secondary teachers (the high school idea was particularly strong in the mid-west because of the comparative lack of firmly entrenched private secondary schools) coupled with the sense of public responsibility in the new institutions clearly stimulated the movement. The University of Iowa, building on a normal department which had been established there in 1855, founded the first permanent

---

[1] Cf. Pangburn, Jessie M. *The Evolution of the American Teachers College.* New York, Teachers College, Columbia University, 1932.

chair in education in 1873. The purpose was specifically 'to prepare students for *advanced* schools'. A number of other universities followed suit soon after, setting up either normal departments or regular professorships of education. After 1900, some, like Columbia University (through its teachers college), New York University, the University of Chicago, and Leland Stanford University, became flourishing centres for the graduate study of education. Liberal arts colleges, stimulated by the leadership of these universities, now gave up some of their former reticence and also instituted teacher education programmes. Some of them even created bachelor of education degrees to cap their courses. So rapidly did the movement advance that by 1890, there were over 100 colleges and universities out of a total of 400 which offered teacher's courses to students; and continued headway was made after the turn of the century.

Education as an Academic Discipline

With the rapid growth of new forms of teacher education and the continuing increase of enrolments in teacher training courses, the content of education as a subject of study also expanded. Pioneering work in the history and philosophy of education was done by Henry Barnard, Horace Mann, William Payne, Paul·Monroe, Ellwood P. Cubberley, and Elmer Ellsworth Brown. Needless to say, these men were significantly influenced by the writings of their European counterparts such as Gabriel Compayré, Karl Schmid, and Karl von Raumer. Similarly, E. L. Thorndike, James McKeen Cattell and others were beginning to lay the foundations of educational psychology, building on the work of Wertheimer and Max Wundt; while Francis W. Parker, William T. Harris, G. Stanley Hall, Frank and Charles McMurry and others were building an educational methodology as well as a new child study movement on the foundation of Pestalozzi, Herbart, Froebel, Rein, and Ziller. At the new graduate centres mentioned above, these scholars were beginning to apply the latest scientific techniques to the study of education, and constructing a new academic discipline through their efforts.

New Forms of Education for Teachers In-service

Another movement with roots in the pre-Civil War period also made rapid advances between 1860 and 1910: this was the effort to improve the work of the teacher already in service. All of the forms which this effort assumed clearly reflected one dominating concept: that working teachers could best be educated by coming into as much contact as possible with academic study and discussion. The teachers' institute—at which one or more permanent lecturers addressed a local group of teachers who then discussed the addresses—had begun in Connecticut as early as 1839, under the sponsorship of Henry Barnard. It was popular throughout the nation until about 1910, when it was generally replaced by more formal agencies. In the last decades of the nineteenth century, university summer sessions and extension courses reached a growing number of practising teachers. The extension course is an arrangement whereby a staff member of the university gives a course away from the university proper, thereby reaching small groups of students who cannot attend the main centre. One of the most interesting innovations was the county training schools in the South which sought to work with teachers of the Negro rural schools. Stimulated by the great philanthropic funds established after the Civil War to aid education in the war torn states, these schools fought the obstacles of apathy and antagonism and worked toward improving the pitifully poor Negro rural schools of the South.

HEIGHTENING CONTROVERSIES IN TEACHER-EDUCATION THEORY

The development of theory in teacher education was enriched during the years after 1860 by an influx of European ideas. Numerous American educational leaders went to France, Germany and Switzerland to learn first hand of new developments in educational philosophy, psychology, and method. Through them, these currents found their way into teacher-training institutions. Thus, for example, Edward A. Sheldon was greatly influenced by Pestalozzian teaching, and made the 'object method' the core of the programme at the Oswego (New York) State Normal School after 1860. After 1875, Froebel's ideas began to enter teacher training, particularly in the preparation of kindergarten teachers; and shortly thereafter, Herbart's theories captured the attention of dozens of men of the stature of Charles de Garmo, President of Swarthmore College, Charles McMurry of the Northern Illinois Normal School, and Frank M. McMurry of Teachers College, Columbia University.

These new influences resulted in sharp and significant differences of opinion. The pre-Civil War position held by many liberal arts educators, that the standard college programme was the best preparation for teaching, continued as before. While many of these men had come to grant the efficacy of the normal school in training elementary teachers, they stood fast on their argument with respect to the secondary teachers.[1] The second and third pre-Civil War positions tended increasingly to coalesce after 1860. As urged by many university

---

[1] Cf. Eliot, Charles W. 'The Duty of Colleges to make Provision for the Training of Teachers for the Secondary Schools.' New England Association of Colleges and Preparatory Schools. *Addresses and Proceedings of the Fourth Annual Meeting*. Syracuse, 1889.

professors of education, those who held, this position now saw the education course as a mediating agency between the best of the academic disciplines and the teaching task itself. Such early leaders in the training of secondary teachers as W. H. Payne, Professor of the Science and Art of Teaching at the University of Michigan, Richard G. Boone, Payne's successor at Michigan, and Nicholas Murray Butler of Columbia University, for example, considered that principles and history of education (at this stage essentially a study of Western European educational classics), together with a broad liberal education were the best preparation of a secondary teacher.[1]

The fourth pre-Civil War group, which had argued for major attention to practical methodology as the best preparation for element-ary teachers, after 1860 tended to split into two camps. One began to formalize and elaborate the concept of 'professional treatment of subject matter'. They thought of knowledge gained for re-teaching as quite different from the general education of the teacher, and tried to treat it so in the professional school. Thus, a course in geography in a normal school was quite different from one in a secondary school or college, even though they bore the same title.[2] The other camp continued to emphasize method in the normal school programme almost to the exclusion of everything else. According to this view, the 'practice school' was the heart of professional education, and it is thus not difficult to understand why it was cordially espoused by many of the normal school enthusiasts.[3]

Among the professionals themselves, especially after 1907, the issues were also more sharply drawn. One group tended increasingly to argue for a strong rooting of teacher education in a study of historical and philosophical movements. They seemed quite receptive to the idea that the real body of data from which educational principles were drawn stemmed from the traditional scholarly disciplines. These data, together with an emphasis on educational ends and purposes, were to be the core of any adequate preparation for the teaching task. The other group combined the older 'hints to teachers' with the newer child study, the systematized techniques of the so-called Oswego move-ment, the formalized Herbartian methods, and the primitive laboratory techniques of the early 1900's, to form a scientific and statistical approach to education—seeing this as the real heart of teacher education.

---

1 Cf. Boone, Richard G 'General Culture as an Element in Professional Training.' National Education Association. *Proceedings*, 1900, pp. 351–64.
2 Cf. Parsons, William W. 'The Normal School Curriculum.' National Education Association. *Proceedings*. 1890, pp. 718–24.
3 Cf. Hollis, Andrew Phillip. *The Contribution of the Oswego Normal School to Educational Progress in the United States*. Boston, Heath, 1898. 160 pp.

THE RISE OF STANDARDIZING INFLUENCES

One might well expect that American teacher education, developing as it did in different states with different standards and outlooks, would reveal vast variations in both goals and the means for achieving them. This might have been the case were it not for two important influences: that of state departments of education and that of voluntary professional associations.

The state departments of education representing the administrative arm of state authority, exerted their influence primarily through their powers of certification or licensing of teachers. While the earliest judgments of the adequacy of teacher preparation had been made by local superintendents and/or school boards, state authorities began gradually to take over the function in the latter years of the nineteenth century. In the beginning, the state board or superintendent of education was authorized to establish standards, to supervise certifying examinations, and to grant state-wide certificates. Once this was done, it was a short step to taking away the certifying powers of local authorities. It is easy to see how most state regulations in this respect would clearly influence teacher education. Thus, for example, when states began requiring education courses for prospective secondary teachers, colleges and universities which had formerly scoffed at work in education had to establish such courses to serve the needs of their students. This relationship between certification and teacher education programmes has continued to the present.

A second standardizing influence was exercised by numerous professional associations in the United States. Early teacher groups like the Western Library Institute and College of Professional Teachers (first established in 1829) and the American Institute of Instruction (founded in 1830) gave extensive attention to views on the education of teachers as did the National Teachers Association (founded in 1857), which in 1870 became the National Education Association. There were also organizations of institutions. In 1858, after several informal meetings held intermittently since 1855, the heads of a number of normal schools combined to form the American Normal School Association. This group became the Normal School Department of the National Education Association in 1870. Another group—regional in character—which met annually after 1902, was the North Central Council of State Normal School Presidents. In addition, there were the various voluntary regional associations of colleges and secondary schools, three of which were organized in the decade after 1886 to secure co-operation on common problems of secondary and higher education looking toward the raising of standards.

These several kinds of professional association exerted their standardizing influence in at least three ways. First, and perhaps the earliest and most common, they provided the opportunity for leaders to exchange ideas on theory and practice in general and teacher education. Second, they appointed committees which studied specific problems common to many institutions and made recommendations. For example, the committee reports issued by the NEA's Normal School Department between 1900 and 1910 did much to shape the future of the teacher training schools.

Finally they influenced teacher education by accreditation.[1] While there was no formal accreditation of teacher training institutions themselves until the 1920's, the North Central Association of Colleges and Secondary Schools in the last years of the nineteenth century began to work out standards for colleges and secondary schools, and in 1901 established a commission to accredit secondary institutions. The association published the first list of accredited schools in 1904, and in doing so, not only set a pattern of voluntary accreditation but also turned the attention of secondary schools themselves to the quality and preparation of their faculties.

Thus, by 1910 the pattern for the education of elementary and secondary teachers had developed to the point where a number of things were already clear: first, that American teachers would be trained in a variety of institutions, in a variety of programmes, with a variety of emphases; second, that within a framework of this variation, there were growing influences to standardize teacher education in the work of state departments and voluntary professional associations; third, that many educators already believed that secondary as well as elementary teachers needed professional study to supplement general education and specialized subject matter; and fourth, that in addition to the preparation of pre-service teachers, the education of in-service teachers was becoming an important concern.

AMERICAN EDUCATION SINCE 1910

The expansion of American education continued after 1910, mainly at the secondary, college, and university levels. The elementary school population rose steadily until the early 1930's, when it fell off because the Depression had caused many young couples to delay or limit their families. Elementary enrolment decreased until the end of World War II at which time the rising birth rate associated with the war once again turned the trend upward. By 1950, a total of 28,628,547 boys and girls were enrolled in the elementary and secondary schools of the

---

[1] See Introduction, page 217, for a definition of accreditation.

U.S. The elementary school population stood at 22,201,505, accounting for the total American population of appropriate age. Of this number 19,447,691 were in public schools, 2,723,814 in private and parochial schools. Secondary school enrolments increased to more than seven million by 1940, but were later also affected by the low birth rate of the early 1930's. In 1950, the figure stood at 6,427,042, or just over three-quarters of the total American population of high-school age. Of this number, 5,731,843 were in public schools, and 695,199 in private and parochial schools.[1] In higher education, an enormous expansion took place, enrolments rising from just under 340,000 in 1910 to almost 2,500,000 in 1950.

Arising out of this increased enrolment is the necessity of gearing the supply of teachers to the demands when they arise. One response has been the investigations carried on by Ray C. Maul for the National Commission on Teacher Education and Professional Standards of the National Education Association.[2] Basically, the effort of these studies had been to project the needs of teachers at different levels in light of the changing birth rate, and to study them in the light of statistics on students preparing themselves for various school jobs. The purpose, of course, is to bring about a much needed co-ordination of the two.

NEW FORCES IN TEACHER EDUCATION

The Role of the Universities

One of the clearest movements in teacher education since 1910 has been the rise to pre-eminence of graduate faculties of education. Graduate school professors have been responsible for many of the great theoretical and practical innovations. It would be impossible in these brief pages to recount the story of the many conflicting proposals regarding teacher education which have been argued since 1910. At best, two of the most influential movements can be briefly discussed. The first of these was the educational science movement which dominated the scene during and after World War I; the second was the great reassessment of values in teacher education which gained momentum during the 1930's.

Growing out of the work of such psychologists as G. Stanley Hall, J. McKeen Cattell, Edward B. Tichener, Hugo Munsterberg, Edward L. Thorndike, and Charles H. Judd, three closely related movements in the early twentieth century combined to form a new approach to

---

1 U.S. Office of Education. 'Statistical Summary of Education, 1949–50.' *Biennial Survey of Education in the United States, 1949–50.* Washington, Govt. Print. Off., 1953. Chapter 1.
2 Cf. Maul, Ray C. 'Implications of the 1950 National Study of Teacher Supply and Demand.' *Journal of Teacher Education.* June 1950, vol. I, pp. 95–102.

teacher education: the educational psychology movement, the child study movement, and the educational measurement movement. The new approach might best be termed a scientific approach to the educational process.

It was natural that this new approach would find ready acceptance by American educators. America was undergoing a vast industrial development. Inasmuch as science was thought to be fundamentally associated with this growth, the effort was made to apply its practical methodological tools to every area of activity. Education consequently gave up its traditional character as an academic study closely allied with philosophy, and rapidly became a matter of scientific techniques and skills. 'The science of education', predicted George D. Strayer, professor of education at Teachers College, Columbia University, 'will in its development occupy relatively the same position with reference to the art of healing.'[1] Growing out of this faith came innumerable attempts during the 1920's to break down and analyse the teaching task into its component parts and to build a teacher education around such technical analysis. Other studies asked teachers themselves to appraise the various aspects of their academic preparation according to the extent to which they aided the teaching process.

A second theoretical movement received impetus from the economic depression of the 1930's. As part of a new literature of social criticism, a growing number of educators began to attempt to revive interest in the values and ends of education. Not only how to educate but in what directions to educate became the guiding concern of this new school of thought. The movement had important foundations in the untiring efforts of men like John Dewey and William H. Kilpatrick ever since 1910 to turn the eyes of educators to social values. In one sense, Dewey's *Democracy and Education*, first published in 1916, had been a classic statement of this position. In 1930, George Counts published *The American Road to Culture* in which he counselled: '...until the leaders in educational thought in America go beyond the gathering of educational statistics and the prosecution of scientific inquiry, however valuable and necessary these undertakings may be, and grapple courageously with the task of analysis and synthesis, the system of education will lack direction and the theory of education will reflect the drift of the social order.'[2] Other leaders such as Jesse Newlon, Harold Rugg, and John L. Childs joined him in pointing out the implications of social change for the training of teachers, administrators, and curriculum makers. More and more, the over-emphasis on techniques yielded to new interest in educational sociology, philosophy, and history as well as comparative education.

---

1 Strayer, George D. *Brief Course in the Teaching Process*. New York, Macmillan, 1911. p. 247.
2 Counts, George S. *The American Road to Culture*. New York, John Day, 1930. p. 194.

In the realm of practice, graduate schools of education also assumed leadership. The training of school administrators and supervisors soon became an important part of their programmes, and more and more, the doctorate of philosophy in education was held by public school educators as well as university professors themselves. When, after 1930, the new doctor of education degree (Ed.D.) became widespread— signifying broad professional competence in education rather than research skill—more and more practitioners undertook and completed doctoral work. Not only was this true of administrators, but increasingly of curriculum experts, guidance specialists, and even public school teachers. The sharp increase in the number of doctoral students in education after 1945 presented one of the most pressing problems to graduate faculties which were seeking both to meet genuine educational needs and to maintain high standards.

The Mounting Influence of State Departments of Education

The interrelationship between state certification and teacher education grew steadily after 1910. Certifying authority during these years passed more and more out of the hands of local authorities and into the hands of state agencies and officers. During the same period, there was a tendency to increase the level of education demanded of teachers and to require specific education courses for specific jobs. While these course requirements differed from state to state, they usually included history; principles and problems of education, child development, and educational psychology; educational methods; and observation and practice teaching.

By 1949, 17 of the 48 states required at least a bachelor's degree (or four years of college) for elementary school teachers, 42 required the same degree for secondary school teachers, and four required work beyond the bachelor's degree for the latter. The great majority of states also made some specific requirements with respect to professional education.[1] Many localities made additions to these minima; moreover, many states and localities encouraged teachers by special salary and inducements to go beyond the minimum requirements. Clearly, these advancing standards of certification could not but influence the course of teacher education.

More recent years have also seen a number of newer tendencies in certification procedures. It has been argued that rather than requiring specific college courses, states should simply designate broad fields in which competence is needed, e.g., child development and social sciences, and should encourage teachers to work in these areas. Some states

---

[1] Council of State Governments. *The Forty-Eight State School Systems*. Chicago, The Council, 1949. Chapter 10.

have already begun slowly to move in these directions. Others have begun to give closer attention to the quality as well as the quantity of work in education; while still others are co-operatively attempting to work out ways of making certification reciprocal (for example, a teacher certified in New York will be eligible to teach in New Jersey). 'Single certificates' entitling holders to work both in elementary and secondary schools have already been introduced in the states of Ohio and Washington. It is significant that more than half of the state departments now use advisory councils of professional people in working out improvements. More and more, then, states are beginning to exercise a leadership and guidance function rather than a policeman's role in the use and administration of certifying authority.

Voluntary Associations Play a Larger Part

Just as the leadership influence of state education departments has grown, so has the role of voluntary associations. The National Society of College Teachers of Education, founded in 1902, has for half a century provided the meeting ground and sounding board of the professors. The American Association of Teachers Colleges, organized in 1917, was undoubtedly the most prominent organization of teacher education institutions for many years. In 1923, the organization became a department of the National Education Association. After 1927 this association took a lead in actually accrediting institutions. In 1948, the AATC merged with two other professional associations to form the American Association of Colleges for Teacher Education —also a department of the National Education Association. The new association has strenuously set itself the task of stimulating improvements, defining standards, and accrediting institutions according to them.

'But the profession, too, has been vigorous in seeking higher standards and common goals. The teachers themselves have participated through the National Education Association's Commission on teacher education and professional standards. In November 1952, this body, the AACTE, and agencies representing the state superintendents of education, the state directors of teacher education and certification, and the nation's school boards joined together to create a voluntary co-ordinating agency called the National Council for Accreditation of Teacher Education.'[1]

---

[1] Cf. Peik, W. E. 'The Accreditation of Colleges and Universities for the Preparation of Teachers in the Building of a Profession.' *The Journal of Teacher Education*, March 1950. Vol. I, pp. 14–23.

The National Studies

With teacher education expanding in size and scope, with thousands of local changes and innovations, and with continuing conflicts over fundamental goals and purposes, it is no wonder that a growing number of educators after 1910 turned their attention to the problem of reassessment in an effort to achieve a basic design. One finds any number of individual studies in given institutions and states throughout the 1920's, and several were highly influential regionally and even nationally. Yet, none achieved the interest nor the scope of the National Survey of the Education of Teachers, conducted between 1930 and 1933.[1] The latter was a comprehensive attempt to gather data on 'the qualifications of teachers in the public schools, the supply of available teachers, the facilities available and needed for teacher training, including courses of study and methods of teaching.' The six-volume report of the survey was a massive compendium of these data. Nevertheless, the conclusions—representing a kind of eclectic approach embracing several of the conflicting positions heretofore discussed—were roundly attacked from many sides. In spite of this, the survey did give teacher educators a broad view of the realities on which they had to build.

In 1938, the American Council on Education—a non-governmental organization whose membership includes almost all colleges and universities, many educational and professional associations, private secondary schools and public school systems—appointed a commission on teacher education that served for nearly seven years in a co-operative study with existing institutions.[2] The effort was to work experimentally at helping on-going school systems and teacher education institutions to help themselves. Inasmuch as a good deal of the commission's effort was directed to organizing institutional and state-wide field programmes, its work was but the beginning of several important programmes. An eighth report, *The Improvement of Teacher Education*,[3] published in 1946, adopted a well-balanced approach urging a judicious combination of general and professional education in teacher preparation curricula. Important consideration was also given to means of improving the work of teachers in-service, and to ways in which teacher-education institutions and school systems might co-operate more effectively. The report attracted wide attention as well as some sharp criticism from some who still adhered to the traditional training school approach.

1 U.S. Office of Education. *National Survey on the Education of Teachers.* Washington, Govt. Print. Off., 1932–35. 6 vols.
2 American Council on Education. Commission on Teacher Education. *A Brief Statement of its Origin and Scope.* Washington, 1940.
3 American Council on Education. Commission on Teacher Education. *The Improvement of Teacher Education.* Washington, 1940.

DEVELOPMENTS IN TEACHER PREPARATION

Normal Schools become Teachers Colleges and State Colleges

The evolution of normal schools into teachers colleges, begun in the years before 1910, went rapidly forward during the succeeding period. While the movement initially grew out of the need to prepare secondary teachers with a bachelor's programme, it was given impetus after 1910 by the growing belief that elementary teachers should also have a full college education. By the time of the national survey in 1933, the evolution was well advanced, with 166 teachers colleges and 101 normal schools (including state, city, private, and denominational normal schools) reported for that date.[1] By 1948–49, the number of teachers colleges had risen to 218 while only a sprinkling of normal schools remained.[2]

During this same period, another very interesting development began to occur in the teachers colleges themselves—their evolution into more general collegiate institutions, often into state colleges. While several factors were influential in this change, probably the usual desire of successful organizations to extend their functions, the effort to attract more students to justify continuance, and the tendency of authorities to assign an increasing number of functions to existing public institutions serve to explain much of it. Gradually, then, many teachers colleges began to increase their offerings in general education and specialized fields other than teacher education to the point where they closely resembled liberal arts institutions. Other teachers colleges added graduate work leading to the master's degree and the doctorate. With all these efforts, however, the teachers college in 1948–49 granted less than one half of the undergraduate degrees in education for the nation as a whole.

The Liberal Arts Colleges enlarge their Scope

Where did the remainder of the undergraduate degrees come from? Largely, from schools of education associated with universities (the outgrowths of the early professorial chairs of education) and from liberal arts colleges. The latter have had a curious attitude with respect to teacher education programmes. Many faculties and administrators continued to feel that a liberal arts programme without specific professional experience was still the best preparation for teaching—particularly at the secondary level. Nevertheless, they had entered the

---

[1] U.S. Office of Education. *National Survey on the Education of Teachers.* Op. cit., Vol. 3, p. 2.
[2] U.S. Office of Education. 'Statistics of Higher Education: Faculty, Students and Degrees, 1949–50.' *Biennial Survey of Education in the United States, 1949–50.* Washington, Govt. Print. Off., 1952. p. 3.

245

field of teacher education for secondary schools, and state certification requirements forced them to provide education courses. One senses, however, a good deal of resentment over these state requirements, a view which is supported by the general reluctance of liberal arts colleges to seek national accreditation for their teacher education programmes.

More recently, however, there is some indication of a shift in these attitudes. In a study of 368 liberal arts institutions, 302 of which are engaged in preparing secondary teachers, Van Cleve Morris in 1948 to 1949 found fairly widespread agreement that liberal arts colleges have a responsibility to train secondary teachers, that they are the best fitted to do so, and that such programmes are a vital phase of their curricula.[1] While many of these same institutions had also taken on the responsibility of preparing elementary teachers, there was less agreement that this was within their scope and capacity. There has since been considerable development of their work in this field. By this time, one could also begin to see the effects of pressures from accrediting agencies and other professional groups in stimulating more attention to professional programmes. Nevertheless, when the colleges of Arkansas in 1951 were approached by the Ford Foundation with a plan to prepare teachers by giving a four-year liberal arts programme (including no professional courses) followed by a one-year's internship in professional education, they agreed to participate.

The Universities Experiment with New Plans

Because of their contact with the graduate faculties through which so much creative influence has been exerted since 1910, university schools of education have been in a unique position to experiment with new approaches to teacher education. While experimentation has certainly not been limited to these institutions, they have often been in the forefront. This has particularly been so in more recent years in the effort to build well-designed five-year programmes for secondary, and increasingly for elementary, teachers. A good deal of stimulus for such work came from the work of the Commission on Teacher Education of the American Council on Education. Obviously, other stimuli came from the fact that universities carried on both graduate and undergraduate programmes to begin with.

Because of the size and character of their faculties, universities have also taken the lead in exploring possible contributions of the traditional disciplines to educational theory and practice. Thus, much of the most creative work in educational history, sociology, anthropology, philo-

[1] Van Cleve Morris. 'The Education of Secondary School Teachers in the Liberal Arts College.' (Unpublished Ed. D. project, Teachers College, Columbia University, 1949.)

sophy, and psychology, as well as comparative education has continued to be carried on at university centres. This was particularly true of early efforts to integrate these various approaches into the 'foundations of education' (an interdisciplinary approach to educational principles) during the 1930's and 1940's.

IN-SERVICE EDUCATION GAINS ACCEPTANCE

One of the most characteristic developments since 1910 has been the growing concern for the education of teachers in service. From the comparatively modest beginnings of the nineteenth century, this movement has mushroomed to such proportions that it now touches a high percentage of American teachers though in varying degrees and varying ways. While a number of changes have occurred since 1910, three trends of recent years seem most significant.

First, the earlier idea of using in-service education to fill academic gaps in a practising teacher's preparation has been largely replaced by a conception of in-service education as a process of continuing growth on the part of the teacher. At least two factors seem to have contributed to this reorientation: first, the increasing length and quality of pre-service education; and second, a growing acceptance of the idea that education in general—as well as professional education—is something which does not stop when a person leaves school, but continues throughout a lifetime.

A second tendency in in-service education has been the gradual shift from programmes developed by higher institutions on their own initiative to programmes designed to meet the special needs of particular schools and school systems. It will be recalled that the dominant conception of in-service training in 1910 was that teachers should take formal course work at academic institutions. More recently, in the effort to help teachers to find ways of improving their work, the focus has been shifted to school systems themselves. Thus, in-service education has become more and more the responsibility of the chief school administrator rather than of the professor of education. Even more significant has been the growing co-operation of the two; and in-service teachers have found themselves carrying on 'action research' in their own classrooms under the supervision of their superintendents as well as of consultants from professional schools. State department officials have also often played a helpful role in such developments, especially in relation to rural schools. This has been just one phase of the growing strengthening of ties between professional institutions and the educational agencies they serve; and more and more, public school systems rather than model or practice schools also have become the new centres of school experimentation.

247

A third trend is implicit in the second: as the focus moves from the professional school to the school system, it has also moved from the individual teacher and his personal growth to the teaching staff and its growth as a working unit. Thus, while individual educational development remains important, great emphasis is now placed on the techniques and skills by which school faculties locate their problems, work co-operatively at determining solutions, and finally solve them. Certainly, this new approach has been one of the most fruitful recent developments in teacher education.

Thus the history of American teacher education bequeaths a legacy to the present: first, a varied approach to the preparation of teachers at different levels—both with respect to organization and content; second, a number of increasingly effective standardizing agencies— representing co-ordinated professional effort—to preserve the healthful aspects of variety while preventing a paralysing anarchy; third, a concern for the education of the teacher throughout his professional career; fourth, a healthy controversy over emphases in teacher education; and fifth, a firm commitment that the values of American teacher education programmes are in the last analysis to be judged by the extent to which they serve American society and the schools it supports and cherishes.

CHAPTER II

CONTROL AND FINANCE OF TEACHER EDUCATION IN THE UNITED STATES[1]

The maintenance of a free system of public education in the United States is a vast undertaking. Year by year, it will be expected that the numbers of teachers who man the schools will increase as the population increases, and that they will become better qualified for their important work. What are the forces which determine the kind and extent of training supplied and demanded for the teachers—whether pre-service or in-service; whether institution-centred or system-centred? And what does this training cost, and how is it financed?

In seeking the answers to these questions, it is essential to realize that education is strongly interwoven into the fabric of the American society; that the patterns of control and finance will reflect the democratic process as understood in the United States, and respond with varying degrees of success to the widespread demand of the American people for good schools for their children. The analysis which follows relates to: the current situation in teacher education in the United States; controls for teacher education; finance of teacher education; the role of the Federal Government in education; and, a recapitulation.

THE CURRENT SITUATION IN TEACHER EDUCATION IN THE UNITED STATES

In 1949–50 a total of 28,628,547 boys and girls were enrolled in elementary and secondary schools in the United States. The number of live births in the United States in the year 1951 is estimated at 3,740,759. This compares with 2,367,674 in 1940, an increase of 1,373,085, or 58 per cent. This increase in the birth rate is expected to increase the school population by 10 millions within 10 years; the implications for increasing the supply of trained teachers are apparent.

In 1949–50, as shown in Table 1, there were more than a million teachers employed in elementary and secondary schools in the country;

---

1 From a manuscript prepared by T. L. Hungate.

923,769 in public schools, and 120,989 in private and parochial schools. Forty-four per cent of all these teachers were in secondary schools.

TABLE I. Number of teachers, 1949–50[1]

Type of School	Men	Women	Total
Continental United States[2]	*374 496*	*868 082*	*1 242 578*
Elementary (including kindergarten)	66 052	609 295	675 347
Public	60 495	538 004	598 499
Private	5 557	71 291	76 848
Secondary	*160 922*	*208 489*	*369 411*
Public	142 920	182 350	325 270
Private	18 002	26 139	44 141
Higher Education	*145 861*	*44 492*	*190 353*
Public	66 462	21 245	87 707
Private	79 399	23 247	102 646
Residential schools for exceptional children, public and private[3]	1 148	4 771	5 919
Federal schools for Indians and Alaskans	513	1 035	1 548

1 Statistics provided by Research and Statistical Standards Section, U.S. Office of Education.
2 Does not include teachers of private vocational and trade schools; private non-degree granting schools of art, music, dancing, dramatics, and individual instruction in these fields; private Bible schools; the Armed Forces Institute; and teachers of unorganized individual and adult education.
3 Statistics, 1945–46.

In addition to the teachers a large number of persons were employed to perform administrative or supervisory services—some 48,000 principals and supervisors, 22,500 superintendents and other professional administrative personnel, and 3,700 professional staff members in state Departments of Education.

It is estimated that the demand for new elementary teachers will be at least 90,000 in the fall of 1953 and then 100,000 a year until 1957; for high schools 48,000 in 1953, to continue until 1956, and then rise. There is, in addition, need to replace as soon as possible some 70,000 poorly trained elementary school teachers.[1]

Before examining the supply of teachers, and their training, a brief view of teacher qualifications will be of interest. An analysis of the preparation of elementary school teachers for the year 1951–52 (or 1949–50 or 1950–51) for 34 states, Alaska and the District of Columbia shows that 55 per cent had four years of college training (ordinarily resulting in the award of a bachelor's degree) or better, 33 per cent had two or more (but less than four) years of such training, and only 12 per cent had less than two years. But these averages obscure the

1 Maul, Ray C. 'How Many Teachers Do We Need.' *The Journal of Teacher Education*, Vol. 3, pp. 94, 95, June 1952.

great variation among the several states: for example, in several states less than 25 per cent of the elementary teachers possessed four years of college training, in others over 80 per cent of the teachers were holders of college degrees.[1]

Yet in the past seven years, the states have markedly increased standards for elementary school teachers. In 1946, the bachelor's degree was required of elementary school teachers in 18 states. In 1952, 33 states required the bachelor's degree, or have set future dates when such requirement will become effective.

Now what of the supply of teachers? In 1951–52, 43,267 college and university students completed certification requirements as elementary teachers. Of this number, only 32,443 had completed four years of preparation. It will be seen that the supply of trained elementary teachers falls far short of the estimated demand of 90,000–100,000 a year.

The situation for high schools is different. In 1951–52, 62,692 college and university students completed standard state certification requirements for high school teachers. This is in excess of the estimated demand of 48,000 a year, necessitating transfer of some to other fields of work. This imbalance in supply between the situation confronting elementary and secondary education will be ameliorated somewhat in future years by the growing tendency toward a single salary scale and a single certificate for elementary and secondary school teachers, as well as by new buildings and better working conditions, but other measures are needed to raise the social prestige of elementary school teaching.

Prospective teachers are prepared in several types of institutions. 'In 1949–50 teachers colleges (including state colleges of education and normal schools), public and private, prepared almost exactly one-third of all elementary school teachers, 17 per cent of the high school teachers, and 22 per cent of all teachers. Public colleges and universities (exclusive of those in the category above) prepared 31 per cent of the elementary school teachers, 40 per cent of the high school teachers, and 37 per cent of all teachers. Private colleges and universities (exclusive of those in the first category) prepared 28 per cent of the elementary school teachers, 39 per cent of the high school teachers, and 36 per cent of all teachers. The technical schools and junior colleges combined prepared only 5 per cent of all teachers.'[2] The distribution of institutions and teachers prepared in 1949–50 according to type of institutional control is shown in Table 2. It is important to note that the institutions under public control train 62 per cent of all teachers, private corporations train less than 16 per cent and the denominational colleges but 22 per cent.

1 Ibid., abstracted from Table 6, pp. 102–3.
2 Stinnett, T. M. 'Accreditation and Professionalization of Teaching.' *The Journal of Teacher Education*, Vol. 3, p. 31, March 1952.

TABLE 2. Distribution of institutions and teachers prepared 1949–50 by type of institutional control

Control	No. of preparing institutions	No. of teachers prepared			Percentage of teachers prepared		
		Elementary	Secondary	Total	Elementary	Secondary	Total
Public							
State	315	21 316	49 623	70 939	57.3	57.6	57.57
County or township	27	475	—	475	0.39	—	0.39
Municipal	61	2 646	1 546	4 192	7.1	1.9	3.40
School district	29	660	292	952	1.8	0.3	0.77
Total	432	25 097	51 461	76 558	67.5	59.8	62.13
Private							
Private corporation	189	4 556	14 523	19 179	12.3	16.8	15.53
Denominational	472	7 518	20 063	27 581	20.2	23.3	22.38
Total	661	12 074	34 586	46 660	32.5	40.1	37.86
GRAND TOTAL	1 093	37 171	86 047	123 218	100.0	99.9	99.99

Source: T. M. Stinnett, 'Accreditation and Professionalization of Teaching', *Journal of Teacher Education*, March 1952, p. 34.

THE CONTROL OF TEACHER EDUCATION

THE CONTROL OF TEACHER CERTIFICATION, AND
THE ACCREDITATION OF TEACHER TRAINING INSTITUTIONS

In all except one state (Massachusetts), the legal authority, usually the State Board of Education, fixes minimum requirements for the certification of teachers. These requirements, quantitative and qualitative, together with salary scales for teachers intended to encourage professional improvement, govern admission to and growth in the teaching profession, and indirectly control courses of study in institutions that prepare the teachers.

Certification requirements vary from state to state, and according to teaching field. Moreover there may be temporary certificates, permanent certificates, and even emergency certificates (issued in times of teacher shortages to persons unable to meet normal minimum standards). In 1951 in 17 states the lowest non-emergency certificate to teach in the elementary schools required,four years of college preparation (or bachelor's degree), two or three years in 20, and one year or less in 10; but the fourth-year requirement was scheduled to be adopted in seven additional states (a year later this figure had risen to 16). Completion of college was a minimum requirement for secondary school teachers in all but six states, and four had already begun to demand still a further year of training—with several others on the verge of following suit. The usual requirement specifically relating to professional, i.e. pedagogical, courses for certification at both element-ary and secondary levels was between 15 and 29 semester hours (a four-year college course, leading to the award of a bachelor's degree, will comprise 120 to 128 semester hours of work).[1]

Sometimes the legal authority to charter, supervise and regulate higher educational institutions is exercised in whole or in part by the same body that legally controls teacher certification and institutional approval; but often the channels of legal control of higher educational institutions are separately administered. Increasingly, however, the legal authorities have enlisted the participation of all legitimately interested elements in the educational community. 'The two chief agencies which have been developed in the state, as media for the co-operative formulation and application of teacher-education and certification programmes, are (1) advisory councils on teacher edu-cation and certification and (2) state commissions on teacher education and professional standards'[2]. It is reported that advisory councils on teacher education and certification, created by state educational authorities, are operating in 28 states; state commissions or committees on teacher education and professional standards, self-created in relation with the National Education Association's National Commission, are operating in 40 states. In 18 states, both types of organization exist. Both provide means for representatives of teacher-preparing institu-tions, members of the teaching profession, and laymen to participate in the formulation and application of the state legal authority to teacher education and certification.

In general, the councils serve to advise the state legal authority on needed changes in requirements, and to recommend specific course and certification requirements. They also encourage experimentation in the improvement of teacher education in colleges and school systems. State commissions afford the means for the continuing study by teachers and school administrators particularly of desirable standards for the profession, including those relating to teacher education and certification. They usually conduct one state-wide conference each year, participated in by members of the state and local education associations, as well as by representatives of teacher-training institutions and the state department of education. District and local study are also promoted. Eventually formal recommendations to the state depart-ment may be framed and receive the support of the state association.

---

1 U.S. Office of Education. *A Manual on Certification Requirements for School Personnel in the United States*. (Circular No. 290) Washington, Government Printing Office, 1951, p. 2.
2 Stinnett, T. M., and Umstattd, J. G. 'Patterns of Co-operation in Administering Staff-Teacher Education and Certification Programs', *Journal of Teacher Education*, Vol. 2, p. 272, Dec. 1951.

In those states where both advisory councils and state commissions operate, dual membership and the continuous exchange of viewpoints serve to co-ordinate the work. The two prevailing patterns provide organizations for the democratic and co-operative development and execution of teacher education and certification. These emerging patterns of co-operation assure growing reliance upon action by 'consent of the governed'.

Advisory councils participate in such activities as these: studies of teacher education programmes, certification requirements, teacher-education curricula, standards for teacher education institutions, problems of both pre-service and in-service teacher education, teacher demand and supply; and recommend changes to the legal authority.

State commissions are often engaged in such activities as these: developing the sense of responsibility among teachers, generally for higher professional standards; developing recognition of the value of support of the profession in the field by teacher-training institutions; assisting in revising and upgrading teacher certification requirements; assisting in plans for teacher recruitment, for improving practices in teacher-education institutions.

The state legal authority invites the advice, co-operation and participation of professional groups in the certification of teachers, and also seeks the help of professional groups in the accreditation of teacher-training institutions.

In most states a state education department agency must determine which colleges in the state offer programmes of teacher-preparation accepted as reaching the minimum standard. Most of the best of these will have been accredited on a basis of general quality (without specific reference to the teacher training programme) by one of the voluntary regional agencies. A smaller number will have sought and been granted membership in, hence achieved specific accreditation by, the American Association of Colleges for Teacher Education. As can be discovered from Table 3, in 1949–50 only 18 per cent of 1,093 institutions preparing teachers had obtained all three types of approval, but 52 per cent were approved by both a state and a regional agency, and 4 per cent by both a state and the AACTE, leaving 26 per cent with recognition by a state only. Over half of the teachers' colleges and precisely half of the publicly supported colleges and universities had met all three sets of standards, but only about 3 per cent of the privately supported colleges and universities had done so, although three-quarters enjoyed both state and regional association approval. These facts help explain the current efforts toward co-operation in professional accreditation already noted.

TABLE 3. Distribution of teachers prepared 1949–50 by type of institution

Designation of institutions	Number of preparing institutions [1] by accreditation					Number of teachers prepared			Percentage of teachers prepared		
	S	SR	SA	SRA	Total	Elementary	Secondary	Total	Element-ary	Second-ary	Total
Teachers colleges [2]	38	5	31	85	159	12 475	14 489	26 964	33.5	16.8	21.9
Public colleges and universities	8	84	4	96	192	11 592	34 548	46 140	31.1	40.2	37.4
Private colleges and universities	121	428	3	17	569	10 510	33 533	44 043	28.3	38.9	35.7
Professional and technical schools	20	10	4	1	35	72	3 354	3 426	0.2	3.9	2.8
Junior colleges [3]	96	42	—	—	138	2 522	123	2 645	6.8	0.1	2.1
	283	569	42	199	1 093	37 171	86 047	123 218	99.9	99.9	99.9

[1] S means accredited by state department of education exclusively; SR by state department of education and regional association; SA by state department of education and American Associations of Colleges for Teacher Education; SRA by all three.
[2] Includes all institutions with name 'Teachers College', public or private, state colleges of education operating as separate institutions, and normal schools.
[3] Includes all junior colleges, public and private.

Source: T. M. Stinnett, 'Accreditation and the Professionalization of Teaching', *Journal of Teacher Education*, March 1952.

Concerning the supply of teachers produced in 1949–50, Stinnett presents the following summary: (a) More than 50 per cent of all teachers completing preparation in 1949–50 are products of preparing programmes which have not been professionally appraised through accreditation by the American Association of Colleges for Teacher Education. (b) It is apparent that publicly supported institutions are the chief supporters of professional accreditation in teacher education, furnishing 96 per cent of the membership of the American Association of Colleges for Teacher Education. Of the 432 public institutions engaged in teacher education, 214 or about 50 per cent were members. Of the 661 private institutions engaged in teacher education, only 27 or 4 per cent were members. Included in the 661 private institutions are 472 denominational institutions. Of these 5 or 1 per cent are members. (c) Multi-purpose institutions are preparing 6 of every 10 elementary school teachers, and 8 of every 10 high school teachers. (d) Publicly controlled institutions are preparing 2 of every 3 elementary school teachers, and 6 of every 10 high school teachers. (e) Institutions offering graduate programmes of one or more years are preparing a majority of all teachers—54.1 per cent;

59 per cent of high school teachers, and 42.5 per cent of elementary school teachers. (f) Teacher education below the bachelor's degree level is diminishing rapidly in importance and apparently will be abandoned in the near future. In 1949–50, the 166 institutions not granting degrees prepared only about 3 per cent of the teachers prepared that year.[1]

CONTROL PATTERNS FOR TEACHER EDUCATION INSTITUTIONS

As shown in Tables 2 and 3 above, 22 per cent of new teachers are trained in teachers colleges, most of which are under state control; 37 per cent are trained in other state colleges and universities; 16 per cent in private independently controlled institutions; 22 per cent in denominational colleges, and the rest in public institutions under local government control. The nature of control of these classes of institutions will be described.

For institutions under state control four kinds of agencies or authorities participate in the decision-making process in varying degrees: (a) the legislatures; (b) the governors; (c) the central state administrative agencies, and (d) the boards governing state institutions of higher education.[2] In addition, institutional faculties and administrative officers participate in varying degrees.

The legislature is composed of elected members, and is designed to reflect the views of the constituents in the development of state policies. Legislatures commonly appropriate funds for the support of state controlled higher education.

The governor is also elected, and represents the interests of the entire state. He not only participates in the formulation of state policies but is responsible as the state's chief executive for appointment of officers to head administrative agencies, and for co-ordination of administrative and financial affairs.

Typical of state agencies are those of budget, legal, purchasing and personnel departments. These agencies are not presumed to have special competence in any particular state programme area, but to perform specialized management functions. The degree to which they exercise control over state colleges and universities varies from state to state.

State institutions are governed by a lay or citizen board with full power to manage and direct their affairs except for those powers reserved by law to other agencies. In 10 states, each state institution is

---

1 Stinnett, T. M. 'Accreditation and the Professionalization of Teaching', *Journal of Teacher Education*, Vol. 3, p. 35, March 1952.
2 Council of State Governments. *Higher Education in the Forty-Eight States*, Chicago, The Council, 1952. p. 121.

governed by a separate board. Two other states have only one institution each. In each of 12 states, all institutions(more than one in each state) are grouped under a single governing board. In 19 states, some boards govern one institution each, others govern groups of institutions; and in two states each board governs two or more institutions. In three states, in recent years, a central state co-ordinating board has been established.

About three out of four of all board members of state institutions are appointed by governors. Other members are chosen in a variety of ways—some are selected, some serve ex-officio. The length of term is typically over five years, with overlapping of terms quite general. Twenty-eight per cent of state boards for institutions of higher education are created by state constitutions; the remainder by legislation.

'Generally speaking, boards established to govern state institutions of higher education appear to have two basic qualities or characteristics. First, for the most part, boards are relatively independent, not directly and immediately responsive to the voters of the states, or to popularly elected central state officials. By a variety of means, most of the boards are screened from the direct and immediate influence of voters and the popularly elected state officials. It is apparent that the provisions establishing them and clothing them with authority to operate state institutions of higher education deliberately intended that the boards should possess a degree of autonomy.

'Secondly, the boards have at their command a wealth of institutional faculty and staff personnel of high technical and professional competence. Within each institution certain processes and procedures are established through which the professional competence of institutional personnel may be focused on the academic problems with which the institution is faced.'[1]

While in general a substantial degree of autonomy is allowed to the boards, particularly with respect to programme, much control is retained by the agencies of state government. For example, the budget format is usually prescribed by central state officials, and most budget requests are subject to revision by a central budget authority before presentation to the legislature. Almost two-thirds of the boards report that appropriations may be reduced by administrative action after the appropriation law is enacted. Similarly many boards must purchase materials and supplies through the central purchasing agent who may determine the standards and specifications. Again many boards are subject to personnel policies of the central agencies so far as non-academic personnel is concerned.

Such is the general organization of state institutions of higher education. Private independent institutions—college or university—will

---

1 Ibid., p. 132.

usually operate under a state charter, enjoy privileges of tax exemption of income and real property. They will generally be governed by a board of trustees who are responsible for policy, programme and finance. Denominational colleges are usually small, most of them simple liberal arts colleges. Some of them are controlled directly by church denominations, however, and others are governed by almost independent boards.

While the above general description will serve well for colleges and universities generally, the control pattern for teachers colleges sometimes places the State Board of Education in direct charge of the teachers colleges of the state. This is true in 10 of the states. A separate board of control for teachers colleges is found in six states. In the remaining 32 states, teachers colleges are either individually organized under separate individual boards, or are grouped with other state higher institutions under the authority of a single board.

The teachers colleges are usually so-called 'single-purpose' institutions. They exist to prepare teachers, and the policies and procedures, the staffing and the facilities are all related to this end. But in some, as in the multipurpose state colleges and universities, the private independent colleges and universities, and the denominational colleges, the preparation of teachers is only one of many functions. In these the training of teachers is often incidental to, or at best correlative with the training of scientists, engineers, or specialists in a particular field of knowledge.

CONTROL PATTERNS OF IN-SERVICE TRAINING

For many years, in-service training consisted largely of institution-centred programmes. There were summer sessions at teacher-training institutions, or evening and Saturday classes during the academic year. The cost was generally borne by the teacher, who through better preparation might expect some increase in salary.

Recently in-service education of teachers under the control of the local school system is receiving increasing attention. Consequently the superintendent of schools is becoming a leader in in-service education. Conferences, workshops, inter-visitations, all relating to the development and functioning of the local system are conducted at the expense of the system. Often leadership is provided by professional staff members of teacher education institutions.

FINANCE OF TEACHER EDUCATION

PUBLIC SCHOOL EXPENDITURES

In 1949–50, public school expenditures in the United States amounted to 5.8 billions of dollars. This may be compared with total income of individuals in the continental portion of the nation in 1950 of 217 billions. Such income includes that received by individuals from wages, salaries, net income of proprietors, dividends, interest, net rents, and other items—such as social insurance benefits, and veterans benefits. Thus public school expenditures represented 2.67 per cent of such income.

FINANCE OF TEACHER EDUCATION INSTITUTIONS

Table 4 shows not only the very rapid growth in higher education in the U.S.A. but also gives interesting facts concerning enrolments, and types of institutional programmes.

TABLE 4. College resident enrolments, 1900–50 by control and type of programme

| Year | Control | | Type of programme | | | | Total |
	Private	Public	Junior college	Teacher education	Other undergraduate	Graduate	
1900	147 242	90 968		69 593	162 786	5 831	238 210
1910	180 452	159 126		88 561	241 646	9 371	339 578
1920	230 277	301 062	8 159	135 237	372 683	15 260	531 339
1930	542 453	539 990	54 583	186 579	790 217	51 064	1 082 443
1940	700 868	798 241	149 854	178 807	1 067 172	103 276	1 499 109
1950	1 196 922	1 242 988	226 885	208 421	1 780 818	223 786	2 439 910

Source: *Higher Education in the Forty-Eight States*. Council of State Governments, 1952. Appendix Tables 3, 4, 5, 6 and 7, pp. 172–84.

The distribution of educational and general income, i.e., income available for educational activities, by type of institution for selected years is shown in Table 5 (see page 260).

This distribution shows that the income of higher education has risen rapidly; that public higher education is currently expanding more rapidly than is private; and that despite the actual rise in income of the teachers colleges, the proportion of all income for higher education devoted to teachers colleges has steadily declined from 11.4 per cent in 1918 to 5.8 per cent in 1950.

259

TABLE 5. Distribution of educational and general income of higher educational institutions for selected years

Year	Total amount (thousands of dollars)	Percentage distribution to		
		Public institutions exclusive of teachers colleges	Teachers colleges	All private institutions
1918	121 601	45.8	11.4	42.8
1926	353 626	43.1	9.0	47.9
1934	385 980	41.8	7.9	50.3
1942	618 152	48.0	7.0	45.0
1950	1 815 826	51.1	5.8	43.1

Source: *Higher Education in the Forty-Eight States*. Council of State Governments, 1952. Table 14, p. 205.

The percentage distribution of income for all publicly controlled institutions—including teachers colleges—is shown in Table 6. In 1950 student fees, including veterans' fees, paid by the Federal Government, amounted to 23.9 per cent, substantially higher than in earlier years; Federal payments, mostly for research, had risen; the share from state governments has declined but is currently rising; the share borne by local governments has been falling since 1945; the share covered by gifts and grants is higher than formerly, while the share covered by endowment income has declined.

TABLE 6. Percentage distribution of income from all sources for all publicly controlled institutions, 1918 to 1950

Year	Student fees	Veterans' fees	Other federal payments	State governments	Local governments	Private gifts or grants	Endowment earnings	All other
1918	9.7		8.4	60.1	2.6	0.5	5.3	13.4
1922	13.5		7.5	58.8	3.7	0.7	3.9	11.9
1926	14.3		6.1	56.3	3.4	0.8	4.1	15.0
1930	14.6		6.1	56.8	3.7	1.1	3.8	13.9
1934	19.0		8.4	51.8	8.0	1.5	3.8	7.5
1938	18.4		10.2	49.6	7.9	1.9	3.2	8.8
1942	17.6		12.2	48.0	7.9	2.8	2.9	8.6
1946	12.5	4.5	16.8	44.7	5.9	3.1	2.6	9.9
1950	10.8	13.1	11.6	46.8	5.8	2.5	1.2	8.2

Source: *Higher Education in the Forty-Eight States*. Council of State Governments, 1952. Table 14, p. 205.

The distribution for state teachers colleges alone is shown in Table 7. Here it is evident that the share borne by the state has declined markedly, and fees charged to students including veterans' fees have greatly increased. Even so, the share borne by the state for teachers colleges is currently substantially above the average for all state-supported institutions.

TABLE 7. Percentage distribution of income from all sources for state teachers colleges, 1918 to 1950

Year	Student fees	Veterans' fees	Other federal payments	State governments	Local governments	Private gifts or grants	Endowment earnings	All other
1918	10.6			82.6			1.0	5.8
1922	9.5			85.2			0.9	4.4
1926	12.8			82.4			0.2	4.6
1930	12.1		0.3	84.3			0.2	3.1
1934	18.8		0.2	78.5		0.1	0.4	2.0
1938	19.1		0.1	76.6	2.5	0.2	0.5	1.0
1942	17.9		0.3	77.1	1.6	0.5	0.6	2.0
1946	12.8	3.4	1.2	76.4	1.2	2.0	0.3	2.7
1950	15.1	14.2	0.2	66.4	1.3	0.1	0.2	2.5

Source: *Higher Education in the Forty-Eight States.* Council of State Governments, 1952. Table 14, p. 205.

The distribution of income from all sources for privately controlled institutions is shown in Table 8. Student fees, including veterans' fees paid by the Federal Government were at 58 per cent of the total in 1950, higher than in any other year. The Federal Government since the war has greatly increased its support, primarily for contracted research. There is some tendency for private expendable gifts and grants to rise, but the steady decline in the role of endowment income is to be noted.

TABLE 8. Percentage distribution of income from all sources for all privately controlled institutions, 1918 to 1950

Year	Student fees	Veterans' fees	Other federal payments	State governments	Local governments	Private gifts or grants	Endowment earnings	All other
1918	36.7		0.2	2.7	—	9.9	36.1	14.4
1922	46.3		0.4	2.9	0.1	9.6	27.7	13.0
1926	47.9		0.3	1.1	—	9.1	25.0	16.6
1930	46.5		0.2	1.4	—	9.5	25.2	17.2
1934	52.4		0.5	1.4	0.1	12.7	24.8	8.1
1938	52.3		0.4	1.3	0.1	12.9	25.3	7.7
1942	51.0		3.1	1.2	0.1	13.0	23.1	8.5
1946	36.3	9.2	12.1	1.1	—	14.5	17.2	9.6
1950	36.1	21.9	10.1	1.1	0.2	11.9	10.7	8.0

Source: *Higher Education in the Forty-Eight States.* Council of State Governments, 1952. Table 14, p. 205.

EXPENDITURE PATTERNS

The expenditure patterns of institutions of higher education vary considerably. The distribution of expenditures shown below in Table 9 are averages, and consequently fail to describe the variations.

TABLE 9. Percentage distribution of educational expenditures in all higher institutions and in teachers colleges, 1949–50

	All institutions	Teachers colleges
	%	%
Administration and general	12.5	13.1
Resident instruction	45.7	58.9
Activities related to instructional departments	7.0	2.6
Organized research	13.2	*
Extension	5.1	1.9
Library	3.3	4.1
Plant operation and maintenance	13.2	19.4
	100.0	100.0

* Less than o.1 of 1 per cent.

Source: *Statistics of Higher Education*, Table XI, Chapter 4, Section II, Biennial Survey of Education 1948–50. Federal Security Agency, U.S. Office of Education.

In reviewing the above comparison, it should be noted that organized educational research (research separately budgeted and separately financed) is not common in the teachers colleges. Extension services are not great, and the activities related to instructional departments in the teachers colleges consist for the most part in laboratory or practice schools.

Table 10 compares salaries of teachers professors and instructors in the several classes of institutions.

TABLE 10. Median salaries of teachers in 486 colleges and universities: 1950–51 (Salaries of faculties in professional schools not included)

Category	State universities	Private and endowed	Teachers colleges
	$	$	$
Deans	7 118	5 000	5 600
Professors	5 460	4 300	4 820
Associate professors	4 629	3 800	4 227
Assistant professors	3 900	3 400	3 805
Instructors	3 200	2 850	3 335

Source: Charles Hoff, *College and University Business*, August 1951, p. 31.

The average for professors in the teachers colleges is, thus, generally below that for professors in the state universities, but well above the average for the private institutions, despite the fact that the latter include many well-endowed colleges with salary scales which equal or surpass those of the state universities.

THE PATTERNS OF STUDENT FINANCE

The patterns of student finance in the United States are not nearly as well known as are the patterns of institutional finance. Recent studies in New York State, where costs may be somewhat higher than the average for the nation, show typical costs for an academic year, and the sources of funds to finance the cost.

TABLE 11. Typical budget of student expense, New York State, 1950–51

Typical budget (Sum of medians)	Commuting to college		Resident at college	
	Private colleges	State teachers colleges	Private colleges	State teachers colleges
	$	$	$	$
Tuition and fees	520	80	630	80
Meals, or meals and room [1]	140	100	700	570
Other expenses	590	420	480	400
	1 250	600	1 810	1 050
Number of cases	700	146	1 090	380

[1] Meals and room for resident students; meals only for commuting students. Figures based on students not working for meals or room.

Source: Louis H. Conger, Jr., 'What a College Education Costs in New York State', *College and University Business*, November 1952, p. 49.

It is significant that in New York State the difference in cost for students in residence and for those who live at home is not so great as might at first be supposed. And some of the difference will doubtless include, for the private institutions, expenditures reflecting higher family incomes. In the teachers colleges, the difference is but $450.

The source of funds to pay the cost is shown in Table 12 (see following page).

It is apparent from Table 12 that the role of the family in student finance is predominant. But those enrolled in teachers colleges receive less from this source both actually and relatively than do other students. Moreover, they rely more on themselves, and work to finance their education. While recent evidence indicates that the quality of students

TABLE 12. Percentage of income obtained by students from various sources, New York State, 1950–51

| | Commuting | | Resident | |
	Private colleges	State teachers colleges	Private colleges	State teachers colleges
	%	%	%	%
Family contribution	54	38	68	61
Scholarship	6	4	7	1
Work previous summer	15	23	12	15
Work during school year[1]	11	24	4	7
Gifts	2	2	1	2
Savings[2]	6	6	3	6
Loans or debt[3]	5	2	4	8
Other sources	1	1	1	*
	100	100	100	100

* Less than 0.5 per cent.
1 Including the value of room and meals earned.
2 Savings previously accumulated.
3 Loans already received and debt to be acquired to finance school year 1950–51.

Source: Louis H. Conger, Jr., 'What a College Education Costs in New York State', *College and University Business*, November 1952, p. 49.

in teachers colleges in New York State compares favourably with students in other institutional types, a greater percentage are drawn from families in the lower income groups.

The pattern of financing a teacher's advanced professional training, as a rule, differs from that for his initial basic preparation. Usually, advanced professional training is taken in university graduate schools after a period of successful experience in the field. Many employed teachers take Saturday and evening classes; others enrol in summer schools. A relatively small number are able to enrol full-time in the academic year, financed by savings, borrowed funds, part-time employment, or perhaps from the earnings of a wife who works full time while her husband studies. Thus, in education, unlike other professions, advanced degrees are achieved typically after years of teaching, interrupted by periods of full or part-time study.

In a large college of education in an Eastern university the cost for a married student for an academic year of study is $3,500 or more. $7,000 or more is needed to finance the work for the doctor's degree if the candidate already possesses the master's degree. This high cost affects the length of time it takes those seeking advanced degrees to acquire them. For example, a study at the institution just mentioned revealed that the average time taken to move from a bachelor's to a master's degree was 8¼ years, but as many as 10 per cent took 15 years and more; while 40 per cent were 38 years of age and beyond (a few above 50 years) by the time the doctor's degree was acquired. The cost factor has these effects: (a) it often denies to the profession the leadership of young men; (b) for those who succeed, the long struggle may dampen the ardour, the initiative, the imagination so necessary to leadership (there is also the loss occasioned by those who fail—those who die before they obtain the degree, and those who have not the health or strength to overcome the obstacles); and (c) many potential leaders are undoubtedly diverted into other fields of endeavour.

The long span of professional life spent by potential leaders in acquiring training represents a great waste, both to the individual and to society, and suggests the need of increased assistance to students to help finance advanced training for the teaching profession.

FINANCE PATTERNS IN IN-SERVICE TRAINING

In-service training is of two main types: (a) that taken by the individual for his own personal and professional advancement, usually offered by institutions of higher education or professional associations, and (b) that which looks toward improved performance in a particular local school situation, often undertaken jointly by a group of teachers.

While for the most part, advanced professional training is carried on voluntarily in evening and Saturday courses or in summer sessions by the teachers in service in institutions accessible to them, the local school system generally affords recognition of such training in the salary scale, thus affording the incentive. A few school systems are now granting leaves with some pay for selected staff members to permit them to acquire special competence in a particular field.

Many voluntary professional organizations afford opportunities for teachers and administrators to develop professional insights into current problems, whether general or specific. These organizations hold meetings and conferences and otherwise provide for leadership and discussion. Ordinarily these organizations are supported from dues paid by the membership.

In recent years an increasing emphasis is being placed upon in-service training offered by school systems themselves. In many local systems the need is recognized; time is set aside; the cost is provided in the budget of the local system. Training may be general or specific; it may employ leadership drawn from professional staff of teacher education institutions or may utilize local leadership. The problems dealt with range from curriculum to guidance; from student health to public relations. But in general, the object is to improve the functioning of the particular system, whether in administration, programme pupil adjustment, teacher performance, or public understanding and support. The cost of these programmes is, of course, considerable, but because it is so integrated with the functioning of the systems, particularly the supervisory functions, it cannot be readily or fully identified.

ROLE OF THE FEDERAL GOVERNMENT IN EDUCATION[1]

As noted in the Introduction, the United States Office of Education, Federal Security Agency, is basically a research, informational and consultative organization, designed, in the words of the Act establishing it (1867), to 'promote the cause of education throughout the country'. While in its early history, and until 1917, it did not assume administrative functions, in recent years it has been called upon to administer federal funds under several provisions, such as those for vocational education, both in agriculture and industry, school housing in critical defence areas, the distribution to schools of war surplus property, the management of vocational training for war production workers.

But the Federal Government does not by any means channel all of its educational relations with the states, the institutions of higher education, or the citizens through the Office of Education. For example, the Immigration and Naturalization Service of the Justice Department has fostered and promoted citizenship education; the Treasury Department has promoted school savings projects; the Department of Agriculture through its Forest Service has promoted conservation education; the Public Health Service has stimulated and assisted in state local public health programmes, and has provided grants-in-aid for training of health educators and others; the Federal Security Agency maintains a service of assistance for the education of the blind; the Civil Aeronautics Administration fosters and develops aviation education and air safety education; the Department of Agriculture through its Production and Marketing Administration administers at the national level and through State Departments of Education the school lunch programme, which daily makes available low cost meals to millions of school children; the Office of Indian Affairs of the Department of the Interior operates both day schools and boarding schools for Indian children who live on non-taxable lands in many areas of the country.

In the field of higher education the Federal Government in 1862 made grants of publicly owned lands to each state for support of

---

1 Much of this information is drawn from *Intergovernmental Relations in Education*, by Robert L. Morlan, Minneapolis, University of Minnesota Press, 1950.

colleges of agriculture and mechanical arts; these colleges are required to maintain military training programmes. There are a number of provisions whereby national government personnel are trained in institutions of higher education at government expense; there are federal appropriations for research; but of transcendent importance have been the provisions for the education of veterans, which include both training for rehabilitation, and the general GI Bills granting educational benefits to veterans of both the second world war and the Korean war—provisions of direct benefit to the individual veteran, and permitting choice of institution.

The Federal Government has for many years been concerned with the educational aspects of agricultural extension, and the agricultural experiment station. The role of the Co-operative Extension Service of the Department of Agriculture is to give instruction in agriculture and home economics by demonstrations on farms and in homes, and by means of publications and radio. The programme is co-operatively administered through the land-grant colleges. Also administered through these colleges are extensive research programmes in agriculture operating through agricultural experiment stations, toward the support of which federal funds are appropriated.

It will be seen from this brief recital of activities of the Federal Government, that federal-state relations are complex, and that without doubt federal influence on local programmes is in far greater proportion than the funds provided.

Looking to the future, the role of the Federal Government, if it should be expanded, may include: (a) Federal aid to the states for elementary and secondary education to ensure equality of educational opportunity to all boys and girls, and (b) scholarships for students in institutions of higher education. These two projects if undertaken would greatly extend the participation of the Federal Government in the financing of higher education. Whether such increased participation will result in greater federal control is difficult to estimate. Proponents of such aid are in general agreement that an increase in federal control is not desirable.

CHAPTER III

SOME TRENDS IN CURRICULUM AND INSTRUCTION IN TEACHER EDUCATION[1]

It is a widely-held view in the United States that there is no one best way to educate teachers and that no one type of institution is best fitted for the preparation of teachers, nor is a single curriculum pattern characteristic of any type of institution. Rather, the curriculum and methods of any given teacher education programme are for the most part developed by the personnel of each institution. True, all states have requirements which individuals must meet to be certified to teach, but even these tend increasingly to be qualitative and broad in scope so as to leave determination of the detailed curriculum and teaching methods to the local institution. Organized professional groups, such as the American Association of Colleges for Teacher Education, establish standards to be met by professional schools, but these standards, too, are built to encourage local planning and experimentation.

Admittedly, there are some disadvantages in the diversity among programmes for the preparation of teachers. When the planning of the curriculum and methods is left to local groups, there is a wide difference in quality of programmes developed, so that prospective teachers in one college do not have the same opportunities as those in another. This inequality in opportunity is reflected in the varying degree of competence among beginning teachers, nor are teachers prepared in one state always fully qualified to teach in another.

On the other hand, such diversity encourages each institution to provide the best programme possible since its reputation depends upon the quality of its product rather than upon a minimum programme to meet standardized requirements. The deliberate fostering of diversity of practice implies a faith that teacher educators are sincere in their desire to prepare teachers fitted for the responsibilities they must assume. Moreover, it implies a belief that when groups of people are stimulated to work co-operatively on improvement of their own programmes, the creative solutions to problems are often superior to solutions set up in advance by a central controlling group.

It would be unfair to leave the impression that all the variation in

---

[1] From a manuscript prepared by Margaret Lindsey.

practice in teacher education is due to a faith in human intelligence and to an experimental approach to our problems. As indicated in Chapter I, there have been many conflicts in the history of the preparation of teachers in this country concerning the philosophy of teacher education, and what are the purposes of the public schools, and what type of education teachers need. Conflicts which emerged at the time of the expansion of the normal school to the teachers college still remain. Differences of opinion which emerged as professional education 'came into its own' still persist. The struggle is still going on to resolve some major questions in teacher education, such as:

Should there be special types of colleges where teachers for elementary schools only are educated? Should these colleges be the state teachers colleges? Should teachers for the secondary schools be prepared only in liberal arts colleges and departments or schools of education in universities?

If prospective teachers build a solid understanding of background knowledge in subject matter, is this adequate preparation for teaching? Or, do teachers need more than subject matter; do they need also to develop professional skills related to the job of helping others to learn?

If some professional education is needed, how much? What should it be? Where should it occur in the programme?

Consequently, as teacher educators take positions on such curriculum issues, resulting programmes vary. In the writing of this particular chapter this has forced a choice between (a) striving in wholly inadequate space to portray the whole range of curricular ideas and practices, and (b) developing more fully one influential point of view, with illustrations. The latter alternative has been selected.

The reader should understand that the viewpoint here emphasized is (a) relatively 'progressive'; (b) more influential in university schools of education and teachers colleges than in colleges of liberal arts—especially, perhaps, those under denominational influence—and, hence (c) more influential in the preparation of elementary than of secondary school teachers. It represents the convictions of a growing proportion of professional educationists, but would be criticized by others of this group and by many professors of the humanities, social sciences, and natural sciences. Among some of the varying criticisms that might thus be evoked would be charges that the point of view emphasized tends: (a) to overstress the scientific in contrast to the moral, ethical, and humanistic foundations of education; (b) to overstress the professional in contrast to the academic or subject-matter components in a programme of teacher education; (c) to assume a closer similarity between the purposes and programmes of elementary and secondary education than actually exists—or should exist; (d) to concentrate upon breadth of training and experience at the expense of

269

depth in some particular area or areas; and (e) to demand intellectual and personal qualities in prospective teachers which, in fact, only a small proportion can be expected to possess.

The extent to which these charges are justified and, if justified, compelling, is a matter of debate—a debate for which there is no room here. The presentation to follow is designed to bring into sharp focus ideas and practices which are becoming increasingly influential, but it is not argued that all competing views and patterns are necessarily inferior.

SOME MAJOR IDEAS AFFECTING MANY CURRICULAR AND METHODOLOGICAL PRACTICES

It is widely held in the United States that the purpose of education is not alone to transmit and preserve the culture of which it is a part. Education must also help individuals to meet effectively personal and social needs which evolve as they and their society mature. In this way, education not only performs the function of transmitting the heritage of knowledge and values but also of contributing to the improvement of living. For this reason, the educational programme must respond in content and method to the issues and problems of the times, and anticipate future developments in the social order. Therefore, one of the bases for determining the role education should play at any given time, and hence the kinds of teachers needed at that time, is the nature of the society in which the educational planning is being done.

Furthermore, education is widely viewed in the United States as a science, both pure and applied. This view implies research, experimentation, and study in a continuous effort to make discoveries through which the process of education can be improved. The accumulated findings from scientific study serve as a second basic determinant in selecting and organizing experiences at any educational level. Traditionally, educators have been concerned about and have made use of information discovered through study of the human organism, how it develops and learns. They now also recognize the great value which can be derived when the findings in other related disciplines, such as psychiatry, sociology, anthropology, and social psychology, are applied to education.

Living in the United States today is quite different from the life of yesterday. The United States is, of course, changing very rapidly from an agrarian society to an industrial society, a change which has been accompanied by shifts in location of population, greater leisure time for more people, organized efforts on the part of labour and management to balance power, and the availability of conveniences and devices which enhance living.

The role of education must therefore be to help children to acquire backgrounds of information and to develop attitudes which ensure socially intelligent behaviour as citizens. Throughout the nation, the actual day-to-day experiences of any individual child must be so planned that he is able to work on those problems which are of concern to him at that time. Only in this way can each child be helped to grow toward maturity.

A VIEW OF THE NATURE OF HUMAN GROWTH AND DEVELOPMENT

Much of what is done in both pre-service and in-service education of teachers finds its basis in what is known about how the human organism grows and develops. While much still remains to be learned about this process of growth, research to date has provided an accumulation of knowledge with abundant implications for the curriculum and methods used in the preparation of teachers. We know, for example, that each individual, as he grows toward maturity, encounters a series of tasks which can be identified, many of which are common to an entire cultural group. This knowledge makes it possible to anticipate the needs of children, youth, and adults at given stages in the growth process.

Further, each individual begins his growth from a different starting point, depending upon his heredity and the environment into which he is born and each progresses from one stage of growth to the next at his own pace, within his own capacity, and under the influence of his own experience. Moreover, no individual develops at exactly the same rate in all aspects of growth; each has an irregular profile within his pattern of development. The various aspects of growth within the individual—physical, social, intellectual, and emotional—are so interrelated that each responds to and affects the others, so that it is unwise to consider one without due recognition of the others. Hence, in any educational endeavour the whole individual must be considered in all efforts to guide his development.

A VIEW OF THE NATURE OF LEARNING

Learning is a process through which individuals modify their behaviour in response to given situations and apply what has been learned to new situations. It is a circular process, beginning with a feeling of need or disturbance within the individual, continuing with procedures used to find possible ways to meet that need or quiet the disturbance, progressing to action. Real learning has not been completed, however, until the individual has reflected upon steps he has taken, generalized the results and applied his generalizations to new situations. Throughout this process he will be discovering new needs which he approaches through this same process of learning. In this sense, learning is continuous and no single experience completes the learning process.

Research findings on how the learning process occurs show that certain factors facilitate good learning and other factors prevent the individual from deriving maximum value from experience. For example, it has been established that the basic need for change in behaviour (learning) must reside within the individual; that he must sense a purpose in what he undertakes; that the motivation for action must come from him. Not only must the learner himself define his needs but he must also be an active participant in all steps of the learning process—in making decisions on what he shall do to meet his needs and how he shall do it; in reflecting upon and evaluating his progress; in generalizing from his experience and making application to new situations which confront him.

Research studies have well established the fact that individuals learn best when they are free from tension and fear. When at any level in the educational programme fear is made the controlling factor in behaviour, the chances for effective learning are reduced to a minimum. This implies that at all levels those who guide learning must bear the responsibility for creating atmospheres which enable each individual to learn in ways best suited to him. Excessively rigid standards to be met at a given time by all students, accompanied by threats of low grades and certain kinds of examinations, rigid authoritarian classroom procedures may interfere with the creation of opportunities for maximal learning. This should not be taken to mean that no goals or standards of excellence can be maintained. On the contrary it points to the possibility of greater and more meaningful achievement when sound principles of learning are understood and applied by the teacher.

IMPLICATIONS FOR TEACHER EDUCATION
IN A DEMOCRATIC SOCIETY

Even more than other citizens, it is the responsibility of teachers to try to see as clearly as possible the issues in the local and world society and ways of dealing with them. This calls for teacher education emphasizing a broad general background of knowledge that can serve as a basis for exercising sound judgment. It demands a process of education that helps prospective teachers develop skills of co-operative action. It requires a programme which draws its content of experience from the world in which teachers live, especially as problems of living impinge upon the day-to-day life of teachers-to-be and the young people they will guide.

What are the implications of what is known about the nature of human growth and development and the learning process for the teaching in elementary and secondary school classrooms?; and, secondly, for the education of prospective teachers? The answer to the first question involves such principles as the following: (a) teachers must understand and plan for the unique needs of every child; (b) teachers must know and use effectively in their guidance of individuals and group the accumulated knowledge regarding the learner and the learning process; (c) teachers must have the skills and techniques for increasing their insights regarding human growth and development in general and regarding the particular children with whom they work. If these principles are accepted it becomes apparent immediately that the pre-service programme must *provide both content and procedures through which students may be helped to develop a growing understanding of human growth and development and of the process of learning.* Further, students must have *opportunity to acquire those skills and attitudes which are basic to continuous deepening of insights regarding learners and the learning process.*

Concerning the second question, one of the basic implications is that the same principles of growth apply at all age levels. This is to say that in pre-service and in in-service teacher education *each individual must be considered as a unique personality and the programme of experiences must be geared to helping him meet his needs as they emerge in his day-to-day living and in his progress toward becoming a professional worker, a mature citizen, and a well-rounded personality.*

This implies that when the exact nature of all the experiences individuals should have in preparation for teaching is defined and set up in advance by the college staff without the participation of the learners, the chances for effective progress toward goals are sharply curtailed. When every individual has the same requirements imposed upon him with the accompanying demands for like progress and like results at the same time, the potential for real learning is decreased. When a situation is dominated by fear, threat, and authoritarian control, again there is a poor environment for learning. Since teacher education is designed to help individuals to learn and, further, since these individuals have as their professional goal the guidance of someone else's learning, it is imperative that full use be made of what is known about the complex process of learning.

Information currently available from studies of the nature of contemporary society and the nature of the learner and the learning process is the basis for determining what kind of teachers are needed and what are the fundamental principles for helping young people to become teachers of that sort. As a basis for interpreting the discussion of teacher education programmes as carried forward in the United States an effort is made here to suggest the goals, the kind of product desired.

THE KIND OF TEACHER SOUGHT

A group of educators and laymen in the process of analysing present teacher education programmes in the United States and developing recommendations for improvement of those programmes first defined the kind of teacher needed. In making this definition, they engaged in study of the basic determinants as indicated earlier. They asked themselves these questions: What is the role of education (and of the teacher) in the kind of society in which we live? What do we know about how the human being grows and develops? What do we know about how learning takes place? Having made a study of these questions, they prepared a statement on the kind of teacher needed. They summarized their findings as follows:

We want teachers who can effectively carry those responsibilities necessary in guiding teaching-learning activities of children and youth in schools which assume their significant and complete role in our society, teachers who themselves demonstrate in personal and professional living the values we hold for our society.

This kind of teacher:

1. Is guided in all his thinking and doing by democratic concepts based upon profound respect for the dignity of the individual.
2. Maintains himself in a state of maximum efficiency and promotes the health of others.
3. Is familiar with the various approaches of man to both the qualitative and the quantitative aspects of his work and uses them appropriately in his work and in his leisure time.
4. Has developed his personality for harmonious living with himself and with others.
5. Is conscious of the values in his own and other cultures, continually re-examines and interprets them in the light of new conditions and experiences; is able to work understandingly with those of other cultural groups.
6. Participates effectively in school and community affairs.
7. Has intellectual vigour; has an inquiring mind; is well informed and continues to keep abreast of social and economic information;

sees the relevancy of knowledge and applies his knowledge to specific situations.

8. Has a continuing mastery of subject matter in a subject area and insight into its basic assumptions; has facility in interpreting content to students in terms of their experience.

9. Has adequate facility in communication.

10. Has a thorough knowledge of all relevant aspects of human growth and development and uses of knowledge to create and foster appropriate learning situations.

11. Uses the school as one of several agencies for the purpose of progressive improvement of man.[1]

CURRICULUM AND INSTRUCTIONAL ISSUES IN PRE-SERVICE TEACHER EDUCATION

Seven fundamental questions currently being explored in pre-service teacher education in the United States are briefly discussed on the following pages.

What is the curriculum?

How should we plan for the personal and professional guidance of students? What role should students play in this guidance?

What should be the common components in the programme?

How much and what kind of provision should be made for differentiation?

How should direct experience be utilized?

What provision should be made to facilitate the student's integration of experience?

How should the various parts of the programme be arranged in the total curriculum?

An attempt is made through discussion of these seven problems to share with the reader some of the possible solutions now being tried out in institutions having promising programmes of teacher education. The point of view represents the trend in the thinking of professional educationists. Its implications are not yet fully realized in practice in the majority of teacher-preparing institutions. It is presented not as typical of American teacher education as a whole, but as representing a somewhat advanced position which is gaining increased acceptance.

---

[1] Unpublished report of State Workshops on the Improvement of Teacher Education, Indiana.

WHAT IS THE CURRICULUM

The curriculum is no longer conceived as merely a group of courses organized in certain sequence. Nor is the curriculum made up solely of the experience offered within the classrooms of the college. The curriculum is all those experiences students have for which the college bears any responsibility. Furthermore, since the curriculum is a total of the experiences of students, with the guidance of their college instructors and advisers, it includes some experiences which are common to all and others which are planned on the basis of individual needs, interests, and abilities. In the last analysis, a curriculum is individual in nature, a sum total of the planned experiences of a given student.

What does this concept of the curriculum mean for a teacher of education? First of all, it means extending and using opportunities for learning in all the experiences of college living. To illustrate: in a certain mid-western college, a budget allocation was received for the construction of a new library. The staff of the college was accustomed to searching for opportunities to provide students with rich learning experiences in the many phases of college living and management. Accordingly, they perceived this budget allocation as presenting a chance to invite students to participate in conducting research, making studies, and producing recommendations on the planning and use of the new library. There was nothing mandatory about the invitation. Those students who were interested and who had the time were encouraged to participate as a part of their preparation for teaching. The staff working with the students considered their role to include careful guidance so that a rich learning experience would result for the students and so that the recommendations finally made would be the best possible within the capacities of the entire institution, both students and staff.

In another college it was discovered that a large number of students were carrying on remunerative work to pay their college expenses. In some cases, the types of jobs held by students not only contributed nothing to their preparation for teaching but actually hampered their preparation. As the faculty of this institution considered this problem, they decided that many types of remunerative work could contribute positively to the student's growth as a prospective teacher. With faculty and students working together, a programme was developed in which work experience for which students were paid became an integral part of the college curriculum. Students engaged in such work activities received the same quality of guidance in those activities as they received in courses on the campus.

In many colleges and universities over the country such experiences as the following are considered integral parts of the curriculum for the preparation of teachers: self-management of residence hall living; operation of college book stores and cafeterias; student self-government; part-time employment connected directly with the institutional programme and even participation in decision-making with respect to administrative policies and procedures to improve the college programme.

This concept of the curriculum also implies the selection and organization of experiences on the basis of individual needs, interests, and abilities. Since students in teacher education programmes have a professional goal in common and because they are at approximately the same stage in development as human organisms, there is obviously some identity in their needs. Experiences designed to help meet these needs make up the common elements of the curriculum. In addition, however, each student has needs and purposes which are peculiar to him and which the college should assume responsibility for helping him to meet. Such individual experiences become a part of the curriculum for each student.

When groups of teachers and students develop co-operatively a curriculum designed for a specific educational goal, they tend to be concerned first with forming a general plan for those experiences which they feel should be common to all students working toward that goal. Such planning merely sets a broad flexible framework within which individual curricula can be developed by each student with his advisers. For example: a group of people including college personnel, personnel already engaged in work in the public schools (teachers, principals, supervisors, and administrators), students, and laymen might co-operatively develop a curriculum for the preparation of elementary school teachers. This curriculum would certainly call for experiences in certain broad areas, comprising what is commonly known as 'general education'. An early step would be to reach agreement concerning certain common understandings or competencies in communication with others. Further specific experiences might be provided through which all students could increase their ability in communication. But it would almost certainly be made possible to select special supplementary experiences to meet the needs of the individual student.

PERSONAL AND PROFESSIONAL GUIDANCE OF STUDENTS

Characteristic of methods employed in modern teacher education programmes is the attention given to the personal and professional guidance of students. Such guidance begins at the time of recruitment and initial selection of students and extends through placement in teaching positions and continued contact with teachers on the job. Despite the great variety of ways in which this guidance is organized, it is considered to be an integral part of the curriculum for prospective teachers.

277

Some institutions have special departments called personnel and guidance departments, or 'student life organizations', or counselling divisions. In some cases these departments have administrative officers who are responsible for co-ordinating the efforts of all toward a programme of adequate guidance for students. In other instances, the entire staff of the college assumes responsiblity for helping students to deal effectively with their personal and professional problems.

Programmes of personal and professional guidance may be the central core of the curriculum. For example, in one institution, when a student is admitted he is immediately assigned to a faculty adviser, along with seven other students. This group of eight students and their adviser carry on a 'personal guidance seminar' throughout the four years of their college programme. As part of this seminar, the adviser works with each student in helping him to make a valid appraisal of his strengths and weaknesses, to select courses and other experiences which this appraisal suggests, and to assess continuously his progress toward his professional and personal goals. The student and his adviser consider long-range purposes and procedures as well as immediate steps to be taken. The plans for each student which emerge make use of all the available opportunities for the student's development, many of these naturally falling within a common sequence of college courses. However, such plans may also involve other types of experience falling completely within the realm of the personal-social living of the student.

Whether or not a special sequence of courses or a seminar is planned to provide the guidance students need, it can be said that most institutions of higher education engaged in teacher preparation regard arrangements for guiding students to be one of their major obligations in curriculum planning. Reliance upon careful guidance of students by staff members alone can, of course, result in imposing preconceived needs on all students and thus persuading all toward the same experiences. This result seldom occurs in teacher guidance programmes when an affirmative role is played by students themselves in the guidance process. Students can share in the gathering of information about themselves, in the development of cumulative records, in making decisions regarding experiences they need and in evaluating their own growth as a result of experiences. Such student participation makes regimented guidance less likely. This concept of co-operative democratic procedures is, of course, not always carried out in practice.

COMMON COMPONENTS IN THE PROGRAMME

Regardless of the particular curriculum patterns which are found in teacher education, all programmes have three parts: (1) general education; (2) provision for specialization; and (3) professional education.

General Education

The purposes of general education are well illustrated in the following statement taken from the bulletin prepared by the University of Minnesota for students who are considering enrolment in that university.

The purpose of general education is to help you take your place in contemporary society, whatever your occupation or your interests may be. It should contribute to your total efficiency both when employed and at leisure. More specifically, a sound general education should enable you:

1. To understand other persons' ideas.
2. To attain a balanced social and emotional adjustment.
3. To improve and maintain your own health.
4. To acquire the knowledge and attitudes basic to satisfying family life.
5. To participate as an active, responsible, and informed citizen.
6. To understand the fundamental discoveries of science.
7. To understand and enjoy literature, music, art, and other cultural activities.
8. To develop a set of principles for the direction of personal and social behaviour.
9. To choose a socially useful and personally satisfying vocation.
10. To develop the ability to think critically and constructively.[1]

Experiences in general education are usually organized around major areas of human knowledge—the social sciences, the natural sciences, the arts and humanities. In most instances, the major work in general education is taken during the first two years of the college programme, and is approximately the same for all students. In the university referred to above, the requirement for all students in general education is as follows:

Area	Courses	Semester hours of credit required
Communication	A sequence of three courses called 'Communication' and taken during the first two years	8
Social sciences	A sequence of three courses called 'Introduction to the Social Sciences' and taken during the first two years	12
Natural sciences	Selected courses from: biology, mathematics, physical science, psychology; or a sequence of three courses called 'Introduction to the Natural Sciences'	12

[1] *Bulletin of the University of Minnesota. College of Science, Literature and the Arts*, 1952–53, p. 3.

Area	Courses	Semester hours of credit required
Humanities	Selected courses from: art, music, foreign language, history, literature, mathematics, philosophy, and speech[1]	12

In one of the mid-western state teachers colleges work in general education is organized in this way:

Area	Courses	Semester hours of credit required
Communication	A sequence of three courses in English composition and speech	8
Science	Mathematics, Physical science, Biology	8
Social sciences	Sociology, Economics, Political science	8
Arts and humanities	An integrated course called 'The Humanities'[2]	8

More important than the organization or sequence of courses, is the method employed in guiding experiences in general education. The basic content in such courses may be oriented to a study of the cultural heritage in each of the areas or it may be oriented to current problems of society, in which case the accumulated knowledge in a given area is used to develop understanding of such problems. Study in general education may be oriented to passive acceptance of information and ideas acquired or it may be rooted in a philosophy of constructive democratic action.

As is true of all educative experiences, the content and method of general education is, at its best, based upon what is known about the society and about the nature of the learner and the learning process. Basic assumptions are that learning is facilitated when students deal with situations which are real to them; when they have inner drive to meet problems confronting them; when they are free to learn in their own best ways. Efforts to apply these principles to general education are frequently apparent today in the United States. Students of contemporary civilization often engage in direct analysis of current social issues through surveys, forums, interviews. They may even participate actively in political campaigns, study the procedures employed by pressure groups, and discuss problems relating to minority groups in our culture. It is rather common to find students, as they pursue a study of the physical sciences, establishing a direct relationship be-

---

1 Ibid., p. 7. The credits required have here been translated from 'quarter hours' to 'semester hours'.
2 Indiana State Teachers College, Terre Haute. The credits have here been translated from 'quarter hours' to 'semester hours'.

tween these organized bodies of knowledge and problems of community sanitation, disease prevention, or the use of atomic energy for the improvement of living.

Provision for Specialization

All curricula provide opportunity for students to specialize. Hence, provision for specialization may be called a common element. However, the detailed provisions made differ from one institution to another and within the same institution the nature of specialization differs from one area to another. Students preparing to teach in secondary schools usually make major preparation in one subject matter area and minor preparation in another. For example, a student may major in English and minor in speech; or he may major in the social studies and minor in English; or he may major in science and minor in mathematics. Provision for specialization through majors and minors is made by accepting related and pertinent general education as basic work in the special area, and, in addition, offering a sequence of courses designed specifically for persons building a specialization in a given area. When prospective secondary school teachers have completed their general education, met requirements in their area of specialization and in professional education, they usually are certified to teach in their major and minor subject matter areas.

Students preparing to teach in the elementary school also specialize. Usually, rather than pursue a sequence of courses in a subject matter area, these students are likely to take a series of courses centring around child development and the methods of teaching in the elementary school. In some colleges provision for such specialization is made through offering so-called integrated or interrelated courses, for which large amounts of time are set aside, and in which attention is given to all the activities common to childhood education. In other institutions, there are separate courses in methods, such as: teaching of reading, teaching of arithmetic, teaching of science, and so on. In still others, students are encouraged to develop special competence in an academic subject, in addition to one of the above fields.

Professional Education

All colleges preparing teachers make some provision for professional education in courses which are aimed specifically at teaching as a profession. Although the exact content and sequences of courses vary greatly among institutions, there are invariably common elements in the professional education for prospective teachers of both elementary and secondary schools. For example, most programmes provide for work in the foundations of education, i.e., basic background material relating to the role of education, the nature of human growth and development, the nature of the learning process, and the historical and philosophical concepts influential in moulding educational practices today. In one college students may be required to take a general course in the sociological foundations of education and a similar general course in the psychological foundations. In another institution students may be required to take educational sociology, history and philosophy of education, child (or adolescent) psychology and the psychology of learning. In still another university the foundations of education are treated in a sequence of three courses: the Child, His Nature and Needs; the School and Society; and the Nature and Direction of Learning. In spite of the differences in specific course patterns, most programmes provide for systematic study of the historical, philosophical, psychological and sociological foundations of education.

DIFFERENTIATION IN THE PROGRAMME

The problem of how much of the pre-service education programme shall be common to all prospective teachers is currently under study, as is the nature and placement of differentiated experiences in the total programme. At least two points seem to be agreed: (a) that all teachers need the same basic general education; and (b) that all teachers need opportunities to practise (do student teaching) in an area of specialization. Beyond these two points of agreement there exists much difference of opinion. It would be fair to say, however, that the trend is toward provision for more common experiences and fewer differentiated experiences.

Current developments in reorganization of courses in professional sequences of courses show this trend. In 1947, a certain programme for prospective teachers in elementary education included child psychology, educational psychology, and principles of elementary education. For those preparing for secondary school teaching it included: adolescent psychology, educational psychology, and principles of secondary education. Today, in place of these six separate courses, three for majors in elementary education and three different ones for majors in secondary education, there is a sequence of two courses taken by all prospective teachers: Human Development and Learning, and Principles and Philosophy of Education. This particular reorganization of courses is based upon the assumptions that all teachers should understand human growth and development at all ages and that the principles of learning are the same for all educational levels. Hence, what formerly was differentiated is now common to all preparing to teach.

Further evidence of this trend toward provision for more common experiences is found in practices developed to balance the supply and demand of teachers. Historically, the schools of this country have gone through periods of critical shortages of teachers for some areas while at the same time having an oversupply of teachers for other levels or areas. This imbalance of supply and demand has produced a concerted effort to develop pre-service programmes in which a student might prepare for teaching in more than one field of study and on more than one level of the educational programme. As study has gone forward on this problem, it has become increasingly clear that many competencies are needed in common by teachers of all levels, suggesting common experiences in pre-service teacher education. In some institutions, programmes are so designed that students graduating from them are certified to teach in both the elementary and secondary schools.

Additional impetus toward reduced differentiation in teacher preparation is found in the changing concepts of secondary education in the country. The high school programme is currently regarded more as general education for the masses rather than as college preparation for the few. This type of high school programme calls for teachers capable of working with children of all types and abilities. Hence it is beginning to be held that their preparation should approximate more closely that of preparation for elementary school teaching.

What has been said thus far suggests a movement toward less differentiation in programmes. Provision is made however, for specialization, the degree of specialization depending upon the unique competencies called for by a particular teaching job. For example, students preparing to work in vocational education; in special subjects such as music, art, and physical education; or in programmes for a typical children (handicapped or otherwise abnormal) have a high degree of specialization.

UTILIZATION OF DIRECT EXPERIENCE

In 1945 the American Association of Teachers Colleges undertook a study of the place of direct experience in teacher education for the purpose of setting up qualitative standards which might be used by institutions in appraising their own programmes and which might, at the same time, provide some direction for institutions engaged in improving this aspect of the total curriculum. During this study those working on it (including several hundred people from all types of institutions and all geographical areas) developed a concept of direct experiences—or, as they called them, 'professional laboratory experiences'—which has now become a goal toward which many

283

programmes are striving. This goal is best described in a series of principles suggested as a basis for determining the function and type of direct experiences to be offered the prospective teacher.

The group of teacher educators initiating this study set up two definitions which are significant as background for discussion of principles governing the use of direct experience. *Professional laboratory experiences* were defined to include *all those contacts with children, youth and adults (through observation, participation, and teaching) which make a direct contribution to an understanding of individuals and their guidance in the teaching-learning process.* Within these experiences would be also those known as *student teaching,* which was defined as *the period of teaching when the student takes increasing responsibility for the work within a given group of learners over a period of consecutive weeks.*[1]

On the basis of these two definitions and convictions regarding the importance of direct experience in teacher education, the following principles were developed:

1. The particular contribution of professional laboratory experiences (including student teaching) to the education of teachers is three-fold: (a) an opportunity to implement theory—both to study the pragmatic value of the theory and to check with the student his understanding of the theory in application; (b) a field of activity which, through raising questions and problems, helps the student to see his needs for further study; and (c) an opportunity to study with the student his ability to function effectively when guiding actual teaching-learning situations.

2. The nature and extent of professional laboratory experiences should be planned in terms of the abilities and needs of the student and should be an integral part of the total programme of guidance.

3. Professional laboratory experiences should provide guided contact with children and youth of differing abilities and maturity levels, and of differing socio-economic backgrounds for a period of time sufficient to contribute to functional understanding of human growth and development.

4. The professional programme should be so designed as to afford opportunity for responsible participation in all the important phases of the teacher's activities, both in and out of school.

5. Professional laboratory experiences should be co-operatively developed by the student and his advisers. Adequate supervision and guidance should be provided through co-operative efforts of laboratory and college teachers.

6. Professional laboratory experiences should be integrated with other phases of the student's programme. Professional education is a

---

1 American Association of Teachers Colleges. *School and Community Laboratory Experiences in Teacher Education.* 1948. pp. 6–7. (Available from Mr. Edward Pomeroy, Executive Secretary, American Association of Colleges for Teacher Education, Oneonta, New York.)

responsibility shared by all members of the faculty, each contributing to the maximum development of the student as individual, citizen, and as member of the teaching profession.

7. Evaluation of professional laboratory experiences should be in terms of growth in understandings and abilities needed in the situations faced by the teacher working in our democracy.

8. Physical facilities should be adequate to provide a range of first-hand experiences with children, youth, and adults in varied home, school, and community situations.

9. Professional laboratory experiences should be developed to recognize needed continuity in the pre-service and in-service educational programmes.

It is well known that many persons who demonstrate verbal understanding of theoretical concepts are unable to make application of those concepts. For this reason, students preparing to teach need continuous opportunity to check their understanding of concepts through putting them into action. As individuals mature individual differences among them become greater. Hence, it is important that they be recognized in planning programmes with college students. This implies that students should enter upon professional laboratory experiences, including practice teaching, at different points in their programme. The time devoted to student teaching and the nature of such experiences should be determined by the particular needs of the student.

The task of today's teacher in the classroom with children is more complex than ever in the past. Work in the classroom is only part of the responsibility of a good teacher. He participates in many school activities, he shares in the formulation of administrative policies, he contributes to improvement of the curriculum, and he is an active member in his community. He is also a wholesome, well-adjusted personality. The extension of professional laboratory experiences from the typical student teaching period to varied direct experience over the entire pre-service programme calls for additional use of facilities and their extension. The laboratory or practice school nevertheless remains a very important facility in the teacher education programme. But no single school can meet all the needs of a group of students. Not only are many schools needed but other types of facilities should be available, e.g. various community service agencies, camps, playgrounds, libraries, co-operatives.

There is a growing tendency to eliminate the former sharp distinction between pre-service and in-service teacher education. The trend is toward one continuum of professional education with the college assuming major responsibility in the early years, but with both groups co-operating on programmes for continuous professional development of the teacher during both stages, pre-service and in-service.

Since the initiation of the study mentioned above, college staffs all over the country have been exploring ways to apply these concepts in their programmes of teacher education. Currently, prospective teachers are finding more and more opportunities in their programmes to use direct experience as one way of learning, as one very important way of developing competencies for teaching. A few observations of what has been happening in this respect might serve to point up the significance of this movement.

1. Whereas a few years ago most colleges allotted one hour a day for nine to twelve weeks for student teaching in a single classroom for observing, participating, and finally, teaching in one area of the curriculum, today more and more students have an opportunity to devote a period of weeks or months out of their college programmes exclusively to student teaching, spending full-time in a school, not only assuming the responsibilities of a teacher with a group of children in the classroom but also participating in other school activities of various kinds.

2. Whereas a few years ago most prospective teachers found their only direct experience with children confined to a single limited student teaching experience, today more and more students have many and varied opportunities for professional laboratory experience in several schools or classes throughout their whole college preparation for teaching.

3. Whereas a few years ago the limited experiences provided for students preparing to teach were confined to schools, today programmes are increasingly designed to offer them experiences in community activities.[1]

4. Whereas a few years ago direct or laboratory experiences were almost strictly confined to courses in professional education, today some of the most useful direct experiences are provided in connexion with general education and other academic courses.

---

1 Unfortunately, space does not permit concrete illustration of the types of professional laboratory experiences now being explored by colleges. Such illustrations are available in other publications. For example: The Association for Student Teaching publishes a yearbook which deals with the nature and function of professional laboratory experiences in pre-service teacher education. Each of these yearbooks includes a comprehensive annotated bibliography of publications released during the preceding year. Here one can find reference to numerous periodical contributions which discuss theory behind practice and which describe practices. Publications of this association are available from the office of the Executive Secretary, Dr. Allan D. Patterson, State Teachers College, Lock Haven, Pennsylvania.

Publications of the Commission on Teacher Education of the American Council on Education also present valuable material on current precepts and practices in both pre-service and in-service teacher education in this country. Of special import with respect to the topic under discussion here are: *The College and Teacher Education*, by William Earl Armstrong and others; *The Improvement of Teacher Education*; *Teachers for our Times*; *Helping Teachers Understand Children*; *State Programmes for the Improvement of Teacher Education*, by Charles E. Prall; *Teacher Education in Service*, by Charles E. Prall and Charles Cushman; *Evaluation in Teacher Education*, by Maurice E. Troyer and Charles R. Pace.

These publications, which are listed in the bibliography on page 340, are all available from the American Council on Education, 1785 Mass. Avenue N.W., Washington, D.C.

5. Whereas a few years ago the guidance of direct or laboratory experience was done by a single person (usually a supervisor of student teaching), today several instructors participate in guiding and evaluating co-operatively the professional laboratory experiences of each student.

INTEGRATION OF EXPERIENCES

The theory of integration, or inter-relationship of learning, is that an individual selects from his real learning experiences those factors which have meaning for him, assimilates them, relates them to a larger whole, reconstructs his behaviour in terms of the added factors, and applies this new behaviour to problems he faces. Such integration is an objective of most programmes of teacher education. While this process is purely individual and can be accomplished only by the individual, it is, however, the task of teacher educators to facilitate the likelihood of such integration in every way possible.

Effort is now being made at all levels in education to discover ways of helping individuals to accomplish this integration. Among those teacher education practices which are regarded as most promising are the following: (a) organizing content and experiences so that those courses, subjects, topics, and materials which belong together are considered in co-ordinated and related ways; (b) organizing instruction around concrete problems and offering opportunities for direct action by students; (c) arranging for a continuous contact between students and selected staff members.

The following diagram illustrates steps which have been successively taken by some institutions so as to increase the degree to which related experiences and fields of knowledge are brought together for the student. Of course such a plan does no more than to increase the ease with which the student might achieve his own integration.

Step 1 Curriculum consists of individual methods courses	Step 2 Curriculum consists of area methods courses	Step 3 Curriculum consists of an integrated course
Teaching of reading	} The languages arts in childhood education	
Teaching language		
Teaching of science	} Health, play, science and safety in childhood education	The child and the curriculum
Teaching of safety		
Teaching of arithmetic	Teaching of arithmetic	
Teaching of history and civics	} Social studies in childhood education	
Teaching of geography		

While the steps indicated above and the exact organization are not duplicated in many colleges, they do illustrate one type of movement away from isolated methods courses toward integrated courses. This is a definite trend in curriculum organization in the United States, particularly in programmes designed to prepare teachers for elementary schools. The basic premise is one of providing for the student's own real integration by making it possible for him to organize his experience around a central core of knowledge.

This trend is equally popular in general education where related fields of knowledge are drawn together into a single course (see p. 279). Another way in which some colleges attempt to provide for integration is well demonstrated in certain professional education programmes for the preparation of teachers for secondary schools where courses which were formerly isolated and taught from textbooks are now integrated and based upon actual experiences which accompany the courses.

Once taught as separate courses	Now combined into one integrated course called
Principles of Secondary Education Special Methods (in the student's area of specialization) Educational Psychology	Principles and Methods in Secondary Schools and accompanied by a wide range of direct experiences

With this new organization it is possible for students to discover their needs, to identify real problems, to observe the many manifestations of a problem as they participate in an actual teaching-learning situation. With these observations as their background they are able to plan activities in the light of a total situation and to make effective use of a wide range of resources in attacking real problems.

Close and continuous guidance of individual students is still another way of providing for integration. Since integration is something that takes place within an individual and is conditioned by readiness for experience, it is considered important that each student have a counselor who takes responsibility for knowing the student extremely well, helping him to appraise his readiness and to plan experiences that are right for him at a given time. Of course, it is important that all college teachers know their students and plan with them on the basis of their particular needs. However, it is unrealistic to expect every college teacher to know every student well. Therefore, to insure that each student has guidance in selecting experiences which seem to hold most promise for him at the time, it is found helpful to have some organization of staff counseling that provides for special understanding of each student on the part of at least one staff member. Of course, it is immediately apparent that unless this special understanding is used in planning for all the major activities of the student, it has limited value.

The discussion of curriculum and instruction issues here is not exhaustive. Many more such problems or issues confront teachers or educators in the United States. Some of the issues having a direct bearing on curriculum and methods are administrative in character, e.g. selection of college teaching personnel, budget allocations for various parts of the programme, degree of co-operative planning of administrative policy, initiative and leadership, and quality of human relations.

As to the arrangement of provisions for experiences in the total curriculum pattern, there is no one pattern characteristic of all programmes for the preparation of teachers in the United States. A brief review of some representative curriculum patterns may help the reader to understand the arrangement of courses and the placement of the three common elements—general education, provision for specialization, and professional education—in the programme.

Chart I illustrates a four-year programme designed for the preparation of teachers for elementary schools in which the common elements run concurrently throughout the four years. (See following page.)

This pattern is built upon certain premises, such as the following: (a) students who enter an institution knowing they want to become teachers should have the opportunity to begin immediately working directly toward that goal; (b) the process of developing from an adolescent toward a mature professional person is gradual and therefore attention to this process should be given throughout the college programme; (c) those reponsible for inducting members into the profession should have an opportunity over a period of time to select those students best fitted for the demands of teaching; (d) since general education is the beginning of a process which it is hoped all teachers will continue on their own initiative after college, it seems desirable to have opportunities for experiences in general education throughout the programme. The pattern illustrated here serves as the general curriculum pattern for many institutions, but there is wide variation in the specific development of programmes.

The following features of this pattern are interesting in relation to the curriculum issues discussed earlier: (a) there is no special provision in the sequence of courses for devoting course time to personal and professional guidance of students. In this programme such guidance is considered as part of the obligation of all staff members and, in addition, a system where each student has a faculty adviser is in practice; (b) both general and professional education are part of the work of each of the four years; (c) differentiation is provided for chiefly by the professional sequence—Child Development, The Child and Curriculum I and II, Practicum in Elementary Education (student teaching), and Seminar in Elementary Education. In this college, students preparing to teach in the secondary school would take a different sequence of professional courses; (d) while it is not apparent from the courses

CHART I. Distribution of courses in four-year programme: elementary education (State Teachers College, Oneonta, New York)

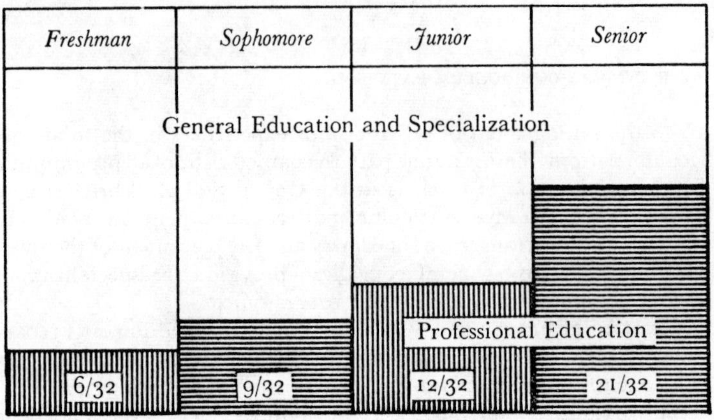

The actual courses in this programme are as follows:

Freshman year	Semester hours of credit	Sophomore year	Semester hours of credit
Essentials of art	4	The child and the curriculum I	6
Child development	6		
Written composition and speech	6	Written composition and speech	6
General mathematics	3	Health education	2
Essentials of music	4	Physical education	0
Physical education	0	Biology	6
Introductory science	3	Contemporary civilization	6
History of civilization	6	Electives	6
	32		32

Junior year	Semester hours of credit	Senior year	Semester hours of credit
Industrial and practical arts	3	Practicum in elementary school teaching	15
The child and the curriculum II	6	Seminar in elementary education	3
English literature	3	Contemporary literature	3
American literature	3	General geography	3
General geography	3	Health protection	2
Physical education	2	Physical education activities	0
American history and government	6	Sociology	3
Electives	6	Electives	3
	32		32

listed, the programme does provide for direct experiences in both general and professional education; (e) one type of arrangement to promote the student's integration is illustrated in the professional sequence, where rather than pursue a series of courses dealing with isolated parts of the curriculum for children, students take two integrated courses—The Child and the Curriculum I and II.

What is commonly referred to as the 'two-two-pattern' in teacher education is illustrated in Chart II. The prospective teacher pursuing a pattern of this type usually devotes the first two years of his college programme to general education and in the last two years devotes a major portion of his time to professional education. Some of the work he does in general education is a basis for his specialization, and he is likely to continue that specialization while he is concentrating on professional education.

CHART II. Distribution of courses in curriculum designed on the basis of two years of general education followed by two years of professional education: secondary education (University of Wisconsin)

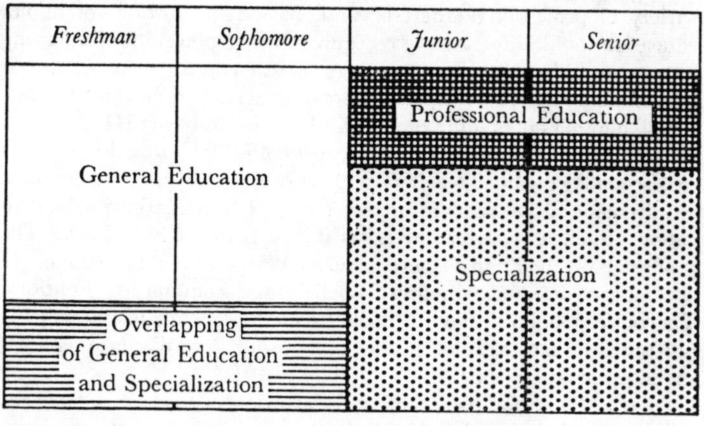

During the junior and senior years the student concentrates on a programme in the School of Education, drawing upon the School of Letters and Sciences wherever he needs to in order to complete his specialization requirements. In the programme of the School of Education he must meet the following requirements:

	Semester hours
The child: his nature and needs	3
The school and society	3
The nature and direction of learnings[1]	5
Methods course (in major field)[1]	5
Elective in education	2
	18

[1] Student teaching is a part of this course.

It is well to note here the concentration of professional education in the last two years of the college programme; that 13 out of the 18 semester hours in the professional education programme are in foundations of education; and that there is considerable overlapping between the general education and work taken in the area of specialization. Colleges and universities whose curriculum is established on this pattern are convinced that many students do not know when they enter college that they want to be teachers, and therefore the programme should permit making that decision later in the college years without penalty of having to make up additional work; if professional choices are made later in college life, opportunities for guiding students into and out of the profession are increased. It frequently happens that institutions following the two-two plan are multipurpose colleges, featuring teacher preparation as only one of their strengths and providing a general education programme designed for all their students. This gives opportunity to make two additional claims: first, it is important that members of all professions be broadened by having the opportunity to live and study with people having a variety of professional interests; and, second, institutions of higher education should increasingly recognize their responsibility for serving a community by providing two years of basic education for all; this is no less valuable as preparation for professional education which follows.

Still another curriculum pattern is illustrated in Chart III. As is true in a few other institutions, the University of Buffalo provides prospective secondary school teachers with two alternatives for meeting a requirement of five years in pre-service teacher education for certification. (Such a requirement exists in the State of New York.) The professional education is here blocked into a unit and planned to accompany direct experiences in school and community situations. This professional unit may be taken by the prospective teacher during his fourth or fifth year of college preparation (the diagram assumes the latter arrangement).

Such a design for the preparation of teachers calls for a five-year programme in which professional education is concentrated in an intensive one-half year block during the fourth or fifth year. Advocates of this pattern hold that the first requisite for successful teaching is a liberal education. They believe that professional choices should be made at a time when students are more mature. They believe that professional education has more meaning and can be accomplished with less waste of time and energy after a student has a base of broad general education. Some believe that all of professional education should be built in and around the job of teaching and therefore incorporated into the fifth-year programme as an internship.

The wide differences of opinion which exist among educators in the United States concerning the nature of the curriculum pattern for the preparation of teachers often promote research and experimentation, encourage educators to find better solutions to their common problems, and stimulate the creativity of all. At the same time all teacher educators and others concerned continue to seek new insights and develop new generalizations which will serve as guides.

CHART III. The curriculum pattern of a programme designed on the basis of a five-year requirement for certification: secondary level (University of Buffalo)

Freshman	Sophomore	Junior	Senior	Fifth Year
General Education and Specialization				Professional Education
				Specialization

Preparation in academic subjects is provided for students in full-time study in the College of Arts and Science where courses in subject matter fields and methods are offered by the various departments. The remaining professional work in education to meet minimum requirements for certification in New York State is concentrated in an intensive integrated programme as follows:
Preparation for Teaching—The Professional Unit in Education—16 semester hours. (An intensive programme closely articulated with observation and supervised student teaching ... including lectures, discussions, laboratory demonstrations, visits to schools, group work, observations, and supervised student teaching.)[1]

[1] *University of Buffalo Bulletin*, Vol. XXXIX, No. 8, p. 224, May 1951.

THE CONTENT AND CHARACTER OF EDUCATION OF TEACHERS IN SERVICE

No matter how adequate the programme of pre-service education may be, no individual ever enters the profession as a finished teacher. Much remains to be learned on the job as the teacher continues to meet new combinations of children, situations, and events with each passing year. Furthermore, the nature of the educational profession is such that new knowledge is being made available all the time. A teacher must run rather hard just to keep abreast of developments, to say nothing of advancing his insights. Therefore it is considered essential that education continue throughout the professional life of the teacher.

As noted earlier in this chapter, programmes of in-service education are no longer designed primarily to fill the gaps left as a result of inadequate pre-service education. Nor are such programmes related solely to courses offered by institutions of higher learning. In fact, in-service programmes are, increasingly, centred in the problems of a local school or school system and characterized by co-operative group attack on common problems.

Because the content and procedures used in in-service education are directly related to a given situation, and since situations differ widely, there results the same diversity in practice as is true of pre-service programmes. However, the processes used by teachers, principals, and other professional educators as they work on their common problems are influenced greatly by the same body of accumulated knowledge and professional opinion on which the curriculum and methodology of teacher education are based. In other words, the same general principles govern both pre-service and in-service programmes in teacher education. Each local school system and often each individual school within a school system makes its own plans and provisions for continued growth on the job by its teachers. While some common required experiences are provided, mostly for the purpose of developing unity and morale in staff groups, programmes of in-service education include a number of voluntary opportunities designed to meet the differing needs of individual teachers.

This relatively new kind of in-service education programme has given rise to new problems for school officials. If classroom teachers are to take responsibility for identifying their own problems, for working on them co-operatively with their peers (drawing upon available leadership and resources as needed), adequate time for this purpose must be provided. Among the many steps taken by some local school systems to solve this problem is that of giving teachers an occasional afternoon so that they may work jointly on school problems. Other school systems set aside three to five days for this purpose at some time during the school year when teachers are freed of other responsibilities. Where such administrative arrangements are made to facilitate co-operative in-service growth of teachers, usually teachers are paid for time spent.

Often, too, special compensations result for teachers who engage in professional growth activities. Such compensations may be in the form of increased salaries, or they may be in the form of payment for special fees involved in the activities. Frequently, school officials make compensations in the form of a budget allocation to a group of teachers to be used in securing the services of special consultants to help on given problems or to secure needed material resources.

While primary responsibility for programmes of in-service education is assumed by the official professional leaders in local community schools, often in co-operation with the teachers, pre-service teacher education institutions share this responsibility in their service area in two ways. First, they usually take considerable initiative in following up their graduates during the latter's first year on the job. There may be visits to teachers in their schools or conferences on the college campus or both. Sometimes, as an additional feature, these first-year teachers may be relieved for a week by student teachers from the college so that they may go back to college for an intensive work conference during the second semester. A second way in which pre-service colleges share responsibility for in-service education of teachers in their area is to offer extension courses, sponsor local workshops (explained below), or serve as consultants to local school systems. These steps are often in addition to the typical later afternoon, evening, Saturday, and summer courses designed to help teachers on the job to advance their professional competence.

As indicated earlier, local school leadership commonly provides opportunities for the teaching group to help plan their own in-service education. When there is a continuous, co-operative effort at curriculum improvement in a school system, teachers secure incidentally much in-service education through group discussion and co-operative planning of a better school programme. Special conferences, courses, workshops, study groups, excursions, and consultant help invariably emerges from the work on the curriculum improvement programme.

Some of the responsibility for in-service education is shared by professional organizations, such as teachers associations, or local branches of professional organizations, such as the Association for Childhood Education International.

Most programmes of in-service education make use at one time or another of consultants from a nearby institution for teacher education, or from state, city, or private universities. Members of the staff of the state department of education are often called in to help with in-service education. Sometimes teachers are sent to outside conferences sponsored by colleges or universities, by the state department of education, or by a professional association.

SOME COMMON FEATURES OF IN-SERVICE PROGRAMMES

The in-service education programme of an active and up-to-date school system in the United States might include any or all of the following features:

Teachers' Meetings

The teachers in one school building or one high school department or those teaching the same grade in different elementary schools usually meet at regular intervals. Here problems are aired, help is exchanged, and curriculum planning is done.

General meetings of all the teachers in a school system or district within a larger system are usually held at the beginning of the year and occasionally during the year. Often a special programme or speaker is brought for such an occasion.

Many school systems have advisory or instruction councils or committees representing the individual schools. Sub-committees may carry out studies or prepare materials for the teaching group as a whole. Committees within an individual school may serve similar functions.

Work Conferences

It is becoming rather common for local school systems to hold a planning conference for new teachers or all teachers for one to five days preceding the opening of school each year. Some school systems provide for so-called work conferences of one or two days one or more times during the school year. Such conferences are highly informal and are focussed on concrete, practical problems. Conferences of this type sometimes provide a few days of evaluation or assessment at the end of the school year and advance planning for the next year.

Workshops

Local school system workshops may be sponsored during the school year or during the summer. These will bring selected—usually self-selected—teachers together, with certain administrative leaders and often a few outside consultants, to work intensively on problems of programme improvement identified by the participants. The aim is to lay the groundwork for early changes in the curriculum or in methods of teaching. Of workshops held during the school year, some meet weekly after school and evenings for a number of sessions; some are concentrated in three to five consecutive sessions, again using the after-school and evening time. In addition to work on specific professional problems, such workshops often provide teachers with an opportunity for direct experiences in creative arts, for conducting science experiments or otherwise increasing their understanding and skills in fields representing personal interests. Commonly, the workshop is devoted to solving problems of classroom management or teaching methods, using discussion, films and audio-visual techniques and other means of learning. Summer workshops of three to five weeks duration often combine all of these features.

Study Groups

Teachers having a common interest in studying a new area such as evaluation of mental hygiene may organize for regular meetings, monthly or bi-monthly.

Those programmes of in-service education judged most successful are those in which administrators, supervisors, and teachers participate jointly and which are co-operatively planned and managed.

The history of this period in teacher education will reflect a number of conceptual conflicts and unresolved issues. At the same time, it will tell of a vast effort to strengthen American education by improving the quality of teaching. This is a period of tremendous experimentation and change. Such a period may presage drastic revisions in both precepts and practices involved in the initial preparation and in the provision for continuous professional growth of teachers.

CHAPTER IV

THE STATUS OF TEACHERS IN THE UNITED STATES

The discussion of the education of teachers in the preceding chapters has touched upon many aspects of the role and status of the public school teacher in American society. In the United States, contrary to the situation in most other countries, the teacher is not a functionary of the national government. He is usually an employee of the local community, with certain rights and privileges deriving from and responsibilities to his particular state. Despite the high degree of de-centralization of educational controls, teachers and the general public hold throughout the country many common fundamental concepts, reflected in wide similarities in school practices. Thus it is possible to generalize somewhat about the economic, social and professional status of teachers.

Typically, the teacher occupies an honoured and enviable position in American life. In the average community the teacher is among the best educated, the most economically secure, and the most highly respected. With the exception of college and university professors, and possibly clergymen, he has more leisure time for travel, cultural pursuits, and professional self-improvement than other professional groups.

While having a lower standard of living than physicians, lawyers, and some engaged in commercial occupations, he compares favourably with them in economic security, as well as in the general respect accorded to his work. The teacher who attains an administrative post, such as a superintendency of a large city school system or a major school principalship, or a supervisory position may achieve a salary, living standard, and social recognition comparable to those of any other profession. Such opportunities are relatively numerous for those with the requisite qualities of leadership, in view of the emphasis in the United States upon the 'science of administration'.

Teachers find it easier than most other occupational groups to change positions at will, even to seek more attractive places to work in distant parts of the country. They have long summer vacations—usually two or two-and-one-half months—which they are free, if they so desire, to devote to supplementary employment. At the same time, they enjoy the various advantages of public service, protected in old age and illness by publicly supported programmes of retirement and insurance benefits. Above all, teachers everywhere have in common the personal satisfactions of living in an atmosphere of social utility. For most of them, no material benefits compare with the satisfaction of serving youth.

These advantages of teaching are, to be sure, balanced somewhat by restraints and limitations. Some of these restraints stem from the teacher's status as an employee of the local community. Local responsibility for education brings the average citizen into close, frequent contact with the schools. The voter, the taxpayer, the parent, the member of religious and civic groups of all sorts has a direct interest and stake in the schools. This interest extending to individual teachers sometimes places them under closer informal surveillance than they would desire. In extreme cases, this may become in the estimation of the teacher an invasion of privacy, or he may view it as interference in professional matters. Such it may well be. But, in the great majority of cases, citizen participation and interest in school affairs is far more advantageous than deleterious, by providing public discussion and support in important matters affecting local education. In the long run, the joint co-operative community action which usually results is in the interest both of the teacher and the community as a whole.

One of the most crucial factors affecting adversely the status of teachers in the United States is the sheer problem of numbers. Even before the recent vast post-war increase in school population, approximately one per cent of all adult citizens were needed to staff the schools and colleges of the country. Teachers constitute the largest professional group in the United States. A related factor affecting the status of teachers is the heavy competition from other professions for the ablest and most personable young people of the nation. These two factors taken together have obviously an adverse effect upon the status of a profession requiring such large numbers of persons with high intellectual and other qualifications. They make it extremely difficult to maintain the high standards desired in the selection of teachers.

The sections of this chapter which follow are adapted from manuscripts prepared by members of the staff of the Research Division of the National Education Association. These sections are designed to bring out some of the implications of the two factors mentioned above, and many others, upon the economic, social, civic, political and professional status of teachers in the United States. They consciously overstress somewhat the *problems* confronting teachers. This reflects a general tendency in the American teaching profession to be highly self-critical as a means toward progressive self-improvement. The studies reported are objective and factual, but were often designed to bring into sharp focus specific conditions which need to be remedied. As with medical and other scientific research, educational research naturally emphasizes problems or obstacles to be overcome rather than the normal healthy situations which present no difficulty. This perspective may be needed in order to interpret accurately some of the studies reported, particularly those based upon very small samples.

Another approach to the status of the teacher is to be found in the growing body of sociological and interdisciplinary research in which an entire community is studied intensively. This approach would provide some of the perspective needed to understand where the teaching profession fits into the complex social and economic structure of the American community. Since such studies cannot readily be generalized for the country as a whole, little use could be made of them for the present purpose.

THE ECONOMIC STATUS OF TEACHERS[1]

As with other aspects of public education, the economic status of teachers varies widely in different parts of the United States. Teachers' earnings and working conditions in general are determined by 48 state legislatures and many thousands of local boards of education. In general, teachers are at about the middle of the economic scale when all earners in the country are considered, but low compared to other professions.

COMPENSATION FOR TEACHING SERVICES

In the calendar year 1939 the average salary of the instructional personnel of the public elementary and secondary schools was an estimated $1,420.[2] This amount is taken as 100 per cent in the comparisons made for other years. The average salary in 1925 was 89 per cent of the 1939 average. It rose slowly but steadily during 1926, 1927, 1928, 1929, and even in 1930 and 1931, as the effect of the 1929 depression did not immediately reach the schools. A three-year downward trend began in 1931, which reached bottom in 1934, when the salary average was only 87 per cent of the 1939 figure. Since 1934 there has been at least a slight increase each year. The average salary is estimated to have been $3,190 in 1951. This amount was more than double—125 per cent higher—the pre-war average of 1939.

Much of this salary increase was only apparent, not real. The war that began in 1939 and included the United States late in 1941 was

---

1 Adapted from a manuscript prepared by Hazel Davis.
2 National Education Association, Research Division. *The Economic Status of Teachers, 1952–53*. Washington, D.C., The Association, 1952, p. 14.

accompanied by great increases in employment, production, and income. Wage rates, prices and taxes rose. Through most of the years from 1939 through 1951, the earnings of teachers failed to keep up with those many upward trends.

Prices were only partially controlled. During several of the war years, the average earnings of teachers were worth less in buying power than during the pre-war period. The value of the average salary dropped again in 1947, after price controls were discontinued and prices rose rapidly. In 1947, however, a great wave of public concern over the plight of the schools found expression in fiscal legislation in almost every state. The average dollar earnings of teachers have risen substantially each year since 1946, and there has been a slight increase in actual buying power. When adjustments are made for the 90 per cent increase in prices since 1939, and the salary is expressed in buying power, it can be shown that the value of the average salary was about 27 per cent higher in 1952 than in 1939. Much of this increase in purchasing power has occurred since 1946.

In addition to prices, increased income taxes have reduced the apparent increase in teachers' salaries. Prior to 1939, employees of state and local governments were exempt from federal income tax. Beginning that year, however, federal income taxes were levied on teachers and other employees of state and local governments. Although the rates are relatively moderate on middle incomes such as those earned by teachers, they take a substantial slice from the teacher's dollar. For example, the public school teacher who in 1951 received the average salary in his profession had about 15 per cent of it withheld for federal income taxes, if he had no dependents. If he had two or more dependents his tax was 7 per cent or less.

DIFFERENCES IN SALARY

The foregoing discussion refers to the national average salary of all instructional personnel in public schools. This emphasis on the average is not meant to obscure the fact that there always have been wide differences in salaries. In part, the wide range between the best paid and the least well paid teachers 25 years ago was to be accounted for by the varying numbers of weeks or months of service rendered in a 'school year'. In 1925 in one state the average school term was 57 days less than the average term in one other state.[1] Within states the school term was often shorter in rural areas than in cities. With both longer school terms and higher monthly salaries favouring urban

---

[1] U.S. Office of Education. *Statistics of State School Systems, 1924–25.* (Bulletin 1927, No. 13). Washington, D.C., Government Printing Office, 1927, p. 22.

teachers, there are still striking differences in the nation as a whole, between the lowest paid rural teachers and the highest paid city teachers. But the extremes are not so great, either within or among states, now as in 1925. Many state legislatures have improved the legal and fiscal structure of the schools, so as to overcome some of the handicaps suffered by the low-income rural areas. A measure of the improvement may be seen in a comparison available for the years 1936 and 1948. In 1935–36, the average salary of urban teachers in 36 states was 2.2 times the average salary of rural teachers. In 1947–48, in the same 36 states, the urban salary was only 1.5 times the rural average.[1]

Money has been made available from state funds to lengthen the school term. Funds are also provided in a majority of states to guarantee a legal minimum salary for the teacher in even the least-favoured rural areas. In 1925, in one state average salaries were 4.4 times the average in the lowest state. This difference between states was reduced by 1950 to a maximum of three to one. The trend toward a narrower range of salaries thus has not been so powerful as to do away with all the diversity among states. But it should be noted that the major differences between states are balanced in part by wide differences in cost of living.

Another type of difference in salaries that is diminishing is the differential between elementary school and secondary school teachers. The NEA Research Division publishes reports biennially on the salaries paid to various groups of teachers in city school systems. Its 1951 report, for example, made comparisons with 1931.[2] To select one group of cities for illustration, the cities regarded as of *average size*, 30,000 to 100,000 in population, may be used. In 1931, the teachers in high schools received median salaries 31 per cent higher than those in elementary schools. But in 1951 the median for high school teachers was only 17 per cent higher.

Differences in the relationship of administrative salaries to those of teachers are also being reduced. In the same group of cities mentioned above over the same 20-year span, the salary advantage of elementary school supervising principals over elementary school classroom teachers fell from 64 per cent higher to only 43 per cent. All groups advanced in salary, but advances were greater for elementary school teachers than for high school teachers. Also the advances were greater for classroom teachers than for supervisory and administrative officers.

Differences between salaries paid in large cities and those paid in small cities and rural areas are also being narrowed. In 1931, the

[1] Smith, Rose Marie. *Education in Rural and City School Systems: Some Statistical Indices for 1947–48*, (U.S. Office of Education. Circular No. 329). Washington, D.C., Government Printing Office, 1951, p. 3.
[2] National Education Association, Research Division. 'Salaries and Salary Schedules of City-School Employees, 1950–51'. *Research Bulletin*, Vol. 29, April 1951, pp. 55–83.

classroom teachers in the 18 largest cities received a median salary that was 90 per cent higher than the median salary in cities of 2,500 to 5,000 population. In 1951 the difference was still great, but had shrunk to 57 per cent.

The relative improvement in salaries of elementary school teachers, and of teachers in rural and small city school systems are directly related to certain factors which are discussed briefly in a later section of this report.

COMPARISONS WITH OTHER OCCUPATIONAL GROUPS

Little reliable information is available on the relative earnings of individuals in various occupations. The teaching profession is unique in the substantial amount of available information. However, the average earnings of all types of employees combined are reported annually both for various industries and for the nation as a whole.[1] Estimates are also available annually on earnings in law, medicine, and dentistry.[2]

In general, it appears that teachers suffered less from the economic depression of the 1930's and profited less from subsequent prosperity than did other employed workers. In 1929 (when information on all employed persons was first compiled) the average employed person earned only about half of one per cent more than the average teacher. In 1939, shortly after the end of the economic depression, the average employed person earned 11 per cent *less* than the average teacher. From 1929 until 1941 the average earnings of teachers exceeded the average for all employed persons.[3]

The United States Bureau of Labor Statistics, at the direction of the Congress, has formulated a budget at a 'necessary minimum' level for the four-person family of a man who works in overalls, lives in rented quarters or owns a modest home, employs no domestic service, but is adequately clothed and fed and enjoys modest comforts, including ownership of an automobile. This annual budget, priced in 34 large cities in September 1951, would have cost an average of about $4,190.[4] This amount exceeds the income of the average teacher by more than one fourth. As mentioned earlier, the incomes of certain professional groups are reported on annually. The largest of the three groups

---

1 'National Income and Product of the United States, 1951', *Survey of Current Business*, July 1952, pp. 8–21, and Table 26, 'Average Annual Earnings', p. 2.
2 'Incomes of Physicians, Dentists, and Lawyers, 1949–51', *Survey of Current Business*, July 1952, pp. 5–7.
3 National Education Association, Research Division. *The Economic Status of Teachers, 1952–53*.
4 U.S. Bureau of Labor Statistics. *Family Budget of City Worker, October 1950* (Bulletin 1951, No. 1021). Washington, D.C., Government Printing Office, 1951, p. 2. Also, *Monthly Labor Review*, May 1952, pp. 520–22.

(dentists, lawyers, physicians) is the legal profession. In 1929 the average net income of lawyers was four times the average salary of teachers. This ratio was reduced in 1951 to three to one. The earnings of medical doctors in both years were close to four times the earnings of teachers. Earnings in dentistry were substantially more than double those of teachers.

One other comparison may be mentioned. The clerical and professional staff of the United States civil service is recruited by competitive examination from all parts of the nation. The great majority are clerical workers and artisans but the average salary consistently exceeds that of public school teachers. The earnings of the federal professional personnel are not reported separately, but the civil service salary schedule throws some light on the relationship. The lowest salary grade to which professional personnel are assigned in the federal civil service is slightly less than the average earnings in the teaching profession. It is not surprising that many former teachers are today in federal employment.

The comparisons between the salaries of teachers and other professional groups would be more favourable to the former if only professional women were considered. Women teachers constitute 79 per cent of the total teaching corps. Although there is a tendency to assign men to the higher paid positions the usual policy is equal pay for men and women in identical positions. Whereas men teachers are paid far less than men in other professions, there is some evidence that women teachers may earn as much as the average professional woman, especially if such occupations as librarianship and social work be included. On the other hand, men teachers are somewhat more likely than women to be assigned to administrative, supervisory, athletic coaching or other supplementary duties involving supplementary salaries.

ADMINISTRATIVE POLICIES THAT DETERMINE ECONOMIC STATUS

Each of the 48 states and each of the many thousand local school districts within states have responsibilities that may affect the economic status of teachers. The state legislatures determine the state and local taxation that provide school support. In addition they establish general policies for the conduct of local school systems and sometimes enact minimum standards and safeguards against discrimination.

Local school boards have the right to adopt salary standards and schedules and to establish the local rules governing the status of the teaching profession, within the limits set by the states.

State laws establish certain standards that must be met by local school districts, and some states use the distribution of state money to local districts as one way of enforcing the standards.

A few states provide very limited state funds for the maintenance of schools; others provide large amounts. On the average, however, about half of the local school budget comes from local taxation, about 40 per cent from the state, and the remainder from county and federal sources.[1] The county is an intermediate unit of government between the locality and the state, serving as a taxing agency in some states but not in all.

Minimum Salary Standards

At present, nearly two-thirds of the states specify some minimum standard for salaries.[2] Owing to the continuing changes in the purchasing price of the dollar, these minimum-salary laws have to be constantly revised. Certain states have old salary laws on the books that are now without influence, owing to the fact that all local school boards are paying salaries in excess of the legal requirements. In other states, however, salary laws are revised at frequent intervals and have a direct influence on the remuneration of many thousands of teachers.

The type of minimum requirement varies from a two-line statute which says that no teacher in the state may be paid less than $2,400 for a year's work, to lengthy and detailed salary 'schedules' covering a great variety of educational positions. About one-fourth of the states have fairly complete minimum schedules of minimum salaries and annual salary increments for classroom teachers. In all of them the salary is determined by the number of years of professional preparation of the teacher, as measured by the teacher's certificate, and by the number of years of experience. In Maryland, for example, only two basic salary classes are established (a) for those without bachelor's degrees, and (b) for those who have bachelor's or higher degrees. The differential between the two classes is $200. Teachers whose certificates are based on the bachelor's degree have a beginning salary of $2,200 and are guaranteed 16 annual increments of $100, thus advancing to a salary of not less than $3,800 for an experienced teacher. In most states, however, more than two levels of preparation are recognized. In only one of the state minimum salary schedules, that of the State of New York, is there variation in the minimum salary requirement as between large and small school districts. Just as the Burnham schedules in England allow a differential for London, the New York State schedule sets a higher requirement for New York City. The New York schedule also includes further variations for the extremely small

---

1 U.S. Office of Education. 'Statistics of State School Systems, 1949–50', *Biennial Survey of Education in the United States, 1948–50*. Washington, D.C., Government Printing Office, 1952, p. 20.
2 National Education Association, Research Division. *State Minimum-Salary Laws for Teachers, 1952–53*. (Special Memo, September 1952). Washington, D.C., The Association, 1952, 39 pp.

systems. In districts employing less than three teachers, a flat minimum salary of $2,500 is specified. In New York City the legal minimum schedule ranges from $3,000 to $5,825.

The adoption of state minimum salary standards and the provisions for state aid to assist local communities of low incomes in meeting the standards have been important factors in reducing the differential between urban and rural school salaries. In every state having a minimum salary schedule, however, the local school boards have the legal right to establish schedules, through the use of local funds, that are higher than the state requirements. Many local school boards in every state, including most of the large cities, do actually exceed the legal state minimum. New York City's local schedule exceeds the state requirements by several hundred dollars.

Teacher Retirement Provisions

Various conditions of teaching employment other than salaries are controlled by the state legislatures. For example, teacher retirement systems are authorized and in part financed by the states.[1] By 1947, all of the states had adopted laws for the establishment of retirement or pension plans for teachers. Recent federal legislation has opened the national social security benefits to local governmental employees under certain conditions. One state abandoned its teacher retirement system for federal social security and two others have developed integrated plans that include both social security and a state teacher retirement plan. The retirement benefits vary from state to state as determined by the particular plan in effect, but in the stronger state systems the benefits are more liberal than under the federal plan.

Sick Leave

One type of state regulation affecting the economic status of teachers is a sick-leave law. About half of the states have passed laws that either authorize or direct local boards of education to grant sick leave for certain maximum periods without loss of pay.[2] In some states funds are provided through state aid to assist in financing these plans. Thousands of local school boards have adopted sick-leave regulations, however, without specific permissive state legislation.

Most teachers now have the protection of paid sick leaves. In 1950–51, 98 per cent of the city school systems reported that sick leave with pay was granted. The median number of days of sick leave was

---

[1] National Education Association, Research Division. 'Public School Retirement at the Half Century', *Research Bulletin*, Vol. 28, December 1950, pp. 115–75.

[2] Yelton, Nathan H. 'Social Security—To Be or Not to Be', *NEA Journal*, Vol. 41, October 1952, pp. 439–40.

11 per year on full pay, and the typical practice was to allow unused days of leave to accumulate for use in case of a protracted illness.[1]

Salary Schedules

In addition to the positive service of establishing and financing minimum amounts of salary and sick leave, state legislatures have enacted certain anti-discrimination laws affecting salaries.[2] For example, the statutes of Illinois say: 'In fixing salaries of certificated employees school boards shall make no discrimination on account of sex.' This is one of 13 states that specifically forbid salary differentials among teachers on the basis of sex. Two other states have laws that are looking toward the elimination of sex differentials at a later date; one state has a law forbidding discrimination on the basis of sex or civil status in the employment of teachers.

Local school systems, as contrasted to the state governments, have served as laboratories in which each new development relating to the economic status of teachers has been experimentally developed. Salary schedules, retirement systems, tenure protection, and sick-leave policies had all been tried in many city school systems before being adopted on a state-wide basis. One significant movement in salary scheduling in the past half-century has been the spread of the practice of paying equal salaries to elementary school and secondary school teachers of equivalent preparation. This policy is called the 'single-salary schedule'. This type of schedule was first adopted in 1920, in the cities of Denver, Colorado, and Des Moines, Iowa. For a number of years there were few imitators among the large cities. The practice grew slowly, however, and in 1945 about 43 per cent of the city salary schedules were of this type.[3] There were many salary schedule revisions in the immediate postwar period and by 1951 only two of the large cities and less than four per cent of any size of city retained the old type of schedule with higher salaries for high school teachers than for elementary school teachers.

All of the 31 state minimum-salary laws provide uniform treatment for teachers at all levels of the elementary-secondary school system. In two states, California and Illinois, separate boards of education maintain high schools in some communities. In these high school districts the salaries are usually higher than in the districts that maintain elementary schools only. In these same two states, however, the cities that maintain unified elementary-secondary school districts almost

---

[1] National Education Association, Research Division. 'Teacher Personnel Procedures, 1950–51: Employment Conditions in Service', *Research Bulletin*, Vol. 30, April 1952, pp. 35–63.

[2] National Education Association, Research Division. *State Laws Forbidding Discrimination in Salaries Paid Men and Women Teachers*. Washington, D.C., The Association, 1950.

[3] National Education Association, Research Division. 'Salaries and Salary Schedules of City-School Employees, 1950–51', *Research Bulletin*, Vol. 29, April 1951, pp. 77–78.

without exception are following single-salary schedules. The adoption of single-salary schedules has helped in the lowering of the differential between the median salaries of elementary school and high school teachers, mentioned earlier.

Although the practice of paying teachers according to a definite schedule is widespread, it is not universal. All except nine per cent of the city school systems that reported to the NEA Research Division on salaries paid in 1951 used a local schedule or were covered by a state schedule for teachers.[1] Each successive study of schedules, however, shows a smaller percentage of districts operating without schedules.

A half-century ago practically all local school systems paid higher salaries to men than to women teachers. This practice is now forbidden by law in some states, and is disappearing in other areas in the absence of laws. Four-fifths of the cities reporting in 1950–51 were paying equal amounts to men and women of like qualifications and work.[2] Salary differentials in favour of white teachers, as compared with Negro teachers, were at one time common in the Southern states but are rapidly disappearing. Less than a tenth of the local school districts maintaining separate schools for Negroes now report higher salaries for white teachers.[3]

The salary schedule for classroom teachers is often used as a point of departure in scheduling salaries of principals and other administrative-supervisory positions. Other differentials may be scheduled; for example, a large majority of school systems provide extra pay for extra duties in such activities as the coaching of after-school athletics. Eight per cent allow salary allowances for teachers with dependents.[4]

A few boards of education have adopted so-called 'escalator clauses' in their salary schedules, which provide that a portion of the annual salary is in the form of a cost-of-living adjustment that varies in amount with the fluctuations of the official government Consumers' Price Index.[5]

An important development in the improvement of both state and local regulations governing the economic status of teachers is the growing participation of teachers themselves. Usually the teachers work through their professional organizations, although in some communities the school administration has organized advisory councils to perform this function. State education associations have led the efforts for legislation to provide better school support and to raise the standards

---

1 National Education Association, Research Division. 'Teacher Personnel Procedures, 1950–51: Employment Conditions in Service', *Research Bulletin*, Vol. 30, April 1952, pp. 35–63.
2 Ibid.
3 Ibid.
4 Ibid.
5 National Education Association, Research Division. *Cost-of-Living Adjustments for Teachers' Salaries, 1950–51*. Washington, D.C., The Association, 1950.

of teacher remuneration. In local school systems it has become typical practice for the school authorities to confer with local organizations of teachers in developing salary schedules. Joint committees of teachers, school board members, and other citizens often work together on the development of such policies, to the mutual benefit of the teaching staff and the community's children.

THE SOCIAL, CIVIC AND POLITICAL STATUS OF TEACHERS[1]

SOCIAL STATUS

Popular images of the teacher occur in the literature of every country. Such images are invariably exaggerations and over-generalizations. Occasionally, they are, however, sufficiently strong to affect somewhat the teacher's social status in the community. The studies reported below are designed to clarify the teacher's actual role in American society.

An important new study now under way by a committee preparing the 1954 Yearbook of the John Dewey Society may be expected to throw considerable light upon the teacher's role in American society. It will deal with the effects of varying types of socio-economic background upon the teacher's adjustment to his work; with the effects of social changes upon the teaching; the conflicts and problems of the teacher; and his professional development. The results will not be available until 1954.[2]

The Social and Economic Backgrounds

A characteristic of American society is the mobility of various socio-economic groups. The general trend of this mobility is upward as technical developments reduce the numbers required in manual labour. Children born in lower economic groups are able, as a result of equal educational opportunities, to enter all professions and occupations.

Based upon several studies of the socio-economic backgrounds of teachers the following points seem well-established: (a) teachers come from a wide variety of backgrounds; (b) a high proportion of teachers in smaller communities derive from older middle-class families of modest means, living in rural areas; (c) a high proportion of teachers

---

1 Adapted from a manuscript prepared by Miss Beatrice Crump.
2 John Dewey Society. Yearbook, 1954. *The Teacher's Role in American Society.* (In preparation.)

in cities derive from city families with foreign-born parents whose children are rapidly moving up the socio-economic scale.

A study[1] of 214 students about to graduate from a school of education of a leading mid-western university showed a quarter of their fathers to be business proprietors, 17 per cent professional men, and 17 per cent farmers. The fathers of 18 per cent of the men and nine per cent of the women were skilled labourers. Other studies supported this general picture of the predominant group of teachers coming from business, professional and farming families but with a substantial minority from families of skilled labourers.

Prospective teachers, coming from families of moderate means, generally earn while they learn. A study[2] of a group of male teachers showed that nine-tenths had engaged in part-time employment by the age of 18, and that they had begun such employment at an earlier age than a similar group of factory workers. The same study showed that the average age of the decision to teach was between 9 and 10, with family influence listed as being the major factor in the decision.

Teachers as They Rate Themselves

One research study[3] reported that teachers identified themselves largely with the middle or upper-middle economic levels. On a Social Class Identification Scale, 726 public school teachers attending summer school at the University of Alabama indicated the groups with which they identified themselves. Two per cent of these teachers identified themselves with the upper levels, 13 per cent with the lower levels, and the remaining 85 per cent were divided between the middle and upper-middle levels about two to one. No teacher identified himself with the highest or 'upper-upper' group or with the lowest or 'lower-lower' group. These findings have significance when these levels are defined. The upper group includes such persons as surgeons, large-city mayors, and corporation lawyers; the upper-middle group, newspaper editors, ministers, civil engineers, and army colonels; the middle group, real estate salesmen, and druggists; and the lower group, factory workers, automobile mechanics, and telephone operators.

Teachers as Rated by Others

A few studies have been made of the standing of public school teachers in the eyes of others. Because youth often choose careers or occupations

1 Best, John Wesley. 'A Study of Certain Selected Factors Underlying the Choice of Teaching as a Profession', *Journal of Experimental Education*, Vol. 17, September 1948, pp. 201–59.

2 Norton, Joseph L. 'A Study of the Development of Vocational Preferences and Early Work Careers', Syracuse University, 1950. (Ph.D. dissertation).

3 Sims, Verner M. 'The Social-Class Affiliations of a Group of Public School Teachers', *School Review*, Vol. 59, September 1951, pp. 331–38.

on the basis of the 'prestige' the occupations have in people's minds, a group of three investigators[1] questioned 1,676 students, mostly first-semester freshmen, at Indiana University. These students were asked to rank 18 occupations according to the amount of prestige they thought they had. The investigators also compared the students' ranking with that made by a similar group 14 years previously.[2] The students ranked the high-school teachers fifth in both studies; they ranked the elementary school teacher seventh in the earlier study and sixth in the later study. In both studies physicians, lawyers, college professors and clergymen (in that order) were ranked above teachers. In both studies the three groups of educators were ranked thus: college professor first, followed by high-school teacher and elementary school teacher.

The study also revealed that teacher prestige was higher in rural areas than in small or large cities. This finding may be partly explained by the fact that teachers in rural areas often have higher cash incomes than other persons in the community. Small communities are very often willing to pay salaries necessary to compete with other communities for competent teachers. State financial aid also tends to raise teachers' salaries to a minimum level which is often relatively good in cash as compared with incomes of many other occupations in rural areas.

Students from families in the higher income brackets ranked teaching lower than students from families of lower incomes. Those who had had some teaching experience ranked teaching higher than did those who had not had teaching experience.

Restrictions on the Teacher's Personal Life

A study[3] of the living and working conditions among teachers in New York State emphasized that community restriction, as well as housing, transport facilities, inadequate salaries, and similar conditions affect teacher morale and competence.

It is generally believed that teachers in smaller communities have considerably more restraints placed upon them than do teachers in larger communities. One investigator,[4] therefore, studies women teachers in 232 communities below 12,000 in population in 34 states, more than half having under 3,000 in population. Eighty-one per cent of the teachers were unmarried. Fifty per cent were living in their

---

1 Richey, Robert W. and others. 'Prestige Ranks of Teaching', *Occupations*, Vol. 30, October 1951, pp. 33–36.
2 Hartman, George W. 'The Prestige of Occupations', *Personnel Journal*, Vol. 13, 1934, pp. 144–52.
3 Brown, Foster S. 'A Study to Ascertain those Living and Working Conditions which Teachers Believe Influence the Quality of their Services and General Morale' (Ph.D. dissertation, Columbia University, 1950), 197 pp.
4 National Education Association, Research Division, 'Teaching Load in 1950', *Research Bulletin*, Vol. 29, February 1951, pp. 3–51.

own homes or apartments, and 45 per cent were living in rooming or boarding houses.

One-third of the teachers reported that they were expected by their communities to attend church services, 14 per cent were expected to be church members, 10 per cent were expected to attend Sunday school. Twenty-nine per cent of the teachers said that they were expected to take part in community activities, this obligation being imposed by the community and by the school board about equally. More than half of the teachers themselves favoured church attendance, church membership, Sunday school attendance, and participation in community activities, but most of them resented having to teach Sunday school. However, almost two-thirds of the teachers did not object to community pressure to engage in other church activities. In more than three-fifths of the communities studied no pressure had been exerted on teachers to engage in any of the activities mentioned above.

Another study[1] found that nearly two-thirds of the teachers were expected to take part in community welfare activities, such as community fund-raising campaigns for local charities, Red Cross work, scouts and other youth organizations. In reporting the sources of such pressure, 41 per cent reported that influential groups in the community insist on such participation; 38 per cent that other classroom teachers urge it; 17 per cent, that school administrators require it; and two per cent, that school board rules require it. Three-fourths of these teachers felt that such participation should be left to the individual teacher; one-fifth that teachers should be urged to take part; and only one per cent that teachers should be required to do so.

Despite possible resentment toward pressure to take part in various community activities, teachers, on the average, spend 3.6 hours per week participating in the work of organizations and in community services according to a recent study.[2] This study showed that 65 per cent of the teachers replying to a questionnaire reported that they took part in parent-teacher association work; 70 per cent, in teachers' associations activities; 67 per cent in church and church school activities; 11 per cent, in the activities of youth-serving groups, and 27 per cent, in other community work. Twenty-four per cent of the women teachers took part in the work of women's groups, and 37 per cent of the men teachers took part in the work of men's groups.

Teachers' participation in most of the activities of the other groups mentioned above was wholly voluntary, but about half reported that they felt some pressure to take part in parent-teacher associations activities, and in teachers' associations activities.

---

1 Lichliter, Mary. 'Social Obligations and Restrictions Placed on Women Teachers', *School Review*, Vol. 54, January 1946, pp. 14–23.

2 National Education Association, Committee on Tenure and Academic Freedom. *The Freedom of the Public School Teacher*. Washington, D.C., The Association, 1951.

Community pressures, or school board rules and policies occasionally forbid certain personal habits for teachers not frowned upon for most people, unless carried to excess. The study[1] mentioned above of a group of women teachers employed in places under 12,000 in population, showed that 55 per cent of the teachers reporting were not permitted to drink alcoholic beverages; 38 per cent are forbidden to smoke; 53 per cent to have social engagements with their male students; 11 per cent were forbidden to wear certain types or styles of dress some of which were considered violations of good taste (slacks, ankle-socks, shorts, etc., on occasions when these are deemed inappropriate); 15 per cent were forbidden to marry while employed by the school. The ban on marriage during the contract period was usually written into the teacher's contract or was based upon an oral agreement with the employer. Disregard of other local taboos was deterred by fear of gossip or even of social ostracism.

Three-fourths of these women teachers objected to the restriction on marriage, but only a quarter or fewer objected to the other taboos. Only 24 per cent objected to the ban on smoking; 12 per cent to the ban on drinking.

In 1951, five years after the study just described, the Committee on Tenure and Academic Freedom of the National Education Association made a nation-wide study[2] of the same types of restrictions. This committee found that drinking alcoholic beverages was most often forbidden—63 per cent of the teachers polled being forbidden to drink alcoholic beverages in public and 19 per cent expected not to drink in private. Twenty-three per cent of the teachers were forbidden to smoke in public. Only in a few extreme cases did communities still forbid women teachers to marry, or impose other restrictions on their personal lives. Slightly more than a quarter of the teachers noted no restrictions whatever.

This latter study revealed that community pressures were responsible for existing restrictions in 35 per cent of the cases; school board rules and policies in 20 per cent; and a combination of school board rules and policies and community pressure in 17 per cent.

It is interesting to compare restrictions on teachers with those of other respected persons in the community. While 71 per cent of the teachers reported pressure to restrict their personal lives, 35 per cent of them reported similar community pressures restricting other respected citizens. It is obvious from the studies reported here that some communities apply a more rigid code of social behaviour to teachers than they do to doctors, lawyers, business men or others in the community. Opinion in the community at large more often imposes the restrictions than does the school board.

---

[1] Lichliter, op. cit..

[2] National Education Association, Committee on Tenure and Academic Freedom. *The Freedom of the Public School Teacher.*

The Employment of Married Women in Teaching

The proportion of married women teachers changes from time to time with changes in economic conditions and the available manpower. A number of local studies have found proportions of married women teachers ranging from 10 per cent to well over 50 per cent. For example, one study[1] in southern Illinois showed that 54 per cent of the women nursery school and primary school teachers studied (first three grades) were married. Three-fifths of the married women teachers were supporting, or helping their husbands to support, dependants, and in addition, many of the single teachers were supporting one or more other persons.

A recent study[2] found that 34 per cent of the urban women teachers and 48 per cent of the rural women teachers were married or widowed. In both urban and rural areas slightly larger proportions of elementary school women teachers than of secondary school teachers were or had been married. The employment of married women as teachers in the public schools has at various times in the past been a subject of controversy. In the 1930's when the supply of available teachers was greater than the demand, married women usually were not appointed as full-time teachers on regular permanent status. Even though some states enacted legislation forbidding the dismissal of women teachers because they married, local communities sometimes discriminated against them by refusing to appoint them. This reflected the feeling that the public owed its available jobs to those needing them most, assuming other qualifications to be equal. It was also based to some extent upon the view that married women might be less effective if they had to divide their time between school and home-making.

Today the situation is quite different with the shortage of teachers of the World War II period only slightly lessened in the last seven years. This shortage of teachers has led most communities not only to retain women teachers who marry while employed by the local school system, but also to give initial appointments to women already married and to provide maternity leave for them. Discrimination against married women teachers is not therefore a serious problem at the present time.

Men Teachers in the Public Schools

Most of the public school teachers during the colonial period were men, but in the nineteenth century women came into the profession in large proportions. Now men make up a very small minority. By 1949–50

---

1 Mott, Sina W. 'The Married School Teacher', *Illinois Education*, Vol. 39, May 1951, p. 351.
2 National Education Association, Research Division. 'The Teacher looks at Personnel Administration', *Research Bulletin*, Vol. 23, December 1945, pp. 93–147.

only 21.3 per cent of all public school teachers were men. It has been estimated that about nine per cent of the elementary school teachers are men.

An investigator[1] found that a large majority of psychologists and educators agree that men teachers are needed in the elementary school classrooms. He found, however, that four out of five male teachers planned to leave the elementary schools because they were dissatisfied with their working conditions, usually with low salaries, with working under women administrators, and/or with lack of the same social recognition given men in other professions.

However, men teachers do have one compensation, as pointed out previously, in that they tend to be appointed to administrative positions much more readily than women teachers.

Teacher Tenure

'Tenure' of teachers usually refers to security or permanency or position. For public school teachers in the United States, tenure varies from state to state. Thirty-eight states have tenure laws which cover some or all the teachers in the state. Some laws provide that when a teacher is not to be re-employed, advance notice must be given by a certain date; other laws protect the teacher against unfair dismissal.

In general, teachers may either be employed under written contract for a specific period of time, usually a year; may be on probation for a period of time after which they come under the provision of a state tenure law; or may be on permanent tenure from the time of employment. Some states require that before teachers are placed on tenure status, they must serve a probationary period of one to five years, three years being the usual length.

Teachers in the public schools are slowly achieving employment security. It is estimated that at the present time 58.5 per cent of the public school teachers in this country are employed under tenure laws. The number of states having teacher tenure laws on the statute book has doubled in the last ten years.

Housing

It adds difficulty to the procurement of teachers when a local community cannot assure teachers of adequate housing. To overcome this tituation, a few school districts provide a house where the teachers of the district may live at nominal cost. Besides providing housing such 'teacherages' reduce the teachers' cost of living. For several years,

---

1 Kaplan, Louis. 'The Status and Functions of Men Teachers in Urban Elementary Schools', *Journal of Educational Research*, Vol. 41, May 1948, pp. 703–9.

many western states, especially Arizona, Colorado, Missouri, Montana, Oklahoma, Texas, and Washington have allowed local school districts to maintain teacherages. In 1948, three more states—Connecticut, Illinois, and Oregon were added to this list.[1]

However, teacherages take care of only a very small proportion of teachers in need of housing. A majority of men teachers own their own homes. A third or more of the single women teachers maintain their own living quarters—owning a home, or renting houses or apartments.

Educational Inbreeding

The local control of education and other community services in the United States has given rise to a sociological phenomenon in some areas known as cultural and educational 'inbreeding'. This refers to the tendency of some communities, particularly in the east, to depend excessively upon their own resources, ideas and personnel to the exclusion of stimulating contacts from other regions. This tendency is, of course, counteracted to a considerable extent by the exceptional mobility of the American population, particularly of the professional groups, and by the extensive utilization of mass media of communications—radio, press and, now, television.

Educational inbreeding has taken on a more specific meaning in recent years. It refers to the tendency in some localities to give preference to teachers of local origin and training, often at the expense of lowered standards. This tendency becomes serious in times of economic depression when teachers are in plentiful supply.

In a study[2] of this sociological problem in 1938, it was discovered that approximately 40 per cent of all teachers in cities of 15,000 to 100,000 are graduates of the local high school, the percentages increasing with the size of the city. However, wide variation was found from city to city in the degree to which local teachers are favoured. In some cities with a very high proportion of local teachers the latter compared very favourably with non-local teachers in training, evidences of professional alertness, initiative, and efficiency. In a few cities, local teachers ranked far below those coming from outside the community. In these relatively few communities exhibiting the effects of harmful educational inbreeding the major factors seemed to be: (a) evidences of undue political influence in teacher selection; (b) low salaries and inadequate teacher selection procedures; (c) special social restrictions upon teachers; (d) rigid, traditional curriculum and narrow conception of the role of the teacher.

---

1 Wright, Grace S. 'The Improvement of Teacher Status', *School Life*, Vol. 30, March 1948, pp. 24–26. May 1948, pp. 21–24.
2 Snyder, Harold E. *Educational Inbreeding*. New York, Bureau of Publications, Teachers College, Columbia University, 1943. 160 pp.

THE CIVIL AND POLITICAL STATUS OF TEACHERS

Many articles and pamphlets have been written about various phases of academic freedom of teachers in the United States but little actual research has been done. Civil and political phases of the teacher's life include many more aspects than are usually encompassed in the term 'academic freedom'. It may include such diverse factors as discrimination in employing teachers on religious or racial grounds, jury duty, and political activities.

An analysis of some of these factors is found in a recent study[1] made by the Committee on Tenure and Academic Freedom of the National Education Association based upon a nation-wide investigation.

Discrimination against Teachers of Certain Types

The Constitution of the United States guarantees freedom to practise the religion of one's choice (or no religion) providing such practice does not infringe on the rights, safety, or welfare of others. Such religious discrimination in the employment of teachers as still occasionally exists is for the most part confined to smaller communities where a single religious faith predominates. The study mentioned above[2] revealed that 53 per cent of the teachers polled reported that a statement of religious affiliations or preferences was still required on applications for teaching positions, while 35 per cent reported that such a question was not asked in their communities. This question does not imply religious discrimination in employment, but many feel that it should not be asked at all. New York and other states now forbid asking applicants what are their religious preferences so as to avoid any danger of prejudiced selection.

The NEA study[3] found that two-thirds of the teachers polled reported that the question of race was asked on applications for teaching positions; one quarter of the teachers reported that this question was not asked in their communities. Since the employing board or superintendent can usually determine a teacher's race by requiring an interview, it is possible that there is more discrimination on the basis of race than appears from this study. Discrimination is still considered to be a problem in communities in those states which do not have racial segregation laws, since the tendency in these states is to employ white teachers.

---

[1] National Education Association, Committee on Tenure and Academic Freedom. *The Freedom of the Public School Teacher.*
[2] Ibid.
[3] Ibid.

Political Activity

For the most part teachers share equally in the political activities of their communities, even occasionally running for public office. However, in some regions teachers refrain from political activity, except voting, because communities and state educational authorities look with disfavour upon such activity. In many communities teachers are protected legally from being asked for contributions to political parties as long as they are on school property. The study[1] cited above found one quarter of the teachers studied reported that the teachers have such legal protection. In a few communities, teachers are restrained either by community opinion or by school board policies from organized political action, particularly that affecting school board policies. A great majority of teachers believe that they should have the same freedom to take part in political activities as other citizens.

Jury Service

Serving on juries is one of the duties of citizens. The law exempts criminals, and the mentally and physically unfit. Those to whom such service would be an unreasonable hardship may also be excused. Some states debar women from such service; this automatically prevents some women teachers from serving. Other states allow teachers to claim exemption from jury duty.

Since 1920, when women were granted the privilege of voting in the United States, 36 states and the District of Columbia have adopted special statutes or amended their constitutions to allow women to serve on juries. About half these states make jury service for women compulsory as it is for men, allowing women the same exemptions as are allowed men. The rest of these states and the District of Columbia allow women to serve on juries if they so wish.

However women are still debarred from jury service in federal, courts as well as in the state courts in 12 states.

Discussion of Controversial Issues

Public school teachers in the United States have always had to struggle for freedom to discuss with students in the classroom highly controversial issues. Since colonial days the teaching of sectarian religion has not been permitted in public schools. During World War I, the teaching of German was forbidden in many schools. The teaching of the theory of the evolution of the human species in classes in the natural

---

1 National Education Association, Committee on Tenure and Academic Freedom. *The Freedom of the Public School Teacher.*

sciences has at various times and places been forbidden. Sex education is currently receiving much attention as a subject of doubtful validity in the minds of many citizens.

Topics which teachers most frequently feel they must avoid include sex, criticism of prominent people, separation of Church and State, race relations, and Communism.

Despite the existence in some places of such restrictions, the NEA study[1] shows that more than two-thirds of the teachers feel that they can present facts on any subject within the limits of good taste, providing they stimulate students to reach their own decisions. Only five per cent of the teachers feel under public pressure to avoid discussing with their students any topic which might possibly offend influential groups in the community because of their religious, social, or political beliefs. Twenty-nine per cent of the teachers polled believe that state and national teachers' associations need to work for more academic freedom in public education, while 26 per cent believe that such activity is not necessary.

Loyalty Oaths for Teachers

As a phase of the current wave of reaction against the alleged infiltration of Communists in public life, doubt has been cast by a few vocal people upon the loyalty of some public school teachers. To check on teachers' loyalty or to assure their loyalty, communities and states now sometimes require teachers to take an oath of loyalty to the United States. These oaths vary in nature from those by which the teacher pledges to fulfil the obligations of his position to those by which the teacher swears that he is not a member of any subversive group, usually defined as one favouring the overthrow of government by force. The reasoning behind this oath is that those testifying falsely can then be prosecuted for perjury, while those admitting undesirable affiliations can be debarred from employment.

An NEA study[2] showed that 48 per cent of the teachers polled reported that an oath of some kind is required of teachers in their communities, 41 per cent of them being required at the time of initial appointment. Of those who reported that an oath was required of teachers, 40 per cent said that the oath included testifying that the teacher was not a member of a subversive group. Many of these oaths are required by state law and are merely administered by the community to conform with state requirements.

Thirty-one per cent of the teachers reporting were subject to special oaths required only of teachers, but 57.5 per cent are subject to oaths

---

[1] National Education Association, Committee on Tenure and Academic Freedom. *The Freedom of the Public School Teacher.*
[2] Ibid.

required of all public officials. A special loyalty oath for teachers is considered by professional agencies to be serious infringement on the teacher's right to academic freedom, carrying a public reflection upon the loyalty of the profession.

According to an NEA study[1] made two years earlier, 26 states required loyalty oaths for elementary and secondary school teachers. Other states prescribe such other requirements as loyalty checks, prohibition of membership in subversive groups, and authorization to dismiss teachers found to be disloyal. This is not a new phenomenon in American education, although currently more common than ever in the past. California enacted such legislation in 1865, and by 1900, two other states also prescribed oaths for teachers. Only 20 states have no state legislation concerning loyalty specifically for teachers, but practically every state has similar general laws applying to all state employees. Twelve states require the teacher to take the oath as a condition for the teaching certificate, nine states require it as part of each employment contract, and eleven states require it at the time of initial local employment.

Many of the facts and comments up to this point may suggest that the status of the public school teachers in the United States is one of tension and petty restraints. It must be kept in mind that studies such as those reported tend to emphasize restraints, problems and issues rather than privileges and opportunities.

In contrast to the medical and legal professions, teaching is a form of public employment. Public employment, particularly under local government, is likely to be hedged about by more restraints than private employment. But public employment is not always unattractive. It offers exceptional security and other advantages. The possibility of anonymous service to the people is such that many gladly teach despite the petty restraints at times imposed.

THE PROFESSIONAL QUALIFICATIONS OF TEACHERS[2]

More than one-fifth of the entire population of the United States is now directly engaged in education, either as students or teachers. After remaining a constant for the two decades prior to World War II, the elementary school population is now growing by an additional million children annually. This rate of increase seems likely to continue so that by 1955 it will begin to affect the secondary schools, which are

---

1 National Education Association, Research Division. 'Teachers in the Public Schools', *Research Bulletin*, Vol. 27, December 1949, pp. 146–47.
2 Adapted from a manuscript prepared by Ray C. Maul.

expected by 1960 to increase by 50 per cent over the enrolment in 1945. Colleges and universities, on the other hand, having declined temporarily in enrolment during the period 1949–52 after the rapid increase owing to the return of students from military service, will not be affected until about 1960 by the wartime and post-war increase in birth rate.

Among the many critical problems confronting American education as a result of this increase in enrolment, is that of securing an adequate number of qualified teachers. This problem has been a serious one for the elementary schools since 1948, in which year it was met in part by an unprecedented number of college graduates. The shortage of teachers has not affected the secondary schools so seriously, but is expected to do so by 1955.

LEGAL REQUIREMENTS FOR TEACHING

It is proposed here to examine the requirements for teaching from the point of view of the teacher's current professional status, even at the risk of some repetition.

Whereas in most countries one central governmental agency is authorized to set up the requirements for teaching, there are at least 49 such authorities in the United States. With each state enjoying complete freedom in the management of its system of free public elementary and secondary schools, qualifications for admittance to the teaching profession vary. Technically, a teaching licence or certificate is valid only in the state issuing it. Freedom of movement of teachers from one state to another is usually easy if the teacher has completed the training prescribed by the state he wishes to enter. As previously shown, the practice of reciprocity among states in the recognition of teacher certificates from other states has grown in recent years.

Most states require at least four years of post-secondary school training for the licence to teach in the secondary school (the only important exception being teachers in some of the vocational subjects, in which successful work experience may be accepted in lieu of regular college or university study), and a few states prescribe a fifth year of training for secondary school teachers of the basic academic subjects, such as languages, mathematics, science and history, although even these states prescribe no more than the baccalaureate degree for secondary school teachers of art, music, industrial arts, physical education and business courses.

To teach in the elementary schools, the designated requirements for the licence vary widely from state to state, ranging from one to four years of college preparation. It is therefore difficult to describe a fully prepared elementary school teacher in the United States in so far as formal education is concerned. However, despite these wide variations in minimum requirements there is a clear trend toward requiring four years of preparation for elementary teachers. The consensus of educational psychologists that the early years of childhood are the most important, and call for the greatest teaching skill, has led to a further tendency toward establishing similar standards of certification for both elementary and secondary school teaching. This contrasts sharply with the earlier view that the elementary school needed only to give the child the simple tools necessary to satisfactory living in a simple, isolated, self-contained society, that the elementary school performed its function if it taught the 'three R's'. Now, the elementary school aims to prepare the child for citizenship in a complex society with its local, national, and international problems. But legal requirements for elementary teaching certificates have just begun to catch up with this conception of elementary education and to demand the cultured, well-trained teacher at all points in the educative process.

With some 650,000 elementary teachers in service, with training requirements varying greatly from state to state, with ideas changing steadily as to what constitutes satisfactory training, and with the number of children to be taught constantly expanding, it seems appropriate to review the current and recent status of the enforcement of the requirements for teaching.

LOWERING OF CERTIFICATION STANDARDS DURING THE WAR

In the early 1940's, after the United States entered World War II, the schools suffered severely. With the rapidly growing demand for manpower, the balance between teacher supply and demand was disrupted and the shortage of teachers with adequate training quickly became acute. In most local school systems, it became necessary to employ persons to teach despite their lack of the prescribed training. These persons were given 'emergency' sub-standard licences. It was necessary to employ teachers who could not meet the requirement of four years of preparation prescribed in certain states, and even many who could not meet the three-year, the two-year, and the one-year standards of other states. Other prospective teachers had attended colleges for the prescribed number of years, but lacked specific training for teaching, or for teaching at the level for which they were employed. At no time was the supply of teachers exhausted, however, for requirements were dropped to the level necessary to obtain the needed number.

This wartime relaxation of standards was authorized and supervised by the regularly constituted authorities. In general, the states with the lowest standards were required to admit the largest proportion of teachers unable to meet even their meagre requirements. The elementary schools admitted proportionally far greater numbers of teachers with sub-standard preparation than did the secondary schools, despite their already lower requirements for teaching. Special emergency licences were granted for one year only, automatically expiring at the end of the school year. As conditions permit, some of the regular requirements are being restored. Generally, teachers with emergency certificates were required to take some kind of professional training during the summer, normally involving college summer-school attendance. Special programmes of in-service teacher education were also frequently conducted by local school systems, aided by the states. Thus many potentially good teachers eventually met all of the requirements for permanent licences.

As early as September 1948, the number of emergency licence holders began to diminish in the secondary schools. By September 1950, they were almost completely eliminated, chiefly in consequence of the increased supply of secondary school teachers made available by the marked upturn in college attendance immediately following the war.

In the elementary schools, on the other hand, at no time since the beginning of the war has there been an adequate supply of fully trained teachers. Since 1945, many states have increased their prescribed requirements for the regular licence, and every state has striven to reduce the number of non-standard licence holders in service. In every state, with but one exception, however, it continued to be necessary in 1952 to staff some of the elementary school classrooms with persons who cannot yet meet the full requirements.

CURRENT STATUS OF EDUCATIONAL QUALIFICATIONS OF ELEMENTARY SCHOOL TEACHERS

Vastly differing definitions of 'full requirements' for teaching certificates prevail from state to state. Most of the statistics in the remainder of the chapter are taken from a recent NEA study of teacher supply and demand.[1]

Of the 650,000 teachers in the elementary schools in 1953, approximately 350,000 have completed the requirements for one or another of the many types of baccalaureate degree granted by the American colleges and universities. These degree holders are technically considered to be 'qualified teachers', meeting the standard which has been advocated by the NEA and other professional agencies for more than 25 years. These 350,000 college graduates are to be found in the largest proportions, as would be expected, in those states which before the outbreak of World War II prescribed a college degree for the standard

---

1 Maul, Ray C., *Teacher Supply and Demand in the United States*. Washington, D.C., National Education Association, 1951. 36 pp. processed.

licence. Even in those states, however, many teachers have not yet met the minimum requirements. There are two reasons for this lag. First, when the educational authorities in a state establish a requirement for the standard licence, the requirements are not made retroactive—do not apply to those teachers already in service, many of whom hold permanent or life certificates. Second, when the licence-issuing authorities in a state raise standards of preparation, it is often difficult, or impossible, to obtain enough qualified candidates to fill all vacancies, necessitating the issue of 'emergency' or non-standard licences for limited periods.

The distribution of all degree-holding elementary school teachers in a state follows an irregular pattern because of the widely differing conditions from community to community. In some of the states most of the population is concentrated in urban centres where salaries tend to be higher, living conditions more attractive, and the teacher often finds better working conditions. Many local school systems have been able to establish and maintain much higher standards than are prescribed by the state as a whole. Localities with greater initiative, interest in education, and resources, have been able to attract superior teachers. Some of these localities have thus been able to develop educational systems recognized as outstanding. On the other hand, local discrepancies make for a tremendous range in educational opportunity for elementary school children living within the same state.

In general, the least well-prepared elementary school teacher has been, and continues to be, in the one-room, one-teacher school. In 1918, there were 196,000 of these small isolated school units scattered throughout the country. Through the last three decades a major movement has developed toward a combination of two or more of these small units into multi-room, multi-teacher schools, commonly called 'consolidated' schools, to which children are brought in special school buses. The consolidated rural elementary school tends to take on much of the form and pattern of its urban counterpart, possessing many of the features necessary to attract and hold better-qualified teachers, i.e. better salaries, lighter teaching loads, better physical plants, more adequate supervision. This growing movement toward consolidation has eliminated a majority of the one-room, one-teacher elementary school units, but in 1952, some 75,000 of the latter remained, mainly in the areas of sparse population. These schools account for a disproportionately large number of teachers having the minimum preparation. However, a recent study shows that one in four of these teachers in one-room schools now holds the bachelor's degree.[1]

A second large group of elementary school teachers consists of some

---

[1] National Education Association. *Research Bulletin*, February 1953.

200,000 who have attended college for two or more years, but have not attained the bachelor's degree. A substantial number of this group are still found in states now prescribing college degrees for new teachers. However, a majority of the teachers with only two or three years of preparation are in the states prescribing less than four years of preparation.

Finally, there are almost 100,000 elementary school teachers in service with less than two years of college preparation. These are largely concentrated (a) in the states maintaining the lowest standards, and (b) in the areas where the one-room, one-teacher schools are found in the greatest numbers.

QUALIFICATIONS OF NEGRO TEACHERS

At this point attention should be directed to an unusual educational situation in the United States. Whereas 31 states have single, unified school systems attended by pupils of all races, religions, and social classes, 17 states maintain separate school systems for white and Negro pupils. Equality of opportunity, as defined in the courts, includes equal preparation of the teacher. In this respect the Negro schools not only equal, but slightly surpass the schools for white children in the same states. Detailed figures are not available for all of the 17 states maintaining separate schools, but the following are indicative. A recent NEA study showed that in the 1951–52 school year, of all white elementary school teachers in service in Maryland, 60.5 per cent held college degrees; of all Negro elementary school teachers in service in the same state, 76 per cent held college degrees. In North Carolina these percentages were: white, 82 per cent, Negro, 97 per cent. In Oklahoma, white, 80 per cent; Negro 95 per cent. In South Carolina, white, 69 per cent; Negro, 58 per cent. In Texas, white, 91.5 per cent; Negro 95 per cent. In Virginia, white, 47 per cent; Negro, 81 per cent.[1]

In five of these six states the Negro non-degree holding elementary school teachers generally have more college preparation than do their white counterparts, according to the same study. In Mississippi and Louisiana, the average preparation of the Negro elementary school teacher is not yet equal to the average of the white teacher. However, in states with separate schools, advances in the level of preparation of Negro elementary school teachers are in general proceeding at a somewhat faster pace than is the case of the white elementary school teachers.

In the secondary schools of states maintaining separate schools for Negro and white children the qualifications of Negro teachers fall

---

[1] Maul, Ray C. *Teacher Supply and Demand in the United States.*

below the college degree requirement less frequently than do the qualifications of white teachers in the same state. The need to employ secondary school teachers having less than a bachelor's degree as a war-induced expediency was somewhat less for Negro schools, and full standards were restored somewhat earlier than in the white or unsegregated secondary schools.

The reasons behind the above differences should be mentioned. In states maintaining separate schools the Negro teacher enjoys relatively higher social and economic status with respect to other Negroes, than do white teachers, with respect to the total white population. A larger proportion of Negro college students prepare for teaching than do white college students. This makes for a more plentiful supply of highly qualified Negro teachers in the areas where segregated schools employ Negro teachers exclusively. In the states not maintaining segregated schools the common practice is still for schools to be staffed predominately with white teachers. Since only limited opportunities for teaching are available to Negroes in states with unsegregated school systems, the tendency is increased for Negroes from the entire country to seek positions in states maintaining separate schools for Negroes.

Teachers' salaries also tend to be more attractive to Negro than to white teachers. The principle of equal pay for teachers of equal qualifications, now firmly established in most states, has been a major factor in the elevation of standards and status of Negro teachers, particularly those in the states with a dual school system.

ANNUAL DEMANDS FOR NEW TEACHERS[1]

Replacement of Those who Leave the Classroom for All Reasons, including Death, Retirement, Other Occupations, Further Study, and Marriage

It has been estimated that nearly one teacher in ten annually leaves the profession. As a result, an estimated 65,000 new elementary school teachers and 30,000 to 35,000 new secondary school teachers are needed annually.

Additional Teachers to Teach the Larger Number of Children Comprising the Whole School Population Each Year

Many elementary school classes were already excessive in size at the beginning of the increase in school population in 1945, and these annual additions will tend to increase still further the size of the existing classes. Nevertheless, it is conservatively estimated that 10,000 more

---

[1] Maul, Ray C. *Teacher Supply and Demand in the United States.*

THE STATUS OF TEACHERS

new elementary school teachers are needed annually, just to meet the annual increase in enrolment. During the 1956–60 period more secondary school teachers will be needed to cope with anticipated enrolment increases.

Teachers to Offer Needed Educational Services Not Now Included in the Programme of Many Elementary Schools

The programmes offered in the 650,000 elementary school classrooms vary tremendously. In many instances instruction is lacking in one or more subjects deemed essential in American schools, such as art, music, handcrafts, remedial reading and speech, domestic arts (home-making), health and safety education. Some of these elements of what has come to be considered a balanced school curriculum are particularly lacking in the one-room elementary schools, where one teacher undertakes to teach all subjects to all pupils in grades one to eight. Even in many urban schools, however, qualified teachers of several of the above subjects are lacking. It is conservatively estimated that 10,000 additional special elementary teachers are needed. Some saving in the total number of teachers needed could be brought about, however, through further consolidation of one-room schools, where a teacher's time is devoted to the instruction of a small group, often less than 10 pupils. Great distances between homes in sparsely populated areas and high transport costs are barriers to the establishment of larger rural schools in many areas, even those where school buses are feasible.

Teachers to Relieve Overcrowded Conditions

Even before the outbreak of the war, many elementary school classrooms were overcrowded. Sometimes, due to lack of classrooms, half-day morning and afternoon sessions were held, with two groups of children using the same facilities at different times. Such conditions have appeared more frequently, year by year, until it is estimated that, in 1953, 500,000 children are affected adversely. Authorities estimate that more than 10,000 additional teachers are needed to relieve overcrowded elementary schools. In the secondary schools, on the other hand, such crowded conditions are relatively rare, and, when found, are usually attributable to a temporary local condition, such as that prevailing during the war, owing to the sudden concentration of large numbers of workers in a war-related occupation.

Attempts at voluntary and legal limitation of class size have in part resulted from voluntary, professional initiative. One important form which such initiative has taken is the effort of the so-called regional accrediting associations. Prominent among the standards of these voluntary accrediting associations is one requiring reasonable control of class size in secondary schools. In general, this standard is 30 students in the regular academic subjects, with smaller numbers suggested in laboratory courses and somewhat larger classes permitted in group music and physical education activities. The influence of these associations has become so strong that class size in secondary schools is a less serious problem than with elementary schools which are not directly affected by the action of regional accrediting bodies.

Qualified Teachers to Replace Under-trained Elementary School Teachers now in Service

With some 300,000 elementary school teachers now in service without having attained the bachelor's degree, full enforcement of the four-year training standard urged by various professional agencies is obviously impossible and unrealistic at the present time. Instead, renewed and diversified efforts are being devoted to the improvement in service of the 200,000 teachers having two or more years of college preparation. This still leaves almost 100,000 persons now teaching with less than one-half of the four-year standard. It is estimated that it would require six to ten years to raise this group to minimum academic standards, if those teachers were willing to devote their summers to college attendance and to take college courses during the school year (on Saturdays and some evenings).

A few educational leaders urge actual replacement of these under-trained teachers but more urge that safeguards be established to prevent the admittance of similarly inadequately prepared persons to the profession in the future. There is also widespread demand for raising the minimum requirements in those states not now requiring the bachelor's degree for entrance to teaching, particularly those not yet prescribing at least two college years. Studies have shown that high requirements tend to attract and hold superior people interested in teaching as a life career, whereas low standards tend to limit the appeal of teaching to those lacking in imagination and ambition, or unwilling to undertake a profession requiring diligent and sustained preparation.

To summarize the need for teachers in the American public school system in the foreseeable future, based upon a study by the NEA:

Secondary schools: 30,000 to 35,000 annually until 1955, then a steadily increasing number commensurate with the expanding enrolment.

Elementary schools: 65,000 annually to replace those who leave the classroom for all reasons; 10,000 or more annually to serve added numbers of pupils; 10,000 to offer vitally important instruction not now included in elementary schools; 100,000 to replace the lower one-third of the 300,000 now in service without the minimum preparation. The last three of these needs, once met, would not recur. The first three are conservative estimates of annual needs.

SOURCES OF TEACHING SUPPLY

The teaching profession in the United States is open to persons from all socio-economic groups. The 12 principal, immediate and potential sources of teachers are:[1]

1. *The Annual Classes of College Graduates*

Students receiving bachelor's degrees of all types in 1952, from all degree granting institutions, without regard to kinds of college curricula pursued, totalled 332,000. Of this number, 95,000 students completed college programmes specifically meeting requirements for standard teaching certificates in states in which the teacher education institutions are located. Of this total group entitled to certificates only 32,500 completed four-year programmes of preparation for elementary school teaching, while 62,500 completed the prescribed programmes of preparation for secondary school teaching. The remaining 237,000 bachelor's degree recipients did not include in their studies the specific subjects required of the teacher.

The 95,000 eligible candidates for teaching were less than the number required to fill available teaching positions of all types. In addition, a majority were prepared only for secondary school teaching, whereas far more new teachers were needed in the elementary schools. To make matters worse, a considerable proportion of these 1952 qualified graduates chose to enter other occupations. Of the 95,000 graduates eligible for teaching 53,000 were women. Many of the women graduates married and did not seek employment. School boards are no longer reluctant to employ married women, but the preference of many of these young women to devote full time to the establishment of homes reduces materially the number available for classroom service. Many of the 95,000 eligibles also elected to enter other occupations in business, government, or other professions.

Taking into account the teachers who were issued standard elementary school teaching licences based upon three years, two years, or even one year of college preparation in certain states, the 1952 total of newly licensed teachers reaches almost 106,000. The distribution of this total number between the elementary and secondary schools, and among the various subject-matter fields taught in the secondary schools

---

[1] Maul, Ray C. *Teacher Supply and Demand in the United States*,

is shown in the following table. This table divides the 1952 group by sex.

TABLE 13. Total number of college and university students completing standard certificate requirements in the 48 states, Alaska, District of Columbia, and Hawaii in 1952, 1951, 1945, and 1941

Type of preparation	1952			Total		
	Men	Women	Total	1951	1945	1941
Elementary School						
4 years	6 280	26 163	32 443	33 782	10 841	15 827
3 years	345	1 470	1 815	1 828	1 815	3 198
2 years	856	6 495	7 351	8 435	5 264	12 186
1 year	227	1 431	1 658	1 752	1 714	3 620
Elementary Total	7 708	35 559	43 267	45 797	19 634	34 831
Secondary School—4 years						
Agriculture	1 923	9	1 932	2 404	318	1 662
Art	885	1 386	2 271	2 296	546	874
Commerce	2 291	2 614	4 905	5 750	2 091	3 874
English	2 389	4 375	6 764	7 782	3 662	5 623
Foreign Language	644	1 317	1 961	2 133	935	1 646
Home Economics	2	4 295	4 297	4 640	3 546	4 682
Industrial Arts	3 373	24	3 397	4 284	268	1 154
Journalism	70	42	112	123	16	48
Library Science	39	311	350	428	177	216
Mathematics	2 313	1 055	3 368	4 118	915	1 825
Music	1 993	2 692	4 685	4 652	1 633	2 761
Physical Ed.—Men	6 987	—	6 987	8 179	459	1 705
Physical Ed.—Women	11	2 567	2 578	2 562	987	1 254
General Science	2 020	541	2 561	2 772	452	1 171
Biology	1 394	682	2 076	2 815	461	1 164
Chemistry	729	201	930	1 342	278	723
Physics	343	54	397	578	87	373
Social Sciences	6 891	3 341	10 232	12 178	3 154	6 695
Speech	621	902	1 523	1 556	347	598
Other	859	507	1 366	2 423	1 245	2 072
Secondary School Total	35 777	26 915	62 692	73 015	21 577	40 120
GRAND TOTAL	43 485	62 474	105 959	118 812	41 211	74 951

Read table thus: Under *Elementary School* in 1952 a total of 6,280 men and 26,163 women college students completed four-year programmes of preparation for elementary school teaching. In 1951 a total of 33,782 college students completed identical programmes of preparation. ... Under *Secondary School* in 1952, 1,923 men and 9 women completed programmes of preparation for the teaching of agriculture as a major subject. In 1951 a total of 2,404 college students completed identical programmes of preparation.

Source: *Teacher Supply and Demand in the United States*—1952. The National Education Association. Washington, D.C. 1952. 40 pp.

2. *Former Teachers of Demonstrated Competence and Adequate Training*

Since the shortage of teachers became critical in 1942, there has been a continuous call for former teachers to return to the classroom, on either a permanent or temporary, full-time or part-time basis. This has done much to fill in the gap between total annual demand and total supply of new, inexperienced candidates. Increasing willingness on the part of local school systems to employ married women has been a great factor in establishing the availability of this important group.

3. *Teachers in Service, but not yet Adequately Prepared*

Two hundred thousand teachers now in active service have more than two but less than four full years of college preparation. Educators are studying ways of identifying and eliminating the factors making for the withdrawal of many of these promising teachers from regular class-room service after only a brief period of teaching. They are also encouraging the participation of these teachers in in-service teacher education programmes, including summer college attendance, educational travel, directed reading, and Saturday and evening classes and seminars, workshops and in many other ways cited in Chapter III.

4. *Former Teachers of Demonstrated Ability but with only Partial Preparation*

Over a period of years many of those teaching despite lack of adequate preparation have developed into highly successful teachers. Many of these, after a brief or extended period of service, have left the profession for various reasons. A considerable number have retained a keen interest in teaching and might be persuaded to return under favourable conditions. But, recognizing their own limited technical training, many of these require special encouragement to return to teaching and special assistance in readjusting to the profession after they have returned.

5. *Teachers Unable to Find Positions in their Preferred Fields of Teaching Specialization*

This group presents an entirely different set of adjustment problems from those rather common to groups 2, 3 and 4, just described. It consists chiefly of recent graduates of teacher educating institutions prepared to teach solely a high school subject in which there are more candidates than vacancies. Notable among these subjects is social science. Annually, more teachers are prepared in this field than there are new positions. In some other high school subjects, notably home economics, the supply has not equalled the demand at any time during the past ten years. Many of these recent college graduates have acquired the background of general education now recognized as an essential element in the preparation of every teacher. In addition, they have completed the basic and specialized professional requirements for teaching. To assist them in shifting to shortage fields, colleges and school systems sometimes offer so-called 'conversion' programmes, designed to impart the knowledge and develop the skills, appreciations and competencies necessary for successful teaching for another grade, level or subject than that for which the teacher was originally prepared. In this way, for example, qualified but unsuccessful candidates for high school social science teaching positions have been 'converted' into competent teachers of other high school subjects or even, occasionally, for service in the elementary schools.

6. College Graduates without any Specific Preparation for Teaching

It has been noted that of the 332,000 recipients of the bachelor's degree in 1952, only 95,000 met requirements for teaching certificates. Some of the remaining 237,000 have pursued highly specialized undergraduate programmes with little relevancy to the teaching profession. But the vast majority of these college graduates have taken a sufficiently broad programme of general education to be eligible for a 'conversion' programme. American educators are increasingly turning to this group for help in solving the mounting supply problem. It is confidently believed that there are many successful teachers among college graduates who were unable for some reason to achieve their primary professional ambitions (e.g. premedical students, only ten per cent of whom, having finished the four-year preparatory course, can gain admission to medical schools).

7. Returning War Veterans with some College Preparation Before Entering Military Service

In times of sudden national crisis, such as those which occurred in 1941, and in Korea in 1950, the sudden demand for manpower depletes the male teaching corps through (a) the loss of male teachers to the armed forces; (b) the entrance of college students and graduates into military service instead of the teaching profession, cutting off the normal supply, and (c) the increased competition for men in other civilian occupations.

Ordinarily, the men constitute only about nine per cent of the total in elementary teaching service; in the secondary schools men comprise about 43 per cent of the teaching staff. To maintain the generally-desired balance between the two sexes, school systems exert special efforts to recruit male teachers. Those returning to civilian life from military duty have become, since the war, the main source of male teachers. Many of these war veterans are relatively mature, capable of pursuing an accelerated college programme to complete their pre-service education in a minimum length of time. It remains, however, a difficult problem to offer salaries and to create other conditions sufficiently favourable to draw substantially larger numbers of men to the profession.

8. *College Students Now Pursuing Teacher Training Programmes*

It might seem that this group needs no particular attention as they have already indicated their intention to teach. But several problems remain. The first is to achieve an equitable balance between these students desiring to teach in the two levels—elementary and secondary. The tendency of those completing college is to prefer secondary school teaching, despite the fact that more openings are to be filled in elementary schools. A second problem is to maintain the interest of this group in teaching in the face of the many other vocational opportunities also open to college graduates. Even those students attending public higher institutions are generally under no obligation, either legal or moral, to enter an occupation merely because of the specific training they have received for it at public expense.

9. *College Students Not Contemplating Teaching*

As shown above, only 95,000 of the 332,000 bachelor's degree recipients in 1952 completed curricula leading to the standard teaching certificate. Of the 237,000 remaining, many entered college without any clear occupational objective, others postponed their choice until the second or even the third year, and a substantial number did not pursue a curriculum culminating in recognized competence for any occupation, taking instead a four-year programme of general education.

During the early stages of college attendance of these 237,000, it is possible that many might have become interested in teaching, had its opportunities, satisfactions and rewards been presented to them more clearly and vigorously by instructors and counsellors and by public school authorities.

10. *Secondary School Graduates of Recent Years*

Slightly more than one-fourth of all secondary school graduates enter college. The remaining three-fourths enter vocations for which college is not considered a prerequisite. A substantial fraction of these are able students, who, despite the low costs of attending public colleges and the generally ample opportunities for earning while learning, decide for some reason against college. Economic reasons, such as need to contribute to family income, often play a part in this decision. Limited facilities in nearby higher institutions sometimes influence the decision not to seek a college education. Not infrequently, after a period of employment, these persons decide to resume their education and some eventually become teachers. The time for this belated shift of object-ives is usually short, however, because such students quickly assume adult responsibilities which prohibit giving up employment to resume formal education.

11. *Students Now Attending Secondary Schools*

The 22,000 secondary schools in the United States are, of course, the source of all college students, including future teachers. Guidance and occupational counselling in the secondary schools are designed to acquaint students with the career potentialities of teaching, as well as other occupations. While this guidance varies widely in effectiveness, it increasingly involves placing the requirements, advantages, and limitations of many occupations, including teaching, before each stud-ent. He is helped in relating this knowledge to his own abilities and interests and his own sense of social responsibility. As the choice of a worth-while career becomes less a matter of chance or whim and in-creasingly a matter of thoughtful planning, teaching may be expected to attract more of the ablest high school students.

12. *Preventable Loss among the Present Corps of Competent, Adequately Prepared Teachers*

Ordinarily, the teacher 'on the job' would not also be classified as a source of supply. But there is an annual loss of some 10 per cent of all teachers from the classroom. This loss is due in part to dissatisfaction, to better economic opportunities in other fields, to marriage, to dis-missal or resignation due to incompetence, and for many other reasons. Elimination of those conditions causing unnecessary loss of teachers who are competent and capable of being retained in the profession could reduce the teaching shortage.

THE PROFESSIONALIZATION OF TEACHING

While the professional status of teachers has been steadily improving, teaching has not yet fully gained in the eyes of the general public of the United States the status of many other professions, such as law, engineering, dentistry, theology, and medicine. Many factors have militated against the professionalization of teaching, among which the following are prominent:

334

The Modest Level of Preparation Required for Admission to Teaching

The relative ease with which licences to teach may be obtained, particularly for the elementary schools, tends to reduce the prestige of teaching as compared with professions requiring greater preparation. Despite the substantial and growing number of extremely competent, well-educated teachers, many remain only partially qualified. The higher qualifications of secondary school teachers are reflected in higher professional status than for elementary school teachers as a group.

The 'High Turnover' in Personnel

The fact that many persons receive elementary school teaching licences with relatively little academic preparation makes it possible for some to enter the profession rather casually, without seriously considering teaching as their career. Many teach for only a short period of years until more attractive positions can be obtained, or, in the case of young women, until marriage. Meagre academic background and lack of serious professional interest account in part for the high proportion of teachers leaving the profession each year, or changing to other teaching positions. This instability of the teaching corps is known as 'high turnover'.

The Predominance of Women

Elementary schools are staffed almost exclusively by women and many young women enter teaching in full realization that their tenure will be brief, often merely an interlude before marriage. On the other hand, a large group of women devote their lives to the profession and constitute the most stable element among both elementary and secondary school teachers. These two groups of women teachers—those who teach only briefly, and those who remain in the profession—constitute so large a majority of all teachers that teaching has become wrongly stereotyped in the public mind as a 'woman's profession'. This stereotype increases the difficulty of attracting competent men into the profession.

The Unfavourable Financial Return

The compensation of teachers bears an unfavourable relation to the earnings of other groups of similar education in the United States. Traditionally, the salary of a teacher has been determined largely by the local school board. Competition for good teachers tends to equalize salaries somewhat, but the states now often find it necessary to participate in the payment of teachers' salaries, and to establish minimum salaries. The states are, more and more, insisting that state funds granted to localities be used to provide equal salaries for teachers, regardless of sex, grade (elementary or secondary), or subject taught. States also generally maintain pension or retirement funds for all teachers. Such state aid is doing much to improve the professional status of teaching, particularly in the elementary schools.

PROFESSIONAL VOLUNTARY ORGANIZATIONS

Voluntary associations have had much to do with the improvement of education. They have also played a large part in the professionalization of the profession of teaching. This is especially true of the various educational associations.

The NEA, founded in 1857, now has almost half a million members, with permanent headquarters in Washington. It has a staff of 500 persons engaged in various fields of educational development and research. In each state there is a parallel state education or teachers association, likewise maintaining a staff and permanent headquarters in the state capital. Affiliated ·vith the state associations and with the NEA, but not controlled by them, are more than 4,000 local teachers associations. All of these groups, national, state, and local are closely interrelated by a common purpose.

Those teachers' associations in which membership is voluntary, strive to improve the working conditions, salaries, and prestige of their own profession, the teachers, administrators and supervisors of the elementary and secondary schools. Many other organizations are a part of the broad structure of the NEA without being under its direct control. Among these are such organizations as the American Association of School Administrators, the National Association of Secondary School Principals, and the National Association of Elementary School Principals, and the National Council for the Social Studies. The teachers of particular subjects or interests, such as mathematics, languages, art, music, English, agriculture, industrial arts, science, or adult education, also have their separate organizations, and are closely interlinked with the parent national association. Their activities are entirely extra-legal and they are not in any way under the control or domination of any legal authority, either national or state or local.

Many other smaller teacher organizations exist. Largest of these is the American Federation of Teachers, directly affiliated with the American Federation of Labor. The membership of the American Federation of Teachers is approximately sixty thousand. In addition several thousand teachers are members of the Union of Professional Workers of the Congress of Industrial Organizations, also a federation of labour unions.

Another important category of professional organizations in education are those whose membership is composed of educational institutions, rather than individuals. Typical are the Association of American Universities, the National Association of Land Grant Colleges, the Association of American Colleges, the Association of Municipal Universities, the American Association of Colleges for Teacher Education, and the American Association of Junior Colleges. Each of these is made up of institutions particularly emphasizing some aspect of higher education, and has nation-wide membership.

Still another type of organization of institutions, already briefly described, is the regional accrediting association, of which there are six, the largest being the North Central Association serving 19 states. These regional associations are made up of higher institutions of all types and of secondary schools. They constitute a voluntary joining together of institutions for a common professional purpose, that of establishing and maintaining high educational standards. The member institutions themselves set the goals, prescribe the methods of procedure, finance their efforts, and establish the criteria for admission.

The American Council on Education is a non-governmental council having as its members almost all of the colleges and universities of the country, as well as most of the educational associations and many schools and school systems. While the ACE has been particularly active in matters pertaining to higher education, its interests extend to every phase of education, both within the United States and abroad. It has organized and sponsored many special studies and programmes designed to solve important educational problems. Among these were the Commission on Teacher Education, the American Youth Commission, and two post-war commissions dealing with international educational relations—the Commission for International Educational Reconstruction and the Commission on the Occupied Areas.

Most professional organizations concerned with public education are more than agencies for the protection of the 'rights' of the profession, although such protection usually remains an important part of their total responsibility. These associations take particular pride in their efforts to raise the standards of American public education, one of their most important functions being to encourage and assist their members to develop in individual professional competence. This includes active programmes designed to enlarge the educational horizons of their members. Thus, professional organizations, as well as higher institutions, engage in a wide variety of programmes for in-service teacher education. These may include professional conferences, seminars, workshops, and special summer courses. They often include special commissions and committees to make professional studies and submit reports. The journals of these organizations, usually issued monthly, are largely devoted to professional self-improvement. They may also issue yearbooks, pamphlets and other publications devoted to particularly important educational problems.

Increasingly, organizations concerned with the professionalization of teaching have transformed their methods from those of mere fact-finding and advocacy to those involving direct action, usually directed toward the solution of a critical problem confronting the profession. Thus, during the mid-1940's, various educational associations joined in a vigorous and successful effort to arouse the American public to the need for greatly increased teachers salaries.

Such joint action by professional voluntary bodies has not been limited to fields directly involving the well-being of their own members. The vast post-war effort in international educational reconstruction was a striking example of decisive humanitarian action by teachers associations and other groups interested in education to meet the urgent needs of teachers and youth in other lands devastated by war. Led by the ACE and the NEA, a joint Commission on International Educational Reconstruction was formed early in 1946 to encourage and assist Unesco to undertake projects for cultural rehabilitation. By the time it completed its programme in 1949, nearly four hundred organizations in the United States had taken part. Their efforts included such diverse projects as the sending of educational materials, the raising of special funds, the provision of scholarships, the organization of cultural missions, the holding of international seminars, the sponsorship of work camps, the affiliation of schools and colleges, and the urging of needed national and international action in areas where voluntary effort proved insufficient. These combined efforts represented a total value of nearly 250 million dollars. But far more important than the dollar value was the provision of urgently needed services abroad and the involvement of millions of individuals in programmes of mutual co-operation across national boundaries.

Although most of these voluntary international professional activities for educational reconstruction as such have terminated, except for those relating to Korea, most of the organizations concerned have remained active in international educational and cultural relations. This is brought out in two recent reports of the ACE, summarizing the current status of voluntary international projects.[1,2]

The growing interest of American teachers in the status of the teaching profession throughout the world and in improved international relations generally is reflected in many other ways, particularly in the work of professional organizations. Some of the forms which this in-

---

1 Snyder, Harold E. *When Peoples Speak to Peoples*. Washington, D.C., American Council on Education, 1953.
2 American Council on Education, Commission on the Occupied Areas. *An Experiment in International Cultural Areas; Report*, by H. E. Snyder and G. E. Beauchamp. Washington, D.C., The Council, 1951. 112 pp.

terest takes are brought out in the 1951 yearbook of the John Dewey Society[1] and in a recent doctoral dissertation at Columbia University.[2] Both studies emphasize the post-war expansion in the conception of the American teacher's role, status and responsibility. They bring out the fact that teachers and their associations are no longer content to limit their concern to purely domestic professional problems. The interdependence of teachers throughout the world is gaining increasing recognition. Unesco's leadership has been an important factor in assisting the gradual progress of the teaching profession of the United States toward world-mindedness.

[1] Arndt, C. O. and Everett, S. *Education for a World Society*. New York, Harper and Brothers, 1951. 273 pp.
[2] Kenworthy, Leonard S. *World Horizons for Teachers*. New York, Bureau of Publications, Teachers College, Columbia University, 1952. 141 pp.

BIBLIOGRAPHY

American Association of Colleges for Teacher Education, Commission on Standards and Studies. *Reports for 1949, 1950 and 1951.* Oneonta, New York.

American Council on Education, Commission on Teacher Education. *The Improvement of Teacher Education.* Washington, D.C., The Council, 1946. 283 pp.

——.——. *Teachers for Our Times.* Washington, D.C., The Council, 1944. 176 pp.

——.——. *Helping Teachers Understand Children.* Washington, D.C., The Council, 1945. 408 pp.

ARMSTRONG, W. E., HOLLIS, E. V. and DAVIS, H. E. *The College and Teacher Education.* Washington, D.C., American Council on Education, 1944. 311 pp.

Council of State Governments. *Higher Education in the Forty-Eight States.* Chicago, The Council, 1952. 317 pp.

ELSBREE, W. S. *The American Teacher.* New York, American Book Company, 1939. 566 pp., illus., plates, diagrs.

MONROE, W. S. *Teaching-Learning Theory and Teacher Education, 1890 to 1950.* Urbana, Ill., University of Illinois Press, 1952. 426 pp.

National Education Association. National Commission on Teacher Education and Professional Standards. *The Education of Teachers.* As viewed by the profession. Washington, D.C., The Association, 1948.

——. *The Teaching Profession Grows in Service.* Washington, D.C., The Association, 1949. 275 pp.

National Society for the Study of Education. *General Education* (Part I of the Society's 51st Yearbook). Chicago, University of Chicago Press, 1952. 377 pp.

PRALL, C. E. *State Programs for the Improvement of Teacher Education.* Washington, D.C., American Council on Education, 1946. 379 pp.

PRALL, C. E. and CUSHMAN, C. L. *Teacher Education in Service.* Washington, D.C., American Council on Education, 1944. 503 pp.

TROYER, M. E. and PACE, C. R. *Evaluation in Teacher Education.* Washington, D.C., American Council on Education, 1944. 308 pp., tables, diagrs.

U.S. Office of Education. *Education in the United States of America.* (Special Series No. 3), Washington, D.C., Government Printing Office, 1939, 55 pp., illus., tables, diagrs.

——. *National Survey of the Education of Teachers.* Washington, D.C., Government Printing Office, 1932–35. 6 vols.